LEGITIMATE EXPECTATIONS IN ADMINISTRATIVE LAW

Legitimate Expectations in Administrative Law

SØREN J. SCHØNBERG

OXFORD
UNIVERSITY PRESS

OXFORD
UNIVERSITY PRESS

Great Clarendon Street, Oxford OX2 6DP

Oxford University Press is a department of the University of Oxford.
It furthers the University's objective of excellence in research, scholarship,
and education by publishing worldwide in

Oxford New York

Athens Auckland Bangkok Bogotá Buenos Aires Calcutta
Cape Town Chennai Dar es Salaam Delhi Florence Hong Kong Istanbul
Karachi Kuala Lumpur Madrid Melbourne Mexico City Mumbai
Nairobi Paris São Paulo Singapore Taipei Tokyo Toronto Warsaw

and associated companies in Berlin Ibadan

Oxford is a registered trade mark of Oxford University Press
in the UK and certain other countries

Published in the United States
by Oxford University Press Inc., New York

First published 2000

British Library Cataloguing in Publication Data
Data available

Library of Congress Cataloging in Publication Data
Data available

ISBN 0-19-829947-8

1 3 5 7 9 10 8 6 4 2

Typeset in Sabon
by J&L Composition Ltd, Filey, North Yorkshire
Printed in Great Britain
on acid-free paper by
T.J. International Ltd., Padstow

Til mormor og morfar

Foreword

The appearance of this study of the protection of legitimate expectations will be widely welcomed, and for a variety of reasons.

One of the many virtues of the book is its illustration of the relevance and value of comparative law. Comparative law is not only of academic interest—very weighty as that interest often is. Today, comparative law is a true source of law. Exchanges of ideas between scholars—and increasingly also between judges and practitioners—can have a profound effect on legal developments.

There are perhaps few better examples than the concept of legitimate expectations. This is a very recent notion in English administrative law. Less than twenty years ago it was scarcely mentioned in the leading textbooks; ten years later, entire chapters were devoted to it. So important is its current place in the fundamental principles of administrative law that a monograph on the subject is fully justified. And a monograph with a comparative perspective is particularly welcome. Although Lord Denning, who referred to the principle as long ago as 1969, was clear that he was not influenced by any European or other legal system, nevertheless in today's climate, with constant and valuable exposure to other systems, any full discussion of the development and proper scope of the principle can now hardly fail to take account of developments in other European jurisdictions and elsewhere.

That is not to say that each of our legal systems must adopt uniform rules on all aspects of public law. That would be wholly unreasonable or, as perhaps one should say in the light of the principle of proportionality, manifestly disproportionate.

There are, it has to be accepted, areas of public law where national legal systems are required to observe the essential principles laid down by EC law; to that extent, the national legal systems of the European Union are necessarily harmonized.

There are also areas where EC law has a welcome 'spill-over' effect. The availability of injunctions by way of remedy against Ministers of the Crown is a well-known example in English public law: it would be anomalous if such a remedy were available in an EC law context, but not in an English law context. Such anomalies could not be allowed to persist.

But there are other areas where no such conclusion need be drawn. The author of this book does not make the assumption that there is an inherent advantage in harmonization. Each case has to be considered on its merits.

In each part of the subject, he draws on the experience of comparative law, and particularly French law and EC law, to illuminate the basic legal and policy issues which arise. What is the rationale for protecting legitimate expectations? How far should that protection extend? Can protection be limited to procedural matters or should it extend to substantive protection?

What are the policy considerations, and how should the competing costs and benefits be assessed?

Perhaps of even greater significance is the potential for the future development of the principle on a question where other systems have advanced further than English law. In practice two fundamental interests are often in apparent conflict: on the one hand, the concern to protect the legitimate expectations of the individual; on the other hand, the public interest and the need not to inhibit a policy which may benefit the public. One possible solution to the dilemma is by the award of damages to the person whose expectations would be frustrated if the public interest is preferred. In general the award of damages for 'public law wrongs' has rarely been seen as an appropriate remedy in English administrative law. It is, by contrast, commonplace in French law. EC law seems to fall somewhere between the other two systems in this respect.

Here as elsewhere, drawing on the experience of other systems, the author points the way in which English law should develop. His book offers not only rigorous jurisprudential analysis and the insights of comparative law, but also practical proposals for the development of the law. Thus it will be of interest to practitioners and judges as well as to all concerned with the principles of public law.

FRANCIS G. JACOBS
Advocate General
Court of Justice of the European Communities

Preface

This book is a substantially revised version of a thesis for which I was awarded the title of D.Phil. at the University of Oxford in February 2000. The research leading to the production of the thesis was generously funded by the Danish Research Academy.

I am indebted to a number of people with whom I have discussed the subject during the last four years. I would like to thank Professor Paul Craig for his encouragement and constructive supervision during my time as a student, and Professors Etienne Picard and Jean-Bernard Auby for invaluable advice on French law. Many others commented on parts of the manuscript. For that I am particularly grateful to Alison Hale, Chris Withers, Dominic O'Sullivan, Georgios Petrochilos, and Phil Syrpis. I have also benefited from constructive criticism by Professor John Bell and Mr Martin Matthews who acted as examiners at the University of Oxford. A special note of thanks is due to Professor Hjalte Rasmussen of the University of Copenhagen who first stimulated my interest in law. Finally, I am deeply indebted to my family and to Cathy for their love and support.

All those working at Oxford University Press have been helpful, efficient, and encouraging during the process of producing this book.

Søren Schønberg

The law is as stated on 20 April 2000.

Outline of Contents

Table of Contents

Abbreviations

Admin LR	Administrative Law Reports
AFDI	*Annuaire français de droit international*
AG	Advocate General
A-G	Attorney-General
AJCL	American Journal of Comparative Law
AJDA	*Actualité juridique. Droit Administratif*
ALJ	Australian Law Journal
Allison	J. W. F. Allison, *A Continental Distinction in the Common Law. A Historical and Comparative Perspective on English Public Law* (Oxford, 1996)
ALR	Australian Law Reports
Art	Article
BJLS	British Journal of Law and Society
BMLR	British Medical Law Reports
Brown & Bell	L. Neville Brown and J. S. Bell, *French Administrative Law*, 5th edn. (Oxford, 1998)
BTR	British Tax Review
Bull	*Bulletin des arrêts de la Cour de Cassation*
BYIL	British Yearbook of International Law
CAA	*Cour administrative d'appel*
California LR	California Law Review
CAP	Common Agricultural Policy
Cass	*Cour de Cassation*
CB (NS)	Common Bench New Series
CC	*Conseil Constitutionnel*
CDE	*Cahiers de droit européen*
CE	*Conseil d'État*
CFI	European Court of First Instance
CFLQ	Child and Family Law Quarterly
Chapus	R. Chapus, *Droit administratif général*, vol. i, 12th edn. (Paris, 1998)
CJALP	Canadian Journal of Administrative Law and Practice
CJQ	Civil Justice Quarterly
CLJ	Cambridge Law Journal
CLP	Current Legal Problems
CLR	Commonwealth Law Reports
CMLR	Common Market Law Reports
CMLRev	Common Market Law Review
comm	*commentaire*

Craig	P. P. Craig, *Administrative Law*, 3rd edn. (London 1999)
Cr App Rep	Criminal Appeal Reports
Crim	*Cour de Cassation, Chambre criminelle*
D	*Receuil Dalloz, Receuil Dalloz-Sirey*
DA	*Droit administratif*
De Smith	S. A. De Smith, Lord Woolf, J. L. Jowell, and A. P. Le Sueur, *Judicial Review of Administrative Action*, 5th edn. (London, 1995)
DF	*Droit fiscal*
DG	Directorate-General
DS	*Droit social*
EAGGF	European Agricultural Guidance and Guarantee Fund
EC	European Community
ECHR	European Convention on Human Rights
ECJ	European Court of Justice
ECLR	European Competition Law Review
ECSC	European Coal and Steel Community
ECtHR	European Court of Human Rights
Ed	*Édition*
EDCE	*Études et documents du Conseil d'État*
Edinburgh LR	Edinburgh Law Review
EEC	European Economic Community
EG	Estates Gazette
EGLR	Estates Gazette Law Reports
EHRLR	European Human Rights Law Review
ELR	European Law Review
EP	European Parliament
EPL	European Public Law
ERPL	European Review of Public Law
ESF	European Social Fund
EU	European Union
EuR	Europarecht
Fasc	*Fasicule*
FIDE	*Fédération Internationale de Droit Européen*
FLR	Family Law Reports
Gaz Pal	*Gazette du Palais*
Harvard LR	Harvard Law Review
HLR	Housing Law Reports
ICLQ	International and Comparative Law Quarterly
ICR	Industrial Case Reports
ILJ	Industrial Law Journal

IRLR	Industrial Relations Law Reports
JC	*Juris Classeur. Droit Administratif*, J.-B. Auby (ed.) (Dalloz, Paris)
JCP	*Juris Classeur périodique, La Semaine juridique*
JEL	Journal of European Law
JILI	Journal of the Indian Law Institute
JITE	Journal of Institutional and Theoretical Economics
JO	*Journal Officiel*
JPL	Journal of Planning and Environment Law
JR	Judicial Review
JSWFL	Journal of Social Welfare and Family Law
LGA	M. Long, P. Weil, G. Braibant, and B. Benevois, *Les Grands Arrêts de la jurisprudence administrative*, 10th edn. (Paris, 1993)
LGR	Local Government Reports
LIEI	Legal Issues of European Integration
LQR	Law Quarterly Review
LS	Legal Studies
MCA	Monetary compensation amount
Med LR	Medical Law Reports
MJ	Maastricht Journal of European and Comparative Law
MLR	Modern Law Review
NHS	National Health Service
NILQ	Northern Ireland Legal Quarterly
NJCL	National Journal of Constitutional Law
NLJ	New Law Journal
NZLR	New Zealand Law Review
NZULR	New Zealand Universities Law Review
OJ	Official Journal of the European Communities
OJLS	Oxford Journal of Legal Studies
Osgoode Hall LJ	Osgoode Hall Law Journal
P&CR	Property and Compensation Reports
PL	Public Law
Quot jur	*Quotidien juridique*
RDP	*Revue de droit public*
RDPE	*Rivista di diritto pubblico europeo*
Rec	*Receuil des décisions du Conseil d'État*
RFDA	*Revue française de droit administratif*
RGDIP	*Revue générale de droit international privé*
RMC	*Revue du marché commun*
RSC	Rules of the Supreme Court
RTDE	*Revue trimestrielle de droit européen*

Rutgers LJ	Rutgers Law Journal
S	*Receuil Sirey*
SA	*Société Anonyme*
Schwarze	J. Schwarze, *European Administrative Law* (London, 1992)
SLT	Scots Law Times
Student LR	Student Law Review
TA	*Tribunal administratif*
Tax J	Tax Journal
TC	*Tribunal des conflits*
TEU	Treaty on European Union (Maastricht Agreement)
Uniform LR	Uniform Law Review
Univ Chicago LR	University of Chicago Law Review
Univ Toronto LJ	University of Toronto Law Journal
UNSWLJ	University of New South Wales Law Journal
Wade	H. W. R. Wade and C. F. Forsyth, *Administrative Law*, 7th edn. (Oxford, 1994)
YEL	Yearbook of European Law

Table of Cases

UNITED KINGDOM

FRANCE

Conseil d'Etat

Cours Administratives d'Appel

Tribunaux administratifs

Tribunal des Conflits

Cour de Cassation

EUROPEAN COMMUNITIES

Cases arranged by number

European Court of Justice

Court of First Instance

EUROPEAN COMMUNITIES

Cases in alphabetical order

European Court of Justice

Grifoni v Commission (Case C-308/87) [1990] ECR I-1203\211
Grimaldi v Fonds des maladies professionnelles (Case C-322/88) [1989] ECR 4407\121
Grogan v Commission (Case 127/80) [1982] ECR 869\97, 145
Hamai v ECJ (Case 92/85) [1986] ECR 3157\122, 141
Hauptzollamt Hamburg-Jonas v Krücken (Case 316/86) [1988] ECR 2213\82
Hauptzollamt München-Mitte v Technische Universität München (Case C-269/90) [1991] ECR I-5469\39, 40
Henri de Compte v EP (Case C-90/95P) [1997] ECR I-1999\72, 77, 79, 80, 98, 99, 100, 101
Herpels v Commission (Case 54/77) [1978] ECR 585\83, 84, 97
Hewlett Packard v Directeur General des Douanes (Case C-250/91) [1993] ECR I-1819\126
Hoechst Chemie v Commission (Joined Cases 46/87 and 227/88) [1989] ECR 2858\37
Hoffmann-La Roche v Commission (Case 85/76) [1979] ECR 461\35, 40
Hoogovens v High Authority (Case 14/61) [1962] ECR 253\72, 97, 98, 100, 101
Houyoux v Commission (Joined Cases 176–177/86) [1987] ECR 4333\221, 227, 228
Ireland v Commission (Case C-238/96) [1998] ECR I-5810\148
Irish Farmers Association (Case C-22/94) [1997] ECR I-1809\127
Kamp v Hauptzollamt Wuppertal (Case C-21/92) [1994] ECR 1619\145
Kampfmeyer v Commission and Council (Joined Cases 54–60/74) [1976] ECR 711\205, 210, 212
Kergall v Common Assembly (Case 1/55) [1955–56] ECR 1\71
Klöckner-Werke v Commission (Joined Cases 303 and 312/81) [1983] ECR 1507\123
Kohll v Commission (Case 137/79) [1980] ECR 2601\222
Kol v Land Berlin (Case C-285/95) [1997] ECR I-3069\126
Kolivas v Commission (Case 40/86) [1987] ECR 2643\138
Kuhl v Council (Case 71/71) [1973] ECR 705\80
Lageder v Amministrazione delle Finance (Joined Cases C-31–44/91) [1993] ECR I-1761\147
Lemmerz-Werke v High Authority (Case 111/63) [1965] ECR 677\73, 98, 100, 101
Leonard v Commission (Case 181/87) [1988] ECR 3823\123
Louwage v Commission (Case 148/73) [1974] ECR 81\7, 59, 133, 135, 138
Lucchini v Commission (Case 1252/79) [1980] ECR 3753\126
Luhleich v Commission (Case 68/63) [1965] ECR 727\206, 212
Lührs v Hauptzollamt Hamburg-Jonas (Case 78/77) [1978] ECR 169\119, 127
Lütticke v Commission (Case 4/69) [1971] ECR 325\178
Lux v Court of Auditors (Joined Cases 129 and 274/81) [1984] ECR 4127\59, 136
Mangera (Case 59/75) [1976] ECR 91\121
Mannesman v High Authority (Case 19/61) [1962] ECR 717\142
Mavridis v EP (Case 289/81) [1983] ECR 1731\118, 223

Court of First Instance

UNITED STATES OF AMERICA

AUSTRALIA

European Court of Human Rights

Table of Legislation

France

United Kingdom

European Community

Treaties and Conventions

Introduction

The simultaneous growth of the welfare state and the information society in the twentieth century have changed the nature of the relationship between public authorities and individuals. In Britain, and in other Western European states, sweeping discretionary powers have been vested in public authorities for the benefit of the general public and vast amounts of information have been compiled in public registers. As a result, administrative decisions and representations have become part and parcel of the population's long-term planning and day-to-day choices. This book is about the legal rules which should apply when public authorities make decisions which differ from what individuals have been led to expect by previous administrative decisions or representations. An example will illustrate the nature of the problem.

Imagine that X is informed in no uncertain terms by an officer of a local planning authority that he will be granted permission to add an extra floor to his house if he makes a formal application, and that X goes on to spend £50,000 reconstructing the house. What happens if the authority subsequently changes its policy and denies X the permission? In this situation, there is a conflict between the principle of government in the public interest and the principle of individual fairness. If the planning authority allows X to add a floor to his house, it will act contrary to the new policy, which has been adopted in the public interest, and contrary to the interests of X's neighbours. If the authority refuses to grant permission, it will disappoint the expectations which its statement created in X, and it will cause X considerable financial hardship.

How should these principles be balanced against each other? In other words, how and in what circumstances should expectations created by administrative decisions and representations be upheld? This question has been a source of academic controversy and complex, sometimes even contorted, legal developments both in Britain and elsewhere. Three different approaches have emerged. First, X can be given a hearing and reasons which will allow him to argue for an exception to the existing policy, as well as permit him to understand why it might be impossible for the administration to do so. This is *procedural* protection of expectations. Second, X can be allowed to hold the planning authority to its statement and proceed with the reconstruction. This is *substantive* protection of expectations. Third, X can be compensated for the £50,000 he lost by relying on the administrative assurance and for the cost of re-establishing the house to its original state. This is *compensatory* protection of expectations.

The aim of this book is to determine how and in what circumstances English law should protect expectations created by administrative decisions and representations. Its working hypothesis is that expectations cannot be adequately protected by a single legal principle: it is necessary to apply a *combination* of procedural, substantive, and compensatory rules to strike a balance between the principles of lawful administration in the public interest and individual fairness. To determine the content of this combination, three questions will be examined.

First, why should administrative law protect individual expectations at all? This question is answered, in Chapter 1, by applying a combination of jurisprudential and socio-legal methods. It will be argued that expectations should be protected for reasons of fairness and trust in administration, and that fairness is intimately linked with the Rule of Law and its requirements of legal certainty and formal equality. Four situations in which legitimate expectations are liable to be disappointed will be distinguished. It will be argued that the justification for protection of expectations differs in these situations, and that different degrees of legal protection are therefore called for.

Second, how are legitimate expectations protected through administrative law today? A detailed comparative study of English, French, and EC law will reveal the extent to which procedural, substantive, and compensatory protection of expectations is provided. In Chapter 2, I will consider how principles of procedural fairness, or 'defence rights' (*droits de la défense*), contribute to the protection of expectations when public authorities depart from what they have previously decided or represented. In Chapters 3 and 4, I look at the general principles (and legislative provisions) which protect expectations created by administrative decisions and representations. In Chapters 5 and 6 I analyse how principles of tort law (and certain other compensatory remedies) contribute to the protection of expectations in administrative decision-making.

Third, is the current approach to protection of expectations in English law satisfactory? This question will be considered in the final sections of Chapters 2–6. It will be argued that English law does not provide sufficient protection of legitimate expectations; it does not fully meet the requirements of fairness and trust in administration. Suggestions for legal reform of procedural, substantive, and compensatory principles will also be made, and the comparative study of French and EC law will be used as a source of inspiration in this context.

Finally, having summed up the various findings and suggestions for reform, the book concludes by presenting a combination of legal principles which is better capable of protecting expectations and of striking a balance between lawful administration in the public interest and individual fairness than existing English law.

Delimitation of the Topic

This book is a study of legitimate expectations created by administrative decisions and representations, and their effects on administrative decision-making in English, French, and EC law. The topic is subject to two main limitations.

First, the book is concerned with individualized decision-making rather than general rule-making. Decision-making and rule-making are subject to different considerations. While it is generally accepted that decision-making is subject to principles of procedural fairness, the application of procedural rights to general rule-making procedures remains a highly contentious issue. It would not be possible to do justice to both areas in a comparative study such as this which deals with not only procedures, but also substantive and compensatory principles.

Second, although principles of legitimate expectations exist in a number of legal systems—such as Australia, Canada, New Zealand, Germany, the Netherlands, and Scandinavia—this book is limited to English, French, and EC law. It does not purport to be an encyclopaedic guide to the principle of legitimate expectations in various jurisdictions.[1] It seeks instead to identify the specific problems which arise when public authorities create expectations in individuals and to develop solutions to those problems. To that end, a comparison of English, French, and EC law is both appropriate and sufficient. For there are striking differences between the approach to legitimate expectations within these three jurisdictions. They differ conceptually: while the concept of legitimate expectations has been recognized for many years in English and EC law, it is not recognized in French law at all. They also differ practically: while English law relies mostly on procedural protection of expectations, EC law relies more on substantive principles, and French law on compensation. German, Dutch, and Scandinavian laws resemble EC law; the Commonwealth jurisdictions resemble English law in this area. Treatment of all or some of those jurisdictions would, therefore, add to the length of the book, create large overlaps, and offer little in the way of new solutions and approaches of interest to English law.

Delimitation of Issues and Methods

Legitimate expectations in administrative law can be studied from a number of different perspectives. This book adopts a contemporary, comparative, practical, and legal perspective. The *contemporary* perspective means that the book will not provide an historical account of the development of the concept of legitimate expectations in English and EC law.[2] The emphasis on *comparative* method means that the description of English, French, and EC law will be concise rather than exhaustive.[3] It also means little use will be made of socio-legal

[1] For general overviews of the topic, see Schwarze ch. 6; J.-M. Woehrling, 'Le principe de confiance légitime dans la jurisprudence des tribunaux', in *General Reports to the XV International Congress of Comparative Law* (University of Bristol, 1998).

[2] For an historical account, see K. J. Smith, 'The Developing Doctrine of Legitimate or Reasonable Expectations in the Public and Private Law of England and Australia', Ph.D. thesis (University of Cambridge, 1994).

[3] For detailed treatment of estoppel in administrative law; see P. M. Brown, 'Estoppel by Representation in Administrative Law', Ph.D. thesis (University of Cambridge, 1989); R. D. Pickard, 'The Doctrine of Estoppel Within Development Control', Ph.D. thesis (Newcastle upon Tyne Polytechnic, 1990).

methodology, and that no attempt will be made to apply law-and-economics methods to test the efficiency of different legal principles.[4] The *practical* perspective means that the book will examine a specific legal problem and the various solutions to it adopted in different legal systems.[5] It will not provide English lawyers with a general description of French law and institutions,[6] and it does not purport to compare methods of legal reasoning, legal cultures, or *mentalités*.[7] Nor will there be a detailed discussion of the phenomenon of convergence or 'spill-over' between European legal systems.[8] Finally, emphasis will be placed on protection of expectations by *formal law* enforceable through the courts. There are, of course, other methods of controlling administrative power and of protecting expectations, such as training and informal socialization of administrative personnel, internal administrative review mechanisms, and the Ombudsmen. Such methods may be very important in practice, but it is impossible to discuss them in the context of this book.[9]

Unlike most administrative law literature, this book draws heavily on comparative legal methodology. It may be useful to explain briefly how that methodology will be applied to the topic. In accordance with the 'basic methodological principle of all comparative law',[10] the book aims to identify and compare functionally equivalent rules in English, French, and EC law. That is, it compares rules which have the *function* of protecting individuals who hold and rely on expectations created by administrative conduct. Whether or not those rules are couched in terms of 'expectations' or 'reliance' is irrelevant. By comparing those rules, the book aims to determine to what extent the three legal systems reach similar *outcomes* in similar cases. For example, if French administrative law does not recognize a principle of legitimate expectations, are there then other rules which protect individuals' reliance on administrative representations, and what is the actual difference between those rules and the English principle of legitimate expectations?

[4] See M. Braunstein, 'In Defense of Traditional Immunity—Toward an Economic Rationale for Not Estopping the Government' (1982) Rutgers LJ 1.

[5] The 'problem' being the conflict between lawful administration in the public interest and individual fairness which occurs when public authorities depart from what their decisions or representations have led individuals to expect.

[6] See F. J. Goodnow, *Comparative Administrative Law* (New York, 1893); H. B. Jacobini, *An Introduction to Comparative Administrative Law* (New York, 1991); Brown and Bell with references in Appendix K.

[7] See H. W. Ehrmann, *Comparative Legal Cultures* (Englewood Cliffs, 1976); V. Gessner, A. Hoeland, and C. Varga (eds.), *European Legal Cultures* (Aldershot, 1996); J. S. Bell, 'English Law and French Law—Not So Different?' (1995) CLP 63; P. Legrand, 'European Legal Systems are not Converging' (1996) ICLQ 52; M. Van Hoecke and M. Warrington, 'Legal Cultures and Legal Paradigms: a New Model for Comparative Law' (1998) ICLQ 495.

[8] See notably J. Schwarze, *Administrative Law under European Influence* (Baden-Baden, 1996).

[9] The Ombudsmen's role in the provision of *ex gratia* compensation will, however, be discussed briefly in chs. 5–6.

[10] K. Zweigert and H. Kötz, *An Introduction to Comparative Law*, 3rd edn. (Oxford, 1998), 34.

Comparative legal research is fraught with difficulty. There are obvious linguistic problems and the different terminologies, concepts, and techniques used by different legal systems often mask similarities at the level of outcomes. Two tools will be used in this book to overcome those difficulties. The general legal problem will, first of all, be divided into more specific categories. A distinction is drawn between four types of situations in which expectations are liable to be disappointed by administrative conduct; namely revocation of administrative decisions, departure from individualized administrative assurances, departure from policy in individual instances, and departure from policy in the light of a general shift in policy. Each of the four categories are then divided into a number of more specific 'fact patterns'. For example, in relation to departure from administrative promises and assurances it is asked whether, and in what circumstances, individuals can hold a public authority to a planning officers' advice, to an informal ruling issued by a tax officer, to a promise granted by the police or a prosecution official to a suspect concerning his criminal prosecution, etc. It will be easier to identify and compare the rules which apply to each of these categories than to tackle the broad question of 'what rules in English, French, and EC law have the function of protecting expectations'.[11] Second, in order to identify the rules which protect expectations within each category or fact pattern, a broad range of legal materials will be considered. For a legal system will (almost) always have some form of solution to a given legal problem if only one digs deep enough to find it.[12] For example, the absence of a principle of legitimate expectations in French tax law might lead one to conclude that the French taxpayer cannot rely on tax rulings issued by competent tax officers. However, an analysis of the detailed French tax statutes and various governmental circulars will reveal a different picture. This book will accordingly be based on a study of case law concerning substantive principles of administrative law, procedural fairness, and tort liability; provisions of primary and secondary legislation; administrative circulars and guidelines; and secondary literature. It will also draw on unpublished legal research;[13] official governmental publications; information obtained from practitioners and judges on e-mail discussion lists;[14] as well as data made available on legal web sites.[15]

[11] Still, it is not practically possible to identify all the possible fact patterns from the outset, they can only be 'discovered' as the research proceeds. It is, therefore, necessary to shift back and forth between the legal systems studied to discover as many permutations of the general problem as possible, and to ascertain how those permutations are dealt with by each legal system.

[12] The relevant 'solution' may be that there is no formal rule which applies, but there is then often an informal regulation which may be as interesting from a comparative point of view.

[13] A useful collection of French doctoral theses is kept at the *Cujas* library in Paris.

[14] The Euro-Lex list is particularly useful for enquiries on European law in a broad sense.

[15] Useful collections of links may be found at www.open.gov.uk and www.legifrance.gouv.fr/citoyen/index.ow.

A Note on Terminology

The terms 'reasonable expectations' and 'legitimate expectations' are used in this book with the following meaning. An expectation is reasonable if a reasonable person acting with diligence would hold it in the relevant circumstances. An expectation is legitimate if the legal system acknowledges its reasonableness and attributes procedural, substantive, or compensatory legal consequences to it.

Chapter 1

Expectations, Fairness, and Lawful Administration in the Public Interest

1 Introduction

The purpose of this chapter is to explain why administrative law should protect expectations created by administrative decisions, representations, and conduct. Once it has been explained why expectations should be protected at all, it will be possible to determine, in the light of a comparative study of English, French, and EC law, how and in what circumstances expectations should be upheld.

It is a trite proposition that administrative authorities have a duty to exercise their powers in the public interest and, in doing so, to stay within the limits set by law. All developed systems of administrative law include principles of auto-limitation (non-fettering) and legality (*ultra vires, légalité*). The former limits the extent to which a public authority may, by making *prima facie* lawful decisions and informal representations, or by the adoption of a fixed practice or policy, disable itself from exercising discretionary powers in individual cases.[1] The latter provides that authorities are not bound by unlawful (*ultra vires*) decisions, representations, and policies. The justification for these two principles is too well-known to require much explanation.[2] Briefly, powers are vested in public bodies by legislative provisions, or by constitutional enactment,[3] on the implicit condition that they be exercised lawfully and in the public interest. Respect for these conditions is therefore a condition for the legitimacy of administrative action.

Legality and administration in the public interest are extremely valuable principles. But they are not absolute.[4] There is growing recognition in Britain that legality and administration in the public interest must be limited by, or balanced against, requirements of morality or fairness, and that it is incumbent on the courts to enforce such limits through principles of judicial review. Public authorities must 'act in a high-principled way, on occasion being subject to a

[1] *R v Home Secretary, ex p Venables* [1998] AC 407, 496–7; CE 11/12–70 *Crédit foncier de France* Rec 750; Case 148/73 *Louwage v Commission* [1974] ECR 81. See De Smith 505–19; Chapus 471–82.

[2] See generally J. D. B. Mitchell, *Contracts of Public Authorities* (London, 1954), 6–15; L. Green, *The Authority of the State* (Oxford, 1990).

[3] Art 34 and 37 of the French Constitution confer important powers upon the administration the exercise of which are not dependent upon statutory delegation. See Brown and Bell ch. 2.

[4] This is well established in EC, German, Dutch, and Danish law. See Schwarze ch. 6 and discussion in Ch. 4.7.C of this book.

stricter duty of fairness than would apply between private individuals'.[5] It follows, it is said, that public authorities should satisfy expectations created by their own representations and conduct.[6] However, while the concept of fairness may provide the underlying rationale, it is too imprecise to provide solutions in individual cases. This lack of precision is, it is submitted, the cause of some confusion about the proper scope of the principle of legitimate expectations in English law. It is therefore desirable to clarify why it is unfair for public authorities to disappoint expectations.

Various specific justifications for why it is unfair, or otherwise undesirable, to disappoint expectations have been suggested. The various justifications proceed from different abstract values, such as autonomy, trust, and economic efficiency. These values are not mutually exclusive. Indeed, public law promotes a range of values at the same time.[7] Consequently, this chapter makes no attempt to justify or rank these abstract values in order of importance. Rather, the objective is to explain how autonomy and other values support the claim that administrative authorities should respect legitimate expectations induced by their own conduct. However, it is necessary, first, to set out more clearly the fact pattern with which these values are actually concerned.

One may identify four situations in which legitimate expectations are liable to be disappointed by administrative decision-making. The first situation arises when a public authority makes a formal decision about a person, or a limited group, which it subsequently seeks to revoke (Situation 1). The second situation arises when a public authority explicitly or implicitly represents that it will follow a certain procedure or policy in relation to a specific individual or group and subsequently makes a decision which differs from the representation (Situation 2). The third situation arises when a public authority makes a general representation about the procedure or policy it will follow in relation to certain types of decisions, but subsequently departs from the procedure or policy in the

[5] *R v Ministry of Agriculture, Fisheries and Foods, ex p Hamble Fisheries* [1995] 2 All ER 714, 724. See similarly *R v IRC, ex p Unilever* [1996] STC 681, 695–6; Lord Woolf, '*Droit Public*—English style' (1995) PL 57, 62.

[6] Ibid. See also the leading United States decision of *Santiago v Immigration Service* (1975) 526 F 2d 488 describing the duty to honour representations as 'a rule of fairness . . . which protect(s) the reliances and expectations of innocent persons from defeat by those who have induced (them).' Several authors also link fairness with expectations, see C. F. Forsyth, 'Wednesbury Protection of Substantive Legitimate Expectations' (1997) PL 375, 384; D. Oliver, 'Underlying Values of Public and Private Law', in M. Taggart (ed.), *The Province of Administrative Law* (Oxford 1997), 217, 230–1; T. R. S. Allan, 'Fairness, Equality, Rationality: Constitutional Theory and Judicial Review', in C. Forsyth and I. Hare (eds.), *The Golden Metwand and the Crooked Cord, Essays in Honour of Sir William Wade* (Oxford, 1998), 15, 31; Craig 614. See also J.-M. Woehrling, 'Le principe de confiance légitime dans la jurisprudence des tribunaux', in *General Reports to the XV International Congress of Comparative Law* (University of Bristol, 1998), 23 arguing that *Billigkeit* (equity or fairness) is the rationale for the German principle of legitimate expectations (*Vertrauensschutz*); J. Héron, *Principes du droit transitoire* (Paris, 1996), 114–15 arguing that immediately effective changes of administrative policy offend against morality and justice (*moralité* and *justice*).

[7] See Oliver, above n. 6, 223–4 for a helpful definition of the notion of values.

particular case (Situation 3). The fourth situation arises when the authority departs from its general representation in the light of a shift in general procedure or policy which has occurred between the initial representation and the decision (Situation 4).[8]

2 Legitimate Expectations, Autonomy, and the Rule of Law

The justification for the legal protection of legitimate expectations which has been most influential in Anglo-European scholarship takes autonomy as its basic premise. There are two types of autonomy-based justifications. A relatively narrow 'reliance theory', which links expectations with the principle of estoppel, and a wider 'Rule of Law theory', which links expectations with the notion of legal certainty.[9]

(A) The Reliance Theory

The reliance theory argues that legitimate expectations should be protected because to do otherwise would inflict harm on individuals who rely upon such expectations.[10] The argument runs as follows. There is a general obligation not to cause preventable harm to others. This obligation derives, first, from our concern to maximize welfare or happiness in society. That is, a utilitarian analysis of societal arrangements suggests that preventable harm should not be tolerated.[11] Second, respect for individual autonomy suggests an obligation not to cause preventable harm, irrespective of what aggregate utility this obligation might have. It follows that the freedom of action of one person may be limited

[8] In all of these situations, it is assumed that the administration does not *deliberately* misrepresent the facts or its intentions. The justification for protection of legitimate expectations set out below applies also to deliberate misrepresentations. However, deliberate misinformation may create an additional element of unfairness because it undermines the recipient's autonomy by interfering with his thinking process, see J. Raz, *The Morality of Freedom* (Oxford, 1986), 377. Deliberate misinformation is also contrary to the requirement, applicable in public and in private law, of good faith; and it damages the legitimacy of administrative action by undermining confidence in public authorities. Moreover, it violates the requirement of 'honesty', which was defined as one of seven fundamental duties of public authorities by Lord Nolan in *First Report of the Committee on Standards in Public Life*, Cm 2850, 1995.

[9] The two theories are here discussed separately for the sake of clarity. However, some authors cite both reliance and general certainty as rationales for the principle of legitimate expectations. See D. Wyatt and A. Dashwood, *European Community Law*, 3rd edn. (London, 1992), 91.

[10] This 'reliance theory' has not been formulated explicitly, but it underlies many judgments and academic writings which equate legitimate expectations with private law principles of estoppel (e.g. R. Pagone, 'Estoppel in Public Law: Theory, Fact and Fiction' (1984) UNSWLJ 267, 275–6; R. Cranston, 'Reviewing Judicial Review', in G. Richardson and H. Genn (eds.), *Administrative Law and Government Action* (Oxford, 1994), 45, 58) or state that expectations only deserve protection if there is detrimental reliance (e.g. Craig 635).

[11] On utilitarianism in general, see J. S. Mill, *On Liberty*, 1859 (London, 1993).

to the extent that its exercise causes harm to others. From this general obligation a further, more specific, principle is deduced, which can be used to justify the legal protection of legitimate expectations. MacCormick states that:

> [I]f a person acts in a potentially detrimental way in reliance upon beliefs about another's . . . conduct, and if the latter person has . . . intentionally or knowingly induced the former to rely upon him [in the sense that he 'thought it likely' or 'ought to have realised' that the other party would rely], the latter has an obligation not to . . . disappoint the other's reliance.[12]

MacCormick developed this principle as an explanation for the morally binding nature of promises and contracts. However, as Joseph Raz has demonstrated, the harm principle also provides a normative justification for the legal doctrine known as estoppel, which applies in the absence of a promissory or contractual relationship between the parties.[13]

The reliance principle may be reformulated as follows: a public authority's freedom to take action in the public interest is limited to the extent that it causes harm to particular individuals. If a public authority has induced a person to rely upon its representations or conduct, realising that such reliance was a real possibility, it is under a *prima facie* duty to act in such a way that the reliance will not be detrimental to the representee. The authority must honour the expectations created by its representation or, at least, compensate the person affected for his reliance loss. This reformulated harm principle has considerable force as a justification for the protection of legitimate expectations. However, it is not an entirely satisfactory justification as it is too narrow and too inflexible.

The reliance theory is too narrow because detrimental reliance is not, and should not, always be a precondition for protection of expectations. As explained further below, procedural protection of legitimate expectations should be available in the absence of reliance whatever the case may be for substantive or compensatory protections. Substantive legal protection may also be required in the absence of reliance. Authorities should be bound not to depart from general policy in an individual case unless there is an overriding policy justification for doing so (Situation 3). Reliance should not be a precondition for the application of this principle.[14] Moreover, the requirement of reliance may lead to unjustified distinctions between similar cases because whether a person relies on the representation or not may be entirely fortuitous. This is aptly illustrated by the *Hargreaves* case.[15] The applicant in this case was one of many prisoners who, under an existing Home Office policy, had been eligible to apply for home leave after serving a certain period of his sentence. When the policy

[12] N. MacCormick, 'Voluntary Obligations and Normative Powers' (1972) Proceedings of the Aristotelian Society, Supplement 46, 59, 67–8.

[13] See J. Raz, 'Voluntary Obligations and Normative Powers' (1972) Proceedings of the Aristotelian Society, Supplement 46, 79, 101.

[14] See section 2.B.

[15] *R v Home Secretary, ex p Hargreaves* [1997] 1 WLR 906.

changed, his personal situation was deeply affected and his expectation of being eligible to apply was defeated.[16] However, this disappointment was not a consequence of his *reliance* upon the existing policy. Still, fairness suggests that the prisoner's expectation was worthy of some form of legal protection and that irrespective of whether one prisoner had, for example, relied on it by buying a cinema ticket for his 'first day out'.

Now it could be argued that the prisoner in *Hargreaves* did 'rely' upon the policy. For although the policy did not lead him to take any physical action or to spend money, he made certain plans for his future life and clearly looked forward to his release. Is the 'emotional commitment' to such plans and hopes not a form of reliance? The answer is as follows. Planning is certainly an extremely important aspect of human life. Indeed, the frustration of a prisoner's plans is (part of) the explanation why it may be unfair to leave him without legal protection. However, if reliance is defined so as to include plans and 'emotional commitments', then the reliance theory collapses into the wider Rule of Law theory, discussed below, according to which planning and certainty provides the rationale for the protection of legitimate expectations. That would obscure, rather than clarify, our understanding of the issue. For there is, it is suggested, an important difference between frustrating a person's plans and causing harm because the person acted in 'real' reliance upon some prior representation or conduct.

The reliance theory is also too inflexible. It suggests that an authority is precluded from disappointing induced foreseeable reliance (or to compensate consequential loss), if the disappointment is preventable. But even the most cautious public authority cannot completely prevent changes of policy from harming, or adversely affecting, individuals. Authorities must be able to change policy in the public interest, even if this causes some harm to individuals. What is required is a fair balance between individual harm and the broader public interest. The notion of 'preventable harm' does not give adequate expression to this balancing.[17] Thus, while the harm principle may provide a convincing justification for the principle of estoppel in private law,[18] the application of that principle to public authorities would be both over- and under-inclusive. The harm principle does, however, provide a convincing justification for the protection of expectations by a more flexible legal principle.

[16] The Court of Appeal accepted that the change had had traumatizing effects upon prisoners.

[17] It might be argued in reply that harm is not 'preventable' if a policy change is justified by the broader public interest. The point is, however, that the theory does not readily support this conclusion.

[18] See M. J. Spence, *Protecting Reliance: The Emergent Doctrine of Equitable Estoppel* (Oxford, 1999), 4–6.

(B) The Rule of Law Theory

Proponents of this theory, influential both in Britain,[19] on the Continent,[20] and in the EC context,[21] see the principle of legitimate expectations as one aspect of the Rule of Law. Like the reliance theory, the Rule of Law theory proceeds from autonomy.[22] For individuals to be autonomous they must, at least, be able to plan ahead and therefore foresee with some degree of certainty the consequences of their actions.[23] Laws, and the actions of those who apply them, are therefore subject to a requirement of predictability and certainty.[24] From an economic perspective, legal certainty is, as Max Weber has shown, a prerequisite for rational enterprise in a capitalist economy.[25] Economic activity, which is an important aspect of autonomous decision-making, can only be carried out if economic operators 'can rely on something'.[26] In a rapidly changing and

[19] See De Smith 563–4; P. P. Craig, 'Substantive Legitimate Expectations and the Principles of Judicial Review', in M. Andenas (ed.), *English Public Law and the Common Law of Europe* (London, 1998), 23, 45–7.

[20] German law in particular stresses the connection between *Rechtssicherheit* and *Vertrauensschutz*. See Schwarze ch. 6.

[21] The ECJ connected protection of legitimate expectations to legal certainty in Case 1/73 *Westzucker v Einfuhr- und Vorratstelle für Zucker* [1973] ECR 723, 729. Consequently, some commentators argue that certainty and predictability is the only, or the most important, rationale for the Court's case law on legitimate expectations. See Schwarze 947; H. G. Schermers and D. Waelbroeck, *Judicial Protection in the EC*, 5th edn. (Deventer, 1992), 52; T. Hartley, *The Foundations of European Community Law*, 4th edn. (Oxford, 1998), 142–3; T. Tridimas, *The General Principles of EC Law* (Oxford, 1999), 163.

[22] See P. P. Craig, 'Formal and Substantive Conceptions of the Rule of Law: An Analytical Framework' (1997) PL 467, 481. This also applies to the French *État de droit* and German *Rechtsstaat* conceptions of this theory. See M. Troper, 'Le concept d'État de droit', in M. Troper (ed.), *L'État de droit* (Caen, 1993), 34.

[23] This is only one of several conditions precedent to an autonomous life. See Raz, above n. 8, ch. 14.

[24] *Black Clawson v Papierwerke AG* [1975] AC 591, 638. This basic requirement is accepted by both proponents of formal and more substantive conceptions of the Rule of Law. On certainty in formal theories see H. W. R. Wade, 'The Concept of Legal Certainty. A Preliminary Skirmish' (1940–1) MLR 183, 185–94; L. L. Fuller, *The Morality of Law*, Revised edn. (New Haven, 1969) 39, 79–80; J. Rawls, *A Theory of Justice* (Cambridge, Mass., 1971), 235–43; J. Raz, *The Authority of Law* (Oxford, 1979), 210–29; R. S. Summers, 'A Formal Theory of the Rule of Law' (1993) Ratio Juris 127, 131. On certainty in substantive theories, see R. M. Dworkin, *A Matter of Principle* (Oxford, 1985), 12–13; *Law's Empire* (London, 1986), 365–9; T. R. S. Allan, *Law, Liberty, and Justice: The Legal Foundations of British Constitutionalism* (Oxford, 1993), 24–5; J. L. Jowell, 'The Rule of Law Today', in J. L. Jowell and L. Oliver (eds.), *The Changing Constitution*, 3rd edn. (London, 1994), 57, 62–8, 75; J. Laws, 'The Constitution: Morals and Rights' (1996) PL 622, 630–2; Craig, above n. 22, 478–9. On certainty in French *État de droit* and German *Rechtsstaat* theory, see Troper, above n. 22, 27, 34; E. Forsthoff, 'Rechtsstaat oder Richterstaat?', in *Rechtsstaat im Wandel: Verfassungsrechtlische Abhandlunger 1954–1973* (Munich, 1976), 242–3.

[25] M. Weber, *Économie et société*, vol. I (Paris, 1971), 350; *L'éthique protestant et l'esprit du capitalism* (Paris, 1981), 23. See also M. E. Streit, 'Economic Order, Private Law and Public Policy' (1992) JITE 675, 693 'legal provisions . . . serve to secure the autonomy of economic agents as a precondition of self-co-ordination on the basis of private contracts'.

[26] See E. Sharpston, 'Legitimate Expectations and Economic Reality' (1990) ELR 103, 106, and section 4.B.

increasingly uncertain world, law is something that operators should be able to, and to a large extent do, rely on.[27]

In administrative law, the importance of certainty is increased by wide-ranging discretionary powers being vested in public authorities.[28] Individuals cannot easily predict how discretionary powers will be exercised because the provisions conferring such powers are linguistically indeterminate and because informal working rules and other constraints, of which individuals are not normally aware, affect their exercise in practice.[29] Representations may create expectations as to the manner of, or criteria for, their exercise. Respect for these expectations therefore makes the exercise of discretion more predictable. However, the importance of the Rule of Law does not stop here. A number of more detailed requirements of the Rule of Law have been derived, most clearly by Joseph Raz, from the basic requirements of predictability and certainty.[30] These requirements have implications for legislators, judges and administrators alike.[31] Two of them are of particular importance for our purposes.

First, the Rule of Law presupposes formal equality.[32] That is, like cases must be treated alike by the correct and consistent application of law. Without formal equality law becomes arbitrary and thus unpredictable and uncertain.[33] Second, the Rule of Law presupposes a certain measure of constancy in the law. The law should ensure that administrative action is based on a mix of short-term exigencies and more long-term considerations.[34] Individual planning becomes difficult or impossible if law and policy are changed too often and too abruptly. Moreover, frequent changes may undermine individual rights by creating uncertainty about the boundaries of those rights.[35]

The legal protection of expectations by administrative law principles is a way of giving expression to the requirements of predictability, formal equality, and

[27] On the uncertainty caused by globalization and the emergence of a 'risk society', see U. Beck, *Risk Society: Towards a New Modernity* (London, 1992); A. Giddens, *The Third Way* (Cambridge, 1998); 'Reith Lectures 1999', available at http: //www.bbc.co.uk/reith99.

[28] See D. J. Galligan, *Discretionary Powers: A Legal Study of Official Discretion* (Oxford, 1986), 154; R. E. Goodin, 'Welfare, Rights and Discretion' (1986) OJLS 231, 244–5.

[29] See K. Hawkins, 'The Use of Legal Discretion: Perspectives From Law and Social Science', in K. Hawkins (ed.), *The Uses of Discretion* (Oxford, 1992), 11, 13, 38–44.

[30] J. Raz, above n. 24, and *Ethics in the Public Domain* (Oxford, 1995), 370–8.

[31] See Raz, above n. 24, 215.

[32] See Wade, above n. 24, 187; A. V. Dicey, *Introduction to the Study of the Law of the Constitution*, 10th edn. (London, 1959), 193; Rawls, above n. 24, 237; Allan, above n. 24. In France equal treatment is also considered an important aspect of the *État de droit*, see Troper, above n. 22, 27 with references. Even critics of the Rule of Law accept that it should, and does, promote formal equality, but they argue that it fails to promote substantive equality, see R. M. Unger, *Law in Modern Society* (New York, 1976), 176–200.

[33] See Raz, above n. 24, 219; Jowell, above n. 24, 76; T. A. O. Endicott, 'The Impossibility of the Rule of Law' (1999) OJLS 1, 3.

[34] Although the right mix is, of course, contested in any society. See Raz, above n. 24, 214–15. See also for discussion of the 'rule of law crisis' in French society caused by frequent regulatory changes; J. Carbonnier, *Flexible Droit*, 7th edn. (Paris, 1992), 165–70.

[35] See Rawls, above n. 24, 235; Carbonnier, above n. 34, 173.

constancy inherent in the Rule of Law. However, it is important to be clear that the requirements apply differently to the four situations identified above.[36]

In the first situation a public authority seeks to revoke a formal decision (Situation 1). This type of action is extremely likely to frustrate the expectations and upset the plans of the addressee. The requirement of predictability in the Rule of Law therefore provides a very strong justification for protecting expectations created by formal decisions. Moreover, to grant this protection, upholding a person's expectation that a formal decision is final, will not normally conflict with the requirement of formal equality. Formal decisions are made according to procedures which ensure that they are, in all but very few instances, made according to prevailing law and policy. Decisions therefore tend to grant their addressee what any other addressee in his situation would obtain. If, on the other hand, the decision is unlawful, the justification for protection is weakened because the principle of lawful administration (legality) requires authorities to act *intra vires,* and because upholding an unlawful decision may lead to better treatment of the addressee than others in similar circumstances. However, the argument for protection of expectations is still valid and forceful. For the principle of lawful administration is not absolute, it should be balanced against the requirement of fairness. To allow the administration to go back on unlawful decisions may be unfair, because individuals are, given the complexity of modern administrative law, rarely in a position to discover that a formal decision is unlawful and will therefore often plan on the presumption that it is final.[37]

In the second situation, a public authority, explicitly or implicitly, represents that it will follow a certain procedure or policy in relation to a specific individual or group and subsequently makes a decision which departs from the representation (Situation 2). Administrative behaviour of this type is very likely to disappoint expectations and disrupt individual planning, as a specific assurance concerned with an individual and a particular set of facts conveys an impression of finality or non-revocability which lasts so long as the relevant facts remain unchanged. There is, therefore, a strong Rule of Law justification for protecting legitimate expectations in these circumstances. But to grant an individual what he has been led to expect is more likely to lead to unequal treatment than in the situation above. Advice given by authorities about specific situations is not normally subject to formal procedures. Consequently, representations are more frequently unlawful or out of line with existing policy than formal decisions. This weakens, but does not override, the justification for upholding expectations based on individualised representations. For individuals are often

[36] The following comments are developed further in the final sections of Chs. 2–4.

[37] And, some might add, it would be impractical to require individuals to verify the legality of decisions. See F. Ansell, 'Unauthorised Conduct of Government Agents: A Restrictive Rule of Equitable Estoppel Against the Government' (1986) Univ Chicago LR 1026, 1032.

unable to discover that advice is unlawful or out of line with policy, and it would not be practical or fair to require individuals to verify administrative advice in every instance.

In the third situation, a public authority makes a general representation about the procedure or policy it will follow in relation to a certain type of decision, but subsequently departs from the procedure or policy in the particular case (Situation 3). This is not only very likely to disappoint the affected person's expectations, there is also a strong egalitarian argument against treating one person differently from others subject to the procedure or policy. There is therefore a very strong Rule of Law justification for protecting legitimate expectations in departure situations.[38] Indeed, the justification for protection of individuals in this situation is as forceful as the justification for protection in Situation 1.

In the fourth situation the authority departs from its general representation in the light of a shift in general procedure or policy which has occurred between the initial representation and the decision (Situation 4). This situation is more complicated. An existing policy may create a reasonable expectation that it will continue to apply for some time or until further notice. The requirement of predictability in the Rule of Law therefore calls for some level of legal protection. The requirement of constancy adds weight to this justification. However, the justification is weakened by two considerations. First, policies should be, and are known to be, impermanent, they cannot reasonably be expected to remain fixed forever. Policies do not bear the mark of finality to the same extent as decisions and individualized representations. Second, the principle of equality does not provide support for protection in this situation. It is true that to decide cases in accordance with a new policy constitutes, compared to those cases decided under previous policy, a form of differential treatment.[39] For example, if a prisoner is refused home leave in February 2000 on the basis of a policy applicable that month, then he is treated differently from a prisoner who was granted home leave in January 2000 on the basis of the policy which operated at that time. However, not all differential treatment offends against the principle of equality or causes unfairness. Different treatment over time is justified, and therefore not a violation of equality, as all legal change would otherwise become impossible. It follows that while there is some normative justification for the protection of legitimate expectations against general changes of policy, it is weaker than in the other three situations.

[38] Whether the authority should be bound by policy is not to be confused with whether discretionary powers should be exercised on a case-by-case basis or be subject to policies and internal rules in the first place. See D. J. Galligan, 'The Nature and Function of Policies Within Discretionary Power' (1976) PL 332; R. Baldwin and K. Hawkins, 'Discretionary Justice: Davis Reconsidered' (1984) PL 570; Jowell, above n. 24, 62–8.

[39] See Allan, above n. 24, 175–6.

(C) The Rule of Law Theory in the English Case Law

It will be seen in the following chapters of this book that the protection of legitimate expectations in English, French, and EC law reflects the varying justifications which apply in Situations 1–4. At this point, it will suffice to illustrate the connection between the case law as it stands and the underlying rationales by a few English cases.

The need to protect individuals against the revocation of lawful administrative decisions (Situation 1) was acknowledged most clearly in *Re 56 Denton Road*.[40] In that case the owner of property at 56 Denton Road in Twickenham challenged the War Damages Commission's revocation of a decision it had previously made concerning his entitlement to statutory compensation for damage caused by enemy action during the Second World War. The court upheld the owner's claim on the grounds that a final administrative decision which affects the rights of a person cannot, in the absence of express statutory power or the consent of the person or persons affected, be altered or withdrawn.

The English courts have also accepted that there are cogent reasons to protect expectations created by specific representations (Situation 2). Thus, in the recent case of *Coughlan* the Court of Appeal held that a local authority could not go back on a promise to a disabled woman that a special housing unit would be her 'home for life' since doing so would violate her legitimate expectations.[41] The court held that while it is not *per se* unlawful for the administration to depart from its own assurances, the courts will intervene whenever the administration has not struck a fair balance between the expectations of the individual and the policy reasons in favour of a cause of action which would disappoint those expectations. The claimant does not have to prove that the administration acted wholly unreasonably or irrationally.

As noted above, equality and legal certainty both speak in favour of individual protection in Situation 3. The English courts accordingly take a strict view of departure from policy in particular instances. For example, in the case of *P* the police had cautioned a juvenile offender although he had not confessed to the crime as required by a prosecution policy circular.[42] The caution was quashed on the grounds that it departed from that policy, and the court did not require the applicant to show that the police had otherwise acted unreasonably or irrationally.[43]

The English courts' approach to Situation 4 is rather different. The relative weakness of the justification for upholding expectations against general changes of policy has led to an almost total denial of judicial protection. This

[40] *Re 56 Denton Rd., Twickenham, Middlesex* [1953] 1 Ch. 51.

[41] *R v Devon Health Authority, ex p Coughlan* [1999] Lloyd's LR Medical 306.

[42] *R v Commissioner of Police of the Metropolis, ex p P* (1996) 8 Admin LR 6.

[43] The applicant will, however, have to show unreasonableness if the administration offers a justification for its decision to depart from policy. See Ch. 4.4.

is best illustrated by the *Hargreaves* case mentioned above.[44] The Court of Appeal held in that case that prisoners affected by a general change of policy concerning their entitlement to home leave would only be able to invoke legitimate expectations, created by the previous policy, if they could show that the new policy, or the immediate application of that policy, was irrational, perverse, or unreasonable. As one might expect, the prisoners did not succeed in passing that high hurdle.

(D) Assessment of the Rule of Law Theory

The Rule of Law theory of legitimate expectations is more comprehensive and convincing than the reliance theory. It explains why the English courts take different approaches to the four situations in which legitimate expectations claims arise. It also explains why expectations are, and should be, protected in the absence of any 'real' detrimental reliance: to respect people's autonomy and to ensure equal treatment.[45] Reliance is only relevant in so far as it strengthens the Rule of Law justification for protection of legitimate expectations. Moreover, the Rule of Law theory is more flexible than the reliance theory. Proponents of the Rule of Law accept that the extent to which a legal system complies with its different strands at any given point in time is a matter of degree. For predictability, equality, and other Rule of Law requirements must be balanced against other important considerations.[46] It is therefore not paradoxical to argue concurrently that the Rule of Law requires protection of legitimate expectations and that such protection is subject to limitations flowing from authorities' duty always to take lawful action in the public interest. The theory has, however, met with both internal and external criticism.

I Internal Criticism

The internal criticism acknowledges the importance of autonomy and legal certainty, but argues that the recognition of legitimate expectations as a principle of administrative law would reduce, rather than increase, certainty for four distinct reasons.

First, 'reasonable' or 'legitimate' expectations are inherently vague[47] standards which introduce unpredictability and uncertainty in the law through the backdoor.[48] This argument is not convincing. Conceptual innovation inevitably

[44] *R v Home Secretary, ex p Hargreaves* [1997] 1 WLR 906.

[45] See Raz, above n. 24, 222.

[46] See Raz, above n. 24, 215. Compare Endicott, above n. 33.

[47] The term 'vague' is used here in the wide sense of linguistic indeterminacy rather than in the strict sense of the so-called Sorites Paradox. See J. Waldron, 'Vagueness in Law and language' (1994) California LR 509.

[48] See *Salemi v Mackellar* (1977) 137 CLR 396, 404; G. Richardson and M. Sunkin, 'Judicial Review: Questions of Impact' (1996) PL 79, 90; Woehrling, above n. 6, 31. For a similar criticism of 'legal certainty' as a principle of EC law, see B. Pacteau, 'La sécurité juridique, un principe qui nous manque?', AJDA 1995 Ed. spéciale, 131, 154.

causes some uncertainty which is gradually reduced as the courts flesh out the content of the relevant standards over time.[49] Indeed, it will be shown in subsequent chapters that the principles of legitimate expectations in English and EC law are today far more precisely defined than even ten years ago and that their application to most situations is relatively straightforward.[50] Moreover, even if the recognition of legitimate expectations does reduce certainty more permanently at a general level, the loss is offset by the gain in predictability and fairness in the treatment of individuals. For example, in the *Ng Yuen Shiu* case the House of Lords held that a promise by British immigration authorities to illegal immigrants in Hong Kong that all applicants would be granted an interview created a procedural legitimate expectation which the authorities were bound to respect.[51] Although the law of immigration became less clear-cut as a whole by this endorsement of the principle of legitimate expectations, those immigrants who had been promised, and come to expect, a certain treatment still gained considerably in their ability to plan and predict their lives.

Second, to protect expectations in change of policy situations (Situation 4), it may be necessary to make transitional provisions. Such provisions introduce uncertainty due to their inherent complexity.[52] An awareness of contemporary administrative practice reveals the weakness of this argument. Transitional provisions are often necessary, and in fact widely used, for practical reasons.[53] The recognition of legitimate expectations merely places policy-makers under an obligation to give proper consideration to the expectations when drafting such provisions.[54] Thus, although transitional provisions can create practical difficulties, the recognition of legitimate expectations is unlikely to increase such difficulties to any great extent.

Third, it is argued that the protection of legitimate expectations would have a 'chilling effect' upon public authorities in the following sense. If public authorities are bound by, or potentially liable in damages for, their representations on the grounds that they generate expectations in individuals, authorities will be much less willing to establish good practices, publish guidelines, and give informal advice lest this conduct be turned against them.[55] Thus, individual

[49] See Craig 646.

[50] See Waldron, above n. 47, 534–40, arguing that vagueness only causes problems in rare borderline cases.

[51] *A-G of Hong Kong v Ng Yuen Shiu* [1983] 2 AC 629.

[52] See AG Roemer [1973] ECR 738; R. Tavernier, 'Le Juge Communautaire et l'application dans le temps des règlements CEE', AFDI 1976, 169, 188; Héron, above n. 6,116, 127.

[53] See e.g. the transitional provisions discussed in *R v Home Secretary, ex p Hargreaves* [1997] 1 WLR 906.

[54] This may cause additional burdens upon the authority's fact-finding, but that is an issue unrelated to the alleged loss of legal certainty.

[55] Such fears are expressed by Ansell, above n. 37, 1046, S. France, 'Legitimate Expectations in New Zealand' (1990) NZULR 123, 140; G. Wignall, 'Legitimate Expectation and the Abuse of Power' (1994) NLJ 1038, 1039; De Smith 568; I. McLeod, *Judicial Review*, 2nd edn. (Chichester, 1998), 345. See also *Brooks and Burton Ltd v Secretary of State for the Environment* (1976) 75 LGR 285, 296.

planning will become more difficult because less information from public authorities will be available and certainty would therefore suffer. There is, however, no empirical evidence for the existence of such a chilling effect in Britain, the US, or in jurisdictions which have developed principles of substantive legitimate expectations (Germany, Holland, Denmark, and the EC) or damages liability for misrepresentation (notably France).[56] The chilling effect is indeed unlikely to pose a real problem for the following reasons.

It is well-known that authorities respond differently to legal constraints, including general principles of administrative law, due to different institutional settings and informal working rules.[57] Chilling would therefore not arise in all administrative sectors. The extent of the chilling effect also depends upon the nature of the principle of legitimate expectations which is adopted. A principle subject to fairly clear and strict limitations is unlikely to deter authorities completely, or even significantly, from giving advice. There is also an increasingly strong movement throughout Europe towards openness and transparency in administration, which is being pressed upon authorities by Ombudsmen,[58] governmental charters and consultation papers,[59] legislative initiatives,[60] as well as EC directives.[61] This movement is likely to counteract much of the alleged chilling effect. Moreover, public authorities derive benefits from providing informal advice and publishing policies because it provides a climate attractive to economic investors.[62] It is, for example, quite unrealistic to assume that a local planning authority would refuse to inform a company about its plans to build a large factory, creating numerous jobs in the region, on the grounds that the authority might be bound by that advice.[63] Finally, even if legal recognition of

[56] See 'Never Trust a Bureaucrat, Estoppel Against the Government', unsigned case note, (1969) Southern California LR 391, 397–401; M. Braunstein, 'In Defense of Traditional Immunity—Toward an Economic Rationale for not Estopping the Government' (1982) Rutgers LJ 1, 32–3; Richardson and Sunkin, above n. 48, 100. The risk of a chilling effect was raised following the decision of *Hedley Byrne v Heller* [1964] AC 465 which accepted banks' negligence liability for economic loss caused by advice about customers' financial situation. However, there is no evidence that banks ceased to give such advice.

[57] Indeed, one administrator, or part of an authority, may respond differently from another. See B. Hadfield, 'Judge-proofing Reviewable Decisions—Should Judges be Entrusted with Review?', in B. Hadfield (ed.), *Judicial Review: A Thematic Approach* (Dublin, 1995), 257; Richardson and Sunkin, above n. 48, 95–7.

[58] In Britain, the Parliamentary Commissioner for Administration's concept of maladministration includes 'neglecting to inform a person of his rights'. See D. J. Galligan, *Due Process and Fair Procedures: A Study of Administrative Procedures* (Oxford, 1996), 304–5. In the EC, openness is a priority for the newly established Ombudsman. See *Annual Report 1996*, [1997] OJ C 272/1.

[59] See notably The Citizen's Charter, discussed by Galligan, above n. 58, 306.

[60] See Draft Freedom of Information Bill 1999; Council Decision 93/731 on access to Council documents, Commission Decision 94/90 on access to Commission documents; *Lois* of 6/1–78 and 17/7–78 on access to public documents and computer registers.

[61] See notably Directive 96/313 (access to environmental information in the member states).

[62] See Sharpston, above n. 26, 106. It also increases legitimacy and compliance as explained in section 3.

[63] Compare *Brooks and Burton Ltd v Secretary of State for the Environment* (1976) 75 LGR 285, 296.

legitimate expectations does lead to a drop in the quantity of information available from public authorities, this must be weighed against the potential gain in the quality of the information which is still made available. Public authorities are likely to take precautions to ensure that representations are factually correct, complete, and not misleading if they are bound by, or liable in damages for what is being represented.[64] Consequently, even given the assumption that people will be given less information, the information actually granted will be more useful as a basis for individual planning and economic decisions. This in turn promotes autonomy. In Britain, incorrect or incomplete advice is one of the most frequent complaints before the Parliamentary Commissioner for Administration[65] and in France it is a very fertile source of administrative court litigation.[66] A loss in quantity would therefore appear to be a price worth paying for a gain in quality.[67]

The fourth, and last, internal criticism of the Rule of Law theory of expectations is that the recognition of a principle of legitimate expectations would cause a flood of judicial review challenges to administrative decisions.[68] This would in turn strain judicial resources, delay the expedition of the case load, and cause legal uncertainty for administrators and individuals who would not know whether it would be safe to rely upon those decisions for fear that they be challenged and eventually overturned.[69] This fear is, at first sight, supported by the fact that judicial review case loads[70] and delays[71] have increased in recent

[64] See 'Never Trust a Bureaucrat' above n. 56, 402; D. Feldman, 'Judicial Review: a Way of Controlling Government?' (1988) Public Administration 21, 27.

[65] See A. R. Mowbray, 'A Right to Official Advice: The Parliamentary Commissioner's Perspective' (1990) PL 68; Galligan, above n. 58, 305.

[66] An electronic survey of CE decisions since 1965 revealed over a hundred complaints of this nature. See Ch. 6.

[67] However, this argument is ultimately inconclusive in the absence of a thorough empirical study comparing the relative gain in quality with the loss in quantity. See section 4.B.

[68] See Ansell, above n. 37, 1045.

[69] Frequent judicial review challenges may also divert administrative resources away from long-term planning, slow down decision-making, demoralize staff, and discourage the pursuit of radical initiatives. See Baldwin and Hawkins, above n. 38, 596–7; Cranston, above n. 10, 54–60. There is, however, little empirical knowledge about the extent of these dangers (Richardson and Sunkin, above n. 48, 82–3) and their importance is cast into doubt by recent literature. See T. Prosser, 'Regulation, Markets and Legitimacy', in J. L. Jowell and L. Oliver (eds.), *The Changing Constitution*, 3rd edn. (London, 1994), 237, 258; M. Loughlin, *Legality and Locality: the Role of Law in Central–Local Government Relations* (Oxford, 1996), 401 f.; A. Barker, 'The Impact of Judicial Review: Perspectives from Whitehall and the Courts' (1996) PL 612, 613; A. H. Hammond, 'Judicial Review: the Continuing Interplay between Law and Policy' (1998) PL 34, 41.

[70] See L. Bridges, G. Mezaros, and M. Sunkin, *Judicial Review in Perspective*, 2nd edn. (London, 1995); Brown and Bell Appendix E–G.

[71] In Britain, the early 1990s saw considerable delays in judicial review procedures, but they have now been reduced to 6–7 months. See Lord Woolf, 'Judicial Review—The Tensions Between the Executive and the Judiciary' (1998) LQR 579, 587. In France, serious delays persist in the CE and the CAAs, and a simple case takes on average 18–24 months to reach judgment. See Brown and Bell 124 and Appendix E reporting that 24 per cent of the cases decided by the CE in 1996 had been pending for more than three years, and 8 per cent for over 5 years.

years and that the principle of legitimate expectations, which has been adopted in English and EC law, has been invoked on numerous occasions.[72] The fear is unfounded for two reasons.

The first reason is that the increase in judicial review applications may be managed by the application of time limits,[73] transfer out of the judicial review procedure of selected categories of cases,[74] simplification of judicial review procedures,[75] and more importantly by improved alternative dispute resolution mechanisms.[76] The retarded development of principles of fair and good administration is hardly an appropriate response to problems caused by increasing case loads.

The second reason is that there is in fact no direct causal connection between the acceptance of legitimate expectations as principles of judicial review and the increasing case load.[77] At a general level, the increase in applications for judicial review may be linked with the emergence of a more litigious and rights conscious culture,[78] the extension of legal aid schemes,[79] the gradual recasting of the traditional welfare state,[80] inadequate administrative appeal systems in

[72] A Lexis search in September 1999 found over 500 British, 750 EC, and eight French judicial review decisions in which legitimate expectations arguments were discussed. Until 1992 at least 118 EC judgments had dealt with legitimate expectations claims in substance, and in 1995 over 300 had mentioned it in some form, see M.-H. Planchon, 'Le principe de la confiance légitime devant la Cour de Justice des Communatés Européennes', Revue de la Recherche Juridique—Droit Prospectif 1994, 447; J.-P. Puissochet, '"Vous avez dit confiance légitime?"', in *Mélanges Guy Braibant* (Paris, 1996), 581, 585. See also for useful information on early English case law, R. E. Riggs, 'Legitimate Expectations and Procedural Fairness in English Law' (1988) AJCL 395.

[73] Strict time limits already apply in Britain, France, and the EC to protect public bodies and individuals the uncertainty caused by judicial review. See Supreme Court Act 1981, s 31(6); *Code des tribunaux administratifs et des cours administratives d'appel* Art R102; Art 230 EC.

[74] See C. Harlow, 'Why Public Law is Private Law: An Invitation to Lord Woolf', in A. A. S. Zuckerman and R. Cranston (eds.), *Reform of Civil Procedure: Essays on 'Access to Justice'* (Oxford, 1995), 201, 208–9 mentioning tax and family cases.

[75] See Lord Woolf, *Access to Justice: Final Report to the Lord Chancellor on the Civil Justice System in England and Wales* (London, 1996), 24, 250–60.

[76] In Britain, appeal rights are to be improved in immigration and housing cases both of which have generated much litigation. See *Access to Justice*, above n. 75, 217. See also the calls for an Administrative Appeals Tribunal by Lord Woolf, 'Judicial Review: A Possible Programme for Reform' (1992) PL 221, 230; A. E. Boyle, 'Sovereignty, Accountability, and the Reform of Administrative Law', in G. Richardson and H. Genn (eds.), *Administrative Law and Government Action* (Oxford, 1994), 102. In the EU, the Ombudsman may also lead to a drop in the number of judicial review actions.

[77] In France, where a principle of legitimate expectations has not been accepted, case loads have also risen rapidly in the last 30 years; see footnote 70. It is unclear to what extent a general tendency towards more strict judicial scrutiny of administrative action contributes to the case load. Compare Lord Woolf, above n. 5, 60; Allison 183.

[78] See Loughlin, above n. 69, 415. H. M. Kritzer, 'Courts, Justice and Politics in England', in H. Jacob (ed.), *Courts, Law, and Politics in Comparative Perspective* (New Haven, 1996), 81, 125–35 found on the basis of wide-ranging statistical material that the litigious culture in Britain is today comparable to that of the USA.

[79] See C. Harlow and R. Rawlings, *Pressure Through Law* (London, 1992), 295.

[80] Causing pressure in particular on local authorities in areas such as housing and education. See Bridges, Mezaros, and Sunkin, above n. 70, 43–5.

certain areas,[81] privatization and contracting-out,[82] central–local government litigation,[83] increasing interest group action,[84] and possibly a general decline in respect for the law in modern government.[85] More specifically, a survey of over 500 British, French, and EC court decisions referring to legitimate expectations reveals that expectations claims are often used as 'make-weights' in cases concerned with other issues.[86] This 'over-use' of expectations arguments in judicial review is partly the result of the conceptual uncertainty which initially followed the acceptance of legitimate expectations both in Britain and the EC.[87] In the EC, judicial control of retroactive rule-making is based on principles of legal certainty and legitimate expectations.[88] This inflates the number of 'expectations cases' compared to France and Britain where retroactivity is controlled without explicit reference to the notion of expectations.[89] The incongruence between the protection of expectation in situations covered by EC law and purely domestic situations,[90] and the absence hitherto of an effective British human rights protection also contribute to the 'over-use' of legitimate expectations claims.[91] However, all of these factors are now becoming less important. As will be shown in subsequent chapters, the limits of the principle of legitimate expectations both in English and EC law are now significantly less uncertain than before and the incongruence between English and EC law is diminishing. Thus, the recognition of expectations as a principle of administrative law has not, in and of itself, created large numbers of judicial review

[81] In Britain, immigration and housing cases make up a large proportion of all judicial review applications and this has been linked with inadequate appeals. See Bridges, Mezaros, and Sunkin, above n. 70, 31.

[82] See S. James, 'The Political and Administrative Consequences of Judicial Review' (1996) Public Administration 613, 614; C. Scott, 'The Jurifidication of Regulatory Relation in the UK Utilities Sector', in J. Black, P. Muchlinski and P. Walker (eds.), *Commercial Regulation and Judicial Review* (Oxford, 1998), 55–6.

[83] In Britain, this type of litigation make up 4–5 per cent of all cases. See Bridges, Mezaros, and Sunkin, above n. 70, 37.

[84] See generally Harlow and Rawlings, above n. 79.

[85] See Lord Woolf, 'Public Law–Private Law: Why the Divide?' (1986) PL 220, 221–2; Barker, above n. 69, 613. See further on the shift from legalistic values towards efficiency and effectiveness in British administration under the 'New Public Management', N. Lewis, *Choice and the Public Order: Rising Above Politics* (London, 1996); D. Woodhouse, *In Pursuit of Good Administration: Ministers, Civil Servants and Judges* (Oxford, 1997).

[86] See Sharpston, above n. 26, 160; Puissochet, above n. 72, 585–6.

[87] In Britain, this uncertainty has been prolonged by the courts' gradual extension of the principle from procedure to substance over a period of over 20 years. See Ch. 4.2.A.

[88] e.g. Case 98/78 *Racke* [1979] ECR 69. There are many such cases as the economic nature of much EC regulation necessitates frequent resort to retroactive action.

[89] See F. A. R. Bennion, *Statutory Interpretation*, 3rd edn. (London, 1997), 235–43 and on the principle of *non-rétroactivité*, P. Delvolvé, 'Le principe de non-rétroactivité dans la jurisprudence économique du Conseil d'Etat', in *Mélanges Marcel Waline*, vol. II (Paris, 1974), 355.

[90] See section 4.A.

[91] e.g. *CCSU v Minister for the Civil Service* [1985] AC 374 (violation of the right to union membership attacked successfully on grounds of legitimate expectations). Thus, the incorporation of the ECHR by the Human Rights Act 1998 may cause a drop in challenges based upon legitimate expectations.

applications. The potential uncertainty caused by judicial review of administrative action is therefore hardly a persuasive reason to reject the adoption, or further extension, of a principle of legitimate expectations.

II External Criticism

The Rule of Law based justification for legitimate expectations may also be criticized on the grounds that the values of autonomy and economic freedom, from which it proceeds, are not an adequate foundation for a modern theory of constitutional and administrative law.[92] This external criticism is no more convincing than the internal criticism discussed above. First, it is thought that autonomy remains an important, if not the only, value which should be promoted by constitutional and administrative law.[93] Second, the Rule of Law is perhaps less dependent upon adherence to autonomy than some of its critics assume. Jürgen Habermas has developed an interesting Rule of Law theory, discussed below, which takes social co-ordination problems rather than autonomy as its starting point. Finally, the justification for protection of legitimate expectations is wider than the Rule of Law considerations discussed so far. It is supplemented by other important considerations as will be explained in sections 3 and 4.

(E) An Alternative Rule of Law Theory

The traditional Rule of Law theory, with its requirements of certainty, formal equality, and constancy, was used above to justify the legal recognition of legitimate expectations. The starting point for that theory is autonomy. Jürgen Habermas has developed a Rule of Law theory which takes a different starting point.[94]

According to Habermas co-ordination problems are central to social life.[95] Social interactions are subject to conditions of 'double contingency', which make planning and predictions about the outcome of choices uncertain.[96] Co-ordination is achieved in two ways. In the first instance, individuals develop 'behavioural expectations' about how nature works (the sun will rise tomorrow) and how others will act (if I agree to a dinner you will expect me to show up). Relying on these expectations, individuals then engage in discourse which, under certain conditions of rational argumentation, takes the form of 'communicative action'.[97] The role of law is to reinforce the existing

[92] See J. F. Handler, *The Conditions of Discretion: Autonomy, Community, Bureaucracy* (New York, 1986), 7; N. Lacey, 'The Jurisprudence of Discretion: Escaping the Legal Paradigm', in K. Hawkins (ed.), *The Uses of Discretion* (Oxford, 1992).

[93] See Oliver, above n. 6.

[94] J. Habermas, *Between Facts and Norms* (Cambridge, 1996). See on the place of autonomy in Habermas's work, R. Alexy, 'Habermas's Paradigm of Law' (1994) Ratio Juris 231.

[95] See Habermas, above n. 94, 139.

[96] See N. Luhmann, *A Sociological Theory of Law* (London, 1985), 24–31.

[97] See J. Habermas, *The Theory of Communicative Action* (Boston, 1984), 273–337; above n. 94, 17–18, 26.

co-ordination[98] by stabilizing behavioural expectations[99] and by institutionalizing the conditions of rational discourse.[100] Habermas writes that the contribution of a modern legal system is:

> [T]o engender a legal certainty that enables the addressees of law to calculate the consequences of their own and others' behaviour. [Therefore] legal norms must [be] general and . . . applied to all persons and all comparable cases in the same way.[101] [Thus] established law guarantees the enforcement of legally expected behaviour and therewith the certainty of law.[102]

Thus, if one accepts that law is a system which reinforces existing co-ordination,[103] it follows that law should be certain, predictable, and applied consistently (with formal equality).[104] These requirements are, despite their root in co-ordination and communicative action theory, similar to those developed by Joseph Raz and others on the basis of autonomy.[105] It was explained above how those requirements justify the recognition of legitimate expectations in the four situations.[106]

3 Legitimate Expectations, Trust, and Good Administration

So far, the discussion has been primarily concerned with fairness and control of administrative decision-making. The Rule of Law justification for protection of legitimate expectations has a certain 'red-light' quality.[107] However, recognition of legitimate expectations is not only about fairness to the individual and control of administrative power, it is also a powerful means to administrative efficacy.[108] Administrative efficacy is an aspect of the wider notion of good administration, the enforcement of which is an important part of modern judicial review.[109]

[98] See similarly Galligan, above n. 58, 141: law is 'not just a system of control imposed from above, . . . but a system of regulation occurring within social relationships'. Compare the depiction of law as a system which *establishes* co-ordination by coercion and regulation in Rawls, above n. 24, 235.

[99] See Habermas, above n. 94, 143 and similarly Luhmann, above n. 96, 29.

[100] This institutionalization takes the form of (democratic) procedures. See Alexy, above n. 94.

[101] Habermas, above n. 94, 143–4.

[102] Ibid. 198.

[103] For this view, see J. Raz, *Practical Reasons and Norms* (Oxford, 1975), 64, 159; G. J. Postema, 'Coordination and Convention at the Foundations of Law' (1982) Journal of Legal Studies 165; J. Finnis, 'Law as Co-ordination' (1989) Ratio Juris 97.

[104] See Habermas, above n. 94, 125.

[105] See references above n. 24.

[106] See section 2.B.

[107] On red and green light theories of administration, see C. Harlow and R. Rawlings, *Law and Administration*, 2nd edn. (London, 1997), chs.1–2; M. Loughlin, *Public Law and Political Theory* (Oxford, 1992), ch. 4.

[108] See Loughlin, above n. 69, 398 arguing that efficacy is related to the Rule of Law requirements inherent in Lon Fuller's concept of the inner morality of law.

[109] See D. Oliver, 'Is the *Ultra Vires* Rule the Basis of Judicial Review?' (1987) PL 543; J. Laws, 'Judicial Remedies and the Constitution' (1994) MLR 213; Lord Woolf, above n. 5, 65–7; P. P. Craig,

Why is it, as Lord Fraser pointed out, in the 'interest of good administration' that public authorities should respect expectations they have created?[110] The reason is that administrative power is more likely to be perceived as legitimate authority if exercised in a way which respects legitimate expectations.[111] Perceived legitimate authority is more efficacious because it encourages individuals to participate in decision-making processes, to co-operate with administrative initiatives, and to comply with administrative regulations.[112] Greater compliance will in turn improve the administration's ability to solve co-ordination problems, and that may actually make its exercise of authority more legitimate. The acceptance of principles of administrative law, which require authorities to respect legitimate expectations, is therefore not merely in the interest of individuals. It is, very much, in the interest of the administration itself. Three points will illustrate this proposition.

First, public authorities are unlikely to be perceived as trustworthy if they are free to, and do in fact, go back on representations with impunity.[113] Legal protection of legitimate expectations therefore promotes trust and confidence in authorities which in turn encourage individuals to participate, co-operate, and comply.[114]

Second, the recognition of legitimate expectations is likely to make public authorities anxious to provide quality information to avoid liability for disappointment of expectations. Thus, the availability of reliable public information will increase. This may in turn facilitate the public's acceptance of administrative policies, because disagreement with public policies and actions is often fuelled by a lack of information about the facts on which those policies are based. For example, the relatively unknown extent of the danger caused by genetically modified food products adds to the fierce debate over the licensing of such products. If more reliable information on this danger were available, a source of discontent with GM food policies would be reduced. Public co-operation and compliance would arguably increase as a result.

Third, legal protection of legitimate expectations requires that policies are not changed too abruptly.[115] Those affected by a change in policy must be given

'*Ultra Vires* and the Foundations of Judicial Review' (1998) CLJ 63. Compare C. F. Forsyth, 'Of Fig Leaves and Fairy Tales: the Ultra Vires Doctrine, the Sovereignty of Parliament and Judicial Review' (1996) CLJ 122 for the more traditional view that courts are concerned with enforcing parliamentary intent (the *ultra vires* theory).

[110] *A-G of Hong Kong v Ng Yuen Shiu* [1983] 2 All ER 311, 350. See similarly *R v Devon Health Authority, ex p Coughlan* [1999] Lloyd's LR Medical 306; Case 105/75 *Giuffrida v Commission* [1976] ECR 1395 para 17.

[111] See 'Never Trust a Bureaucrat', above n. 56, 403. See also J. Waldron, 'The Rule of Law in Contemporary Liberal Theory' (1989) Ratio Juris 79, 94; Summers, above n. 24, 131.

[112] See Hawkins, above n. 29, 29.

[113] This was realised at an early stage in French writings, see G. Jèze, 'Essai d'une théorie générale des fonctionnaires de fait', RDP 1914, 48, 55. See also Forsyth, above n. 6, 384.

[114] See 'Never Trust a Bureaucrat', above n. 56, 402–3; J. F. Handler, 'Discretion: Power, Quiescence, and Trust', in K. Hawkins (ed.), *The Uses of Discretion* (Oxford, 1992), 331, 341.

[115] See above section 2.B.

adequate advance warning, or transitional measures must be adopted. This also increases co-operation and compliance as those subject to the policies are given time to acquaint themselves with, and adapt their behaviour to, the new policy.

4 Other Justifications for the Protection of Legitimate Expectations

(A) The Legal Osmosis Theory

An impressive body of literature has in recent years explored the phenomenon of spill-over or 'osmosis' of legal principles and concepts within the European Union.[116] The importance of this phenomenon for present purposes is as follows. Public authorities have a duty to comply with general principle of EC law in situations which have an EC law dimension.[117] This occurs where the authority implements or applies secondary EC law[118] or derogates from the free movement provisions of the EC Treaty on grounds of public policy.[119] The protection of substantive legitimate expectations is one of the most important of these EC law principles. It follows that, in so far as the EC principle provides greater protection of expectations than domestic law, a situation arises in which expectations issues are subject to 'better' treatment in cases with an EC dimension than in purely domestic cases.[120] There is growing recognition that this type of 'two-speed justice'[121] is problematic for a number of reasons.[122]

The most obvious and cogent reason why cases falling within purely domestic law should not be treated differently from cases with a Community law dimension is that it is highly impractical for administrators and courts to operate two systems of law in what may be closely intertwined factual matters.[123] This may lead, at best, to an increased cost of administration and, at worst, to wrong decisions. It may also create a bulk of judicial review applications because litigants and practitioners push to close the gap between EC

[116] For a few recent contributions; see J. Schwarze (ed.), *Administrative Law under European Influence* (Baden-Baden, 1996); J. S. Bell, 'Mechanisms for Cross-fertilisation of Administrative Law in Europe', in J. Beatson and T. Tridimas (eds.), *New Directions in European Public Law* (Oxford, 1998), 147; W. Van Gerven, 'Mutual Permeation of Public and Private Law at the National and Supranational Level' (1998) MJ 7.

[117] See P. P. Craig and G. De Búrca, *EU Law: Text and Materials*, 2nd edn. (Oxford, 1998), 317–30.

[118] Case 5/88 *Wachauf v Germany* [1989] ECR 2609.

[119] Case C-260/89 *ERT v DEP* [1991] ECR I-2925.

[120] In subsequent chapters I will seek to ascertain whether there is in fact a significant difference in the way expectations are protected and, if so, whether the EC principle of legitimate expectations should be adopted in English law.

[121] Bell, above n. 116, 160.

[122] See I. Ward, 'The Anomalous, the Wrong, and the Unhappy: UK Administrative Law in a European Perspective' (1994) NILQ 46; Forsyth, above n. 6, 381; Lord Irvine, 'The Development of Human Rights in Britain under an Incorporated Convention on Human Rights' (1998) PL 221, 230–2.

[123] See e.g. *R v Minister of Agriculture, Fisheries and Food, ex p First City Trading* The Times 20/12–96.

and domestic situations.[124] Harmonization of national law principles of administrative law with EC law principles may therefore promote efficient administration.

Other arguments advanced in favour of spill-over are far less convincing. Walter Van Gerven has asked: why should individuals be treated less favourably under national law than under EC law? Would different treatment of domestic and EC situations not offend against substantive equality[125] and thereby the Rule of Law in so far as it is taken to include substantive, as well as formal, equality?[126] The answer is that differential treatment does not violate the principle of equality, as it is justified by two considerations.

First, when a national authority acts within the sphere of EC law, it acts as 'the arm of the EC', while when it acts in a purely domestic situation, it acts as the arm of the British government. This, it is thought, presents a relevant difference, which may justify different treatment. Now it may well be that the population does not generally perceive this difference as relevant, and that the courts will therefore come under increasing pressure to change national law in the direction of Community law. However, it is important not to confuse this socio-legal pressure with a morally compelling argument derived from equality. Second, to treat one individual less favourably often improves the situation of some other individual or the general public. For example, to protect the expectations of the holder of a licence to discharge chemicals in the environment may be to the detriment of the environment and other licence applicants. Thus, the choice between EC law principles, which may emphasise individual rights and interests, and national principles, which may leave public authorities more room to regulate in the public interest, is not a choice between good and bad law. It is a choice between different conceptions of the relation between individual and community. If one agrees with those who favour a legal system which emphasizes the individual's autonomy, rights and interests, this should be stated explicitly and principles like legitimate expectations justified on that basis. Simple assertions that EC law principles are 'better' are not helpful.

Harmonization of domestic and EC principles is also said to promote what Ronald Dworkin has termed the integrity of law.[127] Integrity presupposes the coherent application of law in accordance with a set of moral principles. By giving legal recognition to expectations in cases with an EC dimension, but not in others, the legal system fails to apply coherently the moral principles which justify this recognition. However, for this argument to have any real force, it must be shown that the moral principle which justifies the EC principle is better, and

[124] This phenomenon is well known in English law. See *M v Home Office* [1993] 3 All ER 537; *Woolwich BS v IRC* [1993] AC 70. Litigants have also attempted, so far unsuccessfully, to persuade the French administrative courts to develop a domestic principle of legitimate expectations. See Ch. 4.2.B.

[125] Van Gerven, above n. 116, 23–4.

[126] Most British Rule of Law theories only include formal equality, see references in n. 24.

[127] R. M. Dworkin, *Law's Empire* (London, 1986), ch. 6.

indeed more applicable in Britain (or France or any other Member State), than the moral principle which justifies the different principle of English law. Thus, it is necessary to explicate, as I have attempted to do in section 2, what the justification for recognition of legitimate expectations actually is. In and of itself, the integrity argument is of little assistance.

Finally, whether spill-over from European law to national law should take place depends upon one's view of the respective roles of the EU and the nation states. Implicit in arguments based on equality, integrity, and so on is an ideological preference for the political goal of European integration. The national courts are seen as participants in the formation of a European federation with a harmonized legal system. It is, however, doubtful to what extent national courts should be involved in the process of harmonization and integration.[128] Integration is only one aspect of the emerging federation as the insertion of the principle of subsidiarity into the EC Treaty clearly acknowledged.[129] While EC law principles like legitimate expectations may function as a very valuable source of inspiration, their spill-over into national law is only justified if such principles are actually better than national equivalents in the national context.

(B) Legitimate Expectations and Economic Efficiency

Economists have shown that societal arrangements, including legal institutions and principles, which promote economic efficiency also stimulate growth and prosperity. Efficiency is therefore a value which administrative law should promote, albeit not without due recognition of what is perceived as fair.[130] The question is which legal principle will increase efficiency: a principle which leaves authorities free to change policies and decisions in the light of changing societal circumstances, or a principle which places limitations on changes through the protection of expectations?

Economic efficiency may be defined as the exploitation of economic resources in a way which maximizes value.[131] Resources are to be allocated to, and ultimately consumed by, those individuals who value them most highly.[132] Economic operators take decisions in a state of imperfect information because there are costs associated with the acquisition of information.[133] This creates

[128] This issue, and the related issue of the role of the Community courts as the motor of European integration, is beyond the scope of this book. See H. Rasmussen, *On Law and Policy in the European Court of Justice* (The Hague, 1986).

[129] Art 4 (previously 3B) EC.

[130] See C. G. Veljanovski, 'The New Law-and-Economics: A Research Review', in A. I. Ogus and C. G. Veljanovski, *Readings in the Economics of Law and Regulation* (Oxford, 1984), 12, 22–3; C. E. Goodhart, 'Economics and the Law: Too Much One-Way Traffic?' (1997) MLR 1, 16.

[131] See Veljanovski, above n. 130, 17–22; A. Mas-Colell, M. D. Whinston and J. R. Green, *Microeconomic Theory* (Oxford, 1995), ch. 5.

[132] 'Valuing' is measured by the individual's willingness to pay, either in money or kind, to acquire the resource. See Veljanovski, above n. 130, 17.

[133] See J. Hey, *Uncertainty in Microeconomics* (Oxford, 1979), 56.

inefficiencies in two ways. First, the transaction costs inherent in information gathering inhibit the allocation of resources to the person who values them most highly. Second, the imperfection of information actually gathered means that some resources are 'by mistake' not allocated to the person who value them most highly.

The legal recognition of legitimate expectations would have an effect upon transaction costs and efficiency, but the nature and extent of this effect is difficult to predict. Some authors state that the protection of legitimate expectations would increase efficiency. If operators were able to rely safely upon representations by public bodies, knowing that their expectations based on such representations would be protected, the cost of information gathering would be reduced and more efficient allocation of resources would occur.[134] Others take the opposite view that if public authorities knew that they were bound by their representations, they would less inclined to give advice and publish policies. Consequently, less than perfect information would be available for economic operators causing an increase in transaction costs and inefficient allocation decisions.[135] Which of these views is more in tune with reality can only be decided on the basis of a thorough empirical study, beyond the scope of this book, of the impact of legitimate expectations upon the behaviour of public officials.[136] However, as explained above, the experience of Continental jurisdictions suggests that the adoption of a principle of substantive legitimate expectations would not make administrators much less inclined to advise and communicate with citizens. In any event, any loss in the quantity of information provided by public authorities must be weighed against the potential gain in the quality of such information.[137]

5 Preliminary Conclusion

The justification for the legal protection of legitimate expectations engendered by administrative decisions, representations, and conduct may now be stated more precisely.

Fairness requires protection of expectations for two reasons. First, because a disappointed expectation may cause considerable harm to an individual who has relied upon its fulfilment (the reliance theory). Second, because expectations are central to autonomy and planning of one's life (the Rule of Law theory). Fairness is supplemented by two practical considerations of great importance. Protection of legitimate expectations will in the long term promote trust in public authorities and thereby also their perceived legitimacy and

[134] See 'Never Trust a Bureaucrat', above n. 56; Tridimas, above n. 21, 163.

[135] See Braunstein, above n. 56, 32–5, and Sharpston, above n. 26, 105 stating that 'in the general economic interest . . . there should probably be a presumption of legislative freedom.'

[136] See Braunstein, above n. 56, 32; Ansell, above n. 37, footnote 80.

[137] See section 2.

efficacy. Moreover, in so far as the EC principle of legitimate expectations differs from its equivalent in domestic law, recognition along the lines of EC law will add simplicity and thereby efficiency to domestic law. Finally, it is possible, but not certain, that recognition of legitimate expectations will enhance economic efficiency.

It follows that the normative justification for legal protection of legitimate expectations is very strong.[138] However, as pointed out above, this is only one side of the equation. This protection of legitimate expectations is subject to the requirements of lawful government in the public interest. In the following chapters I will consider how a balance between fairness, legality and flexibility may be struck by a combination of procedural, substantive, and compensatory rules. It will then be possible to determine more precisely, in the light of a comparative analysis of English, French, and EC law, how and in what circumstances administrative law should uphold expectations created by administrative decisions and representations.

[138] See also P. Roubier who ranked certainty over both justice and progress (cited by Carbonnier, above n. 34, 172).

Chapter 2

Procedural Protection of Legitimate Expectations

1 Introduction

It was argued in Chapter 1 that public law should, primarily for reasons of fairness and trust in administration, protect legitimate expectations created by administrative decisions, representations, and conduct. In this chapter I will examine how principles of administrative procedure contribute towards meeting those requirements. The connection between procedures and expectations may be explained as follows.

First, procedures may reduce the risk that expectations will *actually* be disappointed in a way which causes unfairness or mistrust in government, because they affect the outcomes of administrative decision-making processes.[1] If persons affected by administrative action are given advance notice, they may adapt their expectations and act so as to avoid or limit loss caused by reliance upon previous administrative representations and conduct. If affected persons are consulted or heard, their expectations and reliance can be brought to the administration's attention, and arguments against action which will disappoint those expectations may be presented. If decisions which affect expectations are followed by reasons, the administration will be forced to consider the justification for disappointing those expectations.

Second, procedures may reduce the *feeling* of unfairness and mistrust which a person whose expectations are disappointed often experiences. For if the holder of an expectation is granted a notification, a say in the process, and a justification for why his expectation cannot be upheld, the administration acknowledges that its action affects his autonomy and personal dignity.[2]

It will now, with these general comments in mind, be considered to what extent legitimate expectations are subject to procedural protection in English,[3]

[1] Although it remains uncertain *how* effective procedures are at affecting outcomes. See D. J. Galligan, *Due Process and Fair Procedures* (Oxford, 1996), 360–1.

[2] See J. L. Mashaw, *Due Process in the Administrative State* (New Haven, 1985), 104–55; R. M. Dworkin, *A Matter of Principle* (Oxford, 1985), 79–84; T. R. S. Allan, 'Procedural Fairness and the Duty of Respect' (1998) OJLS 497. Compare Galligan, above n. 1, 75–82, 122–7.

[3] See generally R. Baldwin and D. Horne, 'Expectations in a Joyless Landscape' (1986) MLR 685; G. Ganz, 'Legitimate Expectation', in C. Harlow (ed.), *Public Law and Politics* (London, 1986), 145; P. Elias, 'Legitimate Expectations and Judicial Review', in J. L. Jowell and D. Oliver (eds.), *New Directions in Judicial Review* (London, 1988); C. F. Forsyth, 'The Provenance and Protection of Legitimate Expectations' (1988) CLJ 238; R. E. Riggs, 'Legitimate Expectations and Procedural Fairness in English Law' (1988) AJCL 395; P. P. Craig, 'Legitimate Expectations: A Conceptual Analysis' (1992) LQR 79; R. Singh, 'Making Legitimate Use of Legitimate Expectations' (1994) NLJ 1215; De Smith 417–30; R. Singh and K. Steyn, 'Legitimate Expectations in 1996: Where Now' (1996) JR 17; B. Schwehr, 'A Study in Fairness in the Field of Community Care' (1997) JSWFL 159, 247.

French,[4] and EC law.[5] The discussion will be structured as follows. First, a comparative overview of administrative procedures in English, French, and EC law will be given. Second, I will analyse the procedural protections which apply when administrative authorities revoke decisions or go back on informal representations (Situations 1–4). Due to the limited space available only the most important aspects of fair procedures will be discussed (namely notice, hearing, and reasons).[6] Finally, the results of the comparative survey will be summed up and proposals for reform of English law will be presented.

2 Procedural Fairness in English, French, and EC Law: A Comparative Overview

Administrative procedure has traditionally played a more important role in the common law than in Continental legal systems. While the British courts had by the seventeenth century devised principles of 'natural justice' to control administrative power, the French courts have traditionally relied more upon substantive principles of judicial review and damages liability for this purpose.[7] A number of historical, ideological, and socio-legal factors may explain this difference. Two explanations are particularly important for our purposes.[8]

[4] See generally R. Odent, 'Les droits de la défense', EDCE 1953, 55; 'De la décision Trompier-Gravier à la décision Garysas', EDCE 1962, 43; M. Waline '*Audi Alterem Partem*', in *Livre Jubilaire du Conseil d'État du Grand-Duché de Luxembourg* (Luxembourg, 1957), 495; R. Hostiou, *Procédures et formes de l'acte administratif unilatéral en droit français* (Paris, 1974), ch. 2; D. K. Allen, '*Audi Alterem Partem* in France' (1980) PL 288; *LGA* 350–4; B. Genevois, 'Principes généraux du droit', in F. Gazier, R. Drago and A. Dupie (eds.), *Encyclopédie Dalloz: Répertoire de contentieux administratif* (Paris, 1996), nos. 350–92; C. Eude-Guias in *JC* Fasc. 107–20; Chapus 1020–54; H. Zeghbib, 'Principe du contradictoire et procédure administrative non contentieuse', RDP 1998, 467.

[5] See generally C.-D. Ehlermann and D. Oldekop, 'Due Process in Administrative Procedure', in *Reports to the 8th F. I. D. E. Congress*, vol. III (1978), 11.1–11.20; V. Korah, 'The Rights of Defence in Administrative Proceedings Under Community Law' (1980) CLP 73; O. Due, 'Le respect des droits de la défense dans le droit administratif communautaire', CDE 1987, 383; D. Curtin, 'Constitutionalism in the European Community: The Right to Fair Procedures in Administrative Law', in J. O'Reilly (ed.), *Human Rights and Constitutional Law: Essays in Honour of Brian Walsh* (Dublin, 1992), 293; Schwarze 1320–71; K. Lenaerts and J. Vanhamme, 'Procedural Right of Private Parties in the Community Administrative Process' (1997) CMLRev 531; H. P. Nehl, *Principles of Administrative Procedure in EC Law* (Oxford, 1999), 70–99; T. Tridimas, *The General Principles of EC Law* (Oxford, 1999), 244–75.

[6] Thus, the right to be granted adequate time to prepare answers, access to files, opportunity to make oral representations, opportunity to call and cross-examine witnesses and opponents, legal representation, and the right to have a decision decided without bias will not be discussed.

[7] It is debated in France to what extent French procedural principles differ from their English counterparts. See Waline, above n. 4, J. Lemasurier, 'Vers une démocratie administrative: du refus d'informer au droit d'être informé', RDP 1980, 1239, 1245. Compare Barthelemy in *JC* Fasc. 590–1 nos. 20–2; G. Vedel and P. Delvolvé, *Droit Administratif*, 12th edn. (Paris, 1992), 472.

[8] See also Tridimas, above n. 5, 245 noting the connection between the Diceyan *ultra vires* doctrine and the preference for procedural rather than substantive judicial control of administrative action.

First, administrative procedures reflect judicial procedures because they are largely the product of case law. In Britain, administrative procedures have to a large extent been developed by analogies from the *audi alterem partem* principle which has since ancient times applied in ordinary court proceedings.[9] This adversarial, formal, and technically elaborate procedure was, and is still to some degree, viewed as an ideal for administrative decision-making.[10] Similar analogies were less influential in France. French administrative law is largely the work of the separate division of administrative courts, the origins of which may be traced back to the seventeenth century.[11] The procedure in the administrative courts, headed by the Conseil d'État, is subject to a principle of 'contradiction' (*contradictoire*),[12] which encapsulates the basic idea of *audi alterem partem*, but it is overall more inquisitorial, informal, and based on written evidence than English judicial procedures[13] (and also more so than French private law court procedures).[14] This difference between judicial procedures may explain the development of different administrative procedures in Britain and in France.

Second, the rationale for procedural rights affects their scope and content in practice.[15] In France, the value of procedures is generally seen to be their contribution to correct outcomes. That is, their rationale is almost exclusively seen as instrumental.[16] Thus, a decision vitiated by a procedural error will in France *only* be annulled by a reviewing court if it appears that the error made an actual difference to the substantive decision made.[17] By contrast, legal writers[18]—and

[9] On the historical background, see Galligan, above n. 1, 161–86.

[10] See e.g. H. W. R. Wade, 'Law, Opinion and Administration' (1962) LQR 188, 192; J. R. Lucas, *The Principles of Politics* (Oxford, 1966), 196–9; J. L. Jowell, 'The Rule of Law Today', in J. L. Jowell and L. Oliver (eds.), *The Changing Constitution*, 3rd edn. (London, 1994) 69; Galligan, above n. 1, 240–7. Compare N. Lacey, 'The Jurisprudence of Discretion: Escaping the Legal Paradigm', in K. Hawkins (ed.), *The Uses of Discretion* (Oxford, 1992), 371–6.

[11] See J. Mestre, *Introduction historique au droit administratif français* (Paris, 1985), 99–103. Excessive judicial interference by the ordinary French courts (*Parlements*) prior to the 1789 Revolution led to an almost total exclusion of judicial competence over administrative matters (Law of 16–24/8 1790, repeated in the Constitution of 1791, Art 203). The administrative courts in their present form developed to fill the vacuum created by this exclusion. See Allison 138–46; J. H. Merryman, 'The French Deviation' (1997) AJCL 109; C. Duval, 'Les Justifications de la raison d'être et du maintient de la juridiction administrative en France au 19e siècle' (1998) Jahrbuch für europäische Verwaltungsgeschichte 55.

[12] See R. Chapus, *Droit du contentieux administratif*, 6th edn. (Paris, 1996), 676–84; Zeghbib, above n. 4.

[13] See J. S. Bell, 'Reflections on the Procedure of the Conseil d'État', in G. Hand and J. McBride (eds.), *Droit sans frontières: Essays in Honour of L. Neville Brown* (Birmingham, 1991), 211; Allison ch. 10; Brown and Bell ch. 5.

[14] See R. Chapus, 'De l'office du juge: contentieux administratif et nouvelle procédure civile', 1977–78 EDCE, 11.

[15] See generally Craig 402–3.

[16] See Fratacci *conclusions* CE 22/3–96 *Société NRJSA* RDP 1996, 1768; C. Yannakopoulos, *La notion de droits acquis en droit administratif français* (Paris, 1997), 376–7; Chapus 1033.

[17] e.g. CE 5/11–52 *Le Moigne* Rec 487. See J. Moreau, 'Les conséquences des illégalités procédurales en droit administratif français' (1993) ERPL, special edn. 85, 90–1; and for recent criticism of this approach, Hubert *conclusions* CE 3/2–99 *Montaignac* AJDA 1999, 631.

[18] See footnote 2.

increasingly also the courts—in common law countries have adopted non-instrumental rationales for procedures.[19] Procedures are seen to promote democratic participation, dignity, and autonomy as well as legally correct outcomes. Consequently, decisions vitiated by a procedural error will normally be quashed in judicial review proceedings without it being necessary to show a causal link between procedure and substance.[20] The recognition of non-instrumental rationales in Britain may explain why the scope of procedural rights is still wider than in France.[21]

The difference between the English and the French courts' approach to judicial control of administration has diminished somewhat over the last twenty years. The British courts have begun to develop more refined and searching substantive principles of review, and procedural protection has since 1978 been extended in France by legislative codes concerning hearings, reasons, and access to files.[22] However, important differences remain both in the conceptualization and substance of procedural rights. To understand these differences, and their significance for the protection of legitimate expectations, it is necessary to be clear about three basic features of English, French, and EC law: what are the sources, the scope, and the content of such rights?

(A) The Sources of Procedural Protection

The *sources* of procedural protection are largely similar in English, French, and EC law, although the practical importance of different sources vary.[23] General principles based on case law remain, in all three systems, the primary source. In English law, procedural protection derives from the two pillars of natural justice (*audi alterem partem* and *nemo judex in re sua*)[24] now known simply as the principle of procedural fairness.[25] In French and EC law, the functionally equiv-

[19] e.g. *R v Home Secretary, ex p Doody* [1994] 1 AC 531. For further examples, see G. Richardson, 'The Legal Regulation of Process', in G. Richardson and H. Genn (eds.), *Administrative Law and Government Action* (Oxford, 1994); D. Woodhouse, *In Pursuit of Good Administration: Ministers, Civil Servants and Judges* (Oxford, 1997), 161–7.

[20] *John v Rees* [1970] Ch 345, 402; *R v Chief Constable of North Wales Police force, ex p Evans* [1982] 1 WLR 1155, 1160–1; *R v Chief Constable of the Thames Valley Police Force, ex p Cotton* [1990] IRLR 344. See Craig 420–1.

[21] It remains somewhat unclear to what extent the CFI and ECJ see the right to be heard as serving non-instrumental values. Decisions are only annulled if the failure to grant a procedural entitlement 'might have influenced' the outcome. See Cases C-142/87 *Belgium v Commission* [1990] ECR I-959; T-30/91 *Solvay v Commission* [1995] ECR II-1775 para 68; T-290/97 *Dordtselaan v Commission*, 18/1–2000 para 47; Nehl, above n. 5, 97–8; Tridimas, above n. 5, 244–5, 259–62.

[22] See Zeghbib, above n. 4, 478 and further below.

[23] See on sources in English law Galligan, above n. 1, 291–313; in French law Chapus 27–58; in EC law Lenaerts and Vanhamme, above n. 5.

[24] Or, the right to be heard and to have a decision made without bias. The latter is not discussed in this book. See generally Galligan, above n. 1, 437–47.

[25] It not entirely clear whether natural justice and procedural fairness are synonymous terms (Wade 515) or whether natural justice connotes a higher level of protection applicable in a more restricted area than fairness (Craig 409–12; Galligan, above n. 1, 186).

alent principles are known as the rights of the defence (*droits de la défense*)[26] and impartiality (*impartialité*).[27] The French principle of *droits de la défense* originates in nineteenth-century legislation and case law concerning disciplinary measures against public employees.[28] Procedural rules developed in this area were from the 1930s[29] broadened into a general unwritten principle established finally in 1944 by the famous case of Ms *Trompier-Gravier*.[30] The EC law principle of defence rights also emerged in employment cases,[31] but in the *TMPA* case from 1974 the ECJ confirmed its status as a generally applicable norm which is binding upon all the EC institutions and valid at a higher level than all secondary measures.[32]

General principles of procedural fairness are supplemented by specific statutory procedures in areas such as immigration, social welfare, planning, and licensing. The growing practical importance of such procedures has been noted both in England and France.[33] A survey of EC legislation reveals a similar picture; some form of hearing provisions apply in many,[34] but not all of the areas in which the community institutions exercise direct administrative authority.[35] Legislative provisions of more general application are also important sources of procedural protection. The EC Treaty contains a few references to the right to a hearing[36] and a general rule in Art 253 that all the Community institutions must give reasons for legally binding measures.[37] In Britain and in France, statutory procedural requirements apply to appeal tribunals and public

[26] This principle is in French law supplemented by the principle of *parallélisme des formes et procedures*. The latter principle is subject to numerous exceptions and its practical relevance is limited. See M. Basset, 'Le principe dit de 'l'acte contraire' en droit administratif français', Doctoral thesis (Paris, 1967), 217–45; Chapus 1040–2.

[27] Impartiality is not discussed in this book. See generally Hostiou, above n. 4, 265–8.

[28] e.g. CE 19/6–1839 *Ledochowski* Rec 452. Art 65 of the Law of 22/4–1905 fuelled the development by providing a right for civil servants to comment on the file in disciplinary proceedings. See Waline, above n. 4, 500–4.

[29] CE 27/11–30 *Ribeyrolles* Rec 76.

[30] CE 5/5–44 *Trompier-Gravier* Rec 133 confirmed by CE 26/10–45 *Aramu* Rec 213; CE 22/5–46 *Mailou* D 1946 III 52.

[31] Cases 32/62 *Alvis v Council* [1963] ECR 49; 26/63 *Pistoj v Commission* [1964] ECR 2071; 35/67 *Van Eick v Commission* [1968] ECR 329.

[32] Case 17/74 *Transocean Marine Paint Association v Commission* [1974] ECR 1063. See also Cases 85/76 *Hoffmann-La Roche v Commission* [1979] ECR 461 para 9–11; C-49/88 *Al-Jubail Fertilizer v Commission* [1991] ECR I-3187 para 17; T-260/94 *Air Inter v Commission* [1997] ECR II-997 para 60.

[33] See A. P. Le Sueur, 'Legal Duties to Give Reasons' (1999) CLP 150, 161–6; Zeghbib, above n. 4, 486–91.

[34] e.g. staff discipline: Art 25(1), 26, 87 and Annex IX Regulation 259/68 (hereafter: 'EU Staff Regulations'). Competition law: Art 19 Regulation 17/62; Art 2 Regulation 99/63. Mergers Art 18 Regulation 4064/89; Art 11–15 Regulation 2367/90. Anti-dumping: Art 6, 20 Regulation 384/96; Art 8, 21 Regulation 3284/94. Trade marks: Art 5, 56(1) Regulation 40/94; Regulation 2100/94. Investment aid: Art 7 Regulation 1168/86; Art 7 Regulation 1116/88, Art 44(1) Regulation 4028/86. Financial grants under the EAGGF: Art 7 Regulation 99/64, Art 22(2) Regulation 17/64.

[35] e.g. financial grants under the ESF Regulations 2052/88 and 4255/88, see text at footnote 144.

[36] Art 88(2), 226(1). See also Art 36(1), 46(2), 54(4), 66(5), 88(1) ECSC; Art 5(2), 46(2), 141 EURATOM.

[37] See also Art 15 ECSC; Art 162 EURATOM.

enquiries.[38] More importantly, the French Law of 11 July 1979 grants the right to reasons for all 'unfavourable' administrative decisions made by both state and local authorities,[39] and an administrative decree[40] from 1983 grants a right to notice and hearing for those affected by unfavourable decisions made by state administrative bodies.[41]

(B) The Scope of General Principles of Procedural Fairness

Different legal systems delineate the *scope* of procedural fairness or 'defence rights' by reference to criteria, which differ widely both in linguistic and conceptual terms. Despite these differences, it is clear that three questions arise in all legal systems. First, what *types of interests* deserve procedural protection? Second, how *intensively* must such interests be affected to attract protection? Third, what *additional conditions* must be fulfilled for protections to apply? The answers to these questions in English, French, and EC law may be set out as follows.

I What Types of Interests?

The first question is what *types of interests* are protected by procedural principles. There are similarities, but also important differences, between English, French, and EC law in this respect. The English courts distinguish between rights and interests. Traditionally, it was assumed that a decision which takes away a legal right must comply with procedural fairness.[42] However, the concept of rights was never clearly defined,[43] and it is now accepted that a decision which affects an interest of a substantial, as opposed to trivial, kind must also comply with procedural fairness.[44] The French courts never distinguished between rights and other interests in the context of administrative procedures, and French writers do not attempt to discern precisely what interests are actually protected. A decision which affects the *situation* of a person adversely

[38] Tribunals and Inquiries Act 1992, s 10; Decree of 23/11–58; Decree of 14/5–76; Law of 12/7–83 completed by Decree of 25/4–85. See L. N. Brown, 'Tribunal Adjudication in Britain: Model Rules of Procedure' (1993) ERPL, special edn. 287; J.-C. Helin and R. Hostiou, *Droit des enquêtes publiques* (Paris, 1993).

[39] Law no 79–587 of 11/7–79, JO 1979, 1711 as amended by Law no 86–76 of 17/1–86, JO 1986, 888.

[40] French administrative rule-making takes a number of forms, such as *décret, règlement,* and *ordonnance.* Following Brown and Bell 11 this book uses the term 'decree' as a shorthand way of referring to all of these.

[41] Art 8, Decree (*Ordonnance*) no 83–1025, 28/11–83, JO 1983, 3492. This provision is shortly to be codified by primary legislation. See Art 22, *Projet de loi relatif aux droits des citoyens dans leurs relations avec les administrations* available at http://www.legifrance.gouv.fr/citoyen/actualite/preparation/citoyen.htm.

[42] *Cooper v Wandsworth Board of Works* (1863) 14 CB (NS) 180; *Ridge v Baldwin* [1964] AC 40.

[43] Craig 413. See also Wade 555 (equating livelihood with rights); De Smith 410–11 (distinguishing livelihood from rights).

[44] *Bushell v Secretary of State for the Environment* [1981] AC 75. Similarly De Smith 410–11.

must, it is said, comply with the principle of *droits de la défense*. The ECJ does not distinguish between rights and other interests either, and it is common ground that the EC rights of the defence apply when a decision 'affects the *interests* of a person adversely'.[45]

A reading of case law and secondary sources reveals that the interests protected by the French and the EC principles 'defence rights' are in fact not significantly different from the 'rights and interests' protected by procedural fairness in Britain.[46] There is a certain core of interests, which attract protection under all of the different concepts of rights, interests, and 'situations'. They include, in particular, property,[47] liberty,[48] immunity from penalties,[49] livelihood,[50] and reputation.[51] Thus, a decision which affects one or more of these interests with a certain intensity (see below) will normally require notification and some form of hearing under English, French, and EC law. There is also growing recognition that procedural protection is required if a decision has serious financial implications, although it does not threaten the livelihood of the addressee.[52] So far, the scope of procedural protection in the three legal systems is quite similar.

There is, however, one very important difference between English, French, and EC law. The English courts accept that a decision which affects a person's *legitimate expectations* must comply with procedural fairness.[53] Expectations are distinct from rights and interests.[54] Expectations are, as explained further below, based on some administrative representation or conduct, and it is this representation rather than the expectation itself, or the scale or context of the

[45] Cases C-142/87 *Belgium v Commission* [1990] ECR I-959 para 46 (state aids); C-49/88 *Al-Jubail Fertilizer v Commission* [1991] ECR I-3187 para 17 (anti-dumping); C-48 and 60/90 *Netherlands v Commission* [1992] ECR I-565 para 44 (public undertakings); C-135/92 *Fiskano v Commission* [1994] ECR I-2885 para 39 (fishing licences); T-450/93 *Lisrestal v Commission* [1994] ECR II-1177 para 42 (ESF); T-305–307/94, 313–316/94, 318/94, 325/94, 328–329/94 and 335/94 *Limburgse v Commission*, 20/4–99 para 260 (competition).

[46] See notably Hostiou, above n. 4, with numerous examples and text below at footnote 47 ff.

[47] *Cooper v Wandsworth Board of Works* (1863) 14 CB (NS) 180; *R v Ealing Magistrates' Court, ex p Fanneran* (1996) 8 Admin LR 351.

[48] *Hopkins v Smethwick Local Board of Health* (1890) 24 QBD 713; *R v Parole Board, ex p Wilson* [1992] 1 QB 740; *R v Home Secretary, ex p Doody* [1994] 1 AC 531.

[49] *Bagg's Case* (1615) 11 Co Re93b; *Abbott v Sullivan* [1952] 1 KB 189, 198; CE 24/6–49 *Nègre* Rec 304; Cases 46/87 and 227/88 *Hoechst Chemie v Commission* [1989] ECR 2858; 374/87 *Orkem v Commission* [1989] ECR 3283.

[50] *R v Barnsley MBC, ex p Hook* [1976] 1 WLR 1052; *R v Wear Valley DC, ex p Binks* [1985] 2 All ER 699; CE 5/5–44 *Trompier-Gravier* RDP 1944, 257; Case C-135/92 *Fiskano v Commission* [1994] ECR I-2885.

[51] *McInnes v Onslow-Fane* [1978] 1 WLR 1520, 1527–8; *Rees v Crane* [1994] 2 WLR 476; CE 12/1–56 *Chapon* Rec 473; Case T-346/94 *France-Aviation v Commission* [1995] ECR II-2843 para 36.

[52] *R v Secretary of State for Transport, ex p Sherriff* The Times 18/12–86; *R v Secretary of State for Health, ex p US Tobacco* [1992] QB 353; Cases C-142/87 *Belgium v Commission* [1990] ECR I-959 para 46; C-32/95P *Commission v Lisrestal* [1996] ECR I-5373.

[53] *Schmidt v Secretary of State for Home Affairs* [1969] 2 Ch 149, 170.

[54] See Craig 414; De Smith 418, 422–3; Galligan, above n. 1, 320. See however *R v Devon CC, ex p Baker* [1995] 1 All ER 73, 88–9.

decision, which justifies the imposition of procedural fairness.[55] In French and EC law, expectations are not recognized as sources of procedural protection. A decision which does not by itself affect a person's interests adversely, but which disappoints an expectation created by an administrative representation, does not attract procedural guarantees. It is examined further below how the absence of a *concept* of procedural legitimate expectations affects the actual *protection* of expectations in France and the EC.

The historical development in English law of the concept of legitimate expectations is intimately linked with the distinction between decisions which affect rights, and therefore attract procedural protections, and other decisions.[56] A number of early twentieth-century judgments distinguished in a formalist way between, on the one hand, administrative and judicial functions and, on the other hand, between rights and privileges.[57] This led to quite severe restrictions on the scope of procedural fairness. Decisions which depended upon the exercise of discretion by the administration were often considered not to be subject to procedural protections. The restrictions upon procedural fairness were to some extent, but not entirely, abandoned in 1964 in the landmark decision of *Ridge v Baldwin*.[58] The concept of legitimate expectations developed as a way of bridging the remaining gaps caused by the traditional distinctions.

This development began in the famous *Schmidt* case from 1969, in which a foreign student sought review of a refusal to extend his temporary permit to stay in Britain. While rejecting his claim that he should have been afforded a hearing, Lord Denning stated *obiter* that the situation would have been different had the permit been revoked before its expiry. For in that situation, the student would have had a legitimate expectation, which deserved procedural protection.[59] This statement fits into the context of procedural fairness as it stood at the time.[60] It was, despite the ruling in *Ridge v Baldwin,* doubtful

[55] *CCSU v Minister for the Civil Service* [1985] AC 374, 401, 409.

[56] For detailed treatment of the early development of the doctrine of procedural legitimate expectations, see articles cited in footnote 3.

[57] *Local Government Board v Arlidge* [1915] AC 120; *Errington v Minister of Health* [1935] 1 KB 249; *Nakkuda Ali v Jayarante* [1951] AC 66.

[58] *Ridge v Baldwin* [1964] AC 40. See M. Loughlin, 'Procedural Fairness: A Study of the Crisis in Administrative Law' (1978) Univ Toronto LJ 215; Galligan, above n. 1, 328–30.

[59] *Schmidt v Secretary of State for Home Affairs* [1969] 2 Ch 149, 170 (the right to a hearing 'all depends upon whether he has some right or interest, or, I would add, some legitimate expectation of which it would not be fair to deprive him without [a] hearing.')

[60] Some commentators have argued (Mackenzie Stuart, 'Recent Developments in English Administrative Law—The impact of Europe?', in F. Capotorti *et al.* (eds.), *Liber Amicorum Pierre Pescatore* (Baden-Baden, 1987); S. James, 'The Political and Administrative Consequences of Judicial Review' (1996) Public Administration 613, 632) that Lord Denning drew inspiration from EC law, but he maintains that the idea 'came out of his own head' (Forsyth, above n. 3, 241). There is no reason to doubt Lord Denning's account given that the UK was not a member of the EEC at the time, that the European doctrine of legitimate expectations is not concerned with procedural protection, and that the ECJ's seminal expectations cases were not decided until the early 1970s. Scattered reference to legitimate expectations existed in ECSC case law, but it was available only in

whether procedural fairness applied to the revocation of such a discretionary benefit. Lord Denning could not, without overstepping the bounds of *stare decisis,* hold that discretionary decisions are in general subject to procedural fairness. It appears, then, that he introduced the notion of legitimate expectations as a malleable instrument which would allow a gradual extension of procedural fairness into areas not previously covered by the concept of rights.[61]

The French and the EC courts never distinguish sharply between rights and privileges in relation to procedural fairness. As explained above, procedural protections were predicated upon interference with 'interests' in a wide sense. Indeed, the ECJ always took the view that decisions made subject to wide discretionary powers should be subject to *more*, rather than less, procedural protection.[62] The French and EC courts did not, therefore, need legitimate expectations as a 'tool' to extend the scope of procedural principles. This, it is suggested, explains why the concept of procedural legitimate expectation did not develop in these jurisdictions.[63] An added factor, of importance in the EC law context, is that procedural legitimate expectations are not widely accepted in the laws of the Member States. The Community courts may have been reluctant to endorse such a principle, because their development of general principles relies heavily upon comparative analysis of those laws.

II How Intensively Must the Decision Affect the Interest?

The second question is *how intensively* a decision must affect a person's recognized interests to give rise to procedural guarantees. A cursory look at English, French, and EC law suggests that the systems differ considerably in this respect. In English law, where the question of intensity is not always distinguished clearly from that of the nature of the affected interest, procedural fairness is said to apply when a decision impacts 'gravely'[64] or 'vitally'[65] upon a legally

French in 1968 and hardly well known even to Lord Denning. Continental and EC law has, however, *subsequently* influenced English doctrine and case law. See *R v Ministry of Agriculture, Fisheries and Foods, ex p Hamble Fisheries* [1995] 2 All ER 714; *R v Devon Health Authority, ex p Coughlan* [1999] Lloyd's LR Medical 306.

[61] This interpretation is confirmed by Lord Denning's use of the concept in later cases like *Breen v Amalgamated Engineering Union* [1971] 2 QB 175, 191; *R v Liverpool Corporation, ex p Liverpool Taxi Fleet Operators' Association* [1972] 2 QB 299.

[62] Cases 19/70 *Almini v Commission* [1971] ECR 623 para 10–11; C-269/90 *Hauptzollamt München-Mitte v Technische Universität München* [1991] ECR I-5469 para 13–14; T-290/97 *Dordtselaan v Commission,* 18/1–2000 para 46.

[63] For the view that the concept of expectations is alien to French public law reasoning, due to a preference for 'objective' rather than 'subjective' concepts, see J. M. Woehrling, 'Le principe de confiance légitime dans la jurisprudence des tribunaux', in *General Reports to the XV International Congress of Comparative Law* (University of Bristol, 1998), 32. A discussion of the nature of continental and common law *styles, mentalités,* or legal reasoning is beyond the scope of this book. See generally J. S. Bell, 'English Law and French Law—Not So Different?' (1995) CLP 63; P. Legrand, 'European Legal Systems are not Converging' (1996) ICLQ 52.

[64] See Wade 514.

[65] *R v Secretary of State for Education, ex p London Borough of Southwark*, 24/1–94 (Laws J, Lexis transcript).

protected right or interest. The formulation in French and EC law is more generous. According to the oft-cited *Cruse* case, the French principle of *droits de la défense* applies when a decision affects a person's interests 'sufficiently seriously' (*suffisamment grave*),[66] and the ECJ recently held in *Lisrestal* that the principle of defence applies when a decision affects a person's interests adversely and to a 'significant extent'.[67]

A comparison of the outcomes of decided cases reveals that the intensity requirement is, despite the different formulations, not applied very differently. For example, while the revocation of a favourable decision, such as a sizeable financial grant, is normally considered sufficiently 'grave' or 'significant' both in English, French, and EC law, applicants for licences or financial grants are normally not entitled to procedural protection in any of the three jurisdictions.[68] A hearing is only required if a refusal would cast a slur on the applicant's reputation, as can happen where the application for renewal of a grant, position, or licence is dismissed on grounds of misconduct or failure to perform the position in a satisfactory manner,[69] or the application raises particularly difficult technical issues on which the applicant has specialized knowledge.[70]

III Additional Conditions

The third, and last, perennial question concerns the *additional conditions* which restrict the scope of procedural protections. On this point, English, French, and EC law still differ considerably. In contemporary English and EC law, procedural protection applies whenever a decision has a 'grave' or 'significant' effect upon legally recognized interests.[71] In French law, it is a necessary but not sufficient condition that the decision has such an adverse effect upon a person's interests. Protection is also conditional upon the *motives* of the decision-maker. Procedural rights (*droits de la défense*) only apply if the deci-

[66] Genevois *conclusions* CE 9/5–80 *Cruse* AJDA 1980, 483; Fratacci *conclusions* CE 22/3–96 *Société NRJSA* RDP 1996, 1767–8. Similarly Hostiou, above n. 4, 91; *LGA* 351; Zeghbib, above n. 4, 477.

[67] Cases C-32/95P *Commission v Lisrestal* [1996] ECR I-5373 para 21; T-218/95 *Le Canne v Commission* [1997] ECR II-2055 para 48; T-290/97 *Dortselaan v Commission*, 18/1–2000 para 46. Compare the more generous formulation in Case 17/74 *Transocean Marine Paint Association v Commission* [1974] ECR 1063 para 15 ('perceptively affected'), and the more limited formulation in Case 85/76 *Hoffmann La-Roche v Commission* [1979] ECR 461 ('proceedings in which sanctions, in particular fines and periodic penalties may be imposed'). In staff discipline cases a stricter 'serious detriment' test is applied, probably because the general principle of defence is utilized to supplement elaborate statutory procedures in this context, see e.g. Case 125/80 *Arning v Commission* [1981] ECR 2539. An even narrower test of 'grave prejudice' (Case 121/76 *Moli v Commission* [1977] ECR 1971 para 19–21) has however been abandoned in staff cases.

[68] *McInnes v Onslow-Fane* [1978] 1 WLR 1520, 1527–8; CE 15/7–57 *Union Mutuelle* Rec 296; Case T-109/94 *Windmillpark v Commission* [1995] ECR II-3007.

[69] *McInnes v Onslow-Fane* [1978] 1 WLR 1520, 1529; CE 4/5–62 *Ruard* Rec 296; Case T-346/94 *France-Aviation v Commission* [1995] ECR II-2843 para 32.

[70] Cases C-269/90 *Hauptzollamt München-Mitte v Technische Universität München* [1991] ECR I-5469; T-42/96 *Eyckeler v Commission* [1998] ECR II-401. See further Nehl, above n. 5, 80–6.

[71] See above, section I.

sion is based on an assessment of the affected person and/or his conduct (*mesures prises en consideration de la personne*). This includes administrative penalties and 'sanctions' (*sanction*), but excludes decisions made solely on the basis of 'objective criteria' unrelated to the affected person, notably the protection of public safety, order, and health (*mesures de police administrative*). For example, the CE held in *Tigrini* that a market stall licence could be revoked without a hearing because the revocation purported to maintain public order in general rather than to respond to the applicant's unmeritorious behaviour.[72]

The requirement of a personalized element owes its existence to both historical developments and the rationale for procedural protection. First, the fact that the principle of *droits de la défense* had its origins in the disciplinary law of the civil service led to the idea that its scope is, more generally, confined to measures which present an analogy with disciplinary sanctions.[73] Second, it is deeply embedded in the French legal tradition that the administration must have powers to uphold public order, safety, and health (*l'ordre public*).[74] The fast and efficient exercise of these powers is, or has been, perceived as incompatible with procedural rights.[75] Third, a hearing is more likely to contribute to a correct outcome if the decision is based on the personal circumstances of the affected person rather than public interest consideration of which he has no special knowledge. It follows that, on the narrow instrumental rationale for procedures which dominates in France, a hearing is only required where personal circumstances are on the decision-maker's mind.

(C) The Content of Procedural Protections

The *content* of procedural protection depends upon a balancing of a number of factors;[76] it is 'infinitely flexible'.[77] Amongst these factors, the relative importance of the affected person's interest and the administrative cost of observing the procedure in question are particularly important. Other factors, such as confidentiality, national security, urgency, the decision's preliminary or final nature, and the statutory context also affect the content of procedural protection. A detailed analysis of these factors is beyond the scope of this book, but it is important to note that, in English law, the existence of a legitimate expectation created by administrative representations or conduct may affect the

[72] CE 9/11–94 *Tigrini* Rec 1139. See further section 3.B.

[73] See Allen, above n. 4, 291.

[74] The leading precedent is CE 8/8–19 *Labonne* Rec 737. See J. S. Bell, *French Constitutional Law* (Oxford, 1992), 83, 96.

[75] See *Études du Conseil d'État: Les pouvoirs de l'administration dans le domaine des sanctions* (Paris, 1995), 39; Genevois, above n. 4, no. 356. It is not hereby suggested that the French administration has extensive privileges or legal protections at a more general level as claimed by A.V. Dicey in *Introduction to the Study of the Law of the Constitution*, 10th edn. (London, 1959), ch. 12. For discussion of Dicey's view, see Allison 18–23 with further references.

[76] See Craig 412–25; Schwarze 1360.

[77] De Smith 431.

content, as well as the scope of, procedural fairness. Thus, expectations have a dual function in the realm of procedural fairness.[78]

3 Procedural Protection of Legitimate Expectations (I): Revocation of Decisions

The revocation of favourable administrative decisions, such as planning permissions, licences, or social benefits, can deeply affect the rights and interests of individuals. Moreover, individuals often assume that formal and favourable decisions are final and irrevocable. Revocation may therefore disappoint expectations and cause the affected person to suffer a reliance loss. Fairness, therefore, suggests that persons affected by the revocation of a favourable administrative decision should be entitled to some degree of procedural protection. It will now be examined to what extent this requirement is met by English, French, and EC law.

(A) English Law

English statutes often prescribe written notice and some form of hearing prior to the revocation of favourable decisions, such as planning permissions and licences.[79] In the absence of statutory provisions, the revocation of a favourable decision will normally attract procedural fairness, because it affects the rights or interests of the affected person.[80] Fairness applies, in particular, if the revocation affects significant economic interests or takes the form of a sanction because it carries an implication of personal misconduct.[81] The *Binks* case is a classic example. In this instance, an administrative decision to revoke a street trader's licence to sell food under an informal arrangement with the local authority, and therefore his livelihood, was quashed for lack of notice, hearing, and reasons.[82] In other cases, the English courts have applied procedural fairness to the dismissal from a public office or employment[83] and the revocation of discretionary financial grants, of a certain size, awarded to undertakings by local authorities.[84]

[78] e.g. *R v Secretary of State for Health, ex p US Tobacco International Inc* [1992] QB 353 (see text at footnote 164).

[79] e.g. Licensing Act 1964, s 20A, 153A (liquor stores); Betting, Gaming and Lotteries Act 1963, Sch 1 para 27; Gaming Act 1968, Sch 2 para 37–38; Local Government Act 1982, Sch 3 para 17 (sex shops); Public Passengers Vehicles Act 1981, s 23 (bus drivers); Broadcasting Act 1996, s 5; Gas Act 1986, s 29; Electricity Act 1989, s 33; Railway Act 1993, s 56. Compare Theatres Act 1968, s 13; Cinemas Act 1985, s 12; Local Government Act 1982, Sch 1 para 12(4) (night clubs).

[80] See A. Rubinstein, *Jurisdiction and Illegality* (Oxford, 1965), 31; De Smith 411.

[81] See Wade 555.

[82] *R v Wear Valley DC, ex p Binks* [1985] 2 All ER 699. See also *R v Barnsley MBC, ex p Hook* [1976] 1 WLR 1052; *McInnes v Onslow-Fane* [1978] 1 WLR 1520, 1527–8.

[83] e.g. *Ridge v Baldwin* [1964] AC 40; *R v BBC, ex p Lavelle* [1983] 1 WLR 23.

[84] *R v Secretary of State for Transport, ex p Sherriff* The Times 18/12–86; *R v Secretary of State for Health, ex p US Tobacco International Inc* [1992] QB 353.

Procedural fairness has, in certain instances, been implied on the grounds that the revocation of a favourable decision disappointed a legitimate expectation. For example, in the case of *D* a decision to place a baby girl permanently in the care of a foster-parent, who had already raised a son of the girl's mother, was revoked when the child's mother, who had harmed other children, became aware of the foster-parent's address. The court found that the foster-parent had a legitimate expectation of, at least, being consulted before it was decided to remove the child.[85] While the result in this case seems correct, the reasoning is problematic. A decision which affects a person adversely and with some intensity should, it is submitted, attract procedural fairness on grounds of interests independently of the proof of expectations. To use legitimate expectations as a synonym for the type of interest on the basis of which everybody can, or should be able to, claim procedural protections causes conceptual confusion and carries a risk that decision-makers will undermine fairness by warning applicants that a fair hearing will not be granted.[86] The concept of expectations should be confined to those rare situations where a hearing *would not otherwise* be available to a person at the receiving end of a revocation.[87] The case of *S* is illustrative of this approach. In this case it was characterized as a clear breach of procedural fairness that an independent school had revoked a pupil's assisted place without prior notice. The adverse effect upon the child's education and general welfare sufficed to justify this result. The judge found, rightly, that it was immaterial that the decision was not a reaction to the pupil's misconduct, and therefore did not affect personal reputation, and that reference to the concept of legitimate expectations was not relevant in the circumstances.[88]

The modification of licences and other favourable decisions will normally attract procedural fairness in the same way as complete revocation, although countervailing considerations of cost and urgency may lead to a different result.[89] For example, it was held in *Fitt* that when an industrial tribunal utilizes its statutory power to vary a decision previously made, it must first hear any party prejudiced.[90] Where a decision is merely suspended temporarily, procedural fairness may apply, but this is always subject to the degree of urgency, the duration of the suspension, whether it implies a finding of guilt, and whether it entails a financial loss.[91] In *Rees v Crane* the Privy Council held that in the absence of serious

[85] *R v Hereford and Worcester CC, ex p D* [1992] 1 FLR 448. See also *O'Reilly v Mackman* [1983] 2 AC 237, 275.

[86] The risk that legitimate expectations might be used, more generally, to deny procedural protection has so far not materialized, see Forsyth, above n. 3, 246–7.

[87] Thus, imposing fairness solely on grounds of rights or interests, *R v Wandsworth LBC, ex p P* [1989] COD 262 and cases cited in footnote 82 f.

[88] *R v Cobham Hall Schools, ex p S* The Times 31/12–97. See also (where misconduct was alleged against the pupil) *R v London Oratory School, ex p Regis* The Times 17/2–88; *R v Fernhill Manor School, ex p Brown* (1993) 5 Admin LR 159; *R v Governors of Dunraven School, ex p. B* The Times 3/2–2000; and (for exclusion of parents) *Wandsworth LBC v A* The Times 28/1–2000.

[89] See De Smith 411.

[90] *Times Newspapers v Fitt* [1981] ICR 637.

[91] *R v Secretary of State, ex p Pegasus* [1988] 1 WLR 990. See De Smith 411–12.

urgency, a judge could not be suspended without prior hearing when serious allegations were made against him.[92] This decision suggests that modification or suspension by a favourable decision must, at least in the absence of significant countervailing considerations, be preceded by a fair hearing.

The scope of the right to be given reasons for the revocation or modification of a favourable decision is more limited than the right to notice and hearing.[93] While some British statutes prescribe reason to be given for revocation of, for example, licences and public housing,[94] many areas of administration remain exempt from such duties.[95] There is, moreover, no general statutory[96] or common law[97] duty to provide reasons or guidance about rights of appeal to those adversely affected by administrative decisions.[98] Still, the important *Doody* case established for life prisoners a right to reasons for decisions by the Home Secretary about the minimum period of time which these prisoners must serve before parole may be considered.[99] Following this decision, it has become generally accepted that fairness requires reasons to be granted if an administrative decision has a profound impact upon an important interest, such as liberty, livelihood, or reputation,[100] if it appears aberrant,[101] or otherwise if the context demands that reasons be given.[102] Reasons must therefore often be

[92] *Rees v Crane* [1994] 2 WLR 476. See also *R v Portsmouth CC, ex p Gregory* (1990) 2 Admin LR 681; *R v P BC, ex p S* [1999] 2 WLR 777.

[93] See generally G. Richardson, 'The Duty to Give Reasons: Potential and Practice' (1986) PL 437; Justice—All Souls Review Committee, *Administrative Justice: Some Necessary Reforms* (Oxford, 1988), 29–32, 46–68; P. P. Craig, 'The Common Law, Reasons and Administrative Justice' (1994) CLJ 282; D. Toube, 'Requiring Reasons at Common Law' (1997) JR 68; M. Fordham, 'Reasons: The Third Dimension' (1998) JR 158; P. Neil, 'The Duty to Give Reasons', in C. Forsyth and I. Hare (eds.), *The Golden Metwand and the Crooked Cord: Essays in Honour of Sir William Wade* (Oxford, 1998), 161; Le Sueur, above n. 33.

[94] *R v Royal Borough of Kensington and Chelsea, ex p Grillo* (1996) 8 Admin LR 165. See further Craig 311.

[95] See Galligan, above n. 1, 434–5; Schwehr, above n. 3, 255–7.

[96] Statutory tribunals and ministers deciding upon statutory public inquiries must, however, give reasons. See Tribunals and Inquiries Act 1992, s. 10.

[97] *R v Home Secretary, ex p Doody* [1994] 1 AC 531; *R v Mayor Commonalty and Citizens of the City of London, ex p Matson* (1996) 8 Admin LR 49; *R v Criminal Injuries Compensation Board, ex p Moore* [1999] 2 All ER 90.

[98] A limited duty to provide reasons *to the reviewing court* has long been established where the facts point 'overwhelmingly' towards another decision than the one made. See *Padfield v Minister of Agriculture Fisheries and Food* [1968] AC 997; *R v Secretary of State for Trade and Industry, ex p Lonrho Plc* [1989] 1 WLR 525. See also *R v Lancashire CC, ex p Huddleston* [1986] 2 All ER 941; *R v ICI, ex p Coombe and Co* (1989) 1 Admin LR 1.

[99] *R v Home Secretary, ex p Doody* [1994] 1 AC 531.

[100] *R v Parole Board, ex p Wilson* [1992] 1 QB 740; *R v Mayor, Commonalty and Citizens of the City of London, ex p Matson* (1996) 8 Admin LR 49; *R v Home Secretary, ex p Al Fayed* [1997] 1 All ER 228; *R v Ministry of Defence, ex p Murray* [1998] COD 134; *Stefan v General Medical Council* [1999] 1 WLR 1293.

[101] *R v Civil Service Appeal Board, ex p Cunningham* [1992] ICR 816, 832; *R v Higher Education Funding Council, ex p Institute of Dental Surgery* [1994] 1 WLR 242.

[102] *R v Civil Service Appeal Board, ex p Cunningham* [1992] ICR 816, 831; *R v Mayor Commonalty and Citizens of the City of London, ex p Matson* (1996) 8 Admin LR 49, 63–4. Compare *R v Kensington LBC, ex p Grillo* (1996) 8 Admin LR 165.

granted when favourable decisions are revoked.[103] Thus, in the *Binks* case mentioned above the revocation of a street traders' licence was quashed *inter alia* because the licensing authority had failed to give reasons.[104] It may be added that the development towards a *de facto* presumption in favour of a right to reasons for administrative decisions is likely to be pushed even further by the Human Rights Act 1998. Under this Act, the courts will have to review the 'necessity' of administrative action, which interferes with rights protected by the ECHR. The courts may find it very difficult to fulfil this task if they do not have detailed reasons from the administration at hand.

(B) French Law

French statutes grant procedural rights to individuals affected by the revocation of administrative decisions in a number of areas.[105] The general rules, which cover situations falling outside the scope of specific statutory provisions, are somewhat complex because the state and the local administration are subject to different procedural requirements: the general decree of 1983, mentioned above,[106] obliges public authorities to grant hearings in a wide range of situations. However, this decree only applies to the state administration.[107] Local authorities such as *régions*, *départements*, and *communes* are not bound by its provisions, nor is the Ministry of Justice.[108] This is practically important because much administrative decision-making power rests with local authorities, particularly in areas such as social welfare and licensing. In these areas, the only procedural protections which apply flow from the general principle of 'defence rights' (*droits de la défense*) and specific statutory procedures.

The *state* administration is, by Art 8 of the 1983 decree, obliged to grant persons affected by an 'unfavourable' decision prior notice, an opportunity to make written observations, and an interview if this is requested. The definition of unfavourable decisions, set out in Art 1 of the Law of 11/6–79, is very wide. Decisions can therefore rarely be revoked or modified to the disadvantage of a person without compliance with Art 8.[109] Unfavourable decisions include all

[103] See Wade 544 and *Stefan v General Medical Council* [1999] 1WLR 1293 where the Privy Council noted that 'what was once seen as exceptions to the general rule may now becoming examples of the norm'. Compare De Smith 411, 421.

[104] *R v Wear Valley DC, ex p Binks* [1985] 2 All ER 699. See also *Breen v Amalgamated Engineering Union* [1971] 2 QB 175; *Congreve v Home Office* [1976] QB 629; *Wheeler v Leicester City Council* [1985] AC 1054; *R v Burton-upon-Trent Justices, ex p Hussain* (1997) 9 Admin LR 233. Compare *McInnes v Onslow-Fane* [1978] 1 WLR 1520, 1532.

[105] See Brown and Bell 296.

[106] See footnote 41.

[107] In this context, the state administration includes central administration (the ministries) and bodies attributed to the state by statutory provisions (*établissements publics d'État*).

[108] Prison authorities are therefore not subject to the Decree's requirements, see TA Rouen 25/5–99 *Aït-Taleb* DA 1999 no. 211.

[109] By way of contrast, an applicant for a beneficial decision is not entitled to a hearing under Art 8.

administrative penalties and 'sanctions'; decisions taken in the interest of public health, safety, and morality (*mesures de police*); and decisions revoking a previous decision which 'created rights' for its addressee.[110] The courts have considered 'unfavourable', for example, the dismissal, forced retirement, or transfer of civil servants from full-time to part-time positions;[111] the revocation of planning permissions,[112] financial grants for housing improvement,[113] licences to open and run pharmacies,[114] authorizations for orphanages to care for minors at the expense of the social welfare system,[115] marketing licences for medical and food products;[116] the suspension of bar licences;[117] and the restriction of taxi licences to certain geographical areas in a city on grounds of the driver's unmeritorious behaviour.[118]

The principle of defence requires *all public authorities*, both state and local, to grant the addressee of a decision notice and an 'effective' opportunity to answer by written representations.[119] However, this principle does not invariably apply to the revocation of favourable decisions. It must be determined in each case whether the revocation is a 'sanction' or a *mesure de police*, since defence rights only attach to the former.[120] Sanctions are 'repressive'; they are based upon an assessment of the affected person's conduct and imply unmeritorious conduct or a failure to live up to legal obligations. *Mesures de police* are 'preventive'; they purport to protect the public order, health, and security and do not involve an assessment or sanctioning of the addressee. This distinction may be illustrated by two leading cases.

In the seminal case of *Trompier-Gravier* a newsagent's licence was revoked without a hearing on the grounds that the licensee had sought to extort money from the person managing the shop. The CE held that a decision made on this ground amounted to a 'sanction' and established the general principle that persons subject to sanctions (broadly defined as decisions taken on the basis of a person's individual circumstances) must be given notice and an opportunity to make written representations.[121] By way of contrast, in the *Canu* case, the applicant's bar licence had been suspended for six months under a statutory provi-

[110] Most favourable decisions 'create rights', see chapter 3.2.B. Art 1 also refers to decisions which restrict public liberties; refusals of authorisations; grants of authorizations on restrictive conditions; and refusal of advantages which the applicant qualifies for under specific statutory conditions.

[111] CE 27/1–89 *Carluer* Rec 36; CE 22/2–89 *Fontenille* Rec 444; CE 21/11–86 *Vergne* no 63.226. Compare CE 27/5–87 *Centre Hospitalier du Rouvray* no. 53.688.

[112] TA Montpellier 26/3–82 *Laurent* Rec. 478.

[113] CE 25/4–90 *Figueréo* Rec 546.

[114] CE 12/6–95 *Scremin* no. 117.244.

[115] CE 21/10–91 *Association d'enfants de Clerlande* no. 89.158.

[116] CE 7/6–85 *Société ACOPASA* Rec. 177.

[117] CE 6/3–92 *SARL Société du spectacle de la Place Blanche* Rec 106 (the licence was revoked by the prefect of Paris, i.e. by a state authority, and it was therefore subject to the 1983 decree).

[118] TA Montpellier 26/3–82 *Laurent* Rec 478; CE 29/7–94 *Commune de Laval* no. 115.680.

[119] CE 24/7–46 *Neveu* Rec 211 and several later judgments. Oral hearings are not normally required, see Zeghbib, above n. 4, 477–8.

[120] See text at footnote 72.

[121] CE 5/5–44 *Trompier-Gravier* RDP 1944, 257.

sion, which gives licensing authorities the power to act in response to *either* the licensee's violations of certain statutory provisions *or* a more general threat to public order.[122] The CE held that while a suspension ordered on the former ground would be a 'sanction', a suspension purporting merely to protect the public order was a *mesure de police* which could be taken without procedural formality.[123]

A survey of case law reveals that a right to notice and representations is normally implied where, as in *Trompier-Gravier*, the revocation, modification or suspension has a significant impact upon the person's financial or personal situation.[124] It applies, for example, to the withdrawal of French nationality,[125] a scholarship,[126] or a place in a state school or other educational institution on grounds of misbehaviour or poor academic performance,[127] unemployment benefit when the recipient rejects a job offer,[128] and the legally privileged status of charitable association (*association d'utilité publique*).[129] Similarly, dismissal from public office on grounds of incompetence or ill health attracts a right to be heard,[130] as does the revocation of licences to carry out a professional activity,[131] tax exemptions,[132] and sizeable financial grants.[133] The only exception to this general rule is where, as in *Canu*, the statutory framework refers explicitly to the requirements of public order, security, or health.[134] Such references are, however, not uncommon, especially in licensing statutes. Thus, in the recent case of *Tigrini* the applicant's licence to use a market stall for the sale of

[122] Art L62 *Code des débits de boisson.* [123] CE 18/6–75 *Canu* Rec 362.

[124] This author surveyed some 350 decisions reported in the Lexis database referring to '*autorisation de police*' or '*mesure de police*'. See similarly Hostiou, above n. 4, 97; Allen, above n. 4, 296; Genevois, above n. 4, no. 369; Zeghbib, above n. 4, 477.

[125] e.g. CE 7/3–58 *Speter* Rec 152; CE 10/1–92 *Hammi* Rec. 11.

[126] CE 27/11–30 *Ribeyrolles* Rec 76.

[127] e.g. CE 8/7–36 *Hoarau* Rec 743; CE 16/5–75 *Abba Sidick* Rec. 835.

[128] CE 10/12–62 *Camarasa-Marsol* Rec 672.

[129] CE 31/10–52 *Ligue mères abandonnées* Rec 480; CE 19/10–56 *École de Commerce de Bastia* Rec. 657; CE 16/4–75 *La Comédie de Bourges* Rec 234.

[130] CE 24/6–49 *Nègre* Rec 304; CE 9/12–55 *Garysas* Rec 585; CE 26/10–84 *Chapuis* Rec 342. See also CE 19/5–93 *Notin* DA 1993 no. 324.

[131] e.g. CE 20/6–47 *Gamard* Rec 276; CE 19/5–50 *Fondation d'Henqueville* Rec 293; CE 7/1–55 *Association Chaumière des Pastorelles* Rec 11; CE 8/1–60 *Rohmer* Rec 12; CE 8/11–63 *Société coopérative d'insémination artificielle* Rec 532; CE 19/5–76 *SA du Château de Neuvecelle* RDP 1976, 1385; CE 16/6–78 *Pignol* Rec 687; CE 28/10–83 *Fogelgesang* DA 1982 no. 457; CE 25/11–94 *Palern* no. 129.381; CE 20/5–96 *Société Vortex* no. 171.423. Compare CE 22/3–96 *Société NRJSA* RDP 1996, 1768.

[132] CE 25/10–85 *Société des plastiques d'Alsace* Rec 300; CE 8/1–93 *Siegel* Rec 570.

[133] CE 11/12–92 *Société Inefor* Rec 439.

[134] For revocations and modification, see e.g. CE 22/4–55 *Association franco-russe* Rec 202 (authorization of charitable association); CE 25/4–58 *Société Laboratoires Geigy* Rec 236 (marketing licence for medical product); CE 12/6–59 *Prat Flottes* Rec 361 (health sanatorium); CE 27/1–82 *Bardin* RDP 1982, 1707 and CE 22/12–89 *SARL Résidence Gambetta* no. 71.097 (rest homes); CE 27/6–97 *Société Lille-Tax* no. 161.412 (taxi licences); TA Rouen 25/5–99 *Aït-Taleb* DA 1999 no. 211 (permission to visit prisoner). For suspensions, see e.g. CE 18/6–75 *Canu* Rec 362 (bar licence); CE 7/11–86 *Edwige* Rec 350 (suspension of civil servant to 'preserve' situation pending disciplinary proceedings); CE 10/5–95 *Auriol* no. 121.113 (drivers licence suspension on medical grounds).

bread and cakes had been revoked because he had also sold alcohol. The CE held, first, that since the revocation had been decided by the mayor of a local authority (a *commune*) the 1983 decree was inapplicable. Second, since his decision was based on a statutory power to maintain order in public markets and places, it was a *mesure de police*. Notice and hearing was therefore not required although the decision was not urgent.[135]

The exclusion of *mesures de police* from the principle of defence is, as *Tigrini* illustrates, problematic both in conceptual and practical terms. Decisions are often made for a variety of reasons related both to the addressee and the public interest. The distinction between 'sanctions' and *mesures de police* is therefore difficult to apply consistently in practice.[136] More importantly, the expectation which a licensee may have of maintaining a licence until it is up for renewal, may be disappointed without a hearing. This does not sit well with the serious impact upon the licensee's livelihood and reputation which the revocation may have.[137] Some form of hearing should, as in English and EC law, be afforded unless there is real urgency.

In French law, the right to receive reasons is much wider than the right to be heard. Although the French courts have shied away from imposing a general duty to give reasons under the general principle of *droits de la défense*,[138] the Law of 1979 prescribes for both state and local authorities that reasons be given for all 'unfavourable' decisions.[139] It was seen above that this notion is broadly defined, and revocation of favourable decisions must therefore nearly always be followed by written reasons and guidance about rights of appeal.[140]

(C) EC Law

Revocation and modification of favourable decisions require notice and, at least, an opportunity to make written observations in EC law. This follows directly from specific legislative provisions in many areas of community competence.[141] In other areas the right to a written hearing flows from the principle of the rights of the defence. In the important case of *Lisrestal* the ECJ held that the Commission's decision to reduce a financial grant, granted by the European Social Fund (ESF), was unlawful because the Commission had failed to ask the

[135] CE 9/11–94 *Tigrini* Rec 1139.

[136] Compare e.g. CE 30/1–48 *Ablon* Rec 52; CE 22/3–63 *Lorde* Rec 193. Similarly Chapus 1036; Zeghbib, above n. 4, 477.

[137] Similarly Hostiou, above n. 4, 93–4 noting that the hardship caused by the exclusion of *mesures de police* was acknowledged already in 1955 by *Commissaire de Gouvernement* Chardeau.

[138] CE 26/1–73 *Lang* Rec 72; CE 21/10–88 *SA TF1* Rec 365. Certain collegiate bodies are subject to a general reasoning requirement, CE 27/11–70 *Agence maritime Marseille-fret* Rec 704. See Hostiou, above n. 4, 180–6. The courts may also require reasons to be provided *to the court* if a decision appears to be unlawful, see CE 28/5–54 *Barel* Rec 308; CE 26/1–68 *Société Maison Genestal* Rec 62.

[139] Art 1, Law of 11/7–79. See footnote 39.

[140] Certain authorities, such as sporting associations, do however escape the provisions of this law. See Case 222/86 *UNECTEF v Heylens* [1989] ECR 4097.

[141] See footnotes 34–5.

Member State to invite comments from affected persons.[142] Importantly, the Court found that although the ESF regulation only prescribes hearing of the Member State, and not the person(s) benefiting, when the Commission purports to revoke or suspend a financial grant,[143] additional procedural protections must be implied to satisfy the principle of defence.[144] Moreover, the ECJ reaffirmed that the EC institutions' duty under the Treaty to give reasons includes decisions which revoke prior and more favourable decisions.[145]

4 Procedural Protection of Legitimate Expectations (II): Informal Representations

Informal representations may create reasonable expectations in individuals in much the same way as formal decisions. For example, a written assurance that planning permission will be granted on the satisfaction of certain conditions may create a reasonable expectation of a favourable decision. If the authority goes back on the assurance, the expectation will be disappointed, the applicant's plans will be upset, and he may suffer a reliance loss. The imposition of some degree of procedural protection is therefore warranted, even if the relevant decision does not otherwise gravely affect the applicant's rights and interests. It will now be examined to what extent English, French, and EC law protect expectations, created by informal representations, by procedural entitlements. For the sake of clarity, a distinction will be drawn between the three situations identified in Chapter 1 (Situations 2–4).

(A) English Law

English law provides extensive procedural protection of expectations created by administrative representations. Legitimate expectations were, as explained above, acknowledged as a separate basis of procedural fairness in 1969[146] and a widely ramified doctrine concerned with expectations has subsequently developed. In the recent *Behluli* case the Court of Appeal reaffirmed that the principle of legitimate expectations has:

[142] Case C-32/95P *Commission v Lisrestal* [1996] ECR I-5373 (approving Cases T-450/93 *Lisrestal v Commission* [1994] ECR II-1177 para 42; T-109/94 *Windmillpark v Commission* [1995] ECR II-3007 para 50).

[143] Art 8 Regulation 4255/88, Art 24 Regulation 4253/88. The requirement of state consultation has been rigorously enforced. See Cases C-304/89 *Oliveira v Commission* [1991] ECR I-2283; C-199/91 *Foyer culturel du Sart-Tilman v Commission* [1993] ECR I-2667; T-432–434/93 *Socurte v Commission* [1995] ECR II 503.

[144] For implication of procedural guarantees, see also Cases C-49/88 *Al-Jubail Fertilizer v Commission* [1991] ECR I-3187; C-135/92 *Fiskano v Commission* [1994] ECR I-2885; T-260/94 *Air Inter v Commission* [1997] ECR II-997.

[145] Art 253 EC.

[146] *Schmidt v Secretary of State for Home Affairs* [1969] 2 Ch 149.

achieved an important place in developing the law of administrative fairness. It is an expectation which, although not amounting to an enforceable legal right, is founded on a reasonable assumption which is capable of being protected in public law. It enables a citizen to challenge a decision which deprives him of an expectation founded on a reasonable basis that his claim would be dealt with in a particular way.[147]

The principle of procedural legitimate expectations applies to both procedural and substantive expectations. The terms of an administrative representation may entitle the person to a hearing or some other procedural protection,[148] or a particular outcome or benefit of a substantive nature.[149] In either case, the expectation created by the representation will attract a duty of procedural fairness or enhance the level of procedural protection which must be granted under statutory provisions.[150]

As indicated by the quote above, the application of procedural fairness presupposes that the applicant holds an objectively *reasonable* expectation. It must be shown that an ordinary[151] or reasonable[152] person would hold the expectation taking into account the form, wording, and context of the representation on which it is based. The notion of reasonable expectations will be discussed in Chapter 4. Here it will suffice to note two things.

First, reasonable expectations may be based on a wide range of representations. The form of a representation is relevant to the reasonableness of expectations, but it is not of paramount importance. Expectations may reasonably be based on both *explicit* representations such as letters,[153] published notices and departmental circulars,[154] ministerial speeches in Parliament,[155] public resolutions of local authorities,[156] and probably even oral assurances,[157] *implicit* repre-

[147] *R v Home Secretary, ex p Behluli* [1998] COD 328, 330.

[148] e.g. *R v Liverpool Corporation, ex p Liverpool Taxi Fleet Operators' Association* [1972] 2 QB 299; *Cinnamond v British Airport Authority* [1980] 1 WLR 582; *A-G of Hong Kong v Ng Yuen Shiu* [1983] 2 AC 629; *CCSU v Minister for the Civil Service* [1985] AC 374, 409; *R v Brent LBC, ex p Gunning* (1985) 84 LGR 168. Compare *Jaramilo-Silva v Home Secretary* [1994] Imm AR 352.

[149] e.g. *Schmidt v Secretary of State for Home Affairs* [1969] 2 Ch 149; *R v Home Secretary, ex p Kahn* [1984] 1 WLR 1337; *R v Secretary of State for Health, ex p US Tobacco International Inc* [1992] QB 353; *R v Secretary of State for Transport, ex p Richmond upon Thame LBC* [1996] 1 WLR 1460.

[150] *R v Secretary of State for Health, ex p US Tobacco International Inc* [1992] QB 353. See text at footnote 164.

[151] *R v Home Secretary, ex p Hargreaves* [1997] 1 WLR 906, 922.

[152] *R v Swale BC, ex p Royal Society for the Protection of Birds* (1990) 2 Admin LR 790; *R v Home Secretary, ex p Behluli* [1998] COD 328, 329.

[153] *Costain Homes Ltd v Secretary of State for the Environment* [1988] JPL 701.

[154] *R v London Borough of Ealing, ex p Lewis* [1993] COD 291.

[155] *R v Home Secretary, ex p Katoorah* [1996] Imm AR 595.

[156] *R v London Borough of Bexley, ex p Barnehurst Golf Club Ltd* [1992] COD 382; *Pelham Homes v Secretary of State for the Environment* [1995] JPL 816.

[157] *R v Home Secretary, ex p Oloniluyi* [1989] COD 275. Compare *R v Home Secretary, ex p Mowla* [1992] 1 WLR 70; *R v Local Government Commission, ex p Cambridgeshire DC* [1995] COD 149.

sentations derived from the decision-maker's conduct or settled practice,[158] and *combinations* of implicit and explicit representations.[159] For example, in the famous *CCSU* case civil servants at the Government Communications Head Quarters were found to have a legitimate expectation of consultation before their union rights were severely curtailed because a practice of consultation had existed for over thirty-five years.[160]

Second, the wording of a representation is of major importance for its ability to create reasonable expectations which will generate procedural entitlements. A representation must normally be 'clear, unambiguous, and devoid of relevant qualification'.[161] While this requirement is applied very strictly when individuals seek to enforce expectations substantively, the courts appear to be somewhat more lenient in procedural cases.[162] The explanation for this difference is that while the imposition of procedural fairness may be costly and inconvenient for the authorities, it normally does not restrict the application of discretionary powers in the same way as when an expectation is upheld in substance. *US Tobacco* is a pertinent example.[163] In this case the applicant company had, strongly encouraged by the Conservative government, built an oral snuff factory in Scotland. Some years later the government proceeded to ban oral snuff entirely. The court found that US Tobacco did not have a substantive legitimate expectation that its financial interests would override the interest in public health. However, given the history of dealings with the government, it had an expectation which attracted procedural protection so that access to, and opportunity to comment on, the scientific evidence on which the ban was based should have been granted.[164]

The existence of a reasonable expectation is a necessary, but not a sufficient condition for the right to procedural fairness. The expectation must also be *legitimate*. This requirement has at least three ramifications.

158 *Breen v Amalgamated Engineering Union* [1971] 2 QB 175; *R v Home Secretary, ex p Bennett* The Times 18/8–86; *R v Brent LBC, ex p Gunning* (1985) 84 LGR 168, 187–96; *R v Secretary of State for the Environment, ex p NALGO* (1993) 5 Admin LR 785; *R v Birmingham City Council, ex p Dredger* [1993] COD 340. Compare *R v Greater London Council, ex p The Lord Mayor and Citizens' of the City of Westminster* The Times 24/3–86.

159 e.g. *Lambeth LBC v Secretary of State for the Environment* [1990] JPL 196; *R v Rochdale MBC, ex p Schemet* [1993] COD 113; *R v British Coal Corporation, ex p Vardy* [1993] ICR 720; *R v Lord Chancellor, ex p Law Society* The Times 25/6–93.

160 *CCSU v Minister for the Civil Service* [1985] AC 374, 401, 409. Contrast where consultation had been granted on one or a few occasions: *R v Greater London Council, ex p The Lord Mayor and Citizens' of the City of Westminster* The Times 24/3–86; *R v Secretary of State for Health, ex p Alcohol Recovery Project* [1993] COD 344.

161 *R v IRC, ex p MFK Underwriting Agencies Ltd* [1990] 1 WLR 1545, 1569; *R v Devon CC, ex p Baker* [1995] 1 All ER 73, 88; *R v Home Secretary, ex p Hargreaves* [1997] 1 WLR 906, 922.

162 See Ch. 4.3.A.I.

163 *R v Secretary of State for Health, ex p US Tobacco International Inc* [1992] QB 353. See also *R v Barnet LBC, ex p Pardes House School* [1989] COD 512 (an applicant 'left with [an] impression' had a procedural legitimate expectation).

164 *R v Secretary of State for Health, ex p US Tobacco International Inc* [1992] QB 353.

First, expectations are not protected if a procedure would be incompatible with the decision-maker's statutory duties.[165] The English courts take the view that reasonable expectations must always yield to the principle of legality (*ultra vires*).[166] Although procedures are rarely denied on this ground, it may occur where the relevant statute prohibits the expected procedure or makes it clear that the procedures provided are exclusive.[167] Thus, in *Bartlam* the Court of Appeal held that a council's policy of publicizing proposed telecommunications developments, which are exempt from the requirement of planning permission, created a procedural legitimate expectation for the neighbours. But that expectation could not override the statutory provisions which deemed the developer to have an implied permission after 28 days of notifying the council.[168]

Second, the decision-maker must *balance* a reasonable expectation against the cost involved in granting procedural protection and other considerations, such as urgency, confidentiality, and national security. The fact that an applicant can show a reasonable expectation does not immunize his procedural claim from these countervailing considerations.[169] In *CCSU* the House of Lords upheld the government's decision to change union rights without consultation. Although consultation was expected by the affected persons, prior notification of the change could have triggered a strike in the GCHQ which would in turn have jeopardized national security.[170]

The impact which it will have upon the affected person if the expectation is disappointed, is also a relevant circumstance in the balancing. The fact that the person has relied upon the expectation and would suffer some financial detriment is therefore relevant; as is the nature and extent of that reliance. However, detrimental reliance is not, and should not be, an absolute condition for *procedural* protection.[171] The fact that a decision which disappoints a reasonable expectation undermines the affected person's planning and trust in the administration is sufficient to merit some degree of procedural protection.[172]

Another important factor in the balancing is whether the holder of the expectation is 'worthy' of legal protection. This will not be the case if the administrative representation was procured by fraud or the person failed to disclose

[165] *A-G of Hong Kong v Ng Yuen Shiu* [1983] 2 AC 629.

[166] For criticism of this view, see section 5.

[167] See De Smith 410.

[168] *R v Staffordshire Moorlands DC, ex p Bartlam* (1999) 77 P and CR 210

[169] *R v Devon Health Authority, ex p Coughlan* [1999] Lloyd's LR Medical 306.

[170] *CCSU v Minister for the Civil Service* [1985] AC 374, 401, 409.

[171] *R v Home Secretary, ex p Kahn* [1984] 1 WLR 1337; *A-G of Hong Kong v Ng Yuen Shiu* [1983] 2 AC 629; *R v Home Secretary, ex p Ruddock* [1987] 1 WLR 1482; *R v IRC, ex p MFK Underwriting Agencies Ltd* [1990] 1 WLR 1545, 1569; *R v Ministry of Agriculture, Fisheries and Foods, ex p Hamble Fisheries* [1995] 2 All ER 714, 725; *Pelham Homes v Secretary of State for the Environment* [1995] JPL 816. Similarly Elias, above n. 3, 48; De Smith 427; M. Beloff, 'Natural Justice and Fairness—the Audi Alterem Partem Rule', in M. Supperstone and J. Goudie (eds.), 2nd edn. *Judicial Review* (London, 1997), 8.29. The position may be different for *substantive* protection, see Ch. 4.

[172] See Ch. 1.

clearly relevant facts.[173] Moreover, it may not be considered unfair to withdraw an implicit[174] or explicit representation[175] without procedural formality if the procedure would, in the court's *ex post facto* view, make no difference to the outcome. For example, in *Jaramilo-Silva* the Home Secretary had informed in writing two Colombian men, convicted of drug offences, who were subject to deportation orders, that they would have a right of appeal against a final deportation order. More than a year later, the Home Office confirmed the deportation subject to a provision which grants no right of appeal. The Court of Appeal found no breach of procedural fairness. Both applicants had submitted written and oral observations with the help of solicitors, and there was therefore no 'detriment' or reason to believe that an appeal would succeed.[176] The result in this case may appear correct, but it is thought that the courts should not readily deny relief on the ground that a hearing would not have made a difference.[177] The courts are ill-equipped to foretell the impact of a procedure upon the outcome of a case, and respect for the affected person's dignity and trust in the administration may require an expected procedure to be granted independently of its effect upon the outcome.

The balancing of expectations, costs, and other considerations is in the first place for the public authority which has by its representations created expectations in individuals. It is, however, subject to judicial control. In the realm of procedure, the courts are the 'author and sole judge' of what is required.[178] They will review the balancing of expectations and countervailing considerations and intervene if it is felt that there is a an imbalance, or lack of proportion, between the interests at stake.[179] This approach differs from situations where individuals seek to enforce expectations substantively. As will be explained in Chapter 4, the courts will only uphold expectations substantively on grounds of *Wednesbury* unreasonableness.[180] This means that the courts will intervene only if there is a very serious imbalance between a person's reasonable expectation and the wider public interest in a decision which will disappoint it.

The balancing of expectations, fairness, and cost is of considerable importance for the scope and practical usefulness of the principle of procedural legitimate expectations. Still, it is far from always reasoned through in a sufficiently

[173] *R v IRC, ex p MFK Underwriting Agencies Ltd* [1990] 1 WLR 1545; *Matrix Securities Ltd v IRC* [1994] 1 WLR 334.

[174] *R v Secretary of State for Foreign and Commonwealth Affairs, ex p Samuel* The Times 17/8–89.

[175] *R v Home Secretary, ex p Jaramilo-Silva* [1994] Imm AR 352; *R v Newport CBC, ex p Avery* [1999] JPL 452.

[176] Ibid. The Court also found that the applicant's solicitors should have detected the error.

[177] See footnote 20.

[178] *R v Panel on Take-Overs and Mergers, ex p Guinness* [1990] 1 QB 146, 183. See also *R v Devon Health Authority, ex p Coughlan* [1999] Lloyd's LR Medical 306.

[179] On the relationship between the principles of proportionality and legitimate expectations, see Ch. 4.7.B.

[180] *Associated Provincial Picture Houses Ltd v Wednesbury Corporation* [1948] 1 KB 223.

clear and open fashion by the courts. A comparison of the *Gunning* and *Kent* cases illustrate this problem. In *Gunning* parents of pupils were found to have a legitimate expectation of consultation about a decision to close a school on the grounds that on two previous occasions, over a period of about two years, consultations had taken place and that a settled practice had therefore emerged.[181] By way of contrast, in *Kent* a practice, adopted by many local authorities for a considerable period of time, of consultation with neighbours in planning cases did not give rise to a legitimate expectation.[182] The different outcomes in these cases is best explained by the fact that while planning decisions are made in great numbers, school closures are a relatively rare occurrence. To impose a duty of neighbour consultation in planning cases would therefore have been far more costly than in school closure cases.[183] However, this cost consideration was not explicitly stated in any of the two judgments.

In the light of these general comments about the principle of procedural legitimate expectations, it is possible to explain more precisely how it applies in the three situations identified in Chapter 1.

The first situation is where a public authority explicitly or implicitly represents that it will follow a certain procedure or policy in relation to a specific individual or group (Situation 2). If the representation is procedural, the authority will normally be obliged to honour it.[184] It may, for example, have to consult with groups or bodies not otherwise entitled to consultation,[185] extend the duration of a statutory consultation exercise,[186] hold a ballot amongst tenants,[187] or a public inquiry on a planning matter,[188] give written reasons,[189] or grant the holder of the expectation a meeting[190] or a personal interview.[191]

[181] *R v Brent LBC, ex p Gunning* (1985) 84 LGR 168. See also *R v Gwent CC, ex p Bryant* [1988] COD 19 and P. Meredith, 'Legitimate Expectation and School Closures' (1988) PL 4.

[182] *R v Secretary of State for the Environment, ex p Kent* [1988] JPL 706 (confirmed by the Court of Appeal [1990] JPL 124). See further De Smith 435–6.

[183] In both cases it was accepted that the legislative framework encouraged consultation and that the consultation practice had been formalized by departmental circulars. See also May LJ's comment in the Court of Appeal that the failure to consult Mr Kent caused injustice [1990] JPL 129.

[184] Though, due to countervailing factors, what is deemed legitimate may not always coincide precisely with what an individual reasonably expected.

[185] e.g. *R v Liverpool Corporation, ex p Liverpool Taxi Fleet Operators' Association* [1972] 2 QB 299; *R v Home Secretary, ex p Bennett* The Times 18/8–86; *R v Brent LBC, ex p Gunning* (1985) 84 LGR 168; *R v Birmingham City Council, ex p Dredger* [1993] COD 340; *R v Lord Chancellor, ex p Law Society* The Times 25/6–93. Compare *R v Greater London Council, ex p The Lord Mayor and Citizens of the City of Westminster* The Times 24/3–86; *R v Secretary of State for the Environment, ex p NALGO* (1993) 5 Admin LR 785.

[186] *Lambeth LBC v Secretary of State for the Environment* [1990] JPL 196; *R v Falmouth and Truro Health Authority, ex p South West Water Services* The Times 6/5–99.

[187] *R v London Borough of Bexley, ex p Barnehurst Golf Club Ltd* [1992] COD 382.

[188] *Pelham Homes v Secretary of State for the Environment* [1995] JPL 816.

[189] *R v Home Secretary, ex p Duggan* [1994] COD 258.

[190] *R v London Borough of Bexley, ex p Barnehurst Golf Club Ltd* [1992] COD 382.

[191] *A-G of Hong Kong v Ng Yuen Shiu* [1983] 2 AC 629.

Thus, in the case of *Ny Yuen Shiu* the rejection of a Chinese immigrant's application for leave to stay in Hong Kong was quashed on the grounds of legitimate expectations. The Privy Council held that while applicants for leave have no claim to be heard on rights or interests grounds, the British government had to honour a promise to interview all immigrants and treat their cases on their merits. Allowing an applicant only to answer questions, and not to state his case, was therefore a violation of procedural fairness.[192]

Similarly, if the administration makes a substantive representation, i.e. about a policy or outcome in the particular case, it must normally give the affected person(s) notice and the opportunity to make written representations before going back on it. For example, in *Costain Homes* the Secretary of State for the Environment had written to the applicant, who had appealed against a refusal of planning permission, that he would grant permission, all that was left for 'confirmation' was the completion of an agreement between the appellant and the local planning authority. The court found that the Secretary of State could not go back on this letter without hearing the applicant first.[193]

The second situation is where a public authority makes a general representation about the procedure or policy it does, or intends to, follow in relation to a certain type of decisions, but subsequently departs from it in the particular case (Situation 3). Procedural fairness normally applies in these 'departure situations'. The authority must notify the person adversely affected by the departure and allow him an opportunity to make written observations.[194] For example, in the oft-cited *Kahn* case the Court of Appeal held that the Home Secretary could not depart from criteria, published in the form of a circular, for the treatment of applications for permission to adopt children without granting the applicant a hearing.[195] Moreover, the recent *Gangadeen* case reaffirmed previous dicta to the effect that reasons must also be given to justify a departure from policy.[196]

The third, and last, situation is where the authority departs from its procedure or policy representation in the light of a shift in general policy which has occurred between the initial representation and the decision (Situation 4). The

192 Ibid.

193 *Costain Homes Ltd v Secretary of State for the Environment* [1988] JPL 701. See also *R v Enfield LBC, ex p Unwin* (1989) 1 Admin LR 51; *R v Devon Health Authority, ex p Coughlan* [1999] Lloyd's LR Medical 306.

194 *R v Home Secretary, ex p Kahn* [1984] 1 WLR 1337; *Conteh v Home Secretary* [1992] Imm AR 594; *R v Secretary of State for Transport, ex p Richmond upon Thame LBC* [1994] 1 WLR 74, 92; *R v Secretary of State for the Environment, ex p West Oxfordshire DC* (1993) 25 HLR 417; *R v Secretary of State for Education, ex p London Borough of Southwark* [1994] COD 298, 299. See also *R v Great Yarmouth BC, ex p Botton Brothers Arcades Ltd* [1988] JPL 18 (hearing rights implied in departure situation by liberal interpretation of a planning decision's effect on 'interests').

195 Ibid.

196 *R v Home Secretary, ex p Gangadeen* [1998] 1 FLR 762. Similarly *Westminster CC v Great Portland Estates*, [1985] AC 661, 673; *Wycombe BC v Secretary of State for the Environment* [1988] JPL 111, 112–13 (planning); *R v Home Secretary, ex p Hastrup* [1996] Imm AR 616 (immigration); *R v Islington LBC, ex p Rixon* [1997] ELR 66 (social services); *R v North Derbyshire Health Authority, ex p Fisher* (1998) 10 Admin LR 27, 42 (NHS).

case of *Bates* established that there is no common law duty of consultation or reasoning in the making of general policy and secondary legislation.[197] If it were accepted that an existing policy can create legitimate expectations, which ground a right to be consulted before the policy is changed, the *Bates* principle would be limited to some extent. The English courts have not, so far, been willing to take this step.[198] There is no common law duty to consult on policy, unless a consultation has explicitly been promised or the applicant has benefited from a settled practice of consultation.[199] Thus, in *King* it was said that licensees had no right to be consulted on a change of policy which caused a very substantial increase in licensing fees. The application of the new policy would gravely affect their livelihood and financial interests, but a duty of procedural fairness would only be implied if the licensees could show a *procedural* legitimate expectation of consultation based on a promise or practice.[200] It is doubtful whether this restrictive approach to procedures and changes of policy satisfies the requirements of fairness and good administration, and it will be argued below that a change in the direction of greater participation is required.[201]

(B) French Law

French public authorities are generally free to resile from representations without procedural formality.[202] As explained above, the principle of *droits de la défense* only applies to 'sanctions' (broadly defined as decisions taken on the basis of a person's individual circumstances) which have a 'sufficiently serious' impact. The fact that a decision disappoints expectations does not, in and of itself, make it a serious sanction. Moreover, decisions are not considered 'unfavourable' under the Law of 1979 (reasons) and the Decree of 1983 (hearing) simply because they go back on representations or disappoint expectations.

[197] *Bates v Lord Hailsham of Marylebone* [1972] 1 WLR 1373; *Leech v Deputy Governor Parkhurst Prison* [1988] AC 533, 538. Moreover, since the Rules Publication Act 1893 was repealed in 1946 there has been no statutory procedure for the publication of proposed legislation with a view to comments, as the Tribunal and Inquiries Act 1992 does not apply to measures of a legislative nature, s 10(5)(b). See Galligan, above n. 1, 483–92, 507–13.

[198] *Findlay v Home Secretary* [1985] AC 318; *R v Secretary of State for Transport, ex p Richmond upon Thame LBC* [1994] 1 WLR 74, 93. Compare *R v Liverpool Corporation, ex p Liverpool Taxi Fleet Operators' Association* [1972] 2 QB 299 (Lord Denning). A duty of consultation may, however, be accepted where a policy will affects a strictly limited number of individuals in a direct way. See *R v Rochdale MBC, ex p Schemet* [1993] COD 113, 445–6; *R v Devon CC, ex p Baker* [1995] 1 All ER 73; *R v London Borough of Camden, ex p Hughes* [1994] COD 253.

[199] See footnotes 157–9.

[200] *R v Manchester City Council, ex p King* [1991] COD 422. See also *R v Birmingham City Council, ex p Dredger* [1993] COD 340.

[201] See section 5.

[202] For a few notable examples, see CE 11/5–56 *Société Lesieur-Afrique* Rec. 184; CE 18/10–57 *Bouveret* Rec 542; TA Paris 24/5–60 *Etablissement Millo-Frolich* AJDA 1961, 218; CE 27/2–63 *Société Paramount* Rec 689; CE 1/12–72 *Texierp* Rec 1222; CE 26/10–73 *SCI Résidence Arcole* Rec 601; CAA Paris 13/6–89 *Commune de Bois d'Arcy* Rec 318; CE 29/12–95 *Hurey* no. 122.188.

This may be illustrated by a few leading cases concerned with the three situations identified above.

First, the French administration is not bound by individualized promises to grant a certain procedure or a certain outcome (Situation 2). This is aptly illustrated by the case of *Priolet*.[203] This case concerned a decision to refuse permanent guardianship over eight children, who had been placed temporarily in the care of a couple, and to remove the children from their care. The CE found that since a final decision on the care and placement of the children had not been made, the children could at any time be removed without a hearing. The substantive expectations, which might have been created by the initial placement of the children, were not considered. Moreover, the fact that the director of the social services had allegedly promised the applicants guardianship was, in the Court's view, entirely irrelevant for the application of the principle of defence.

Second, the fact that an administrative decision departs from a general policy or practice does not in and of itself, give rise to a requirement of procedural formality (Situation 3). The CE ruled in the famous *Crédit foncier de France* case from 1970 that decision-makers must not, in the absence of an overriding public interest, depart from a general policy or practice (an internal *directive*) in an individual case as this would violate the general principle of equal treatment (*égalité de traitement*).[204] However, this principle has no procedural implications. On the one hand, if an authority purports to depart from a *substantive* policy in a particular applicant's case for reasons of public interest, it is not obliged to seek the applicant's view on this justification. The applicant's only remedy is to contest the departure on substantive grounds *ex post facto*. On the other hand, general notices, circulars, and internal directives which lay down a *procedure* to be followed, as opposed to a substantive policy, are not considered 'internal directives', which are binding towards individuals under the principle of equal treatment.[205] This was established in the important *Mousset* case, in which the CE held that a published and detailed departmental circular, which set out the Ministry of Justice's interpretation of the Law of 1979 concerning the right to reasons, could not be invoked by individuals against the administration.[206]

Finally, there is no duty to consult prior to, or give reasons for, general changes of policy in French law (Situation 4). The principle of *droits de la*

[203] CE 16/11–77 *Priolet* Rec 435.

[204] CE 11/12–70 *Crédit foncier de France* Rec 750; CE 27/6–73 *Société Gea* Rec 453. See Ch. 4.4.B.

[205] The officer who departs from an internal circular may in theory be subject to disciplinary action for failure to obey the instructions of his superiors. See Vedel and Delvolvé, above n. 7, 261; Chapus 475–7.

[206] CE 25/3–83 *Mousset* Rec 135. See also CE 13/10–82 *Chiquet* no. 13.324 (confirmed by CE 4/7–97 *Seguier d'Agoult* no. 155.649); CAA Lyon 3/11–93 *SARL Institut Artistique de Provence* no. 92LY00225; CAA Lyon 17//11–94 *Alibelli* DF 1995 no. 21 comm 1159; CE 18/4–80 *Comité Lyon-Satolas* no. 8.836; CAA Paris 27/4–95 *Les jardins de Grenade* DF 1995 no. 30 comm 1622.

défense and the procedural codes of 1979 and 1983 apply exclusively to individualized decision-making.[207] The extent to which consultation on policy takes place is therefore, in the absence of statutory consultation provisions, within the discretion of the French administration. It follows that substantive expectations created by an existing policy that the policy will remain in force are not protected by procedural rules in France.

(C) EC Law

The procedural protection of expectations is more developed in EC law than in France, but not as extensive as in Britain. The EC law position resembles French law in that the Community principle of defence applies where a decision affects the interests of a person adversely and to a significant extent. Expectations are not taken into account when the courts apply this test. Going back on a representation is therefore not, in and of itself, a reason for imposing procedural protections in EC law. There is, however, a highly developed doctrine of legitimate expectations in EC law, which originates in ECSC cases from the 1950s.[208] It was always clear in EC law that substantive expectations are enforced substantively and procedural expectations procedurally. In other words, the ECJ takes the perfectly logical view that protection should correspond to what is actually expected by the affected person. If the Community administration made a substantive representation (about outcomes), the affected person may be able to enforce that substantively (see Chapter 4). If the administration made a procedural representation, which created a legitimate expectation, then that procedure must be granted. What does this mean in the three situations?

First, there is no duty to grant a hearing before the administration resiles from an individualized promise of a certain outcome (Situation 2). The applicant's only remedy is to contest the decision on the grounds that it disappointed his *substantive* legitimate expectations. For example, in the striking case of *Pauvert* the applicant had been promised in unequivocal terms that he would be granted employment as a chauffeur, but the Court of Auditors subsequently went back on its promise when it realized that Mr Pauvert did not quite qualify for the job. The ECJ held that while the Commission should have informed the applicant when it realized that it had to go back on the promise, its failure to do so did not in itself constitute a breach of the principle of defence.[209] The out-

[207] CE 4/5–60 *Maréchal* Rec 884; CE 11/1–63 *Syndicat national des administrateurs* AJDA 1963, 289. See P. Delvolvé, 'Acte administratif', in F. Gazier, R. Drago and A. Dupie (eds.), *Encyclopédie Dalloz: Répertoire de contentieux administratif* (Paris, 1996), no. 364 and more generally G. Langrod (ed.), *La consultation dans l'administration contemporaine* (Paris, 1972).

[208] Notably Cases 7/56 and 3–7/57 *Algera v Common Assembly* [1957] ECR 39. See Ch. 3.2.C.

[209] Case 228/84 *Pauvert v Court of Auditors* [1985] ECR 1969 para 16. See also Cases T-46/90 *Devillez v EP* [1993] ECR II-699 para 38; T-493/93 *Hansa-Fisch v Commission* [1995] ECR II-575 para 44–50.

come in this case would presumably have been different if the Commission had represented that it would grant the applicant a hearing or other *procedural* benefit. Although there is no case law in point, there is little reason to doubt that the EC principle of legitimate expectations could be invoked to enforce a procedural expectation in a specific instance.[210]

Second, the distinction between procedural and substantive representations is also important when the Community administration departs from a general policy or practice in an individual case. The ECJ ruled in the *Louwage* case from 1974 that the Community administration must not, without good reason, depart from a general policy or practice in an individual case as this would violate the general principles of legitimate expectations and equal treatment (Situation 3).[211] There is no conceptual link in the EC case law between this duty to apply policy loyally and the right to be heard. A community institution, which considers whether to depart from an existing general policy of a *substantive* nature, is therefore not obliged to grant the affected individual a hearing about the 'good reasons' for which it intends to treat him differently from others subject to the existing policy. The position is, however, different if a community institution made a representation about the *procedure* it intended to follow in certain types of cases. The principle laid own in *Louwage* applies to such general procedural representations, and they must not be departed from in individual cases. Thus, in the *Hercules Chemicals* case[212] the Commission had stated in a report, published in the Official Journal, that it would grant access to certain documents in competition proceedings, and it had for some years it followed a practice of doing so. The CFI held that the Commission had imposed a binding rule on itself. It was obliged on grounds of legitimate expectations and equality to grant access to all applicants, even if in a particular instance several applicants had requested access to a large number of documents.[213]

Finally, while consultation on general changes of EC policy takes place on an *ad hoc* basis,[214] there is no legal duty to consult or give reasons (Situation 4). The Treaty contains no generally applicable consultation provisions and the principle of the rights of defence only applies to persons directly affected by an

[210] In practice procedural expectations are rarely invoked before the community courts. See however Case T-353/94 *Postbank v Commission* [1996] ECR II-921 para 73.

[211] Case 148/73 *Louwage v Commission* [1974] ECR 81 para 12. See Ch. 4.4.B.

[212] Case T-7/89 *Hercules Chemicals v Commission* [1991] ECR II-1711 confirmed by Case T-9/89 *Huls v Commission* [1992] ECR II-499 para 48–49. See also staff Cases 80–83/81 and 182–185/81 *Adam v Commission* [1984] ECR 3411; 129 and 274/81 *Lux v Court of Auditors* [1984] ECR 4127 para 20–23; T-45/90 *Speybrouck v EP* [1992] ECR II-33 para 57–80; T-33/91*Willams v Court of Auditors* [1992] ECR II-2499 para 66–71.

[213] For criticism of this wide-ranging duty of disclosure, see AG Leger [1995] ECR I-888; S. Moore (1996) CMLRev 366.

[214] The Commission publishes a number of Green and White books every year calling for comments on EC policy and legislation.

individual measure.[215] This means that policies and procedures, both as to substance and procedure, can lawfully be changed with prospective effect without procedural formality so long as the change does not affect already lodged applications.[216] In the 1993 Inter-institutional Declaration on Democracy, Transparency, and Subsidiarity, the Institutions proposed a formal notification procedure by which the Commission would publish proposed general measures in the Official Journal with a deadline by which interested parties could submit comments. This interesting proposal is, however, unlikely to be implemented in the near future.[217]

5 Comparison and Suggestions for Reform

It emerges from the comparative survey that the difference between English, French, and EC law in terms of actual procedural protection of expectations is not as great as the markedly different conceptualization might suggest. Despite the absence of a distinct *concept* or doctrine of procedural legitimate expectations in French and EC law, some procedural *protection* of expectations is actually available in both legal systems. This comes about in two ways.

First, a public authority which revokes or modifies a favourable decision must typically comply with procedural guarantees because its decision affects legally recognized interests, such as livelihood and reputation (Situation 1). The only, but important, exception to this common rule is the French notion of *mesures de police* which has the effect that licences can be, and are in fact sometimes, revoked without a hearing.

Second, a public authority which makes a specific or general representation about the *procedure* it intends to follow will, under both English and EC law, be bound to comply with that procedure in individual cases (Situation 3). For departing from the procedure violates the principles of legitimate expectations and equal treatment. Thus, the procedural expectations created by representations are protected in both legal systems. So far, a similar protection has not been available in France.

These similarities apart, the absence of a distinct concept of procedural legitimate expectations does lead to different outcomes in many other situations. *Substantive* expectations created by individualized promises, practices, and general policy representation are not procedurally protected by French and EC law.

[215] Cases 37/81 *Seton v Commission* [1983] ECR 1789 (staff); C-49/88 *Al-Jubail Fertilizer v Commission* [1991] ECR I-3187 para 15 (anti-dumping); C-170/89 *BEUC v Commission* [1991] ECR I-5709 para 19–21 (consumer groups); C-104/99P *Atlanta AG v Council and Commission*, 14/10–99 para 36–38 (CAP).

[216] To apply a new policy to an already lodged application should, and is likely to be, considered a departure from existing policy.

[217] See Report on the Working of the Maastricht Treaty (1995) SEC 731 para 81–82.

In this respect English law provides clearly superior protection as a comparison of *Costain Homes* with *Pauvert* and *Priolet* illustrates.[218] It may therefore be concluded that the explicit recognition of procedural legitimate expectation does contribute significantly to fairness, certainty and trust in administration. Procedural legitimate expectations should therefore remain an important aspect of procedural fairness in English law, and this is a concept which deserves the attention of both the French and the Community courts.

There is, however, room for improvement of English law in three respects. First, there is some suggestion in the case law that procedural fairness only applies when a decision affects a person's interests 'gravely'.[219] This phraseology is unfortunate and it should be acknowledged as a matter of general principle that fairness applies whenever a decision affects a person's interests adversely and *significantly* (Situation 1).[220] This test of implication is cited in EC case law,[221] and the comparison of procedural rights in revocation situations has revealed that English case law is in substance little different from EC law. Thus, intellectual honesty joins arguments of principle in favour of a change of the English formulation. The degree of seriousness of the decision's impact and the relative importance of the affected interest would remain relevant, but they should be reflected in the *content* of the procedure afforded rather than in the scope of the fairness principle itself.

Second, the present approach to changes of policy (Situation 4) is not entirely satisfactory. A policy which has applied for some time can create a substantive and reasonable expectation that it will be continued, at least until further notice. It should be accepted that such an expectation may create a right to some form of consultation.[222] It is thought that this would apply especially, but not exclusively, where the change of policy will have a serious impact upon an individual's rights or interests (apart from expectations). For example, in *Hargreaves* the Court of Appeal found that a change in policy on prisoners' access to home leave had had a 'severely traumatizing effect' upon several inmates. The court should, it is submitted, have considered whether the government's consultation exercise prior to the change had granted the prisoners a say.[223]

To accept a duty of consultation on the grounds of substantive legitimate expectations would not be a major shift towards a more general duty to consult in policy- and rule-making procedures.[224] The *scope* of the duty to consult

[218] See text at footnotes 193, 203, 209. [219] See footnotes 64–5.

[220] *Board of Education v Rice* [1911] AC 179, 182. Similarly De Smith 405; Galligan, above n. 1, 316–7; Beloff, above n. 171, 8.24.

[221] And in Australian law, *Haoucher v Minister for Immigration and Ethnic Affairs* (1990) 169 CLR 648, 653.

[222] See *R v London Borough of Camden, ex p Hughes* [1994] COD 253, 255.

[223] *R v Home Secretary, ex p Hargreaves* [1997] 1 WLR 906.

[224] Whether the courts should impose a general duty of consultation, or leave untouched the existing system of informal *ad hoc* consultations, is a question beyond the scope of this book. See

would be limited, because it would remain open to the courts to find on the facts of each case that expectations are not reasonable or legitimate. It would, in particular, remain open to authorities to warn those subject to policies and practices that they are liable to change. Influential groups and interests which already benefit from consultation practices (the 'insiders' in policy-networks), would therefore not be entitled to claim the continuation of such practices to the detriment of less influential or established interests (the 'outsiders').[225] The *content* of the duty to consult would be limited, because the courts would take into account the practicality of consulting. If a large number of individuals are affected, as in *Hargreaves*, consultation could be limited to allowing written representations from, or a meeting with, representative groups or persons.[226] To accept a duty to consult based on legitimate expectations would, therefore, not make policy-making excessively cumbersome or expensive, as might be the case if the administrations were subjected to a duty to consult on all policy changes which affect individuals adversely.

Third, there is a strong case for accepting that *unlawful* decisions and representations can, in appropriate circumstances, generate enforceable procedural expectations (Situations 1–4). The principle of legality (*ultra vires*) is not absolute; it should be balanced against the requirements of fairness.[227] There may be situations in which the public interest would not be seriously harmed if a procedure were granted against the word or intention of a statute, and fairness should prevail in these situations.[228]

Assuming that the principles of procedural fairness were developed in accordance with these three proposals, would procedures be sufficient by themselves to provide effective protection of legitimate expectations and thus meet the demands of fairness and good administration? The answer is negative for three reasons.[229]

First, a rigid conceptual distinction between procedure and substance cannot be maintained.[230] Once it is accepted that expectations give rise to procedural entitlements, it becomes difficult to deny entirely the possibility that substantive entitlements can also follow. As Sedley J noted in *Hamble Fisheries*, 'it is difficult to see why it is any less unfair to disappoint an expectation that something

generally M. Asimov, 'Delegated Legislation: United States and United Kingdom' (1983) OJLS 253; P. P. Craig, *Public Law and Democracy in the United Kingdom and the United States of America* (Oxford, 1990); R. Baldwin, *Rules and Government* (Oxford, 1995), 74–80, 111–21; Galligan, above n. 1, chs. 15–16; P. Cane, 'The Constitutional and Legal Framework of Policy-Making', in C. Forsyth and I. Hare (eds.), *The Golden Metwand and the Crooked Cord: Essays in Honour of Sir William Wade* (Oxford, 1998), 39.

225 See on policy networks D. Marsh and R. A. W. Rhodes, *Policy Networks in British Government* (Oxford, 1992); B. O'Toole, 'Treating Networks Seriously' (1997) Public Administration 45.

226 See for this approach *R v Devon CC, ex p Baker* [1995] 1 All ER 73.

227 See Ch. 1.

228 See also Chs. 3.5.B and 4.7.C.

229 See Forsyth, above n. 3, 253 and 'Wednesbury Protection of Substantive Legitimate Expectations' (1997) PL 375, 377.

230 See Galligan, above n. 1, 333–4.

will or will not be done by the decision-maker than it is to frustrate a legitimate expectation that the applicant will be listened to before the decision-maker decides whether to take a particular step.'[231]

Second, procedural protection is sometimes impractical for public authorities, partly because it is costly and time-consuming,[232] partly because a notification and hearing may undermine the purpose of the relevant decision. For example, in the *Ruddock* case a police authority had intercepted the applicant's phone in breach of published general policy guidelines. Although this violated the applicant's expectation that these guidelines would be adhered to, prior notice and hearing would obviously have been impractical.[233] In other instances, it may be impractical for individuals to make use of procedural entitlements. To take up a hearing, and present convincing arguments in favour of respecting expectations, requires information, expertise, time, and money which may not be available.[234]

Third, and most importantly, procedural rights do not provide any guarantee of a substantive outcome. Procedures can make a difference,[235] but they will in some instances amount to no more than a formality *unless* they are backed up by substantive principles, which guarantee that the views presented are taken into account and given some weight.[236]

Thus, while procedural protection of legitimate expectations is necessary to provide fair and good administration, it should only be considered a complement to substantive principles of law. It is with such principles that the following two chapters are concerned.

[231] *R v Ministry of Agriculture, Fisheries and Foods, ex p Hamble Fisheries* [1995] 2 All ER 714, 724.

[232] See *R v Secretary of State for the Environment, ex p Kent* [1988] JPL 706 discussed at footnote 182. There is also some evidence that authorities do not always comply with procedural obligations. See Galligan, above n. 1, 360–1.

[233] *R v Home Secretary, ex p Ruddock* [1987] 1 WLR 1482.

[234] Costs are especially problematic if legal advice is sought, as legal aid is unavailable for hearings before most administrative authorities and tribunals. See J. L. Jowell, above n. 10, 70 and further T. Prosser, 'Poverty, Ideology and Legality' (1977) BJLS 39; J. F. Handler, 'Discretion: Power, Quiescence, and Trust', in K. Hawkins (ed.), *The Uses of Discretion* (Oxford, 1992), 331.

[235] Though, as mentioned above in footnote 1, the actual impact of hearings upon outcomes is uncertain.

[236] See Forsyth, above n. 3, 253; G. Cartier, 'La théorie des attentes légitimes en droit administratif' (1992) Revue de Droit Université Sherbrooke 75, 111; P. P. Craig, 'Substantive Legitimate Expectations in Domestic and European Law' (1996) CLJ 289, 296; S. Foster, 'Legitimate Expectations and Prisoners' Rights' (1997) MLR 727, 731; Allan, above n. 2, 31.

Chapter 3

Substantive Protection of Legitimate Expectations (I): Revocation of Decisions

1 Introduction

Individuals often plan their lives and rely financially upon administrative decisions. Revocation of decisions may, therefore, cause legal uncertainty, disappointment of reasonable expectations, and financial loss. For this reason, it is accepted in English, French, and EC law that restrictions must be imposed upon the power public authorities may have to revoke their own decisions.

Revocation is not regulated by constitutional provisions or general legislation in any of the three jurisdictions;[1] the courts have been the driving force in the development of principles in this area.[2] In English law, three principles are cited in cases concerned with administrative revocation; finality of administrative determinations,[3] estoppel by record (estoppel *per rem judicatam*),[4] and *functus officio*.[5] It is not proposed to trace the historical origin of these principles which, with the exception of some relatively insignificant details, impose the same restrictions on administrative revocation.[6] In this book, the principles will be referred to simply as 'the principle of irrevocability'. In French and EC law, the legal terminology is somewhat more consistent. The French courts resolve revocation problems by reference to a broadly defined principle of irrevocability of decisions which 'create rights' (*intangibilité des décisions*

[1] The Interpretation Act 1978, s 12 states that, as a general rule of interpretation, a statutory 'power may be exercised . . . from time to time as occasion requires'. This provision does not imply a general power to revoke administrative decisions. See M. Letemendia, *Retrait et abrogation des actes administratifs individuels en droit communautaire et droit anglais* (Brussels, 1987), 159–60; Wade 261.

[2] Specific statutory revocation provisions do, however, apply in many areas. A detailed survey of such provisions is beyond the scope of this book, but see e.g. in EC law Art 8(3) Regulation 17/62 (competition law exemptions); Staff Regulations Art 85, Art 41 Annex VIII (recovery of salary payments); Art 8 Regulation 4255/88, Art 24 Regulation 4253/88 (structural fund grants); Arts 50–51, 54 Regulation 40/94 (trade marks); in English law the Licensing Act 1964, s 20A (public houses); Social Security Administration Act 1992, s 25–26, 35, 71, 75 (welfare benefits); Taxes Management Act 1970, s 29 (tax assessments); Town and Country Planning Act 1990, s 97, 100 (planning permissions); Prosecution of Offences Act 1985, s 25 (prosecution); and in French law the provisions cited in footnote 162.

[3] *Re 56 Denton Rd., Twickenham, Middlesex* [1953] 1 Ch 51.

[4] *Thrasyvoulou v Secretary of State for the Environment* [1990] 2 AC 273.

[5] *Barons v Luscombe* (1835) 3 Ad and E 589.

[6] See however section 3.D on the requirement of reliance as a precondition for the finality of administrative decisions.

créatrices de droits).[7] Similarly, in Community law, the ECJ has developed a principle of irrevocability of decisions which create or confer 'vested rights'.[8]

On the face of it, English, French, and EC law differ quite markedly in legal terminology, conceptualization, and the actual content of the relevant principles. In this chapter it will become apparent, from a comparison of outcomes of decided cases, that the substantial differences are less marked than they would appear.[9] However, important differences do exist, especially in relation to revocation of unlawful (*ultra vires*) decisions. For the purposes of the comparison, three distinctions should be kept in mind.

First, a distinction may be drawn between decisions which determine whether the addressee has a pre-existing legal right and decisions which confer a benefit that would otherwise not have existed. The former type of decision corresponds to a legal duty on the decision-maker.[10] For our purposes, such a decision may be called *declaratory*, because it does not in principle create a new legal situation for the addressee.[11] The latter type of decision corresponds to a discretionary power in the decision-maker.[12] For our purposes, a decision of this type may be called *constitutive*, because it creates a real change in the legal situation of the addressee.[13]

Second, a distinction may be drawn between prospective and retroactive revocation.[14] Imagine a pensioner was awarded a pension in 1997 for an indefinite period of time. If in 1999 the decision-maker revokes this pension, the revocation may take effect for the future (prospectively) or from the day the pension was initially granted in 1997 (retroactively). While prospective revocation deprives the pensioner of a future benefit, retroactive revocation would logically entail the recovery of sums already paid.

Third, it is important to distinguish between decisions which have a continuous temporal dimension (such as a licence or a pension) and temporally complete decisions the effects of which are exhausted at the time of the decision itself (such as an award of compensation). While a continuous decision can be

[7] CE 3/11–22 *Cachet* Rec 790. Some commentators refer to this principle as the principle of 'acquired rights' (*droits acquis*), while others explain irrevocability in terms of non-retroactivity (*non-retroactivité*). See P. Auvret, 'La notion de droit acquis en droit administratif français', RDP 1985, 53, 56; C. Yannakopoulos, *La notion de droits acquis en droit administratif français* (Paris, 1997), 1–9, 58.

[8] Cases 7/56 and 3–7/57 *Algera v Common Assembly* [1957] ECR 39.

[9] This chapter draws upon the author's survey of some 200 published and unpublished decisions from the three jurisdictions.

[10] The relevant legislation states that a person has a right to some favourable decision when certain, fairly precise, conditions are fulfilled. The administration is under a duty to determine whether the conditions are fulfilled and, if so, to make the decision.

[11] In French law, decisions of this kind are known as *décisions récognitives*, *confirmatives*, *interprétatives*, or *déclaratives*. See Yannakopoulos, above n. 7, 78–9.

[12] The legislation does not set out precisely the conditions under which a person is entitled to a favourable decision, but leaves it to the administration to define those conditions on a case-by-case basis.

[13] In French law, decisions of this kind are known as *décisions attributive*.

[14] In French law, a similar distinction is drawn between *abrogation* and *retrait* of decisions. See Yannakopoulos, above n. 7, 56.

revoked *either* prospectively or retroactively, the revocation of a temporally complete decision is logically always retroactive.[15]

The discussion will be structured as follows. First, the basic principles of English, French, and EC law will be set out. Second, I will consider three more specific issues: what conditions must be fulfilled in the three legal systems for a lawful *(intra vires)* decision to be *prima facie* irrevocable; in what circumstances can *prima facie* irrevocable decisions nonetheless be revoked; and to what extent are unlawful (*ultra vires*) decisions irrevocable? Finally, it will be argued on the basis of the comparative survey that the principle of irrevocability in English law is in need of reform both in relation to lawful and unlawful decisions.

2 A Comparative Overview of Revocation in English, French, and EC Law

(A) English Law: Decisions Which Affect Rights[16]

The principle that administrative decisions are irrevocable was firmly established in English law by the case of *Re 56 Denton Rd*.[17] This case concerned two decisions made by the War Damage Commission. By its first decision, made in 1945, the Commission classified damage to a house caused by enemy action during the Second World War as a non-total loss. However, in 1946 the Commission decided that this decision 'set an awkward precedent' and informed the owner that the house was now classified as a total loss, thereby reducing the amount payable. In other words, the Commission revoked its initial (temporally complete) decision with retroactive effect. Vaisey J found for the owner on the following principle:[18]

> [W]here Parliament confers upon a body such as the War Commission the duty of deciding or determining any question, . . . which affects the rights of the subject, such decision or determination made or communicated in terms which are not expressly preliminary or provisional is final and conclusive, and cannot, in the absence of express statutory power or the consent of the person or persons affected, be altered or withdrawn by that body.

[15] See J. Carbajo, *L'application dans le temps des décisions administratives exécutoires* (Paris, 1980), 131.

[16] See generally G. Ganz, 'Estoppel and *Res Iudicata* in Administrative Law' (1965) PL 237; M. A. Fazal, 'Reliability of Official Acts and Advice' (1972) PL 43, 'Estoppel in English Administrative Law' (1994) JILI 455; A. W. Bradley, 'Administrative Justice and the Binding Effect of Official Acts' (1981) CLP 1; M. Akehurst, 'Revocation of Administrative Decisions' (1982) PL 613; Letemendia, above n. 1; Wade 261–5, 941–2.

[17] *Re 56 Denton Rd., Twickenham, Middlesex* [1953] 1 Ch. 51. See for earlier decisions, none of which provide firm support for the existence of a general principle of irrevocability, *Barons v Luscombe* (1835) 3 Ad and E 589; *R v Fordham* (1839) 11 Ad and E 73; *Cook v Ipswich Local Board* (1871) 6 LRQB 451; *Gould v Bacup Local Board* (1881) 50 LJMC 44; *Livingstone v Westminster Co* [1904] 2 KB 109.

[18] Ibid. 56–7.

In the more recent case of *Thrasyvoulou* this principle was confirmed by Lord Bridge in the following terms:[19]

> In relation to adjudications subject to a comprehensive self-contained statutory code, the presumption, in my opinion, must be that, where the statute has created a specific jurisdiction for the determination of any issue which establishes the existence of a legal right, the principle of *res judicata* applies to give finality to that determination unless an intention to exclude that principle can properly be inferred as a matter of construction of the relevant statutory provisions.[20]

This case concerned the planning authority's repeated attempts to order Mr Thrasyvoulou, the owner of a hotel, to stop using the premises as a hostel. On the first occasion, the owner appealed to an planning inspector who decided that there was in fact no hostel use and that there was no breach of the planning legislation. Some years later the authority made a new decision alleging a breach of planning rules. The House of Lords held that the authority could not, in the absence of a change in the relevant facts, issue a new decision on the basis that the hotel was used as a hostel, nor could another inspector make such a decision.[21]

These decisions establish a principle that administrative decisions which 'affect rights' or 'establish the existence of a legal right' are irrevocable. The question is therefore: what sort of decisions affect rights? A conceptually clear answer cannot be found in the case law, but the decisions of *Parker* and *Rootkin v Kent CC* provide some guidance. In *Parker*, Lord Goddard said that 'the very fact that a licence is granted to a person would seem to imply that the person granting the licence can also revoke it'.[22] In *Rootkin* this was taken further.[23] Ms Rootkin, a girl attending school, had been awarded a season bus ticket by Kent CC. The Council was under a statutory duty to pay such transport if the distance between school and home was over three miles and it had a discretionary power to award transport in all other cases. Initially the Council believed the distance to be over three miles. When this later proved to be incorrect, it informed Ms Rootkin's parent that no bus ticket would be issued for the following seasons. That is, the favourable decision, which had a continuous temporal dimension, was revoked with prospective effect. The Court of Appeal found for the Council. It held that as the distance was in fact less than three

[19] *Thrasyvoulou v Secretary of State for the Environment* [1990] 2 AC 273, 289.

[20] This principle has, unsuccessfully, been invoked in tax and mental health order cases. See *Society of Medical Officers of Health v Hope* [1960] AC 551; *Caffoor v Commissioner of Income Tax* [1961] AC 584, 597–9; *R v South-West Thames Mental Health Review Tribunal, ex p Demetri* [1997] COD 44.

[21] See also *Williams Le Roi v Secretary of State for the Environment* [1993] JPL 1033; *Porter v Secretary of State for Transport* [1996] 3 All ER 693; *Hammond v Secretary of State for the Environment* [1997] JPL 724; *Forrester v Secretary of State for the Environment* (1997) 74 P and CR 434.

[22] *R v Metropolitan Police Commissioner, ex p Parker* [1953] 1 WLR 1150, 1154 (*obiter dictum*).

[23] *Rootkin v Kent CC* [1981] 1 WLR 1186. See D. G. T. Williams, 'Discretion and Estoppel' (1981) CLJ 198.

miles, the Council had a discretion. Ms Rootkin was not *entitled* to a bus ticket and its revocation did therefore not affect her statutory rights.[24]

On the basis of this authority, the position in English law appears to be that while authorities cannot normally revoke decisions which 'establish' or 'affect' rights, they have an inherent discretionary power to revoke decisions which grant licences and other discretionary benefits.[25] In other words, lawful *declaratory* decisions are irrevocable, while *constitutive* decisions are not.[26]

This principle is open to criticism both on practical grounds and on grounds of principle.[27] In practical terms, the line between rights and benefits is not sharp and the principle may therefore be difficult for administrators to operate in practice. In terms of principle, fairness and legal certainty suggest that individuals should be able to plan their lives and rely upon favourable administrative decisions. The general rule should be that a favourable decision is (subject to conditions discussed below and in the absence of subsequent changes in material facts) irrevocable. It should make no difference whether the initial decision was the determination of a statutory right or the exercise of a discretion. Indeed, the vesting of wide-ranging discretion in public authorities appears to call for more, rather than less, protection of legal certainty against the use of such powers to revoke decisions. The importance of legal certainty in relation to discretionary decisions has, as will become apparent, been acknowledged very clearly in French and EC law. Three lines of authority suggest a growing acknowledgement of this view also in English law.[28]

First, in the recent case of *Pierson,* two members of the House of Lords stated that the Home Secretary's decision about the minimum period (tariff) which a mandatory life prisoner must serve cannot be revoked to the detriment of the prisoner once it is communicated, apart from, perhaps, in exceptional circumstances or where the decision-maker has been misled. Although tariff decisions are discretionary (constitutive), Lord Hope found that 'the minimum standard of fairness does not permit . . . a person, once he has been told what his punishment is to be, to be given in substitution for it a more severe punish-

[24] This view was implicitly supported in *Thrasyvoulou.* Lord Bridge drew a distinction between, on the one hand, planning decisions which concern a 'matter of policy and [are made] in the exercise of discretion' from which 'no question of legal right arises' and, on the other hand, decisions which determine a 'matter of legal right'. See also *R v Secretary of State for Social Security, ex p S,* 22/8–97 (an *ex gratia* payment may 'always be reconsidered'); *R v London Borough of Lambeth, ex p Stockwell Law Centre,* 22/5–98 (discretionary funding reconsidered in the light of authority's financial problems).

[25] See Akehurst, above n. 16, 617; Letemendia, above n. 1, 69–128, 139–64; G. Aldous and J. Alder, *Applications for Judicial Review: Law and Practice of the Crown Office*, 2nd edn. (London, 1993), 43–7; Wade 261–5, 941–2; Craig 632–5. Compare Fazal, above n. 16, 463 for the view, unsupported by authority, that only decisions made by a judicial-style *procedure* are irrevocable.

[26] See, however, text at footnotes 153–4.

[27] See Fazal, above n. 16, 463–4; P. Cane, *An Introduction to Administrative Law*, 3rd edn. (Oxford, 1996), 228; Craig 633.

[28] See also *Dean v District Auditor for Ashton-In-Makerfield* [1960] 1 QB 149; *R v Cripps, ex p Muldoon* [1984] 1 QB 686.

ment'.[29] While this dictum does not pronounce a general principle applicable to all administrative decisions, it recognizes that the revocation of constitutive decisions may be unfair, and indeed unlawful, where the affected person's liberty is at stake. A similar recognition is implicit in the recent *Watson* case. The Parole Board had released a sex offender on parole, and he was later recalled to prison (his licence revoked) in the light of new evidence that confinement was 'necessary for the protection of the public'.[30] On appeal the Court of Appeal said that it would be 'absurd' and, it would seem, therefore unlawful to recall 'if nothing had changed'. That is, although the decision to release a prisoner on parole is discretionary, the Minister is not entirely free to revoke it.[31]

Second, the courts have frequently held that planning permissions are irrevocable and that new conditions cannot be attached to a lawfully granted permission.[32] This does not sit comfortably with *Rootkin* because planning permissions are constitutive decisions granted subject to discretionary powers. Again, it reflects that the economic and legal certainty of property owners would be undermined to an unfair and unacceptable extent if planning permissions were freely revocable.

Third, a number of recent decisions suggest, in direct opposition to *Rootkin*, that discretionary welfare benefits cannot be revoked. The most interesting case, *Dennis Rye Pension Fund*, concerned housing improvement grants.[33] The relevant statute provides for both mandatory grants (declaratory decisions) and discretionary grants (constitutive decisions). Authorities can make payment of such grants conditional upon completion of works according to certain technical standards. The Court of Appeal said, speaking of both types of grants, that this gives the grant holder a 'right to payment . . . on compliance with the conditions'. In other words, in the absence of a statutory power to revoke a discretionary grant, the decision-maker was bound to maintain it.[34]

It may be concluded that English law is in a state of flux. It is not unlikely that the courts would, given the opportunity, accept that favourable discretionary administrative decisions are, in the absence of contrary statutory intention, irrevocable to the same extent as decisions which establish or affect rights.

[29] *Pierson v Home Secretary* [1997] 3 WLR 492, 533 (it is unclear whether this opinion was shared by the House's majority). See also *R v Home Secretary, ex p Hindley* [1999] 2 WLR 1253, 1270–1. Compare *R v Home Secretary, ex p Stafford* [1998] 3 WLR 372.

[30] Criminal Justice Act 1991, s 34(4)b.

[31] *R v Parole Board, ex p Watson* [1996] All ER 641. See also on penalties *Patel v Spencer* [1976] 1 WLR 1268; *R v Bloomfield* [1997] 1 Cr App Rep 135. See on immigrants' liberty *R v Home Secretary, ex p Ram* [1979] 1 WLR 148; compare *R v Home Secretary, ex p Choudary* [1978] 1 WLR 1177.

[32] *Heron Co v Manchester CC* (1977) 33 P and CR 268; *Hove BC v Secretary of State for the Environment*, 19/2–90; *London Borough of Havering v Secretary of State for the Environment*, 14/5–97.

[33] *Trustees of the Dennis Rye Pension Fund v Sheffield CC* (1998) 10 Admin LR 112.

[34] Ibid. 118. See also *R v Secretary of State for Education and Science, ex p Hardy*, 27/7–88; *R v Salisbury DC, ex p Helyer*, 4/5–89.

(B) French Law: Decisions which Create Rights[35]

The principle of irrevocability of administrative decisions (*intangibilité des décisions créatrices de droits*) was established in French law by the *Cachet* case in 1922.[36] A French law from 1918 exempted certain categories of tenants from payment of rent and prescribed that landlords be given compensation by local authorities. Ms Cachet made a claim under this legislation which was met only in part by the Department of Rhône. She complained to the Minister of Finance, who rejected her claim for additional compensation and revoked the initial grant altogether. The CE annulled the Minister's decision on the basis of 'a general principle of law' according to which the administration does not have an inherent power to revoke a decision which has 'created rights' (*droits acquis*). Such a decision is irrevocable (*intangible*) unless provisions of primary or secondary legislation explicitly grant the administration the power to revoke it.[37] Thus, in the words of *Commissaire de Gouvernement* Henry

> le principe constamment admis par la jurisprudence est celui de l'intangibilité des effets juridiques des actes individuels qui ont crée des droits.[38]

The scope of the principle of *intangibilité* is wide. Indeed, the French courts never took the view, still prevailing in English law, that the administration has an inherent power to revoke discretionary benefits (constitutive decisions).[39] Most decisions are therefore capable of 'creating rights'.[40] For example, decisions to appoint or promote civil servants,[41] or to employ persons by contract whether indefinitely or for a limited period;[42] building and demolition per-

[35] See generally J. M. Auby, 'L'incompétence ratione temporis. Recherches sur l'application des actes administratifs dans le temps', RDP 1953, 5, 'L'abrogation des actes administratifs', AJDA 1967, 131; F. Batailler, 'Les *Beati Possidentes* du droit administratif', RDP 1965, 1072; J.-Y. Vincent, 'Le retrait des actes administratifs unilatéraux', RTDE 1974, 31; P. Le Mire, 'La stabilité des situations juridiques', AJDA 1980, 203; Carbajo, above n. 15, 151–226; Auvret, above n. 7; *LGA* 221–9; J.-Y. Vincent in *JC* Fasc 108–30; Chapus 1073–8; Yannakopoulos, above n. 7.

[36] CE 3/11–22 *Cachet* Rec 790. Revocation had previously been considered in cases which had failed to establish clear principles. See CE 26/12–1891 *Sohier* Rec 787; CE 1/7–1898 *Brincart* Rec 515; CE 16/2–12 *Abbé Blanc* Rec 224; and further G. Jèze, 'Du retrait des actes juridiques', RDP 1913, 225; T.-X. Girardot and F. Raynaud, 'Chronique générale de jurisprudence administrative française', AJDA 1997, 936, 940–1.

[37] Moreover, the revocation decision (the *acte contraire*) must comply with the procedural and substantive conditions set out in the relevant text. See Yannakopoulos, above n. 7, 440–5.

[38] Henry *conclusions* CE 1/4–60 *Quériad* Rec 245, 247 ('the principle consistently upheld by the courts is that of the inviolability of the legal effects of individualized administrative acts which have created rights').

[39] On the contrary, constitutive decisions are in some respects subject to greater protection in French law than declaratory decisions. See section 5.C.

[40] See Bacquet *conclusions* CE 1/2–80 *Rigal* AJDA 1981, 44; Le Mire, above n. 35, 207; *JC* Fasc 108–30 no 64.

[41] CE 24/2–67 *De Maistre* Rec 91; CE 22/2–89 *Fontenille* Rec 444.

[42] CE 25/1–89 *Dumas* no 66.207; TA Paris 17/1–91 *Luguern* no 8708066; TA Nice 17/10–86 *Jaubert* JCP II 20869. Compare CE 15/2–63 *Turin* Rec 91.

mits;[43] licences to practise a profession[44] or a commercial activity,[45] or to open a shop;[46] decisions to enter into procurement contracts;[47] decisions to grant financial aid to local authorities or persons, directly in money[48] or indirectly by waiving a debt or offering a guarantee;[49] grant of leave to reside in the French territory;[50] and decisions pursuant to which EC milk production quotas are transferred from one farmer to another.[51]

However, the administrative courts never provided a conceptual definition of what decisions 'create rights', and this remains one of the most complex issues in French public law.[52] The key to sanity is to realize that the concept cannot be explained adequately by reference to a single 'logical' criterion or test.[53] It is simply a label which is applied to describe a legal conclusion, namely that a given decision is irrevocable (*intangible*).[54] To determine what decisions 'create rights', one must therefore examine the conditions that decisions must fulfil in order to be irrevocable and in what circumstances decisions may nevertheless be revoked.[55]

(C) EC Law: Favourable Decisions and Vested Rights[56]

When the problem of revocation first arose before the ECJ, in the *Algera* case from 1957,[57] the Court developed a general principle of irrevocability drawing upon a comparative analysis of the administrative laws of the then six Member States. It relied in particular on the French principle of *intangibilité des décisions créatrices de droits* and the dual German principles of legal certainty

[43] CE 20/1–60 *Zagame* Rec 35; CE 1/6–73 *Roulin* Rec 390; CE 6/10–82 *Crédit Lyonnais* DA 1982 no 372.

[44] CE 26/10–88 *Jagord* no 79.185.

[45] CE 3/12–82 *Société continentale de promotion immobilière* Rec 409.

[46] CE 12/6–95 *Scremin* no 117.244.

[47] CE 16/12–88 *SCI Paule* RDP 1989, 1796.

[48] CE 3/11–22 *Cachet* Rec 790; CE 1/12–50 *EDF* Rec 595; CE 25/7–86 *Société Grandes Distilleries les fils d'Auguste Perreux* RFDA 1987, 454; CE 25/4–90 *Figueréo* AJDA 1990, 641.

[49] TA Nantes 29/1–92 *Association Chant La Vie* D 1993, 238; CE 28/7–93 *Association 'Chant' la Vie'* Rec 658.

[50] CE 23/6–95 *Neves* Rec 644; CAA Paris 30/1–97 *Fung* AJDA 1997, 275.

[51] CE 3/7–98 *SARL Matrey* DA 1998 no 269.

[52] This is true despite considerable academic attention devoted to its clarification. See Yannakopoulos, above n. 7, 70–92 and the literature cited in footnote 35. French textbooks also do not provide clear conceptual definitions, e.g. Chapus 1073–4.

[53] See Batailler, above n. 35, 1072; Auvret, above n. 7, 61; P. Delvolvé, 'Acte administratif', in F. Gazier, R. Drago, and A. Dupie (eds.), *Encyclopédie Dalloz: Répertoire de contentieux administratif* (Paris, 1996), no 591.

[54] See Bacquet *conclusions* CE 1/2–80 *Rigal* AJDA 1981, 44, 45. Compare Yannakopoulos, above n. 7, 70.

[55] See sections 3–4.

[56] See generally R. W. Lauwaars, *Lawfulness and Legal Force of Community Decisions* (Leiden, 1973), 309–29; J.-Y. Vincent, above n. 35; Letemendia, above n. 1; Schwarze 970–1032; T. Hartley, *The Foundations of European Community Law*, 4th edn. (Oxford, 1998), 435–9; H. Ragnemalm, 'Confiance légitime et délai raisonnable', in G. C. Rodríguez Iglesias, O. Due, R. Schintgen and C. Elsen (eds.), *Mélanges en hommage à Fernand Schockweiler* (Baden-Baden, 1999), 511.

[57] Cases 7/56 and 3–7/57 *Algera v Common Assembly* [1957] ECR 39. The ECJ had previously touched upon the issue (in Case 1/55 *Kergall v Common Assembly* [1955–56] ECR 1) without developing clear principles.

and legitimate expectations *(Rechtssicherheitsprinzip* and *Vertrauenschutzprinzip)*.[58] Ms Algera was a temporary employee with the Common Assembly who was appointed to a permanent position by a decision of the board responsible for employment matters. Seven months later the Assembly changed its mind in the light of an industrial dispute in which Ms Algera had played a part and sought to dismiss her. That is, it sought to revoke her employment with prospective effect. The ECJ held that as a matter of general principle:

> [A]n administrative measure conferring individual rights on the person concerned cannot in principle be withdrawn, if it is a lawful measure; in that case, since the individual right is vested, the need to safeguard confidence in the stability of the situation thus created prevails over the interests of an administration desirous of reversing its decision.[59]

The Court did not in this case explain more precisely in what circumstances administrative decisions 'confer' individual rights or when such rights become 'vested'. Some commentators argued that the ECJ should follow the French principles of revocation (*retrait*). On this view, the Court would look to the nature of the statutory power to determine whether a decision is irrevocable. While discretionary (constitutive) decisions would be irrevocable, declaratory decisions would be revocable.[60] Others argued that the Court should follow the example of German,[61] Dutch,[62] and Scandinavian law,[63] all of which look more to the effects of the decision than to the nature of the power.[64] A decision would be irrevocable if it conferred a benefit upon a person (a *droit subjectif*), but not if it imposed a burden.[65] While the ECJ failed to address this conceptual issue for several years, the important case of *De Compte* has now provided a clarification.[66]

Like *Algera,* the *De Compte* case arose out of the employment relationship between the EP and one of its civil servants. The applicant developed a serious mental illness which, it was decided by the EP, was work-related, and substantial compensation was awarded. However, three months later, before the money was actually paid, the decision was revoked. The ECJ held, against the decision of the CFI, that Mr De Compte was entitled to rely on the stability of the decision.

[58] Cases 7/56 and 3–7/57 *Algera v Common Assembly* [1957] ECR 56. AG Lagrange also emphasised French and German law in his opinion in this case.

[59] [1957] ECR 55. In the original French edition of the decision, the ECJ said: 'Il est en effet, de principe que les décisions individuelles, lorsqu'elles sont conformes à la loi, ne peuvent pas être l'objet d'un *retrait*: ceux qui en sont l'objet tiennent donc de ces décisions un *droit subjectif* dont ils sont fondés à exiger le respect', Rec. (1957) 81, 154 (emphasis added).

[60] See Hartley, above n. 56, 437 citing Case 14/61 *Hoogovens v High Authority* [1962] ECR 253.

[61] See Schwarze 886 ff.

[62] See Lauwaars, above n. 56, 313–14, 324; Schwarze 926–32.

[63] See K. Loiborg, in W. E. von Eyben (ed.), *Juridisk Grundbog 4* (Copenhagen, 1989), 187–8.

[64] In these legal systems a distinction is drawn between favourable (*begünstigender Verwaltungsakt*) and unfavourable decisions (*belastender Verwaltungsakt*).

[65] See Lauwaars, above n. 56, 311, 324; Letemendia, above n. 1, 46–50. See also Schwarze 988–91, 1009 mentioning both the French and the German approach without explaining which is preferred by the ECJ.

[66] Case C-90/95P *Henri de Compte v EP* [1997] ECR I-1999.

The Court did not use the French terminology of 'creating rights'. Instead, it stated in unequivocal terms that the principle laid down in *Algera* applies to the revocation of 'a *favourable* administrative act'.[67] Thus, it is now settled that the ECJ adopts the German and Scandinavian rather than the French approach. Lawful administrative decisions which are favourable to their addressee cannot, in the absence of statutory provision, be revoked.[68] It is immaterial whether the decision declared the person's statutory entitlement or granted a discretionary benefit.[69]

3 The Scope of Principles of Irrevocability

The principle that administrative decision are irrevocable is subject to a number of specific, and quite similar, conditions in English, French, and EC law. The decision must be favourable (A), unconditional (B), and, with the exception of French law, communicated to the affected person (C). There is also some suggestion in English case law that the affected person must have relied to his detriment on the decision (D).

(A) Favourable Decisions

While it is settled in EC law that the principle of irrevocability applies only to the revocation of favourable administrative decisions, some commentators argue that *unfavourable* decisions can be irrevocable in English and in French law.[70] This view is, with respect, neither accurate nor good in principle.[71] While there are no explicit statements in French or English case law to the effect that a decision must be favourable to 'affect' or 'create' rights, a survey of numerous decisions suggests that this requirement is implicitly and consistently applied. An unfavourable decision, such as the refusal of an application for a licence, is conclusive and binding in the sense that the applicant and other administrative

[67] Ibid. para 35. Previous case law had gradually moved in this direction. See Cases 42 and 49/59 *SNUPAT v High Authority* [1961] ECR 53 ('created a right or a similar advantage'); 111/63 *Lemmerz-Werke v High Authority* [1965] ECR 677 (a decision 'by which a benefit is conferred'); 159/82 *Verli-Wallace v Commission* [1983] ECR 2711 ('an individual right or similar benefits'); T-227/95 *Kraft v Commission* [1997] ECR II-1185 ('a decision granting a benefit to its addressee').

[68] In other words, a favourable decision creates a 'vested right' (or *droit acquis*) which cannot be revoked. See T. Tridimas, *The General Principles of EC Law* (Oxford, 1999), 194; Ragnemalm, above n. 56, 512.

[69] For an early suggestion along these lines, see AG Roemer [1961] ECR 129–30. See further section 5.D about revocation of *unlawful* decisions.

[70] See Wade 264; D. Foulkes, *Administrative Law*, 8th edn. (London, 1995), 231; Chapus 1074. Most French authors note somewhat ambiguously that favourable decisions normally create rights while unfavourable normally do not. See G. Vlachos, *Les principes généraux du droit administratif* (Paris, 1993), 158; *JC* Fasc 108–30 no 64; Delvolvé, above n. 53, no 601; Yannakopoulos, above n. 7, 75.

[71] See A. Rubinstein, *Jurisdiction and Illegality* (Oxford, 1965), 30.

bodies are bound to respect it.[72] However, the decision-maker should be, and indeed is, entitled to make a fresh decision at a later stage, even in the absence of a new application, if this is to the advantage of the applicant.[73] The principle of irrevocability only applies where the authority makes a *less* favourable decision. It is, therefore, paramount to be clear about what constitutes a 'favourable' decision in the first place.

First, the effects of a decision must be assessed relative to what action the administration subsequently takes. This is aptly illustrated by *Gould v Bacup Local Board*.[74] This case concerned a decision by the Board on payment of costs incurred by the paving and sewering of a street. The Board had three options. It could impose the full cost, a 75 per cent contribution, or no payment at all. Initially the Board went for the second option, but later it sought to impose the full cost. The court decided that the Board was not entitled to 'withdraw . . . the benefit offered'. The relativity of the concept of a 'favourable' decision is also accepted in French and EC law. For example, in *Hurtaud* a prefect had used his power to close a bar, which constituted a threat to public order. Initially, he ordered a two-month closure, but after an informal request from a Minister the period was increased to four months. The CE annulled the latter decision on the ground that the first decision had created rights.[75] Similarly, in *Alpha Steel* the ECJ held that a Commission decision to impose a quarterly production quota upon a steel company could not, after some weeks, be revoked and replaced by a smaller quota. For the initial quota allocation had, compared to the subsequent allocation, 'conferred a benefit'.[76] This case also highlights that the nature of a decision depends upon the sum of its favourable and adverse effects. The quota decision affected the applicant's immediate profits adversely, but the Commission's effort to restructure the steel sector had (potential) favourable long-term effects. The Court, correctly, attached greater weight to the immediate effects than to the uncertain long-term effects when deciding on the favourable or unfavourable nature of the decision.

Second, it is also generally accepted that the favourable nature of a decision should be assessed from the viewpoint of its addressee.[77] That is, a decision, which is unfavourable to the addressee but favourable to a third party, does not 'affect' or 'create rights' and the decision-maker is free to reconsider the matter

[72] See Wade 264.

[73] *R v Hambledon DC, ex p Geohan* [1985] JPL 394, 395–6; *Cheung v Hertfordshire CC* The Times 15/7–85; *Thrasyvoulou v Secretary of State for the Environment* [1990] 2 AC 273; *Porter v Secretary of State for Transport* [1996] 3 All ER 693.

[74] *Gould v Bacup Local Board* (1881) 50 LJMC 44.

[75] CE 27/1–71 *Hurtaud* Rec. 68. See also CE 23/7–74 *Gay* Rec. 441.

[76] See also Cases 108/63 *Merlini v Commission* [1965] ECR 1; 2/70 *Riva v Commission* [1971] ECR 97.

[77] See Chapus 1076–7; Yannakopoulos, above n. 7, 75–6, 100–3; Girardot and Raynaud, above n. 36, 943 and cases cited below.

in the applicant's favour. The French *Feng* case is an example in point. Mr Feng was initially refused permission to open a pharmacy, but the decision stated that he could reapply and that it would be preferable to find business premises more than 250 metres away from an existing pharmacy. This decision did not create rights for the owner of the existing pharmacy and a subsequently granted licence to open only 137 metres away was therefore lawful.[78] Applying similar reasoning, the French courts have found that neighbours and economic competitors could not derive rights from refusals to grant, respectively, planning permission[79] and permission to use the title of 'architect'.[80]

The English case law is less rich in examples, but in the recent case of *Helyer* the Divisional Court ruled that a pharmacy licence, which had been granted in breach of certain formalities, was a favourable decision which could not be revoked although it affected owners of existing pharmacies in the area.[81] In EC law, one finds a similar principle in the case of *Kraft,* where the CFI said, with respect to a fine imposed by the Commission for breach of EC competition law, that when 'the decision . . . merely imposes burdens or penalties on the individual concerned, the Commission is not precluded from withdrawing the decision by . . . the principles of . . . legitimate expectation and vested rights'.[82] In other words, although the fine was indirectly favourable to Kraft's competitors, it was unfavourable to the 'concerned' individual.

There may be situations, however, where a limited group of third parties is directly affected to such an extent that the administration should not be free to revoke on the ground that the decision was 'unfavourable' to the addressee.[83] This is acknowledged in French employment law, which is subject to a system of administrative control. A decision which affects public (or private) employees adversely may create rights for other employees,[84] and a decision which refuses a private employer permission to make employees redundant creates rights for the employees.[85] The explanation for this case law is that employees constitute a closed and identifiable group of third parties who are deeply affected by decisions nominally addressed to the employer.[86]

[78] CE 11/1–84 *Feng* no 34.617. See also CE 27/6–47 *Société Duchet* Rec 283; CE 8/11–91 *Coquide* Rec 690.

[79] CE 12/1–62 *Canton* Rec. 23; CE 25/2–83 *UCAIP* Rec 80; CE 9/10–89 *Steiner* no 83.958.

[80] CE 28/5–86 *Conseil régional Rhône-Alpes de l'Ordre des architectes* Rec 385.

[81] *R v Salisbury DC, ex p Helyer*, 4/5–89.

[82] Case T-227/95 *Kraft v Commission* [1997] ECR II-1185 para 91.

[83] See CE 4/5–84 *Poissonier* Rec 162; TA Châlons-sur-Marne 1/2–94 *Société réparation wagons foudres de Touraine* DA 1995 no 271; *Cheung v Hertfordshire CC* The Times 15/7–85.

[84] CE 4/2–55 *Rodde* Rec 72; CE 12/6–59 *Syndicat chrétien du ministère de l'industrie et du commerce* Rec 360. See also CE 4/5–84 *Poissonier* Rec 162.

[85] CE 29/3–68 *Michelin* Rec 217.

[86] Mayras *conclusions* CE 12/6–59 *Syndicat chrétien du ministère de l'Industrie et du Commerce* AJDA 1960, 63. See also Yannakopoulos, above n. 7, 102.

(B) Conditional Decisions

A decision which is explicitly *conditional* upon the addressee's taking a certain action or the materializing of some event does not become irrevocable until this condition is satisfied. In English law such a decision is said to be 'provisional' rather than final. For example, in *Pearce Homes* a planning permission had been granted by a local authority, subject to the condition that the developer agreed to restrict occupation of the building to persons over 60 years of age. As long as the developer had not agreed, the permission remained revocable without compensation being payable under the relevant statute.[87]

French law reaches a similar result, albeit via a conceptually different route. The irrevocability of a conditional decision is said to be 'deferred'.[88] In the leading *Pabion* case the administration had decided, in January 1945, to reinstate the applicant in the civil service position he had had prior to the Second World War. However, the decision was made 'on the condition that Mr Pabion asks for retirement with effect from 1 February 1945'.[89] When the applicant failed to do so, the decision could be revoked some months later.[90] The notion of conditional, or deferred, decisions is sometimes applied quite strictly in France. In a recent case the CE found that a grant for the purpose of conducting a study into the building of an industrial plant, on a site owned by a local authority, could be revoked when the company subsequently decided to build elsewhere. The court held that as the builder had supplied detailed plans for the plant, the grant was 'implicitly conditional' upon the building works actually being carried out.[91]

Again, EC law does not differ appreciably from English or French law in this respect. The *CNTA* case is a pertinent example.[92] The Court held that the grant of an export licence with advance fixing of the amount of monetary refund, which the exporter was entitled to under EC regulations, did not create 'vested rights' until the export was actually carried out. Until that moment, the decision was therefore *prima facie* revocable.[93]

[87] *R v West Oxfordshire DC, ex p Pearce Homes Ltd* [1986] JPL 223 concerning the Town and Country Planning Act 1990, s 107. See also *R v London Borough of Lambeth, ex p Stockwell Law Centre*, 22/5–98.

[88] The decision is said to be subject to a *condition suspensive*. See Auvret, above n. 7, 91; Yannakopoulos, above n. 7, 89–91.

[89] The purpose of this arrangement was to secure the applicant's pension rights.

[90] CE 1/6–56 *Pabion* Rec 218.

[91] CE 26/11–93 *Société industrielle française du tout terrain* Rec 594. See also CE 25/7–86 *Société Grandes Distilleries les fils d'Auguste Perreux* RFDA 1987, 454.

[92] Case 74/74 *CNTA v Commission* [1975] ECR 533.

[93] The Court found, however, that the modification of the refund breached the principle of legitimate expectations. Compare Case 276/82 *De Beste Booter v Produktschap voor Zuivel* [1983] ECR 3321 and see Ch. 4.5.

(C) Communicated or Signed Decisions?

A formal decision comes into existence the moment the decision-making process is ended, typically when a final text is signed by the competent person within the decision-making body or, in the EC context, when it is approved in a Commission or Council meeting.[94] However, in English and EC law the decision does not become irrevocable until it is also communicated to the addressee.[95] For there is normally no risk that legitimate expectations and trust in government will be disappointed by the revocation of a decision which is not known to the person concerned.

The question, then, is what form of communication is required. Where a particular form of communication, such as registration and written notice or publication in an official journal, is prescribed by legislation,[96] the decision is unlikely to be considered binding and irrevocable unless it is complied with.[97] Other decisions can, both in English and EC law, be communicated by a simple letter,[98] although there is in the Community institutions a practice of notification of important matters by registered mail.[99] However, it appears that the addressee of a decision cannot invoke the principle of irrevocability on the basis of an oral notification, in person or via the telephone.[100] Thus, in the *Hardy* case an employee in the Ministry of Education informed a local education authority by telephone that the Ministry had approved its plan to close a school. Evidence showed that the decision had actually been made, and a specific form of communication was not required by statute. Nevertheless, the court held that there had to be a 'formal, precise and published decision'.[101]

French law differs somewhat from English and EC law in this respect. A decision creates rights from the moment it is *signed* by the competent person within the administration.[102] This applies even if a specific form of notification or publication is prescribed by law. Thus, in *Delville* the CE held that a decision to

[94] Case 3/58 *Erzbergbau v High Authority* [1960] ECR 173, 188.

[95] *R v Greater Manchester Valuation Panel, ex p Shell* [1982] QB 255, 264; Case C-90/95P *Henri de Compte v EP* [1997] ECR I-1999. See also *Pierson v Home Secretary* [1997] 3 WLR 492; *R v Home Secretary, ex p Hindley* [1999] 2 WLR 1253, 1273, 1276.

[96] e.g. Art 21 Regulation 17/62. It is unclear whether a decision may become irrevocable once notified to the addressee, but not yet published in the OJ.

[97] *R v West Oxfordshire DC, ex p Pearce Homes Ltd* [1986] JPL 223; *Norsk Hydro v Plastics Processing Industry Training Board*, 29/1–87; *Calder Gravel Ltd v Kirklees MBC* (1990) 2 Admin LR 327. See also *R v Home Secretary, ex p Patel* [1992] 1 WLR 70, 87.

[98] *Re 56 Denton Rd., Twickenham, Middlesex* [1953] 1 Ch. 51; Case 108/79 *Belfiore v Commission* [1980] ECR 1781 para 7.

[99] See Case 42/85 *Cockerill-Sambre v Commission* [1985] ECR 3749, 3756.

[100] Oral representations can, exceptionally, be binding under the principle of estoppel by representation and substantive legitimate expectations. See Ch. 4.3.A.I.

[101] *R v Secretary of State for Education and Science, ex p Hardy*, 27/7–88. Compare Akehurst, above n. 16, 615; Wade 262, 264 (citing *Lamont v Fry Metals* [1985] ICR 566, 567 though in this case the court assumed, without deciding the point, that an orally communicated decision would 'not normally' be binding).

[102] CE 19/12–52 *Mattéi* Rec 594; Pécresse *conclusions* CE 24/10–97 *Laubier* RFDA 1998, 528.

offer a person an employment position in the administration created rights once it was signed by the Minister even though it had not been published as required by the staff regulations.[103] The French rule purports to avoid uncertainty about when decisions become irrevocable. By attaching legal consequences to the signature, which is (almost) always dated, doubt about when and if a letter of notification reached the addressee is immaterial. In practice, the difference between French and English law is rarely significant, because the Law of 17 July 1978 prescribes notification of most administrative decisions.[104]

It is sometimes said that existing, but not yet communicated, decisions may be final and irrevocable also in English law.[105] This view appears to be based on a confusion of two meanings of finality. An uncommunicated decision, which is the result of an otherwise completed decision-making process, may be 'final' in the sense that the heirs of the addressee may claim the benefit which would have been conferred upon him had he not died.[106] However, the decision only becomes 'final', in the sense that it cannot be revoked, once it is communicated.

(D) A Requirement of Reliance?

Individuals should generally be able to trust that lawful decisions which are favourable, unconditional, and communicated will not be revoked. There is, however, some suggestion in English case law that the irrevocability presupposes that the beneficiary relied financially upon the decision in such a way that its revocation would cause him detriment.[107] These dicta contradict the classic statement in *Re 56 Denton Road* that 'reliance is not a condition for the finality of decisions'.[108] They appear to be inspired by the requirement of detrimental reliance in the private law doctrine of estoppel.[109] It is submitted that favourable administrative decisions should be irrevocable irrespective of reliance.[110] This is acknowledged in both French and EC law, and it should be recognized that a requirement of reliance may induce individuals to incur expenses, which in turn makes it more difficult to reach a solution if an authority seeks to revoke or modify an inappropriate decision with the consent of the affected parties. This is not to say, however, that reliance is irrelevant for the question of revocation. Reliance is, or should be, an important consideration

[103] CE 10/1–58 *Delville* Rec 27.

[104] Art 8, Law of 17/7–78.

[105] See Aldous and Alder, above n. 25, 44; Foulkes, above n. 70, 231–2.

[106] *R v Criminal Injuries Compensation Board, ex p Tong* [1976] 1 WLR 1237.

[107] *Porter v Secretary of State for Transport* [1996] 3 All ER 693 cited the *Thrasyvoulou* case for the view that a planning decision can create an estoppel 'if acted upon', although that case did not in fact mention this condition. See also *Cheung v Hertfordshire CC* The Times 15/7–85; *R v Sandwell Family Practitioner Committee, ex p Lloyds Chemists*, 19/12–88.

[108] *Re 56 Denton Rd., Twickenham, Middlesex* [1953] 1 Ch. 51, 56.

[109] See generally S. Wilken and T. Villiers, *Waiver, Variation and Estoppel* (Chichester, 1998), 154–65.

[110] Similarly De Smith 564.

when public authorities contemplate whether to exercise statutory revocation powers to the detriment of particular individuals.

4 On What Grounds can *Prima Facie* Irrevocable Decisions be Revoked?

Administrative authorities may wish to revoke lawful decisions, fully or partially, for a number of reasons. The administration may discover that its decision was unlawful or based on incorrect facts. This problem is examined further below.[111] Again, if subsequently the facts change or the administration changes its policy, it may have strong reasons for wanting to revoke its initial decision. Is this allowed? In other words, what are the exceptions to the general principles of irrevocability? These are complex questions, and the existing case law does not always provide clear answers.[112]

(A) The Classic Exceptions

So much is clear that there are, in English, French, and EC law, two exceptions to the principle of irrevocability. Decisions can, first of all, be revoked with the explicit consent of all the affected parties.[113] This is unsurprising, since the protection of legal certainty and legitimate expectations, which underpin the principle of irrevocability, does not require decisions to be upheld against the wishes of those affected. However, a person's request for reconsideration of a decision should not be interpreted as 'implicit consent'. In *Riva* the ECJ held that a company which had requested 'a further examination' of a decision could not invoke the principle of legal certainty to challenge the (less favourable) result of the examination. However, this decision concerned an *unlawful* decision and should not be applied to lawful decisions.[114]

Decisions obtained by fraud or deception can also be revoked.[115] Fraud is not, in any of the jurisdictions, narrowly defined. The English courts will infer fraud where the person presents obviously incorrect documents, although he did not

[111] See section 5.

[112] See Ganz, above n. 16, 250; Akehurst, above n. 16, 624–5. Compare Rubinstein, above n. 71, 31.

[113] *R v The Justices of Norfolk* (1822) 5 B&A 484, 487; *Re 56 Denton Rd., Twickenham, Middlesex* [1953] 1 Ch. 51, 56–7; *R v Hambledon DC, ex p Geohan* [1985] JPL 394, 395–6. CE 9/1–53 *Desfour* Rec 5; CE 23/7–74 *Gay* Rec 441; CE 9/4–99 *Saunier* DA 1999 no 244. Cases 7/56 and 3–7/57 *Algera v Common Assembly* [1957] ECR 39.

[114] Case 2/70 *Riva v Commission* [1971] ECR 97 para 9. Compare Case T-73/95 *Oliveira SA v Commission* [1997] ECR II-381 mentioning the principle of *reformatio in pejus*.

[115] *Lazarus Estates v Beasley* [1956] 1 QB 702; *R v Dacorum BC, ex p Walsh* (1992) 24 HLR 401. CE 17/3–76 *Todeschini* Rec. 157; CAA Marseille *Morisson* AJDA 1999, 942. Cases 42 and 49/59 *SNUPAT v High Authority* [1961] ECR 53; C-96/89 *Commission v Netherlands* [1991] ECR I-2461; C-90/95P *Henri de Compte v EP* [1997] ECR I-1999 (stating that the applicant had not 'provoked' the unlawful decision).

make any incorrect statements of his own.[116] According to French commentators, fraud is defined broadly in French administrative law, and it is perhaps slightly wider than its equivalent in English law.[117] The French courts regularly find that applicants, having supplied incorrect or incomplete information, acted fraudulently.[118] For example, in *Vettard* a haulage company was found to have acted fraudulently by failing to inform the administration that it had downscaled its capacity after applying for, but before being awarded, transport licences under rules intended to help growing enterprises.[119] In EC law, the scope of fraud appears to be even wider. In *SNUPAT,* the ECJ held that decisions may be revoked if they are obtained by fraud or otherwise rest 'upon wrong or incomplete information from the persons concerned'.[120] This statement, which suggests that even innocent misinformation is equated with fraud,[121] is too sweeping to ensure adequate protection of legitimate expectations. If bad faith cannot reasonably be implied, the administration's power to revoke a favourable decision should not be unlimited.

It is suggested by some commentators that the British administration has a limited power to amend decisions to correct ambiguities or clerical errors.[122] This would seem a practical and reasonable rule, if applied in a way which respects legitimate expectations, but recent precedent suggests that such a power requires a statutory basis.[123] In French law, simple clerical errors may be corrected without such a basis.[124] The actual content of a decision cannot be changed, but congruence between the wording of what was actually decided

[116] See *R v Home Secretary, ex p Huasain* [1978] 1 WLR 700; I. Glidewell, 'Immigration Law and Practice in the United Kingdom', in *Bridging the Channel: The Clifford Chance Lectures*, vol. i (Oxford, 1996), 193, 206.

[117] See M. Lombard, 'Recherches sur le rôle de la bonne et mauvaise foi en droit administratif français', Doctoral thesis (Univerity of Strasbourg III, 1978), 45–6; M. Azibert and M. de Boisdeffre, 'Chronique générale de jurisprudence administrative française', AJDA 1987, 86, 88; Yannakopoulos, above n. 7, 105.

[118] An innocent misrepresentation may cause an error of fact which makes the decision unlawful, but its revocation will then be subject to a two-month time limit, see CE 7/2–73 *Van Lang* AJDA 1975, 248 and section 5.C.

[119] CE 21/1–91 *Vettard* no 64.563. See also CE 19/1–83 *Dalanson* no 21.554; CE 20/5–94 *Masméjean* RDP 1996, 596.

[120] Cases 42 and 49/59 *SNUPAT v High Authority* [1961] ECR 53. See also Case C-96/89 *Commission v Netherlands* [1991] ECR I-2461 para 30; C-90/95P *Henri de Compte v EP* [1997] ECR I-1999 (stating that the applicant had not 'provoked' the unlawful decision).

[121] Later decisions do not clarify the scope of 'fraud' in EC law, as they have all concerned staff members' *deliberate* failure to inform the Commission of changes in their circumstances. See Cases 6/72 *Meganck v Commission* [1973] ECR 527, 534; 71/71 *Kuhl v Council* [1973] ECR 705, 712–3. Compare the strict attitude in the analogous Cases 230/83 *Van Gend en Loos v Commission* [1984] ECR 3763; C-384/89 *Behn v Hauptzollamt Itzehoe* [1990] ECR I-2659.

[122] This is known as the 'slip-rule'. See Wade 262.

[123] *Hove BC v Secretary of State for the Environment*, 19/2–90. See also *R v Cripps, ex p Muldoon* [1984] QB 68; *Preston BC v Secretary of State for the Environment and ELS Wholesale* [1978] JPL 548.

[124] CE 9/7–52 *Lipsky* Rec 236.

and the wording of the communicated decision can be ensured.[125] It remains to be seen whether the ECJ will accept the correction of clerical errors.[126]

(B) Changing Facts and Policy: A Complex Issue

While the three exceptions of consent, fraud, and clerical error are relatively straightforward and well known, the matter becomes more complex where the administration seeks to revoke a decision because the facts on which it was based have changed or the administration has changed its policy. To provide a conceptually clear, and substantively fair, answer to this question, it is important to distinguish between prospective and retroactive revocation.[127] While a subsequent change in fact or policy may, in some circumstances, justify the prospective revocation of a favourable decision, it cannot justify retroactive revocation.[128] For example, a change in the use of a street trader's licence may justify its revocation with effect for the future.[129] But retroactive revocation followed by administrative or criminal sanctions for unlawful trading without a licence would be unacceptable. The question, then, is in what circumstances subsequent changes of fact and policy justify *prospective* revocation.

A change in facts or policy does not, and should not, make a decision unlawful *ex post facto*. The theoretical starting point must be that a decision which satisfied the relevant conditions (favourable, unconditional, and communicated) at the time it was made can be revoked neither retroactively nor prospectively on the ground of new facts or policy. This has been explicitly acknowledged as a principle of French law. In *Kässbohrer* a company asked permission from the administration (an *inspecteur de travail*) to dismiss a shop steward. The application was refused, but a Minister subsequently granted it on the basis of certain, allegedly illegal, union activities which the employee had taken part in after the initial decision. The CE annulled the minister's decision on the ground that a lawful decision which creates rights cannot be revoked on the basis of a subsequent change in the facts.[130] A similar principle is to be found, implicitly rather than explicitly, in EC law.[131] Thus, in *Boizard* the ECJ

[125] CE 5/5–86 *Tissier* Rec 128. See further J.-J. Israel, *La régularisation en droit administratif français* (Paris, 1981), 212–14; J. Petit, 'Contribution à l'étude des conflits de lois dans le temps en droit public interne', Doctoral thesis (Paris II 1993), 613–17.

[126] See in favour of this possibility, Ragnemalm, above n. 56, 512.

[127] *Re 56 Denton Rd.* and *Rootkin* concerned, respectively, retroactive and prospective revocation, but the temporal aspect did not come out in the speeches of either of the two cases, and it is unlikely that it affected their different outcome. Compare Letemendia, above n. 1, 87–8.

[128] See Akehurst, above n. 16, 621, 625.

[129] Alternatively, if the licence is of fixed duration its renewal may be refused.

[130] CE 29/4–87 *Société Kässbohrer-France* Rec 156. See also CE 11/1–35 *Touzet* Rec 43; CE 6/7–90 *Mattéi* Rec 205; CE 12/10–94 *Visconti* Rec 442; CE 10/5–95 *Front Calédonien* no 104.378. Compare CE 8/1–71 *URSSAF des Alpes-Maritimes* Rec 11; TA Nice 27/4–82 *Syndicat intercommunal de la Marana* JCP 1983 II 19930 (decisions can be revoked *prospectively* in the light of subsequent developments).

[131] See AG Lenz [1984] ECR 3911; Schwarze 1024.

held that a pension awarded to the family of a deceased official could not be reduced when a national court subsequently awarded damages against the person who caused the death.[132]

The principle that decisions cannot be revoked in the light of new facts is, however, modified to a considerable extent in both English and French law. In these two jurisdictions, the courts allow the administration considerable flexibility to revoke decisions *prospectively*.[133] While this flexibility is, as explained below, achieved in conceptually different ways, the outcomes of decided cases are often similar. To understand this properly it is necessary to distinguish between three scenarios.

I Changes of Fact: Decisions Granted Subject to Conditions Imposed by the Administration

The first scenario is where a decision is explicitly granted subject to one or more conditions on which its continued validity depends. If such conditions cease to be fulfilled, the decision becomes prospectively revocable. In French jurisprudence, which provides a clear conceptualization of this issue, a decision is said to be subject to 'resolutive conditions' (*conditions résolutoires*) which, when the material facts change, cease to be fulfilled and make it revocable.[134]

Conditions will, and should, normally be listed in the decision text to alert the addressee to the possibility of subsequent revocation. For example, in *Société Afer* a permission to arrange an annual fair next to a busy highway was granted on the explicit condition that the applicant arrange for safe access to the parking area. When this access was not constructed, the permission could be revoked.[135] In EC law, one finds a similar principle in, for example, *Zuckerfabrik Franken* where the ECJ held that a premium for treating surplus EC sugar could be recovered (retroactively revoked) when it emerged that a third party, who had bought the sugar from the applicant, had not used it for animal food as required by the grant decision.[136]

Conditions have also in some cases been *implied* from information supplied by the addressee.[137] In the French case of *Achace* the applicant stated in an

[132] Cases 63–64/79 *Boizard v Commission* [1980] ECR 2975.

[133] See Auvret, above n. 7, 91; Yannakopoulos, above n. 7, 90.

[134] Ibid. See also Carbajo, above n. 15, 207 ff.; Chapus 1077–8; Delvolvé, above n. 53, no 614, 622.

[135] CE 5/11–84 *Société Afer* no 36.043. See also CE 19/6–64 *Société des pétroles Shell-Berre* Rec 344; CE 3/3–65 *Coudert* AJDA 1965, 487; CE 7/3–69 *Association touristique des cheminots* Rec 141; CE 18/3–83 *Siefert* AJDA 1983, 437; CE 7/12–84 *Fons-Sicart* no 20.047; CE 26/11–93 *Société industrielle française du tout terrain* Rec 593; CE 22/3–96 *Société NRJSA* RDP 1996, 1768.

[136] Case 121/83 *Zuckerfabrik Franken v Hauptzollamt Wurzburg* [1984] ECR 2039. See also Cases 124/83 *Direktoratet for Markedsordningerne v Nicolas Corman* [1985] ECR 3777; 316/86 *Hauptzollamt Hamburg-Jonas v Krücken* [1988] ECR 2213; T-451/93 *San Marco Impex Italiana v Commission* [1994] ECR II-1061; T-73/95 *Oliveira SA v Commission* [1997] ECR II-381; T-331/94 *IPK-München v Commission* [1997] ECR II-1665; T-194/97 and 83/98 *Branco v Commission*, 20/1–2000 para 94.

[137] e.g. Cases T-46/98 and T-151/98 *CEMR v Commission*, 3/2–2000 para 68–69.

application for permission to place scaffolding on the public highway that the pavements would be kept free for the use of pedestrians and, when the pavements were in fact blocked, the permission could be revoked.[138] The recent English *Cox* case provides a similar example. In this case, the Ministry of Agriculture was allowed to revoke the allocation of an EC milk quota when the beneficiary failed to comply with a requirement, stated on the application form, to use the relevant piece of land for grazing.[139]

II Changes of Fact: Decisions Granted Subject to Conditions Implied from Statutory Requirements

The second scenario is where a decision, which is not explicitly conditional, is granted subject to specific statutory conditions or requirements. If the facts change in such a way that these conditions are no longer fulfilled, the administration may have strong reasons to wish to revoke the decision. To allow this does not present a major problem for legal certainty; an individual cannot reasonably expect a beneficial decision to remain permanently unchanged if his situation changes so that the decision could not lawfully have been made given that situation. However, there is a strong argument in favour of authorities softening the blow by, as far as possible, granting the individual a transitional period to adapt to the new legal situation.

The French courts utilize the notion of *conditions résolutoires* to allow prospective revocation in this situation. Decisions are considered 'implicitly conditional' upon continuous compliance with the relevant statutory conditions. For example, in *Richoux* the owner of a driving school had his licence revoked because he had used unqualified teachers. While neither his initial application nor the licence itself mentioned a duty to use qualified teachers, the relevant legislation did. The CE therefore held that the licence was implicitly conditional upon compliance with these rules.[140]

The ECJ conceptualizes this problem differently, but the result is similar to that of French law. The ECJ considers the decision *ex post facto* 'unlawful' with the result that it may be prospectively revoked. The leading case is *Herpels*. Mr Herpels, who was a Community employee, received from 1961 a 'separation allowance' because he was living in Brussels and working in Luxembourg. When his place of work was transferred back to Brussels in 1968, payments continued until the mistake was discovered in 1976. Mr Herpels claimed that he had a right to the continuation of the payment, but the ECJ cited its case law

[138] CE 16/6–95 *Achache* D 1995, 179.

[139] *R v Ministry of Agriculture Fisheries and Food, ex p Cox* [1993] CMLR 917. Note, however, that the power to attach conditions is not unlimited. See *Chertsey UDC v Mixnam Properties Ltd* [1965] AC 735; *R v Edmonton Licensing Justices, ex p Baker* [1983] 1 WLR 1000.

[140] CE 15/7–75 *Richoux* Rec 429. See also CE 10/3–67 *Cottore* Rec 111; CE 30/3–79 *Université de Bordeaux II* Rec 141; CE 18/6–82 *Barbe* RDP 1983, 520; CE 9/12–83 *Ville d'Hendaye* Rec 506; CE 1/2–95 *Delprat* Rec 61.

concerning revocation of unlawful decisions and stated that 'the revocation of such a decision as regards the future is always possible'.[141]

The position in English law is somewhat less clear, but it does not appear to differ from French or EC law.[142] Two examples will illustrate this. In the *Thrasyvoulou* case, Lord Bridge held that a planning inspector's decision about the applicant's alleged breach of planning restrictions upon his hotel was irrevocable because 'no subsequent change of use [was] alleged'.[143] In other words, if the relevant facts had actually changed, the planning authorities would not be bound by the initial decision. The *Watts* case is along similar lines. A street trader's licence had been granted for one year: the relevant statute stated that stalls must be supervised personally by the licensee, and when Mr Watts ceased to do so some time during this year, his licence could be revoked.[144]

III Changes of Policy

The third scenario is where the administration wishes to revoke a decision in the light of a change in administrative policy (or general circumstances which have no bearing on the specific legal conditions under which the decision was made). For example, although a street trader's licence is granted for a year the authorities may wish to revoke it during the year in the light of a new policy purporting to clean up the neighbourhood by reducing the number of traders. This type of administrative action is problematic in terms of legal certainty and legitimate expectations. Individuals should, it is submitted, normally be able to rely on decisions remaining in force as long as their personal situation or other material facts remain unchanged. Authorities must, of course, be able to change policy and it may be necessary to revoke decisions to implement policy. However, the courts should not grant authorities the power to take such action *as a matter of general principle*. Insofar as revocation is deemed necessary, it should be incumbent upon legislative bodies to adopt appropriate specific revocation provisions.

The English courts have not, so far, drawn the full consequences of this argument. It is common ground that declaratory decisions (which 'affect rights') cannot be revoked on grounds of a change in policy.[145] In *Re 56 Denton Road*

[141] Case 54/77 *Herpels v Commission* [1978] ECR 585, 598. See also Case 15/60 *Simon v ECJ* [1961] ECR 115.

[142] There is little general case law on this question due to the fact that revocation of temporally continued decisions, such as licences and social benefits, is normally subject to statutory provisions. See footnote 2.

[143] *Thrasyvoulou v Secretary of State for the Environment* [1990] 2 AC 273. See also *R v Home Secretary, ex p Hindley* [1999] 2 WLR 1253, 1273.

[144] *R v Southwark Crown Court, ex p Watts* (1992) 156 JP 154. The Court of Appeal cited a statutory revocation provision, but the result would probably have been identical on general principle.

[145] Presupposing of course that they are favourable, unconditional, and communicated. Similarly Akehurst, above n. 16, 623–4. Compare Ganz, above n. 16, 254–5; Letemendia, above n. 1, 91–3.

the War Damages Commission attempted to revoke an assessment of war damage on the ground that it 'set an awkward precedent', that is on the ground that the Commission had changed its policy and wished to reassess the matter. This attempt was held to be an unlawful breach of the principle of irrevocability.[146] Similarly, in *Pierson* Lord Hope said that a life prisoner's tariff could not be increased 'simply because [the Minister] disagreed with the view formed by his predecessor about the appropriate level of punishment'.[147] However, individuals who benefit from constitutive decisions (which confer discretionary benefits) are not, as the law stands, subject to the same protection. As explained above, the *Rootkin* case limited the principle of finality laid down in *Re 56 Denton Road* by excluding constitutive decisions. Constitutive decisions may therefore, in principle, be revoked in the light of a change in policy.[148]

Still, the fact that the British administration has a power to revoke constitutive decisions on policy grounds does not mean that this power is unlimited. When an authority decides to revoke one of its own decisions, it must do so in a way which complies with the principle of *Wednesbury* unreasonableness.[149] The authority must therefore take into account and, it is submitted, give some weight to the harm which would be caused to the addressee. Moreover, the authority must act only for proper purposes[150] and always within a 'reasonable time',[151] as lengthy passivity can create expectations which should not be disappointed.[152] The importance of these points is aptly illustrated by the *Wheeler* and *Skytrain* cases.[153]

[146] *Re 56 Denton Rd., Twickenham, Middlesex* [1953] 1 Ch. 51.

[147] *Pierson v Home Secretary* [1997] 3 WLR 492, 533–4. See also *R v Dacorum BC, ex p Walsh* (1992) 24 HLR 401; *Thrasyvoulou*, judgment in the Court of Appeal, cited by C. Crawford (1990) MLR 814, 818: 'the administration cannot, in the absence of a material change in the facts, make a new decision by relying on more detailed evidence, by arguing that the initial decision was out of line with usual practice, or that it was simply not good'.

[148] See Ganz, above n. 16, 254–5; Akehurst, above n. 16, 624–5. Compare Fazal, above n. 16, 465, 470.

[149] *Associated Provincial Picture Houses Ltd v Wednesbury Corporation* [1948] 1 KB 223. See Craig 581–5.

[150] i.e. purposes compatible with the relevant statutory framework. See *Padfield v Minister of Agriculture* [1968] AC 997.

[151] *Re 56 Denton Rd., Twickenham, Middlesex* [1953] 1 Ch. 51, 56. In *Rootkin v Kent CC* [1981] 1 WLR 1186 revocation was decided within a few months and the court did not consider the question of delay.

[152] See *Khan v Home Secretary* [1987] Imm AR 543. See also *R v Secretary of State for Foreign and Commonwealth Affairs, ex p Samuel* The Times 17/8–89; *Musah v Home Secretary* [1995] Imm AR 236. Moreover, if the revocation of a decision leads to a criminal prosecution, delay may cause the prosecution to be struck out as an abuse of process. See *R v Telford Justices, ex p Badhan* [1991] 2 WLR 866; *R v Norwich Crown Court, ex p Belsham* [1992] 1 WLR 54; *A-G's Reference (No 1 of 1990)* [1992] QB 630; J. F. Archbold, *Criminal Pleading, Evidence and Practice* (London, 1998), 289–302.

[153] *Wheeler v Leicester City Council* [1985] AC 1054; *Laker Airways Ltd v Department of Trade* [1977] QB 643.

Wheeler concerned the revocation of a rugby club's licence to use land owned by a local authority. The authority had adopted an anti-Apartheid policy and, following certain club members' touring of South Africa, revoked the club's licence. The House of Lords accepted the general proposition that a discretionary licence (a constitutive decision) may in appropriate circumstances be revoked in the light of a new policy. However, it struck down the revocation on the ground, *inter alia*, that the club was being punished where it had done no wrong. The *Skytrain* decision reached a similar result by a different route. An airline company had been granted a licence to run a passenger air service between London and New York and, encouraged by the English government, the company spent £6 million preparing the service. However, before the American authorities had approved the company, a new policy, purporting to protect British Airways, was introduced and the licence was revoked. Again, the courts intervened on general *Wednesbury* grounds finding that the protection of British Airways was not a lawful purpose under the statute.[154]

In French law, the position is slightly more protective of legal certainty and legitimate expectations. The general principle is that the administration does *not* have the power to revoke favourable decisions in the light of a change in policy. Indeed, there is no suggestion in French law that discretionary benefits fall outside the principle of irrevocability. Thus, in the recent '*Chant' la Vie*' case a local authority decided to guarantee, on behalf of a private company, a loan intended to finance the construction of a home for old aged pensioners. Shortly afterwards the authority changed its mind and revoked the decision without alleging any change of relevant facts. The CE found, by examining the minutes of the meeting which had approved the guarantee and the text of the letter notifying the company, that it was not implicitly conditional and held that the authority was therefore bound by its initial decision.[155]

The principle that the administration cannot revoke decisions on the grounds of a change in policy is, however, subject to one very important exception. Numerous activities are in France, as in other societies, subject to licensing requirements. If a licensing law purports to ensure *l'ordre public*, that is either public security and order, health and cleanliness, or morality, the licence is called an *autorisation de police*.[156] The administration has an inherent discretionary power to terminate such licences with prospective

[154] See also *R v Barnsley MBC, ex p Hook* [1976] 1 WLR 1052; *Congreve v Home Office* [1976] QB 629; *R v Secretary of State for Transport, ex p Pegasus Holidays* [1988] 1 WLR 990; *R v London Borough of Lambeth, ex p Stockwell Law Centre*, 22/5–98.

[155] CE 28/7–93 *Association 'Chant' la Vie'* Rec 658. Compare CE 8/2–85 *Marana* Rec 28.

[156] All French administrative bodies have inherent power to protect *l'ordre public* by taking *mesures de police administrative*. The police forces have additional powers to fight crime for which purpose they take *mesures de police judiciaire*. See generally E. Picard, *La notion de police administrative* (Paris, 1984); Chapus 641–86.

effect.[157] This was established in the case of *Constantin*. The case concerned a mayor's permission to allow a bar to stay open for half an hour after the closure of a nearby cinema. Permission should not have been granted, as it violated a general decree, and it was subsequently revoked. In what has become classic terms the CE held that 'nobody has right to the continuation of an *autorisation de police*'.[158]

The scope of the power to revoke licences is wide. The notion of *autorisations de police* is wide-ranging and its contours are far from clear. It includes, for example, licensing of medical laboratories, handguns, public houses, and airfields.[159] It should be added that the French administration has inherent power to revoke licences to exercise trade and other professional activities on public lands and the public highway (*autorisations d'occupation du domaine public*).[160] Thus, the CE held in *Visconti* that the administration can change the fee charged for, or completely revoke, the licence to moor a houseboat in a public marina if the licensee's situation changes or more general societal circumstances cause a change in licensing policy.[161]

It follows that a very large number of licences are in theory at risk of revocation at any given time in France, but in practice the legal certainty of licensees is not greatly affected. Most licensing laws now contain specific revocation provisions which limit the circumstances in which licences may be revoked[162] and the general theory of *autorisations de police* is therefore rarely applied.[163] Moreover, the power to revoke licences is discretionary but not entirely unlimited. The administration must comply with the normal restrictions upon

[157] Several writers state, therefore, that licences do not 'create rights' (e.g. Le Mire, above n. 35, 208; Delvolvé, above n. 53, no 596). However, this oversimplifies the matter. Licences are favourable and constitutive decisions which create rights, and the CE consistently held that licences cannot be revoked with *retroactive* effect. See *JC* Fasc 108–30 no 166–7; Yannakopoulos, above n. 7, 91.

[158] CE 17/7–53 *Constantin* Rec 381. See also CE 2/2–57 *Dupé* Rec 77; CE 4/7–58 *Graff* Rec 414; CE 21/5–82 *Conseil régional d'Ile de France de l'Ordre national des pharmaciens* Rec 523; CE 11/3–87 *Weisbach* D 1988, 55; CE 20/1–89 *Syndicat nationale des pilotes professionnelles* Rec 449.

[159] Ibid.

[160] Such licences are also known as *permissions de voirie*. See R. Chapus, *Droit administratif général*, vol ii, 11th edn. (Paris, 1998) 482–6.

[161] In the absence of any factual change whatsoever in this case, the applicant's claim was upheld, see CE 12/10–94 *Visconti* Rec 442. See also CE 21/2–34 *Soustre* Rec 257; CE 27/4–87 *Berder* DA 1987 no 326.

[162] e.g. CE 25/4–58 *Société Laboratoires Geigy* Rec 236 (medical product's marketing licence); CE 1/2–80 *Rigal* Rec 64 (Art L634 *Code de la santé*); CE 21/5–82 *Conseil régional d'Ile de France de l'ordre national des pharmaciens* Rec 523 (Art L594 *Code de la santé*); CE 10/6–88 *Ministre du redéploiement industriel* Rec 571 (Art 84 *Code minier*); CE 13/6–90 *Pentsch* Rec 161 (Art L62 *Code des débits de boisson*); CE 4/3–91 *Ville de Tourcoing* Rec 74 (Art 123–52 *Code de la construction et d'habitation*); CE 18/12–91 *Pelardy* Rec 1083 (Art L.18 *et seq Code de la route*); CE 25/2–94 *Laboratoires d'Artois* AJDA 1994, 394 (Art 24 *Décret* of 4/11–76 implementing the *Code de la santé*); CE 16/12–94 *SA La Médicale Equipex* no 131.774 (Art 598 *Code de la santé*).

[163] A Lexis search of cases referring to *autorisation de police* and other related terms did not reveal any recent decisions which allowed the revocation of a favourable decision without a specific statutory basis. See also Picard, above n. 156, 754; Yannakopoulos, above n. 7, 110–11.

discretionary decision-making.[164] While there is no suggestion in French case law that the administration must necessarily consider the harm which will be caused to the licensee and his expectations or that it must act within a reasonable time,[165] a revocation decision must at least be based on correct facts and pursue a lawful purpose which is in the public interest.[166] This is aptly illustrated by the *Heitz* case. A licence to move a dental clinic from one locality to another, and run it from the new locality, had been granted for one year only and subject to 'revocation at any moment'. In view of the profound impact of these restrictions upon the business, the CE found them incompatible with the purpose of the legislation, which was to regulate the profession and ensure a rational allocation of clinics.[167] Finally, a person benefiting from the type of licence known as an *autorisation d'occupation du domaine public* may, in certain circumstances, be entitled to financial compensation if it is revoked.[168]

What, then, of EC law? A favourable, notified, and unconditional decision cannot, in the absence of a statutory provision, be revoked due to a change of policy which causes the decision-maker to assess the initial facts differently.[169] In this important respect, EC law is both simpler and more protective of individual's legitimate expectations and legal certainty than either of the two national legal systems. The Community principle was established in the seminal *Algera* case,[170] and it has been maintained since as the recent *Interhotel* case illustrates. In this case the CFI held that the Commission had violated the principle of legitimate expectations by partially revoking a financial grant awarded under the European Social Fund. The Commission argued that certain expenses incurred by the beneficiary fell outside its reimbursement policy, but the CFI found that since the grant decision notified to the applicant was neither explicitly conditional nor restricted to certain types of expenditure, the Commission was bound by it no matter what its initial or subsequent policy was.[171]

[164] However, it appears that these requirements are rarely applied to overrule revocation in practice. See Auvret, above n. 7, 89; Yannakopoulos, above n. 7, 107–8; Chapus, above n. 156, 482–3.

[165] See G. Vedel and P. Delvolvé, *Droit Administratif*, 12th edn. (Paris, 1992), 315.

[166] CE 13/3–03 *Cie d'Orléans* Rec 243: the power to revoke *autorisations d'occupation par le domaine publique* 'n'existe que dans l'intérêt même du domaine sur lequel elles sont été accordées'. See also Auby, above n. 35, 137–8; Yannakopoulos, above n. 7, 107–13.

[167] CE 27/5–60 *Heitz* Rec 370. See also CE 7/1–20 *Cael* Rec 5 and compare CE 13/11–29 *Cie des produits chimiques* Rec 981; CE 6/5–36 *Ministre du Commerce* Rec 497; CE 8/2–57 *Augier* Rec 96.

[168] CE 29/3–68 *Michelin* Rec 217. See Chapus, above n. 156, 494–501 and Ch. 5.3.B.

[169] See Schwarze 1023–4.

[170] Cases 7/56 and 3–7/57 *Algera v Common Assembly* [1957] ECR 39, 55.

[171] Case T-81/95 *Interhotel v Commission* [1997] ECR II-1265. See also Cases T-46/98 and T-151/98 *CEMR v Commission*, 3/2–2000 para 72. Applicants for financial aid may however have to seek clarification of applicable conditions, see Tridimas, above n. 68, 194.

5 Revocation of Unlawful Decisions

(A) The Nature of the Problem

Traditionally, lawyers in most jurisdictions found the idea that an unlawful decision can be revoked illogical. An unlawful decision was considered void[172] and without effect from the time it was made (*ex tunc*). It followed from this premise that 'where there is no act, there can be no question of a power to revoke or rescind it; you cannot alter that which does not exist'.[173] Thus, it was said, the administration can proceed as if the initial decision did not exist.[174]

Later theory has pointed out the logical flaw in this line of reasoning. It relies on a false premise, namely that an unlawful decision is non-existent.[175] In reality an unlawful decision does produce effects until *either* a court (which is asked to review the decision within the relevant time limit by a person who has standing) annuls the decision, *or* it is replaced by a new (lawful) decision. It is therefore entirely logical to ask in what circumstances the administration is empowered to make a new decision once it is discovered that its initial decision was unlawful.

This question causes considerable difficulty because fairness to the individual clashes with the principle of lawful government (*ultra vires, légalité*). On the one hand, the principle of lawful government would require that public authorities must act only where specifically given the power to do so and then only within the limits set by law. To accept that unlawful decisions and representations can create expectations which the authority is bound to uphold runs against this principle. For by making unlawful representations authorities could, deliberately or inadvertently, extend their powers beyond the limits set by law.[176] On the other hand, individuals are, given the complexity of modern administrative law, not well placed to detect that an administrative decision or representation is unlawful, and it is unrealistic to require them to take legal advice every time they rely upon administrative decisions.[177] The absence of any protection of legitimate expectations can, therefore, cause considerable hardship and undermine confidence in public authorities when individuals plan their lives and rely financially upon unlawful decisions.[178]

(B) English Law: Estoppel and the Nature of the Illegality

Faced with the choice between legality and individual fairness, the English courts have generally preferred to uphold legality. The administration can in

[172] On the terminology of void and voidable, see Wade 344.

[173] Rubinstein, above n. 71, 29.

[174] Ganz, above n. 16, 243; Akehurst, above n. 16, 619.

[175] See Wade 339–44.

[176] See *Minister of Agriculture and Fisheries v Hulkin*, unreported but cited in *Minister of Agriculture and Fisheries v Mathews* [1950] 1 KB 148.

[177] See Bradley, above n. 16, 3.

[178] This hardship is acknowledged in the case law. See *A-G for Ceylon v Silva* [1953] AC 461, 480–1.

principle always revoke an unlawful decision, prospectively as well as retroactively, without being subject to any time limit.[179] Thus, in the leading case of *Howell* a company had been granted an oral licence to carry out ship repairs. The licence was a decision made by the competent officer and substantively correct, but it was unlawful because it should have been made in writing according to the statutory provisions. The House of Lords held that the licence was not binding, as no unlawful act, decision, or representation can be binding or create an estoppel by representation.[180]

It is, however, acknowledged that in some situations the hardship caused to an individual may justify a limitation of the principle of legality. Certain *species of illegality* have been singled out in English law as less serious than others and decisions vitiated by such errors may be binding and irrevocable. Conceptually, this binding effect does not flow from a distinct public law principle of irrevocability or legitimate expectations, but from the application of the private law principle of estoppel by representation.[181] Accordingly, an authority is bound by an unlawful decision if the illegality falls within one of the two following categories and the addressee, assuming that the decision was lawful, has relied upon it in a reasonable way such that revoking the decision would cause him financial detriment.

First, an officer may bind the authorities if he acts within powers which, on a proper construction of the statutory framework, could have been *delegated* to him although no formal delegation has actually taken place.[182] However, this

[179] *Re 56 Denton Rd., Twickenham, Middlesex* [1953] 1 Ch. 51 suggested that unlawful decisions should be corrected within a 'reasonable period', but later decisions do not support this view. See Akehurst, above n. 16, 619; Letemendia, above n. 1, 114, 188–90.

[180] *Howell v Falmouth Boat Construction Co* [1951] AC 837, 845, 849. See also *Cook v Ipswich Local Board* (1871) 6 LRQB 451, 462; *R v Brisby* (1849) 1 Den CC 416; *Maritime Electric v General Dairies* [1937] AC 610; *A-G for Ceylon v Silva* [1953] AC 461; *R v Oxford Regional Mental Health Review Tribunal, ex p Home Secretary* [1988] AC 120, 126; *Thrasyvoulou v Secretary of State for the Environment* [1990] 2 AC 273, 289; *R v Greater Manchester Police Authority, ex p Cushion* [1991] COD 327; *R v Arun District Council, ex p Fowler* [1997] EGCS 139. Compare *Holt v Markman* [1923] 1 KB 504; *Algar v Middlesex CC* [1945] 2 All ER 243; *Robertson v Minister of Pensions* [1949] 1 KB 227.

[181] See generally on estoppel by representation in private law Wilken and Villiers, above n. 109, 103–99. On public law estoppel, see footnote 16 and Farrer, 'A Prerogative Fallacy—That the Crown is not Bound by Estoppel' (1933) LQR 511; G. Treitel, 'Crown Proceedings: Some Recent Developments' (1957) PL 321, 335–9; P.P. Craig, 'Representations by Public Bodies' (1977) LQR 398; C. Crawford and T. Reid, 'Planning Officers' Advice and Undertakings: Estoppel and Personal Bar in Public Law' (1982) 3 Scottish Planning Law and Practice Occasional Papers; T. Nöcker and G. French, 'Estoppel: What's the Government's Word Worth? An Analysis of German Law, Common Law Jurisdictions, and of the Practice of International Arbitral Tribunals' (1990) The International Lawyer 409; Wade 371–8; and case notes by A. W. Bradley (1961) CLJ 139, (1971) CLJ 3; J. M. Evans (1971) MLR 335; C. Crawford (1982) MLR 87, (1990) MLR 814; P. Jackson (1983) LQR 499; H. W. Wilkinson (1990) NLJ 168.

[182] *Western Fish Products v Penwith DC* [1981] 2 All ER 204 (approving to this extent *Lever Finance v Westminster City LBC* [1971] 1 QB 222); *Camden LBC v Secretary of State for the Environment* (1993) 67 P and CR 59. Compare *Graham v Secretary of State for the Environment* [1993] JPL 353.

exception is strictly limited. It is not sufficient that the officer appeared to the reasonably diligent observer to be acting on behalf of the authority, for example because the officer was holding a senior office. There must be evidence, such as a long-established practice of (unlawful) delegation, which could lead a person dealing with the administration to expect that delegation had actually taken place. Thus, in *Garner* the court held that a district surveyor did not have sufficient 'ostensible authority' to bind a local council on a planning matter.[183] The delegation exception is clearly of limited assistance in practice.[184] Individuals are often not in a position to know whether an officer is competent or not, or if power has been formally delegated, and the exception does not apply where the decision is outside the powers of the decision-making body itself.

Second, an authority may be bound if it waives *procedural formalities*. What formalities can be waived is not entirely clear, but it is likely to depend upon their importance within the relevant statutory scheme. In *Howell* the House of Lords held that a licensing body was not bound by an orally communicated licence because the statute explicitly prescribed licences to be made in writing.[185] This result may be contrasted with *L's* case, where an authority was bound to consider an application which had been submitted late due to incorrect advice about the statutory time limit,[186] and *Western Fish* which held that planning permission is binding once granted, although the applicant did not use the right application form.[187] However, the formality exception has not always been applied in practice[188] and it does not cover situations where individuals rely upon decisions or representations which are vitiated by a substantive error, for example, an irrelevant consideration, an error of law, or an error of fact.[189]

An exception to the general rule that unlawful decisions and representations can be revoked also flows from the principle of abuse of the criminal courts' process. Thus, in *Bloomfield* the Court of Appeal held that a decision by a Crown Prosecutor to discontinue a criminal prosecution, communicated in court, was binding. Neither the court nor the defendant 'could be expected to enquire whether prosecuting counsel had authority to conduct a case in court in any particular way and they were therefore entitled to assume in ordinary circumstances that counsel did have such authority'.[190] This decision bears some

183 *Garner v Secretary of State for the Environment* (1998) 75 P and CR 273.

184 See Craig 644.

185 *Howell v Falmouth Boat Construction Co* [1951] AC 837. See similarly *R v Home Secretary, ex p Mowla* [1992] 1 WLR 70, 87.

186 *Re L* [1971] 3 All ER 743.

187 *Western Fish Products v Penwith DC* [1981] 2 All ER 204 (approving to this extent *Wells v Minister of Housing and Local Government* [1967] 1 WLR 1000, 1007).

188 *Graham v Secretary of State for the Environment* [1993] JPL 353.

189 *Rootkin v Kent CC* [1981] 1 WLR 1186.

190 *R v Bloomfield* [1997] 1 Cr App Rep 135. See also *R v Croydon Justices, ex p Dean* [1993] QB 769, 777 approved in *R v Horseferry Road Magistrates' Court, ex p Bennett* [1994] 1 All ER 289, 124.

resemblance to the delegation exception mentioned above, but goes further towards protecting the legitimate expectations of individuals because there is no requirement of 'extra factors', such as seniority and a practice of delegation. This should not come as a surprise. Criminal prosecutions deeply affect the interests and rights of individuals. The courts are therefore more likely to review decisions intensively and to accept inroads into the *ultra vires* principle. However, the practical relevance of the abuse principle is limited to the criminal law context.

On the whole, these exceptions to the principle that unlawful decisions can always be revoked are very limited. If they were applied to the letter, the individual's reasonable expectations would often be disappointed. To avoid this outcome, the courts have sometimes resorted to a variation, or manipulation, of the concept of legality itself. The reviewing court may then be seen to uphold principle while doing justice to the individual.[191] This pragmatic 'solution' is exemplified by *Lever Finance*. In this well-known case Lord Denning held that a planning officer's decision, to the effect that planning consent was not required for a modification of a development, was binding under the 'delegation' exception. However, the planning legislation did not, at that time, allow delegation of planning decisions at all. It was not, as the judge pretended, a case of missing formal delegation, but a case of a completely unlawful decision.[192]

This form of 'variation' of the principle of legality is hardly a satisfactory solution to the problem of unlawful decisions. It is likely to confuse administrators about the extent to which they are bound to respect unlawful decisions, it forces applicants to seek judicial review to obtain by the back door what the law will not grant by the front door, and by concealing the injustice caused by a rigorous adherence to legality, it prevents consideration of the more general problem of reconciling legality with legal certainty.

(C) French Law: A Fixed Time Limit

I The General Principle

The French courts accept, as do the English and EC courts, that to uphold the principle of legality (*ultra vires, légalité*), the administration must have an inherent discretionary power to revoke a decision if it is discovered that it is unlawful. However, the CE held in *Cachet* that this power must be limited to protect legal certainty and legitimate expectations.[193] The Court accepted that the principle of lawful government is not absolute; it must be balanced against individual fairness and trust in government.[194]

[191] See Craig 646.

[192] *Lever Finance v Westminster City LBC* [1971] 1 QB 222. For a more recent example of manipulation of legality, see *Ejaz v Home Secretary* [1995] COD 72.

[193] See Pécresse *conclusions* CE 24/10–97 *Laubier* RFDA 1998, 528; Yannakopoulos, above n. 7, 436–40.

[194] See Girardot and Raynaud, above n. 36, 937.

How, then, is the power to revoke unlawful decisions limited? The CE consistently held that this power is a reflection of the administrative judge's power to annul unlawful decisions.[195] Revocation of a decision which has created rights[196] is therefore only possible within the time limit for seeking judicial review or, if the addressee (or a third person with *locus standi*) appeals or seeks review, until a final appeal decision or judgment has been made.[197] After the expiry of this time limit, the decision remains forever final and irrevocable. It is for this purpose irrelevant whether the decision was unlawful on procedural or substantive grounds.[198]

The time limit for judicial review is in France very short, namely two months.[199] If a specific form of publication is not prescribed by law,[200] the period is calculated from the moment the initial decision was notified to the affected person.[201] The principle of *intangibilité* therefore provides a considerable degree of legal certainty. Individuals can expect that, after two months, favourable decisions can be revoked only with their consent or by reference to a specific statutory provision. However, if judicial review is sought, the certainty provided is much reduced; partly because the proceedings can be very lengthy,[202] partly because there is no system to ensure that the addressee of a favourable decision is informed when an administrative decision is challenged by a third party.[203]

The principle of *intangibilité* strikes a balance between fairness and legality by imposing a time limit upon the power to revoke unlawful decisions. The

[195] CE 3/11–22 *Cachet* Rec 790.

[196] That is, a favourable and unconditional decision which is not procured by fraud.

[197] CE 12/6–33 *Kremer* Rec 638; CE 10/2–82 *Angeletti* Rec 62 (review); CE 12/1–77 *Dalbos* Rec 19 (appeal). In EC law, a decision is revocable if challenged by the affected person, but it is unclear whether this extends to third-party challenges. See Case 14/81 *Alpha Steel v Commission* [1982] ECR 749 para 10.

[198] Although decisions may, in extreme circumstances, be deemed non-existent in which case they may always be replaced by a lawful decision. See CE 15/5–81 *Maurice* Rec 221; CE 31/5–57 *Girard* Rec 355; CE 3/2–56 *De Fontbonne* Rec 45; and further J.-M. Auby, *L'inexistence des actes administratifs: étude de contentieux administratifs* (Paris, 1951); *LGA* 553–60; Yannakopoulos, above n. 7, 83–9.

[199] This time limit is based on a general principle, now codified by the Decree of 11 January 1965. See Chapus 736–7.

[200] In which case these requirements must be complied with. See CE 18/2–94 *Wrobel* DA 1994 no 180.

[201] A case law (CE 6/5–66 *Ville de Bagneux* Rec 303; CE 14/11–69 *Eve* Rec 498) according to which decisions could always be revoked so long as third parties had not been notified has now been overruled. See CE 24/10–97 *Laubier* RFDA 1998, 527; CAA Bordeaux 8/3–99 *Centre Sanitaire de Saint-Clar* DA 1999 no 187; Girardot and Raynaud, above n. 36. The overruling may be codified shortly, see Art 21 of *Projet de loi relatif aux droits des citoyens dans leurs relations avec les administrations*, available at http://www. legifrance.gouv.fr/citoyen/actualite /preparation/citoyen.htm.

[202] Based on 1997 figures, a decision will on average remain revocable for just under two years if challenged before a first instance administrative court (*Tribunal Administratif*). Appeal to a *Cour d'Appel Administratif* takes on average another fourteen months and a further appeal to the CE an additional two to three years. See Brown and Bell Appendix E.

[203] See Études du Conseil d'État: *Urbanisme—pour un droit plus efficace* (Paris, 1992), 98–9.

doctrine known as *fonctionnaire de fait* fulfils a similar role, though it is less practically important.[204] The doctrine is somewhat similar to, but narrower than, the English doctrine of estoppel by representation.[205] While the estoppel doctrine starts logically from the individual and asks whether he can prevent (estop) the administration from taking a different course of action from that which it decided or represented, the *fonctionnaire de fait* doctrine starts from the person who made the representation and asks whether he should in the circumstances be considered a *de facto* decision-maker whose decisions are lawful and therefore binding and irrevocable. Much has been written about the *fonctionnaire de fait* doctrine, but it remains unclear to what extent it is actually applied in practice.[206] The administrative courts never mentioned it explicitly,[207] but some judgments appear to be based implicitly on it. The doctrine may apply in two types of situations.

First, a decision which is made by a person who was unlawfully appointed or elected is, in principle, unlawful, but a number of decisions have accepted that an illegality of this kind may be 'without influence'[208] or 'cannot be invoked'[209] as a reason for revoking the decision. For example, in *Commune de Moules* the CE held that a local authority (*commune*) could not revoke a decision to employ a civil servant, 'although [the matter was] decided upon by an unlawfully elected mayor'.[210]

Second, it is argued by some authors that an officer may bind the authorities if he acts within powers which have been unlawfully delegated to him,[211] and a reasonably prudent individual would have assumed that the officer acted in a normal and legal capacity.[212] There is, unfortunately, no support for this sensible view in recent case law, and it is doubtful whether the French courts would in practice uphold a decision made in excess of lawful delegation.[213]

[204] See generally L. Ledoux, 'Essai d'une théorie sur la fonction de fait', Revue générale d'administration 1912 II 397, III 22; G. Jèze, 'Essai d'une théorie générale des fonctionnaires de fait', RDP 1914, 48; Auby, above n. 198, 235–51; V. Jouve, 'Recherches sur la notion d'apperance en droit administratif français', RDP 1968, 283; M. M. Moustakas, 'La confiance de l'administré et son influence sur le régime juridique des actes administratifs unilatéraux', Doctoral thesis (Paris II, 1993), 18–70.

[205] The seminal French studies appear to have been inspired partly by English law. See Jèze, above n. 204, 51.

[206] Leading textbooks mention the doctrine only very briefly. See e.g. Chapus 946.

[207] This is admitted by Jouve, above n. 204, 291–2; Moustakas, above n. 204, 44 and confirmed by a search on the Lexis database.

[208] CE 24/6–53 *Perchel* Rec 312.

[209] CE 2/11–23 *Bosquié* Rec 699. Similarly CE 21/11–34 *Nicod* Rec. 1087; CE 20/2–57 *Zahoual* Rec 831; CE 2/12–83 *Charbonnel* Rec 474.

[210] CE 27/10–61 *Commune de Moules* Rec 920.

[211] See Jouve, above n. 204, 295 ff. drawing upon the writings of Jèze.

[212] See Auby, above n. 198, 55; A. de Laubadère, J. C. Venezia and Y. Gaudemet, *Traité de droit administratif*, vol. i, 14th edn. (Paris, 1996), 672.

[213] One case (Cass Civ 7/8–1883 *"Les Mariages de Montrouges"* D 1883 II 49) is said to support the view, but a close reading reveals that the court did not rely upon the *fonctionnaire de fait* theory as suggested by the Court's *Procureur général* Barbier. Compare CE 18/5–45 *Société auxiliaire de Gestion et d'Avances* Rec 99; CE 13/5–49 *Couvrat* D 1950, 77.

II Exceptions: Declaratory Pecuniary Decisions

The principle that unlawful decisions may be revoked only within two months may have serious financial implications for public authorities because it excludes the recovery of sums unlawfully paid. To alleviate this problem, the principle established in *Cachet* has been limited to some considerable extent.[214]

The CE has consistently held, at least since 1927,[215] that unlawful declaratory decisions (*décisions déclaratifs*) are not irrevocable in the same way as constitutive decisions (*décisions attributives*).[216] A decision is constitutive if it is based on a discretionary power, whether statutory or inherent.[217] Conversely, a decision made on the basis of precise legal provisions is declaratory. The French courts reason that only the former is capable of *creating* a new situation for the addressee. The latter merely declares what is already his statutory right and it does, therefore, not 'create rights' protected against subsequent revocation. It is, as pointed out in the discussion of English law above, very difficult to distinguish clearly between declaratory and constitutive decisions and the distinction has been the subject of much litigation in France.[218] Two examples may illustrate how the courts draw the line.

In the leading case of *Buissière,* the CE held that a farmer who had received a greater pension than he was legally entitled to could not invoke the two-month time limit to prevent the administration from terminating the overpayment and recovering sums already paid. The relevant statute gave applicants an entitlement to pension on completion of a set of precisely defined conditions[219] which left the decision-maker no discretion in the matter.[220] Consequently, the decision which awarded the pension was considered 'declaratory' and therefore revocable. The fact that the farmer had ceased production in reliance upon the

[214] While the CE never stated explicitly that financial concerns underpin this case law, this is evident from the conclusions of Labetoulle in CE 15/10–76 *Buissière* Rec 428.

[215] CE 11/3–27 *Lehoux* Rec 322.

[216] See Prétot *conclusions* CE 25/4–90 *Figuereo* AJDA 1990, 641; M. Nauwelaers and L. Fabius, 'Chronique générale de jurisprudence administrative française', AJDA 1976, 557; M. Lefondre, 'Le retrait des aides financières publiques aux enterprises privées' (1993) Revue Administratif 131; Yannakopoulos, above n. 7, 137–8.

[217] The French administration has considerable inherent powers under Art 34 of the Constitution.

[218] See Labetoulle *conclusions* CE 15/10–76 *Buissière* Rec 428; Le Mire, above n. 35, 211–12; Yannakopoulos, above n. 7, 136–43.

[219] The pension consisted of a basic amount, intended as a supplement to the normal state pension, and an additional amount intended to speed up the restructuring of the agricultural sector. Award of the basic amount presupposed, first, that the applicant had reached a certain age, was a farmer and undertook to cease production; second, that the farm was of a certain size; third, that the person taking over the farm was already a farmer. The restructuring amount was subject to additional conditions, namely, that the farm was of a larger size and that it be merged with another farm. Mr Buissière did not fulfil the additional conditions and the restructuring proportion of the pension was revoked.

[220] The relevant land sizes were determined by implementing regulations, see Rec 420.

decision and received money for about a year in good faith did not inspire the CE to take a different view.[221]

The *Consorts Machet* case concerned an establishment grant awarded to two young farmers. These grants were also subject to specific legislative conditions concerned with the applicant's citizenship, age, and plans to develop a farm of a certain minimum size. In the light of *Buissière*, one might expect grants made on the basis of these rules to be declaratory. However, the rules did not state that an applicant 'must' or 'does' benefit if the conditions are fulfilled; only that he *can* benefit. It follows that the decision-maker had a discretionary power to refuse applications even where the basic conditions were fulfilled.[222] Consequently, the CE held that the grant was constitutive and thus irrevocable even though it had emerged that the applicants did not fulfil all the relevant conditions.[223]

The exclusion of declaratory decisions from the principle of *Cachet* is unfortunate from the point of view of legal certainty. Declaratory unlawful decisions may create legitimate expectations in individuals in the same way as constitutive decisions, and considerable hardship may therefore, as the *Buissière* case illustrates, result from their retroactive revocation.[224] It should, as proposed by judge Labetoulle, be recognized that all *favourable* pecuniary decisions are subject to the principle of irrevocability.[225]

(D) EC Law: Balancing on a Case-by-Case Basis

I The General Principle

Drawing upon both French and German jurisprudence, the ECJ has developed a conceptually sophisticated public law principle which purports to strike a balance between the requirements of legality and fairness to individuals who plan their lives and rely upon unlawful decisions. This principle does not iden-

[221] CE 15/10–76 *Buissière* Rec 428. See also CE 5/5–50 *Clemencelle* Rec 265 (a decision fixing the amount of interest to be paid on a compensation claim); CE 14/4–61 *Cazes* Rec 232; CE 15/10–69 *Forasetto* Rec 437; CE 29/5–96 *Secrétaire d'État à la Mer* Petites Affiches 1996 no 127 (building improvement grants); CE 2/10–81 *Vipal* Rec 347 (EU export restitution); CE 5/12–94 *Pétillon* Rec 774 (cessation of milk production grant); CE 16/10–96 *Vuillecard* no 116.867 (award to a civil servant of a complementary allowance until his retirement).

[222] This interpretation was supported by the fact that the administration was required to carry out a general feasibility study before deciding on each application.

[223] CE 16/3–90 *Consorts Machet* Rec 69. See also CE 31/1–36 *Bouzy* Rec 142 (discretionary social benefit); CE 27/4–45 *Brousser* Rec 82; CE 10/3–67 *Société Samat et Cie* Rec 112 (discretionary tax concession); CE 12/1–77 *Dalbos* Rec 19 (housing improvement grants); CE 30/3–79 *Université de Bordeaux II* Rec 141 (ministerial funding of university teaching); CE 8/2–85 *Marana* Rec 28 (water works grants to companies); CE 25/7–86 *Société Grandes Distilleries les fils d'Auguste Perreux* RFDA 1987, 454 (production restructuring grant); CE 8/3–93 *Morange* Rec 594 (professor's discretionary supervision allowance).

[224] See Le Mire, above n. 35, 210–11; Auvret, above n. 7, 76–7.

[225] *Conclusions* CE 15/10–76 *Buissière* Rec 428; D. Labetoulle, 'Principe de légalité et principe de sécurité', in *Mélanges Guy Braibant* (Paris, 1996), 403, 409–10.

tify *specific species* of illegality, which may give rise to an estoppel (as in English law), nor does it impose a *fixed time limit* upon revocation (as in French law).[226] The Community approach is more subtle and flexible. An important distinction is drawn between prospective and retroactive revocation.

An unlawful decision is always *prospectively* revocable.[227] For example, in the leading *Algera* case the Assembly had granted the applicant permanent employment and conferred upon her a certain grade which determined her salary. While the appointment itself was lawful and irrevocable, the grading violated certain staff regulations and it could be revoked. That is, the Assembly's decision to place Ms Algera in a lower category with effect for the future did not violate any general principle of EC law.[228] This principle is not above criticism. There is a risk that individuals rely upon unlawful decisions, such as licences, in a way which cannot be reversed without a certain transitional period. Prospective revocation of a decision with immediate effect may therefore disappoint legitimate expectations and cause hardship. This is acknowledged in French law where decisions become retroactively as well as prospectively revocable after two months.[229] Unfortunately, the ECJ has not proved receptive to this argument so far.[230]

Unlawful favourable decisions are not always *retroactively* revocable. The institutions have inherent power to revoke with retroactive effect only if, in the circumstances, the public interest in revocation outweighs the private interest in seeing the measure upheld and the revocation is carried out within a 'reasonable period' from the time it was notified. In other words, when purporting to revoke an unlawful decision, the institution must *balance* the principle of legality against the principle of legal certainty.[231]

The balancing principle was established in *SNUPAT* and *Hoogovens*. These are two of several cases concerned with the so-called metal scrap equalization

[226] AG Lagrange urged the ECJ to adopt a similar principle, but the Court did not follow his advice. See Case 14/61 *Hoogovens v High Authority* [1962] ECR 253.

[227] See Letemendia, above n. 1, 200–10; Hartley, above n. 56, 435. Compare Schwarze 1003–7 for the unsubstantiated claim that this only applies to decisions which do not create rights.

[228] Cases 7/56 and 3–7/57 *Algera v Common Assembly* [1957] ECR 39. See also Case 159/82 *Verli-Wallace v Commission* [1983] ECR 2711 para 8–11 (unlawful decisions 'can always be revoked as regards the future'); and similarly Cases 15/60 *Simon v ECJ* [1961] ECR 115; 54/77 *Herpels v Commission* [1978] ECR 585; T-498/93 *Dornonville v Commission* [1994] ECR-SC II-813 para 48.

[229] In German law both retroactive *and* prospective revocation require a *balancing* of legality and legal certainty. See Schwarze 886 ff.

[230] The ECJ acknowledged the problem in a case about the revocation of a lawful general regulation, whereby staff members' pensions were reduced by 50 per cent. Although a general regulation cannot be irrevocable as such, the Court found on grounds of legitimate expectations that the reduction could not be implemented without a transitional period of more than ten months. See Case 127/80 *Grogan v Commission* [1982] ECR 869.

[231] Decisions may however be deemed non-existent if vitiated by an extremely grave form of illegality. In this case, the administration may proceed as if the decision were never made. See Cases 7/56 and 3–7/57 *Algera v Common Assembly* [1957] ECR 39; 15/85 *Consorzio Cooperative d'Abruzzo v Commission.* [1987] ECR 1005 para 10–11.

scheme.[232] This scheme imposed a levy on metal scrap with an exception for scrap resulting from a company's own production. One of SNUPAT's competitors, Hoogovens, received scrap from a company within its business group and the Commission decided that this was 'own' production. When SNUPAT failed to obtain a similar exemption for scrap it had received from the car manufacturer Renault, it asked the Commission to revoke Hoogovens' exemption with retroactive effect. When the Commission failed to do so, SNUPAT sought judicial review. The ECJ found that the exemption awarded to Hoogovens was indeed unlawful and the question arose whether it should therefore be revoked. The ECJ held that:

> [T]he principle . . . of legal certainty . . . must be combined with . . . the principle of legality; . . . which of these would prevail in each particular case depends upon a comparison of the public interest with the private interests in question, that is to say: on the one hand, the beneficiaries' . . . good faith and . . . reliance. On the other hand, the interest of the Community . . . [233]

The Commission subsequently revoked Hoogovens' exemption with retroactive effect. When this was in turn challenged by *Hoogovens* the ECJ found for the Commission. The Court reaffirmed that retroactive revocation is, and should be, restricted to situations where prospective revocation is without real effect:

> [I]n weighing up the conflicting interests on which the choice between the *ex nunc* and *ex tunc* revocation of an illegal decision is to depend, it is important [for the Commission] to bear in mind the actual situation of the parties concerned.[234]

However, in this case the whole equalization scheme had subsequently been wound up. Nothing would therefore have been achieved by a decision to reimpose the levy for the future and the retroactive revocation was therefore lawful.

As these cases illustrate, the balancing of legality and legitimate expectations is in the first place for the administration, but it is reviewable by the Community judicature.[235] The ECJ has described this review as 'strict',[236] but a survey of the case law reveals that the Community courts give legality concerns considerable weight and that they will interfere only if there is a serious lack of proportion between the public and private interests at stake.[237] Five considerations are important in deciding whether a decision may be revoked retroactively.

First, revocation is barred only if the person in favour of whom the decision was made had a legitimate expectation that the decision finally settled the

[232] Cases 42 and 49/59 *SNUPAT v High Authority* [1961] ECR 53; 14/61 *Hoogovens v High Authority* [1962] ECR 253; 111/63 *Lemmerz-Werke v High Authority* [1965] ECR 677; 14/81 *Alpha Steel v Commission* [1982] ECR 749.

[233] *SNUPAT*, 87.

[234] Case 14/61 *Hoogovens v High Authority* [1962] ECR 253 para. 5.

[235] See also Case 111/63 Lemmerz-Werke v High Authority [1965] ECR 677.

[236] Case C-90/95P *Henri de Compte v EP* [1997] ECR I-1999 para. 35.

[237] Retroactive revocation has been held unlawful only on two occasions; Cases 15/85 *Consorzio Cooperative d'Abruzzo v Commission.* [1987] ECR 1005 only; C-90/95P *Henri de Compte v EP* [1997] ECR I-1999.

matter. The concept of a legitimate expectation is discussed in detail in Chapter 4. For present purposes, the following comments will suffice. The question is whether a person in possession of the applicant's general knowledge and expertise could reasonably expect the decision to finalize the matter.[238] A legitimate expectation will more easily be accepted if it is difficult to spot that the decision was unlawful than if it violates specific statutory provisions or fundamental procedural or substantive principles.[239] Thus, when the Commission informed a private organization that it had been awarded a grant of four, rather than three, billion lire, the difference could not be recovered some two and a half years later. For while the Commission could have discovered its mistake in a matter of days, the recipient had no way of detecting it.[240] However, even if a person could reasonably expect a decision to be final, his conduct may reveal that he did not in fact hold such an expectation. If the person challenges the unlawful decision by judicial review, he can, in the Court's view, have no reasonable expectation whatsoever.[241] It follows that, as in French law, a decision may remain uncertain and subject to revocation for a considerable period of time if judicial review is sought.[242]

Second, if it is established that the person had a legitimate expectation, the institution must consider the affected person's interest in the decision. It is particularly important whether the affected person relied financially on it,[243] and only one case has ever been won in the absence of reliance.[244] However, financial reliance is neither necessary nor sufficient.[245] The real question is what consequences, in a wide sense, it would have if the decision were revoked. Thus, in the *Alpha Steel* case the Commission had revoked a quarterly production quota although seven weeks of the quarter had already lapsed.[246] The ECJ emphasized that although Alpha Steel had started production pursuant to the quota, it had used up only about 10 per cent of it when it was revoked. In other words, although the company had relied financially on the decision, it would still be able to adapt its production to the new decision.

[238] See the ECJ's reference to the concept of a prudent trader in Case 74/74 *CNTA v Commission* [1975] ECR 533. See further E. Sharpston, 'Legitimate Expectations and Economic Reality' (1990) ELR 103.

[239] See Case 112/77 *Töpfer v Commission* [1978] ECR 1019 and AG Lagrange citing German law for this view in the *Hoogovens* case, [1962] ECR 277.

[240] Case 15/85 *Consorzio Cooperative d'Abruzzo v Commission.* [1987] ECR 1005.

[241] Case 14/81 *Alpha Steel v Commission* [1982] ECR 749 para. 10.

[242] Reliable data about the average duration of actions before the Community judicature is not available, but in 1998 29 per cent (54 of 188) of all direct actions, excluding staff cases, before the CFI took over twenty-nine months to reach final judgment.

[243] See Lord Mackenzie Stuart, 'Legitimate Expectations and Estoppel in Community Law and English Administrative Law' (1983) LIEI 53, 60. Reliance was mentioned explicitly in Cases 42 and 49/59 *SNUPAT v High Authority* [1961] ECR 53; 14/81 *Alpha Steel v Commission* [1982] ECR 749; 15/85 *Consorzio Cooperative d'Abruzzo v Commission* [1987] ECR 1005.

[244] Case C-90/95P *Henri de Compte v EP* [1997] ECR I-1999.

[245] See Ragnemalm, above n. 56, 521.

[246] Case 14/81 *Alpha Steel v Commission* [1982] ECR 749.

Third, the importance, or weight, of the principle of legality must be taken into account. The more serious the illegality is, the more likely is it that the decision can be revoked. A decision which violates fundamental rights is more likely to be revocable than a decision which is procedurally flawed or based on an erroneous interpretation of an ambiguous legislative provision. In the *De Compte* case, the ECJ found that an award of compensation which was based on an erroneous interpretation of the concept of 'work-related' illness could not be revoked. This was, correctly it seems, considered a relatively minor legal error which did not justify revocation to the detriment of a person who had already suffered enough.[247]

Fourth, it must be taken into account how third parties will be affected if the unlawful decision is allowed to stand. For example, in *Hoogovens* the ECJ held that a metal scrap levy exemption could be revoked, *inter alia* because all other steel producers had paid the levy. To allow the exemption to stay in force would therefore have a distorting effect on competition.[248] However, the effect on third parties must be fairly direct to carry any weight in the balancing. *De Compte* is, again, an example in point.[249] Who would be harmed by the unlawful decision to grant Mr De Compte compensation for his (non)-work-related illness? Only the Community's finances; that is the total number of European taxpayers. There were no colleagues in comparable circumstances who might be directly 'harmed' or discriminated against as a result of the unlawful award.[250]

Finally, the time which has lapsed between the decision and its revocation must be taken into account. Retroactive revocation must always be carried out within a 'reasonable period'. The length of this period depends upon, notably, how difficult it was for the institution and the affected person to discover that the decision was unlawful, how soon the affected person was warned that the institution might revoke the decision, and the nature of the statutory scheme. These criteria are rarely spelled out explicitly by the ECJ and they may pull in different directions. Consequently, it is not possible to say precisely what is 'reasonable', although a few weeks will almost always be accepted.[251] A few examples will illustrate the Community judicature's approach.

In *Lemmerz-Werke* the ECJ accepted the Commission's decision to require full payment with retroactive effect of a levy, which it had failed to impose from 1956 to 1963. Advocate General Roemer explained that people cannot in general expect not to be subject to late claims in the field of tax regulations and that it had been difficult for the Commission to detect the illegality. Nevertheless, he found the delay too long to be reasonable. The Court disagreed but it did not

[247] Case C-90/95P *Henri de Compte v EP* [1997] ECR I-1999.

[248] Case 14/61 *Hoogovens v High Authority* [1962] ECR 253, 269–70.

[249] Case C-90/95P *Henri de Compte v EP* [1997] ECR I-1999.

[250] See also Case 15/85 *Consorzio Cooperative d'Abruzzo v Commission* [1987] ECR 1005.

[251] See Case T-336/94 *Efisol v Commission* [1996] ECR II-1343 para 34.

explain why.[252] This case, and other related cases, demonstrate that the delay can be very lengthy if all the criteria are in the institution's favour.[253] The ECJ has, however, taken a stricter attitude in some recent cases. In *Consorzio d'Abruzzo* a delay of two and a half years was considered unreasonable. In this instance all the criteria were in the applicant's favour: the Commission could easily have discovered the error, while the applicant could not, and there is no general presumption that financial grants are subject to revision in the same way as tax rulings. Similarly, in *De Compte* the Court found a delay of merely two months and twenty-five days unreasonable. These decisions show that the notion of 'reasonable delay' is inextricably linked with the balancing of legitimate expectations and legality. As explained above, the *De Compte* case involved strong interests in favour of the applicant, weak legality arguments, and no risk of harm to third parties. Consequently, to ensure an overall fair result the ECJ shortened the 'reasonable' period considerably.[254]

II Exceptions? Declaratory Pecuniary Decisions

The French principle of irrevocability is, as explained above, subject to the rule that pecuniary declaratory decisions may always be revoked. The ECJ suggested in *Hoogovens* that the EC law principle is subject to a similar exception. The Court held, considering the Commission's retroactive revocation of an exemption from payment of a metal scrap levy, that the principle of irrevocability 'is of less significance where [the decision is] purely declaratory' than where the revoked decision creates rights. In this case, 'the exemption granted to [Hoogovens] did not . . . create rights, as the High Authority has no power to grant derogation or exemptions . . . but power only to declare . . . the obligation to pay'.[255]

This statement, which is clearly unfortunate in terms of legal certainty and legitimate expectations, was never repeated by the Community courts. In subsequent decisions concerned with scrap levies, the Court avoided the terminology of declaratory decisions.[256] Moreover, in the recent *De Compte* case the ECJ reaffirmed that a decision to award compensation for work-related illness was a *favourable* measure which could not be revoked. It is significant that the Court made no mention of the notion of declaratory decisions, as the compensation was awarded on the basis of precise statutory provisions and might therefore be have been considered 'declaratory'.[257] It may be concluded that

[252] Case 111/63 *Lemmerz-Werke v High Authority* [1965] ECR 677.

[253] See also Cases 54/65 *Châtillon v High Authority* [1966] ECR 185; T-73/95 *Oliveira SA v Commission* [1997] ECR II-381.

[254] Compare Case C-248/89 *Cargill v Commission* [1991] ECR I-2987 para 22–3.

[255] Case 14/61 *Hoogovens v High Authority* [1962] ECR 253 para 6.

[256] This is significant in view of the fact that the AGs' opinions continued to use the terminology. Compare the judgment and AG Roemer's opinion in Case 111/63 *Lemmerz-Werke v High Authority* [1965] ECR 677.

[257] Case C-90/95P *Henri de Compte v EP* [1997] ECR I-1999. See also Case T-142/97 *Branco v Commission*, 15/8–98 para 103–7.

pecuniary declaratory decisions are today irrevocable to the same extent as other favourable decisions.[258]

6 Comparison and Suggestions for Reform

(A) Revocation of Lawful Decisions

It emerges from the comparative survey of English, French, and EC law that the conceptual differences between the three legal systems do not lead to radically different outcomes in relation to the revocation of *lawful* decisions. It is generally accepted that decisions must be favourable, communicated, and unconditional to benefit from the protection of the principle of irrevocability. It is also common ground in the three jurisdictions that decisions may be revoked on grounds of fraud and deception, consent from the affected person, and changes in material facts. Still, it has been seen that there is one very significant difference between English law and EC law.

The *scope* of the principle of irrevocability is narrower in English law than in French and, especially, EC law. In English law, the principle applies only to favourable decisions which 'declare' or 'affect rights'. Consequently, licences and other discretionary favourable decisions can be revoked prospectively in the light of an *intra vires* error of fact or a subsequent change in administrative policy. In French law, the principle of irrevocability is wider, and it applies also to discretionary benefits, but the administration still has wide-ranging powers to revoke licences prospectively under the notion of *autorisation de police*. By contrast, the ECJ has held that *all* favourable decisions are *prima facie* irrevocable. The Community administration does not have inherent power to revoke licences and other discretionary benefits.

It is submitted that the English courts should reconsider traditional case law in the light of EC law. It should be accepted that formal, communicated, unconditional and *favourable* decisions are as a matter of general principle irrevocable.[259] That is, the scope of the principle of irrevocability should depend upon the *effects* of decisions upon individuals rather than upon the nature of the power under which the decision was made. The principle of irrevocability should also be 'objective' in the sense that the affected person should not be required to show that he has a reasonable or legitimate expectation that a lawful decision is final or that he relied upon it. The courts ought also to delimit the existing exceptions to the principle of irrevocability more carefully. The administration should not, as a matter of principle, have the power to revoke

[258] Similarly Lauwaars, above n. 56, 311, 324; Letemendia, above n. 1, 46–50; Ragnemalm, above n. 56, 517. Compare Hartley, above n. 56, 436–8 and the contradictory statements in Schwarze 988–91, 1009.

[259] Similarly Fazal, above n. 16, 463–4; Cane, above n. 27, 228; Craig 633.

decisions on the grounds of *intra vires* errors of fact, even if caused by an innocent misrepresentation by the affected individual, or subsequent changes in administrative policy.[260]

Reform along these lines would promote legal certainty, and legitimate expectations, in the relation between the administration and the citizen. This would in turn, as explained in Chapter 1, promote fairness and good administration. It might, however, be objected that the administration's flexibility to take action in the public interest would be restricted too much by a reform along these lines. This objection is unconvincing for two reasons.

First, the fact that the administration's ability to act flexibly in the public interest is restricted is not, in and of itself, a compelling argument. Government in the public interest must, as explained in Chapter 1, be limited by, or balanced against, the requirements of fairness, legal certainty and good administration. The question is therefore not *if*, but *to what extent*, restrictions are justified.

Second, to accept that favourable decisions are *prima facie* irrevocable clearly does not take away all flexibility. There is no empirical evidence that the EC institutions' ability to take effective and flexible action has been hampered to any significant extent by the principle that all favourable decisions are *prima facie* irrevocable. Moreover, decisions which have a continuous temporal dimension, such as licences, may be granted for a fixed period of time and subject to specific conditions. This allows the administration some flexibility to change policy in a way which is foreseeable to the affected individuals. Specific statutory revocation provisions may also be adopted to enable the administration to revoke decision in areas where the legislative authority considers such a power necessary.

Revocation provisions should, however, be carefully drafted not to undermine the general principle of irrevocability and the underlying requirement of fairness and certainty in administration. Three types of considerations ought to guide the drafting of such provisions. First, the temporal dimension should be taken into account. A power to revoke lawful decisions retroactively should never, or only very exceptionally, be granted. The power to revoke prospectively decisions granted for a fixed period of time should also be more restricted than the power to revoke decisions granted for an indefinite period of time. This is so because individuals will typically expect that a definite decision will remain in force until its expiry date. Second, revocation provisions should prescribe the granting of a warning, some form of hearing and, if at all possible, a transitional period within which the affected person may adapt to a new situation. Third, the conditions in which decisions may be revoked should be described as precisely as possible to allow individuals to foresee when revocation may occur, and it should in every case be considered whether compensation should be

[260] Ibid.

made available for those who suffer the revocation of a favourable decision, such as a licence, in the wider public interest.[261]

(B) Revocation of Unlawful Decisions

There are, in relation to revocation of *unlawful* decisions, differences between English, French, and EC law at the level both of theory and practice. While English law grants the administration unlimited power to revoke (replace) unlawful decisions, only subject to the limited application of estoppel by representation, French law imposes a strict two-month time limit on revocation. In EC law, revocation is subject to an *ad hoc* balancing of individual and public interests under the principle of legitimate expectations.

These different legal principles reflect the fact that while the British courts perceive the principle of legality (*ultra vires*) as sacrosanct, French and EC courts have accepted that the principle of legality must be limited to protect individual fairness, legal certainty, and trust in the administration. English law has, in this respect, much to learn from French and EC law. It should be acknowledged that legality is not absolute, but rather an important *aspect of* the legal system, the consequences of which are subject to important countervailing considerations.

How, then, should legality be limited to provide fairness and certainty? The imposition of a fixed and strict time limit on revocation, as in France, clearly provides great certainty for individuals. However, it is arguably too mechanical and restricts administrative flexibility too much. A fixed time limit does not take into account that upholding a decision may, in some instances, have a very detrimental effect upon third parties and the wider public interest, and that some species of illegality are more difficult to accept than others. Indeed, it was explained above that the French courts have felt 'forced' to develop the notoriously difficult notion of declaratory pecuniary decisions to alleviate some of the consequences of the strict time limit.

The Community principle of revocation within a 'reasonable period', subject to protection of legitimate expectations, is a more desirable model. By imposing a duty upon the administration, subject to judicial review, to weigh individuals' legitimate expectations and reliance against the principle of legality, a fair balance can be struck on a case-by-case basis.[262] However, the suggestion that the individual and public interest should be balanced under a principle of legitimate expectations has met with a number of objections in Britain. Three of these objection deserve some attention at this juncture.

The first objection to 'Community style' balancing of legality and legitimate expectations is that such balancing would create more, rather than less, legal

[261] See Ch. 5.3.D.

[262] A balancing approach was first suggested by Craig, above n. 181.

uncertainty because the concept of legitimate expectations is vague. This objection was considered, and rejected, in Chapter 1.[263]

The second objection is that the principle of legality would be completely subverted if it were accepted that the administration may be bound by unlawful decisions or representations. For officials would, it is argued, make large numbers of unlawful decisions, deliberately or inadvertently, which would be binding upon them.[264] This objection is, on reflection, unconvincing for two sets of reasons.[265]

First, the classic image of officials as power-hungry, untrustworthy, or even corrupt, expounded by Montesquieu and adopted by many public law scholars and judges, is not in tune with the reality of modern British administration.[266] Officials do generally purport to make lawful representations and decisions. Quantitatively, the problem of unlawful action is therefore small. The possibility of legitimate expectations based on unlawful representations would not change that. There is no evidence that authorities in France and the EC deliberately make unlawful decisions to extend their powers through the principle of irrevocability.[267] Indeed, the possibility that an authority may be bound, on grounds of substantive legitimate expectations, is likely to *increase* the care taken in the making of representations and decisions.[268]

Second, the acknowledgement that unlawful decisions or representations can create legitimate expectations does not imply that expectations will always be upheld. The seriousness of the unlawfulness is part and parcel of the circumstances which must be balanced against the harm that would be caused to individuals by insisting rigidly on the principle of legality. A decision vitiated by a formal or procedural error, such as failure to use a written form or improper delegation, is therefore more likely to be upheld than a decision vitiated by a substantive error, such as an irrelevant consideration or plainly irrational reasoning.[269]

A third objection to the introduction into English law of a 'Community style' balancing principle is that this principle would not sit well with existing constitutional arrangements. According to the traditional Rule of Law theory, developed by Professor Dicey, Parliament is sovereign and the justification for judicial review of administrative action is that the courts enforce Parliament's

[263] See Ch. 1.2.C.I.

[264] *Minster of Agriculture and Fisheries v Hulkin*, unreported but cited in *Minister of Agriculture and Fisheries v Mathews* [1950] 1 KB 148. See similarly Wade 376; Cane, above n. 27, 227.

[265] See Craig 640–3.

[266] See D. J. Galligan, 'Judicial Review and the Textbook Writers' (1982) OJLS 257, 259–60.

[267] See also R. Berger, 'Estoppel Against the Government' (1954) Univ Chicago LR 680, 684; M. Braunstein, 'In Defense of Traditional Immunity—Toward an Economic Rationale for Not Estopping the Government' (1982) Rutgers LJ 1, 28; Craig 642. Compare E. Campbell, 'Agreements About the Exercise of Statutory Powers' (1971) ALJ 338.

[268] Though the extent of this increase is, of course, difficult to predict.

[269] See Bradley, above n. 16, 13; Cane, above n. 27, 227.

intentions. Adherence to this theory of sovereignty and *ultra vires* makes it nigh impossible to accept that the courts should *depart from* Parliament's intentions to achieve fair or just results by balancing legality and expectations.[270] This objection is, again, unconvincing for two reasons.

First, there is growing recognition that the British courts are not only, and should not only be, concerned with enforcing Parliamentary intent.[271] Standards of fair and good administration, and protection of rights *against* Parliamentary intent have become part of modern judicial review as the doctrines of Parliamentary sovereignty and *ultra vires* have, for good reasons, come under attack.[272]

Second, the need to balance legality against other considerations is *already* recognized in at least three areas of English administrative law. The courts have the power to limit the retroactive effect of judgments which hold administrative decisions unlawful by categorizing them as voidable rather than void;[273] to withhold discretionary remedies;[274] and to refuse judicial review if claims are not made within strict time limits.[275] In every case the full consequences of the principle of legality are limited to avoid otherwise unacceptable consequences for authorities and/or individuals. That is, legality is implicitly balanced against other considerations. The only real difference between this type of balancing and the balancing in legitimate expectations cases is that while time limits etc. work against the individual litigant, balancing of legitimate expectations and legality works to his advantage.[276]

There are, admittedly, other objections to the adoption in English law of a balancing principle to limit revocation of unlawful decisions. It will, for reasons which will become apparent, be more convenient to examine, and reject, these objections in the following chapter, which is concerned with substantive protection of legitimate expectations created by informal administrative representations.

[270] See Allison 183–5.

[271] *A-G of Hong Kong v Ng Yuen Shiu* [1983] 2 All ER 311, 350; *R v Lancashire CC, ex p Huddleston* [1986] 2 All ER 941, 945.

[272] See D. Oliver, 'Is the *Ultra Vires* Rule the Basis of Judicial Review?' (1987) PL 543; J. Laws, 'Law and Democracy' (1995) PL 72, 78–9; Lord Woolf, '*Droit Public*—English style' (1995) PL 57, 65–7; J. L. Jowell, 'Politics, Principle, and Judicial Review' (1997) CLP 189, 196–7; P. P. Craig, '*Ultra Vires* and the Foundations of Judicial Review' (1998) CLJ 63, 'Competing Models of Judicial Review' (1999) PL 428; T. R. S. Allan, 'Fairness, Equality, Rationality: Constitutional Theory and Judicial Review', in C. Forsyth and I. Hare (eds.), *The Golden Metwand and the Crooked Cord, Essays in Honour of Sir William Wade* (Oxford, 1998), 15. This is not to deny that the theory of *ultra vires* is convenient, or that it may serve a 'decorative' function. See C. F. Forsyth, 'Of Fig Leaves and Fairy Tales: The Ultra Vires Doctrine, the Sovereignty of Parliament and Judicial Review' (1996) CLJ 122; Allan, op cit. 20, 23.

[273] See Craig 660–70.

[274] e.g. *R v Secretary of State for Social Services, ex p AMA* [1993] COD 54. See Bingham LJ, 'Should Public Law Remedies be Discretionary?' (1991) PL 64.

[275] Supreme Court Act 1981, s 31(6); Order 53 r 4.

[276] See P. P. Craig, 'Substantive Legitimate Expectations and the Principles of Judicial Review', in M. Andenas (ed.), *English Public Law and the Common Law of Europe* (London, 1998), 23.

Chapter 4

Substantive Protection of Legitimate Expectations (II): Informal Administrative Representations

1 Introduction

It was seen in Chapter 3 that the administration's power to revoke its own decisions has been limited to promote fairness, legal certainty, and trust in government. People do not, however, rely only on formal administrative decisions. Informal representations such as advice given to citizens and circulars setting out administrative policy are also an important part of the information on the basis of which lives are planned and choices made.[1] In this chapter, the substantive principles of law which protect those who rely upon expectations created by such representations will be studied and evaluated.

The discussion will be structured as follows. First, the basic content of the relevant principles in English, French, and EC law will be set out. It will be seen that the three legal systems appear to differ markedly in their approach to administrative representations (section 2). Second, a more detailed account of the scope and practical application of these principles will be provided. It will become apparent that the marked conceptual differences between English, French, and EC law do not always lead to different outcomes in practice. The detailed analysis will look at expectations aroused by *lawful* individualized representations and assurances (section 3); by generalized policy representations from which the decision-maker departs in a particular instance (section 4); and by generalized representations which are changed with effect for all those affected (section 5). Third, the principles which apply to expectations created by *unlawful* representations will be described (section 6). Finally, some limited proposals for reform of English law will be presented (section 7).

[1] Representations take a variety of forms. For our purposes, representations may be defined as explicit or implicit administrative pronouncements of fact, law or intent which cannot be categorised as final decisions or determinations.

2 The Binding Effects of Administrative Representations: A Comparative Overview

(A) *English Law*

Whether, and in what circumstances, authorities can be held to informal representations is the subject of some confusion in English law because various principles, such as estoppel by representation,[2] *Wednesbury* unreasonableness,[3] legitimate expectations,[4] substantive fairness,[5] abuse of process,[6] and consistency[7] have been applied to similar fact-patterns.[8] To resolve this confusion, it is necessary first of all to set out the basic content of these principles.

[2] See generally on estoppel by representation in private law S. Wilken and T. Villiers, *Waiver, Variation and Estoppel* (Chichester, 1998), 103–99 and in public law Farrer, 'A Prerogative Fallacy—That the Crown is not Bound by Estoppel' (1933) LQR 511; G. Treitel, 'Crown Proceedings: Some Recent Developments' (1957) PL 321, 335–9; M. A. Fazal, 'Reliability of Official Acts and Advice' (1972) PL 43, 'Estoppel in English Administrative Law' (1994) Journal of the Indian Law Institute 455; P. P. Craig, 'Representations by Public Bodies' (1977) LQR 398; C. Crawford and T. Reid, 'Planning Officers' Advice and Undertakings: Estoppel and Personal Bar in Public Law' (1982) 3 Scottish Planning Law and Practice Occasional Papers; T. Nöcker and G. French, 'Estoppel: What's the Government's Word Worth? An Analysis of German Law, Common Law Jurisdictions, and of the Practice of International Arbitral Tribunals' (1990) The International Lawyer 409; Wade 371–8; and case notes by A. W. Bradley (1961) CLJ 139, (1971) CLJ 3; J. M. Evans (1971) MLR 335; C. Crawford (1982) MLR 87, (1990) MLR 814; P. Jackson (1983) LQR 499; H. W. Wilkinson (1990) NLJ 168.

[3] See generally Craig 581–5; J. L. Jowell and A. Lester, 'Beyond Wednesbury, Substantive Principles and Administrative Law' (1987) PL 368; P. Walker, 'What's Wrong With Irrationality?' (1995) PL 556.

[4] See generally R. Baldwin and D. Horne, 'Expectations in a Joyless Landscape' (1986) MLR 685; P. Elias, 'Legitimate Expectations and Judicial Review', in J. L. Jowell and D. Oliver (eds.), *New Directions in Judicial Review* (London, 1988); C. F. Forsyth, 'The Provenance and Protection of Legitimate Expectations' (1988) CLJ 238, 'Wednesbury Protection of Substantive Legitimate Expectations' (1997) PL 375; W. Hinds, 'Estopping the Taxman' (1991) BTR 191; P. P. Craig, 'Legitimate Expectations: A Conceptual Analysis' (1992) LQR 79, 'Substantive Legitimate Expectations in Domestic and European Law' (1996) CLJ 289, 'Substantive Legitimate Expectations and the Principles of Judicial Review', in M. Andenas (ed.), *English Public Law and the Common Law of Europe* (London, 1998), 23; R. Singh, 'Making Legitimate Use of Legitimate Expectations' (1994) NLJ 1215; De Smith 563–76; R. Singh and K. Steyn, 'Legitimate Expectations in 1996: Where Now' (1996) JR 17, 'Legitimate Expectation Update 1997' (1997) JR 33; Y. Dotan, 'Why Administrators should be Bound by their Policies' (1997) OJLS 23; K. Markus and M. Westgate, *Unilever* and *Hargreaves*: A Cross-Analysis (1997) JR 220. See also case notes by A. R. Mowbray (1985) PL 558, (1990) LQR 568; C. Lewis (1986) MLR 251; J. Woolf (1989) Tax J no 33, 4, (1994) Tax J no 254, 6; B. Schwehr and P. Brown (1991) PL 163; D. Sandler (1994) CLJ 273; G. Wignall (1994) NLJ 1038; G. Himsworth (1996) PL 46; R. J. F. Gordon and T. Ward (1996) NLJ 1663; T. R. S. Allan (1997) CLJ 246; S. Foster (1997) MLR 727.

[5] See M. Poole, 'Legitimate Expectations and Substantive Fairness: Beyond the Limits of Procedural Propriety' (1995) NZLR 426; N. Bamforth, 'Fairness and Legitimate Expectation in Judicial Review' (1997) CLJ 1.

[6] See J. F. Archbold *et al.*, *Criminal Pleading, Evidence and Practice* (London, 1998), 4.48.9–10.

[7] See K. Steyn, 'Consistency—A Principle of Public Law?' (1997) JR 22.

[8] *R v Devon CC, ex p Baker* [1995] 1 All ER 73, 89.

Estoppel is an ancient principle of English private law, which is applied in a wide variety of circumstances.[9] The particular aspect of the principle which is of interest here is known as estoppel by representation. This rule prevents one party from disputing the truth of a statement previously made to another if three conditions are met. First, the representor must make a clear and unequivocal but untrue statement of fact. Second, the statement must be communicated to the recipient (or a class of which he is a member) with the intention that it be relied on or knowledge that it is likely to be relied on. Third, the recipient, assuming reasonably that the statement is true, must rely upon it in a way which is not unreasonable, thereby suffering some financial detriment.

Lord Denning suggested in the *Robertson* case from 1949 that estoppel may apply to public authorities.[10] This would have the effect of preventing the administration from making a decision which differs from what it had represented, for example, to a land owner who had inquired about the need to obtain planning permission for a development. However, the House of Lords rejected this suggestion and it is now common ground that public authorities *are not* subject to estoppel by representation.[11] There are only two, strictly limited, exceptions to this rule which will be discussed further below.[12]

Following the rejection of estoppel in public law, Lord Denning turned his attention to the concept of legitimate expectations which had, since his judgment in the *Schmidt* case, begun to play an increasingly important role in the context of procedural fairness.[13] Lord Denning suggested that authorities may be bound by administrative representations and conduct, as doing otherwise would disappoint expectations and be an abuse of power. For example, in *HTV v Price Commission* he said that a public authority which had led traders to rely on one interpretation of a statutory provision could only adopt another interpretation if there was 'an overriding public interest' in doing so.[14]

These statements led some commentators to suggest that the principle of legitimate expectations could in certain circumstances give rise to substantive as well as procedural entitlements.[15] This suggestion created considerable debate.

[9] See Wilken and Villiers, above n. 2, 103–5.

[10] *Robertson v Minister of Pensions* [1949] 1 KB 227.

[11] *Howell v Falmouth Boat Construction Co* [1951] AC 837.

[12] See section 6 and Ch. 3.5.B.

[13] See Ch. 2.2.

[14] *HTV v Price Commission* [1976] ICR 170, 185. See also *R v Liverpool Corporation, ex p Liverpool Taxi Fleet Operators' Association* [1972] 2 QB 299; *Laker Airways v Department of Trade* [1977] QB 643, 707.

[15] See Baldwin and Horne, above n. 4, 706; Lewis, above n. 4, 252–3; Elias, above n. 4, 45–9; Forsyth (1988), above n. 4; De Smith 514–15, 575; Craig, above n. 4; Singh, above n. 4; Singh and Steyn, above n. 4; Allan, above n. 4, 247. Compare the more cautious statements in P. Cane, *An Introduction to Administrative Law*, 3rd edn. (Oxford, 1996), 144, 225–7.

Some judges[16] and commentators[17] rejected the idea of substantive protection of expectations for fear that it would lead the courts to review the merits of administrative decision-making, restrict (or 'fetter') the exercise of statutory powers, and undermine the principle of legality (*ultra vires*) by upholding expectations created by unlawful representations.[18] The tension between proponents and opponents of substantive protection of expectations is also evident in the case law. There are three issues which have divided the judiciary in this area.

The first issue is whether the concept of substantive legitimate expectations forms part of English administrative law at all.[19] This issue has now been resolved. There is eminent support in the case law, both implicitly and explicitly, for the proposition that substantive legitimate expectations is indeed part of English law.[20] Implicit support may be found in a number of decisions concerned with taxation, such as *Matrix Securities* and *Unilever*, which accepted that it may amount to an abuse of power to go back on a precise and unqualified representation because doing so is unfair.[21] Although these decisions are couched in terms of substantive fairness rather than legitimate expectations they do indeed lead to substantive enforcement of expectations created by administrative representations. The decisions only make sense once it is realised that the reason why the administration's actions were deemed unfair was that representations had created expectations which in turn affected individual planning and reliance.[22]

[16] *R v Secretary of State for the Environment, ex p Barratt* The Times 3/4–89; *R v Home Secretary, ex p Mowla* [1992] 1 WLR 70, 88; *Keung v Home Secretary* [1992] Imm AR 201; *R v Secretary of State for Transport, ex p Richmond upon Thame LBC* [1994] 1 WLR 74; *R v Panel on Take-overs and Mergers, ex p Fayed* [1992] BCC 524, 530.

[17] See G. L. Peiris, 'Wednesbury Unreasonableness: The Expanding Canvas' (1987) CLJ 53, 80; S. France, 'Legitimate Expectations in New Zealand' (1990) NZULR 123, 142; M. Purdue, 'The Scope for Fact-Finding in Judicial Review', in G. Hand and J. McBride (eds.), *Droit sans frontières: Essays in Honour of L. Neville Brown* (Birmingham, 1991), 193; R. Cranston, 'Reviewing Judicial Review', in G. Richardson and H. Genn (eds.), *Administrative Law and Government Action* (Oxford, 1994), 45, 57–8; Poole, above n. 5, 431–5; M. Beloff, 'Natural Justice and Fairness—the Audi Alterem Partem Rule', in M. Supperstone and J. Goudie (eds.), *Judicial Review*, 2nd edn. (London, 1997), 8.27; J. W. F. Allison, 'Transplantation and Cross-fertilisation', in J. Beatson and T. Tridimas (eds.), *New Directions in European Public Law* (Oxford, 1998), 175.

[18] For an assessment of these arguments, see section 7.

[19] The debate over this issue was not helped by the uncertainty about what is meant by a concept or principle being recognized in public law. For a helpful definition, see J. M. Woehrling, 'Le principe de confiance légitime dans la jurisprudence des tribunaux', *General Reports to the XV International Congress of Comparative Law* (University of Bristol, 1998), 3.

[20] This author surveyed some 950 decisions (reported on Lexis) referring to 'legitimate expectations'.

[21] *R v IRC, ex p Preston* [1985] AC 835; *R v IRC, ex p MFK Underwriting Agencies Ltd* [1990] 1 WLR 1545; *Matrix Securities Ltd v IRC* [1994] 1 WLR 334; *R v IRC, ex p Unilever* [1996] STC 681.

[22] A number of other decisions also proceeded on the assumption that substantive legitimate expectations claims might be upheld in appropriate circumstances, e.g. *R v Bristol City Magistrates' Court, ex p Willsman* [1991] RA 292; *R v Joint Committee on Higher Medical Training, ex p Goldstein* (1993) 11 BMLR 10; *R v Funding Agency for Schools, ex p Bromley LBC* [1996] COD 375; *Home Secretary v Abdi* [1996] Imm AR 148; *R v CEC, ex p Littlewoods Ltd* [1997] STC 317.

Explicit support for substantive protection of expectations is also considerable. In the *Kahn* case Parker LJ drew upon Lord Denning's earlier dicta and held that a public authority can only go back on reasonable expectations after granting a hearing and then only if 'the overriding public interest demands it'.[23] Other judgments have accepted that the distinction between procedural and substantive expectations is neither useful nor relevant,[24] and in *Ruddock* it was said that fairness may require more than procedural protection. Consequently, the applicant was entitled to expect that the police would comply with its own published policy on telephone tapping.[25] Relying on these precedents, the Court of Appeal recently confirmed the principle of substantive legitimate expectations in *Coughlan* holding that:

> [if] a lawful promise or practice has induced a legitimate expectation of a *benefit which is substantive*, not simply procedural, authority now establishes that the court will in a proper case decide whether to frustrate the expectation is so unfair that to take a new and different course will amount to an abuse of power.[26]

The recognition of substantive legitimate expectations as part of English law has direct implications for administrative decision-makers. It is incumbent upon administrators to ascertain whether their own promises, practices, and other representations have aroused objectively reasonable expectations in persons who will be affected by administrative decisions. If reasonable expectations are at stake, then those expectations are a mandatory consideration,[27] which must be taken into account, given a certain weight, and balanced against the public interest in a course of action which will disappoint them.[28] If this balancing tips

[23] *R v Home Secretary, ex p Kahn* [1984] 1 WLR 1337, 1344. See also *R v Home Secretary, ex p Oloniluyi* [1989] COD 275.

[24] *R v Secretary of State for Transport, ex p Richmond upon Thame LBC* [1994] 1 All ER 577, 595; *R v Ministry of Agriculture, Fisheries and Foods, ex p Hamble Fisheries* [1995] 2 All ER 714, 723.

[25] *R v Home Secretary, ex p Ruddock* [1987] 1 WLR 1482, 1487 (approved *obiter* in *Chundawadra v Immigration Appeal Tribunal* [1988] Imm AR 161). See also *R v IRC, ex p MFK Underwriting Agencies Ltd* [1990] 1 All ER 91, 107; *R v London Borough of Ealing, ex p Denny* (1994) 26 HLR 424; *R v Devon CC, ex p Baker* [1995] 1 All ER 73, 89–90; *R v Ministry of Agriculture, Fisheries and Foods, ex p Hamble Fisheries* [1995] 2 All ER 714, 724; *R v Gaming Board, ex p Kingsley* [1996] COD 241, 242. For Divisional Court decisions upholding substantive legitimate expectations, see *R v Brent LBC, ex p MacDonagh* [1990] COD 3; *R v Northamptonshire CC, ex p Commission for the New Towns* [1992] COD 123.

[26] *R v Devon Health Authority, ex p Coughlan* [1999] Lloyd's LR Medical 306, 322.

[27] The term 'mandatory consideration' is preferred to 'relevant consideration' to avoid confusion with the existing principle of relevancy according to which an interpretation of the statutory power itself will single out certain considerations as relevant. This principle is—as noted by D. Wright, 'Rethinking the Doctrine of Legitimate Expectations in Canadian Administrative Law (1997) Osgoode Hall LJ 139, 184—independent of the doctrine of legitimate expectations.

[28] *R v Beatrix Potter School, ex p Kanner* [1997] ELR 468; *R v DPP, ex p Burke* [1997] COD 169; *R v Shropshire CC, ex p Jones* (1997) 9 Admin LR 625; *R v The Bloody Sunday Inquiry, ex p B* The Times 5/4–99; *Devon Health Authority, ex p Coughlan* [1999] Lloyd's LR Medical 306. Similarly A. W. Bradley, 'Administrative Justice and the Binding Effect of Official Acts' (1981) CLP 1, 18; De Smith 575–6.

in favour of the individuals' expectations, they are deemed legitimate and must be respected by the decision-maker.

The second issue which has divided the judiciary is whether substantive legitimate expectations is a separate ground of judicial review differing conceptually from the traditional ground of *Wednesbury* unreasonableness or irrationality as it is now often called.[29] The traditional view has been that legitimate expectations is not conceptually distinct, but rather 'a head of *Wednesbury* unreasonableness'.[30] More recently, however, the Court of Appeal has held that it is 'not necessary to explain the modern doctrine of legitimate expectations in *Wednesbury* terms' since the traditional grounds of review are the major, but not the sole instances of how public power may be misused.[31]

The third issue concerns the role of the courts in reviewing the administration's balancing of expectations and countervailing policy considerations. The view which dominated the cases until recently was that the balancing is a matter for the administration rather than the courts. On this view, the courts will not check what weight is attached to the different considerations. They will only intervene if the administration has entirely ignored a reasonable expectation, or if there is a very serious imbalance, or lack of proportion, between the interests at stake.[32] In other words, the balancing is subject to the low intensity review which applies generally to discretionary decision-making in English law. This traditional position has been expressed in two ways. Some decisions, like *Preston*, held that the courts will interfere only if disappointing an expectation is so unfair that it amounts to an abuse of power[33] while others, like *Hargreaves,* have stated that the decision must be irrational, perverse, or *Wednesbury* unreasonable.[34] The use of different phraseologies is apt to cause confusion, but a survey of the case law suggests that the practical difference is negligible. Both lines of authority are, it is submitted, emanations of the basic requirement of fairness in relations between public authorities and private agents and both

[29] *CCSU v Minister for the Civil Service* [1985] AC 374, 410.

[30] *R v IRC, ex p Unilever* [1996] STC 681, 695. Similarly *R v Joint Committee on Higher Medical Training, ex p Goldstein* (1993) 11 BMLR 10; *R v Home Secretary, ex p Hargreaves* [1997] 1 WLR 906; *R v Beatrix Potter School, ex p Kanner* [1997] ELR 468.

[31] *Devon Health Authority, ex p Coughlan* [1999] Lloyd's LR Medical 306. See similarly *R v Home Secretary, ex p Urmaza* [1996] COD 479.

[32] On the relationship between the principles of proportionality and legitimate expectations, see section 7.B.I.

[33] e.g. *R v Home Secretary, ex p Kahn* [1984] 1 WLR 1337; *R v IRC, ex p Preston* [1985] AC 835; *R v West Glamorgan CC, ex p Gheissary* The Times 18/12–85; *R v Home Secretary, ex p Ruddock* [1987] 1 WLR 1482; *Matrix Securities Ltd v IRC* [1994] 1 WLR 334; *R v IRC, ex p Unilever* [1996] STC 681, 691; *R v CEC, ex p Kay* [1996] STC 1500; *R v DPP, ex p Burke* [1997] COD 169.

[34] *R v Home Secretary, ex p Hargreaves* [1997] 1 WLR 906, 924. Similarly *R v Secretary of State for Health, ex p US Tobacco International Inc* [1992] QB 353, 368–9; *R v Joint Committee on Higher Medical Training, ex p Goldstein* (1993) 11 BMLR 10; *R v Walsall MBC, ex p Yapp* [1994] ICR 528; *R v Secretary of State for Transport, ex p Richmond upon Thame LBC* [1994] 1 WLR 74, 94; *R v IRC, ex p Unilever* [1996] STC 681, 695; *R v Beatrix Potter School, ex p Kanner* [1997] ELR 468; *Boyle v Secretary of State for the Environment,* 31/3–99.

express the courts' traditional and cautious attitude to review of discretionary power. [35] A different view of the courts' role has recently emerged in the case law. In the recent and important case of *Coughlan* the Court of Appeal held that, when faced with a claim based on legitimate expectations,

> the courts will have the task of weighing the requirements of fairness against any overriding interest relied upon [by the public authority] for the change of policy and that it is for the court to determine whether there is a sufficient overriding interests to justify a departure from what has previously been promised.

This approach draws upon Sedley J's judgment in *Hamble Fisheries*, where he said that the court should intervene if the expectation 'has a legitimacy which in fairness outtops the policy choice'.[36] The *Hamble* approach was rejected as 'heresy' and 'wrong in principle' by the Court of Appeal in *Hargreaves,*[37] but that case was distinguished in *Coughlan* on the grounds that while *Hargreaves* concerned expectations based on a general policy which was subsequently changed,[38] *Coughlan* concerned a specific representation addressed to a limited class of persons.[39]

There is an important difference of principle between the deferential *Wednesbury* approach applied in cases like *Hargreaves* and the more intensive fairness based standard of review applied in *Coughlan.* Still, this difference may be reduced in some instances because the actual application of the traditional *Wednesbury* test will be intensified where, in addition to affecting a reasonable expectation, the decision affects human rights as enshrined in the common law or the ECHR.[40]

On the basis of these authorities, one may conclude that the principle of substantive legitimate expectations is now well established in English law.[41] However, the precise relationship between legitimate expectations and other grounds of review, and the intensity of judicial scrutiny, remain highly contentious issues. Clarification from the House of Lords is urgently needed, and suggestions as to how the matter should be dealt with will be considered below.[42]

[35] Indeed, substantive fairness and *Wednesbury* unreasonableness were treated as interchangeable in *R v Home Secretary, ex p Hargreaves* [1997] 1 WLR 906.

[36] *R v Ministry of Agriculture, Fisheries and Foods, ex p Hamble Fisheries* [1995] 2 All ER 714, 731 also cited with approval in *R v Gaming Board, ex p Kingsley* [1996] COD 241, 242.

[37] *R v Home Secretary, ex p Hargreaves* [1997] 1 WLR 906, 921.

[38] This is what was called 'Situation 4' in Ch. 1 of this book. See further section 5.

[39] This is what was called 'Situation 2' in Ch. 1 of this book. See further section 3. It was also said that *Hargreaves* is confined to the context of prison policy, see [1999] Lloyds LR Medical 326.

[40] e.g. *R v Ministry of Defence, ex p Smith* [1996] QB 517, 554; *R v Home Secretary, ex p Turgut* The Times 15/2–2000. See M. Beloff and H. Mountfield, 'Unconventional behaviour? Judicial Uses of the Convention in England and Wales' (1996) EHRLR 5; F. Klug and F. Starmer, 'Incorporation through the Back Door?' (1997) PL 223, 228–32; Lord Woolf, 'Judicial Review—The Tensions Between the Executive and the Judiciary' (1998) LQR 579, 590–1.

[41] *R v Shropshire CC, ex p Jones* (1997) 9 Admin LR 625, 633.

[42] See section 7.A.

It may be added that substantive protection of expectations is not only available through the doctrine of legitimate expectations. The doctrine of abuse of process leads to similar results.[43] A criminal prosecution may be rejected as an abuse of the courts' process if it is clearly unfair to proceed with it.[44] This may be due to unjustifiable delay or, more importantly for our purposes, because the police or the prosecution service had informed the accused that he would not be prosecuted. Expectations created by such information must, together with the public interest in upholding the integrity of the criminal justice system, be balanced against the public interest in seeing detected crimes prosecuted.[45] As the liberty of the accused is at stake, this balancing is subject to more intensive judicial scrutiny than ordinary *Wednesbury* unreasonableness. 'Weighing countervailing considerations of policy and justice, it is *for the judge to decide* whether there has been an abuse of process.'[46] Thus, in *Dean* the prosecution of a young offender was struck out as abusive because he had been treated as a witness by the police for five weeks and, after being assured that he would not be prosecuted, granted considerable assistance to the police.[47]

(B) French Law

French public law draws a rigid distinction between administrative decisions and more informal representations. Decisions are considered legal acts (*actes administratifs*) which are binding and, subject to the principle of *intangibilité*, irrevocable.[48] Representations are considered 'legally relevant facts' (*faits juridiques*). This means that while the administration may be under an obligation to compensate loss caused by reliance upon informal representations, it is not obliged to act in accordance with what it has represented.[49]

The reasoning behind this distinction is, interestingly, very similar to the arguments presented by opponents of substantive protection of legitimate expectations in English law. In the leading case of *Compagnie franco-algérienne*, *Commissaire de Gouvernement* Romieu argued that the administration should never be bound by informal representations because this would restrict its exercise of discretionary powers and undermine the principle of legality as, by mak-

[43] See footnote 6.

[44] *R v Croydon Justices, ex p Dean* [1993] QB 769, 777 (approved in *R v Horseferry Road Magistrates' Court, ex p Bennett* [1994] Cr App R 114, 124); *R v Bloomfield* [1997] 1 Cr App Rep 135; *R v Bretscher and Townsend* [1997] 2 Cr App Rep 540; *R v Liverpool Stipendiary Magistrate, ex p Slade* [1998] 1 WLR 531. Compare *Doyle v Leroux* [1981] RTR 438.

[45] *R v Latif* [1996] 1 All ER 353, 361.

[46] Ibid. 360 (emphasis added).

[47] Ibid. Compare *R v Horseferry Road Magistrates' Court, ex p DPP* [1999] COD 441.

[48] See Ch. 3.2.B.

[49] See J.-M. André, 'La responsabilité de la puissance publique du fait des diverses formes d'engagements non contractuels de l'administration', AJDA 1976, 20; L. Tallineau, 'Les tolérances administratives', AJDA 1978, 3, and Ch. 6 of this book.

ing representations, public authorities could do what they could not otherwise lawfully have done by a formal decision.[50]

The French courts have applied this reasoning in various contexts, such as land planning,[51] licensing,[52] education,[53] social welfare,[54] and public employment.[55] For example, in *Bouveret* the applicant had, following a job competition, been offered a position by a letter signed by the mayor of a French town and he had resigned from a position elsewhere. When the mayor subsequently refused to confirm the appointment, the CE held the local authority liable in damages. However, it found that the applicant could not demand to be employed, nor could he challenge the employment of another person.[56]

The principle that administrative authorities are not bound by informal representations is not modified by notions of estoppel, legitimate expectations, or abuse of process. The only principle which, in certain circumstances, has the effect is that of equal treatment (*égalité de traitement*).[57] Although French private law contains principles of ostensible authority and good faith (*apparance* and *bonne foi*),[58] the administrative courts never applied these principles, directly or by analogy, to informal administrative representations.[59] The CE has not accepted a principle or concept of 'legitimate expectations' as part of French law either.[60] The *Tribunal Administratif* of Strasbourg applied a principle of legitimate expectations (*confiance légitime*) in an innovative judgment from 1994 as the basis of administrative no-fault liability,[61] but this decision was overturned on appeal.[62] Applicants have subsequently sought to invoke legitimate expectations in a number of cases before the French administrative courts,

[50] Romieu *conclusions* CE 20/1–1899 *Compagnie franco-algérienne* D 1899 III 41; confirmed by Teissier *conclusions* CE 15/5–07 *Le Bigot* Rec 460.

[51] CE 27/2–63 *Société Paramount* Rec 689; CE 26/10–73 *SCI Résidence Arcole* Rec 601; CE 16/3–77 *SA de construction* Rec 958; CAA Paris 13/6–89 *Commune de Bois d'Arcy* Rec 318.

[52] CE 11/5–56 *Société Lesieur-Afrique* Rec 184; TA Paris 24/5–60 *Etablissement Millo-Frolich* AJDA 1961, 218; CE 17/12–86 *Syndicat de l'Armagnac* no 76.115.

[53] CE 27/1–88 *Cadoret* no 64.941.

[54] CE 6/5–66 *Feutren* no 65.301; CE 27/5–88 *Brenac* no 90.896.

[55] CE 18/10–57 *Bouveret* Rec 542. See similarly CE 1/12–72 *Texierp* Rec 1222; CE 29/12–95 *Hurey* no 122.188.

[56] Ibid.

[57] See section 4 and G. Pélissier, *Le principe d'égalité en droit public* (Paris, 1996); N. Belloubet-Frier, 'Le principe d'égalité', AJDA 1998 Ed. spéciale, 152.

[58] See J.-M. Auby, *L'inexistence des actes administratifs: étude de contentieux administratifs* (Paris, 1951) 234–9; V. Jouve, 'Recherches sur la notion d'apparence en droit administratif français', RDP 1968, 283, 285–9.

[59] The public law doctrine of *fonctionnaire de fait* draws upon these concepts, but it is only applied to formal decisions. See Ch. 3.5.C.I.

[60] The EC law principle of legitimate expectations has been mentioned briefly, but never applied in favour of an applicant, in cases concerning French administrative measures which implement EC legislation. See e.g. CE 19/6–92 *FDSEA des Côtes-du-Nord* Rec 783; CE 30/11–94 *SCI Résidence Dauphine* RJF 1995 no 132; CAA Bordeaux 15/6–97 *ONIL* no 94BX01801 CE 30/11–99 *SA Chagnaud* AJDA 1999, 96.

[61] TA Strasbourg 8/12–94 *Freymuth* AJDA 1995, 555. See M. Heers, 'La sécurité juridique en droit administratif français: Vers une consécration du principe de confiance légitime?', RFDA 1995, 963.

[62] CAA Nancy 17/6–99 *Freymuth* AJDA 1999, 950.

but they have all been decided on the basis of traditional case law,[63] and the CE recently confirmed in *Rouquette* that if the decision or legal provision, which the applicant has challenged

> is not implementing provisions of European Community law, the applicant's claim that the CE should overrule this provisions [or decision] on the grounds that it is contrary to the principle of legitimate expectations has no validity.[64]

Finally, there is no French equivalent to the English principle of abuse of the criminal court's process.[65] The French prosecution service (*Procureur de la République)* decides on information laid by the police whether to prosecute and it informs the suspect of its decision.[66] Such a decision may, just as more informal assurances, be revoked at the discretion of the prosecution service, which need not give reasons or point to new facts.[67]

Why has the CE, against the advice of influential French commentators,[68] refused to embrace the principle of legitimate expectations? Regrettably, the court's terse judgments do not give the answer to this question, but it is submitted that four considerations are in play. First, it is deeply embedded in the tradition of French administrative law that the administration must be granted sufficient freedom from legal constraints to be able to act effectively in the public interest and that it has certain prerogatives, such as the inherent power to take measures designed to uphold *l'ordre public*, which it is incumbent on the courts to protect in the same way as they protect the rights of individuals.[69] Within this tradition, the principle of legitimate expectations might appear problematic because it restricts the administration's freedom to develop policy to some extent.[70]

Second, it has been noted that French public lawyers prefer to resolve issues of fairness by legal principles or statutory rules which are, or appear to be, clear and objectively defined. Thus, as seen above in Chapter 3, the CE laid down a

[63] CE 16/3–96 *Association des élèves* DA 1998 no 11; CE 30/12–96 *Brockly* Rec 526; CE 17/10–97 *Doujon* DA 1998 no 19; TA Paris 14/10–97 *Société Batignolle* DA 1998 no 118.

[64] CE 5/3–99 *Rouquette* RFDA 1999, 370. The Conseil Constitutionnel has also ruled that the principle of legitimate expectations is not part of the French constitution, see CC 30/12–96, no 96–385, *Receuil* CC 141; CC 7/11–97, no 97–391, *JO* 11/11–97, 16390.

[65] See *JC* Procédure Pénale, Art 31–44, no 278–304.

[66] Art 40, *Code de procédure pénale.*

[67] Cass Crim 6/6–52 Bull Crim no 142; Cass Crim 5/12–72 Bull Crim no 375. The power to revoke a prosecution decision is, however, subject to a time limit.

[68] See G. Le Chatelier, 'Les Incidences du droit communautaire sur le droit du contentieux administratif', AJDA 1996 Ed. spéciale, 97; M. Fromont, 'Le Principe de sécurité juridique', AJDA 1996 Ed. spéciale, 178; P. Delvolvé, *Droit public économique* (Paris, 1998) no 170; J.-M. Woehrling, 'Le Principe de confiance légitime dans la jurisprudence des tribunaux', *General Reports to the XV International Congress of Comparative Law* (University of Bristol, 1998); E. Fatôme, 'Audaces et prudences en matière de responsabilité de la puissance publique', AJDA 1999 Ed. spéciale, 94.

[69] See Brown and Bell 221–2 and Ch. 2 at footnote 74.

[70] See Fatôme, above n. 73, 95. For criticism of this 'fettering of policy' argument, see section 7.B.I.

fixed time limit of two months for the revocation of unlawful decisions rather than a flexible period based on what is 'reasonable' or 'fair' in the circumstances. That fixed time limit enhances predictability and ease of application at the cost of flexibility and fairness in some cases. And as seen in Chapter 2, the CE defined the scope of the principle of *droits de la défense* by reference to the dichotomy between administrative 'sanctions' and *mesures d'ordre public* rather than by asking what is, in each instance, required by procedural fairness. In the light of this preference for clarity and objectivity, the CE appears to consider that the notion of legitimate expectations is too imprecise and, therefore, incompatible with the conceptual structure of French administrative law.[71]

The third reason why, it is submitted, the CE has declined the invitation to adopt a principle of legitimate expectations is that French law needs such a principle less than English and EC law. On the one hand, there are—as will be seen below—a number of statutory provisions, notably in the areas of taxation and planning, which resolve some of issues dealt with by the principle of substantive legitimate expectations in English and EC law. On the other hand, the French principles of administrative liability are, as will be shown in Chapters 5 and 6, more generous than the equivalent principles of English law. Individuals who suffer loss by reliance on administrative decisions and conduct are more likely to be compensated, and the need for a principle designed to protect legitimate expectations substantively is therefore less pertinent.[72]

Finally, the CE's stance may reflect its pride in the existing principles of *droit administratif*, which are the product of its own creative jurisprudence. The CE may be seeking actively to maintain the central aspects of that body of law intact despite increasing pressure, in a number of other areas, from the law of ECHR and the European Communities.

(C) EC Law

The EC law approach to administrative representations is conceptually simpler than English law. The ECJ holds the Community institutions to their representations by a well-established principle of legitimate expectations,[73] which is

[71] See J.-P. Puissochet, '"Vous avez dit confiance légitime?"', in *Mélanges Guy Braibant* (Paris, 1996), 581; Fatôme, above n. 73, 94; P. Vincent, 'Chronique de jurisprudence', AJDA 1999, 880, 882. For criticism of this vagueness argument, see Ch. 1.2.C.I.

[72] See P. Vincent, above n. 71, 880, 882. The generosity of the French principles of administrative liability is however not unlimited and, as the *Freymuth* case illustrates, they do not cover all the situations which might be caught by the EC law principle of legitimate expectations.

[73] See generally Mackenzie Stuart, 'Legitimate Expectations and Estoppel in Community Law and English Administrative Law' (1983) LIEI 53; F. Hubeau, 'Le principe de la protection de la confiance légitime dans la jurisprudence de la Cour de Justice des Communautés Européennes', CDE 1983, 143; E. Sharpston, 'Legitimate Expectations and Economic Reality' (1990) ELR 103; Schwarze 1079–93; C. Naômé, 'La notion de sécurité juridique dans la jurisprudence de la Cour de Justice et du Tribunal de Première Instance des Communautés Européennes', RDPE 1993, 223; M.-H. Planchon, 'Le principe de la confiance légitime devant la Cour de Justice des Communatés

supplemented by a principle of equal treatment.[74] The expectations principle, which was drawn predominantly from German law,[75] developed initially in cases concerning revocation of administrative decisions.[76] It was applied for the first time to a situation where an institution went back upon an informal 'statement', rather than a formal decision, in the *Châtillon* case from 1966. On this occasion the ECJ ruled that the High Authority could depart from its initial statement 'subject to the protection of legitimate expectations'.[77] In the *Staff Salaries* case, the ECJ confirmed that an undertaking by the Council to apply for three years a particular system of adjusting the salaries of Community staff was 'in the absence of circumstances sufficient to justify the abandonment . . . of the system [binding upon the Council by virtue of the] rule of protection of the confidence the staff could have that the authorities would respect undertaking.[78] The ECJ subsequently held that breach of legitimate expectations can be a ground for annulment under Art 230 EC,[79] that the principle is binding upon all the Community institutions, and that it may benefit 'any individual who is in a situation in which it is apparent that the Community administration has led him to entertain reasonable expectations.'[80]

The content of the expectations principle can, as its English equivalent, be broken down into three propositions. First, it is incumbent upon the Community administration to ascertain whether its own representations have created objectively *reasonable* expectations in persons who will be affected by a decision. To do so, the administration must consider, in particular, the nature of the representation, those persons' knowledge, and the regulatory context. Second, if reasonable expectations have been created, the administration must *balance* the policy reasons in favour of departing from the representation against the harm which will be caused to the person by doing so. If this balance is in favour of the individual interest, the expectation is *legitimate* and must be respected by the administration.[81] Third, the duty to take into account expectations and balance them against the public interest is subject to review by the Community courts. However, the Community courts have never stated explicitly how *intensive* this review is. It is therefore not immediately clear whether the courts will substitute

Européennes', Revue de la Recherche Juridique—Droit Prospectif 1994, 447; Craig, above n. 4; J.-P. Puissochet, above n. 71, 581; T. Tridimas, *The General Principles of EC Law* (Oxford, 1999), 169–201.

[74] See generally H. G. Schermers and D. Waelbroeck, *Judicial Protection in the EC*, 5th edn. (Deventer, 1992), 69–76.

[75] See J. Usher, 'The Influence of National Concepts on Decisions of the European Court' (1976) ELR 359; G. Nolte, 'General Principles of German and European Administrative Law—A Comparison in a Historical Perspective' (1994) MLR191.

[76] See Ch. 3.2.C.

[77] Case 54/65 *Châtillon v High Authority* [1966] ECR 185, 196.

[78] Case 81/72 *Commission v Council* [1973] ECR 575, 584–5. The term 'expectations' has been preferred to 'confidence' in the translation of later case law. See AG Warner [1973] ECR 729–30.

[79] Case 112/77 *Töpfer v Commission* [1978] ECR 1019.

[80] Cases 289/81 *Mavridis v EP* [1983] ECR 1731; T-534/93 *Grynberg v Commission* [1994] ECR-SC II-595 para 51.

[81] e.g. Case 81/72 *Commission v Council* [1973] ECR 575, 585.

their judgment for that of the administration or whether they will only intervene if there is significant, serious, or even extreme imbalance between the public and private interests at stake. As will become apparent, the Community courts do *not* substitute judgment in legitimate expectations cases, and claims based on legitimate expectations are very rarely upheld in practice.[82]

3 Departure from Individualized Representations (Situation 2)

A public authority which makes a representation concerning the situation of one individual or a specific group is normally entitled to go back on it and make a decision which differs from what it initially represented. This is the starting point both in English, French, and EC law. In English and EC law, the authority may however be bound by its representation if it has aroused a reasonable expectation (A), which it would be unfair to disappoint (B).[83] In French law, statutory provisions impose a duty upon planning and tax authorities to respect certain individualized representations (C).

(A) Reasonable Expectations in English and EC Law: A Narrow Concept

The administration is only bound by a statement if it has thereby created a *reasonable* expectation of a certain outcome. This is an objective test. In English law, the question is what an ordinary[84] or reasonable[85] person would expect in all the circumstances. The Community courts refer to what a prudent, diligent, or *bonus pater familias* person would expect.[86] In practice, these formulations do not lead to different outcomes as both the English and the Community courts' take a strict view of what people can reasonably expect of public authorities.[87] Two sets of conditions must in both jurisdictions be fulfilled for a reasonable expectation to arise. These conditions relate to the nature of the representation (I) and the recipient's situation (II).

[82] In a total of over 750 cases referring to 'legitimate expectations', sixteen claims have been upheld (of which eleven were separate instances).

[83] The English principles of estoppel by representation and abuse of process are only considered briefly in the following due to their limited scope. See further on estoppel Ch. 3.5.B.

[84] *R v Home Secretary, ex p Hargreaves* [1997] 1 WLR 906, 922.

[85] *R v CEC, ex p Kay* [1996] STC 1500, 1527; *R v Home Secretary, ex p Behluli* [1998] COD 328, 329.

[86] Cases 78/77 *Lührs v Hauptzollamt Hamburg-Jonas* [1978] ECR 169 para 6; 265/85 *Van den Bergh en Jurgens v Commission* [1987] ECR 1155 para 44; AG Van Gerven [1994] ECR I-5757 para 11. See also Sharpston, above n. 73, 156, 158–9.

[87] See Planchon, above n. 73, 495; Puissochet, above n. 71, 593; R.-C. Papadopoulou, *Principes généraux du droit et droit Communautaire* (Brussels, 1996), 233, 236–7.

I The Nature of the Representation

Reasonable expectations only arise, in English law, if the administration made a representation which was 'clear, unambiguous, and devoid of relevant qualification'.[88] In EC law, the administration must have made a 'precise and specific assurance'.[89] A survey of the case law reveals that these two tests are applied in much the same way in practice. The form, wording, and statutory context in which the representation was made are all relevant criteria in this respect.[90]

There are no strict rules as to *form*. Expectations may, in both English and EC law, be supported by almost all forms of explicit representations. For example, letters,[91] faxes,[92] and 'agreements';[93] circulars,[94] reports,[95] 'communications',[96] and 'codes of conduct'[97] setting out existing policy; white papers and other documents indicating future policy;[98] administrative statements made by a minister in Parliament or by a Community institution in the EP (in so far as they are sufficiently clear);[99] and probably even general informative material like a 'Taxpayers' Charter'.[100] However, the Community institutions and the English government cannot, as a general rule, be expected to implement a legislative proposal in the form in which it was initially published.[101] Similarly, the Community institutions cannot be expected to comply with a resolution adopted by the EP or to adopt measures for which money has been set aside

[88] *R v IRC, ex p MFK Underwriting Agencies Ltd* [1990] 1 WLR 1545, 1569; *R v Home Secretary, ex p Hargreaves* [1997] 1 WLR 906, 922; *R v IRC, ex p Unilever* [1996] STC 681, 693; *R v Newport CBC, ex p Avery* [1999] JPL 452, 453.

[89] Cases T-123/89 *Chomel v Commission* [1990] ECR II-131 para 26; T-465/93 *Murgia Messapica v Commission* [1994] ECR II-361 para 67; T-571/93 *Lefebvre v Commission* [1995] ECR II-2379 para 72–74; T-521/93 *Atlanta v Council* [1996] ECR II-1707 para 57.

[90] The importance of the statutory context may be greater in English law than in EC law. See *R v Home Secretary, ex p Behluli* [1998] COD 328, 329; *R v Devon Health Authority, ex p Coughlan* [1999] Lloyd's LR Medical 306, 322, 326.

[91] *R v Home Secretary, ex p Kahn* [1984] 1 WLR 1337; *Matrix Securities Ltd v IRC* [1994] 1 WLR 334; *R v Devon Health Authority, ex p Coughlan* [1999] Lloyd's LR Medical 306; Cases 144/82 *Detti v ECJ* [1983] ECR 2439; T-587/93 *Ortega Urretavizcaya v Commission* [1996] ECR-SC IA-349/II-1027.

[92] Cases T-46/98 and T-151/98 *CEMR v Commission,* 3/2–2000 para 79–80.

[93] *R v CEC, ex p Kay* [1996] STC 1500.

[94] *R v Home Secretary, ex p Ruddock* [1987] 1 WLR 1482.

[95] *R v Panel on Take-overs and Mergers, ex p Fayed* [1992] BCC 524; Case 265/85 *Van den Bergh en Jurgens v Commission* [1987] ECR 1155.

[96] Case T-7/89 *Hercules Chemicals v Commission* [1991] ECR II-1711.

[97] Cases 310/85 *Deufil v Commission* [1987] ECR 901; C-313/90 *CIRFS v Commission* [1993] ECR I-1125 para 32–52; C-400/92 *Germany v Commission* [1994] ECR I-4701 para 27–29.

[98] *R v Secretary of State for Transport, ex p Richmond upon Thame LBC* [1996] 1 WLR 1460.

[99] *R v Home Secretary, ex p Hammersmith and Fulham LBC* [1991] 1 AC 521; *R v Home Secretary, ex p Batemann* The Times 1/7–94; *Samir v Home Secretary* [1993] Imm AR 551; *Musah v Home Secretary* [1995] Imm AR 236. Cases 424–425/85 *Frico v VIV* [1987] ECR 2755 para 32–33; T-229/94 *Deutsche Bahn v Commission* [1997] ECR II-1689. Compare *R v DPP, ex p Kebilene* The Times 31/3–99 (noting that such statements are often very general).

[100] *R v IRC, ex p Mead* [1993] 1 All ER 772.

[101] *R v Secretary of State for the Environment, ex p NALGO* (1993) 5 Admin LR 785; Cases C-13–16/92 *Driessen v Minister van Verkeer* [1993] ECR I-4751 para 31–34.

on the Community budget.[102] The status of other 'soft-law' measures,[103] such as interpretative Council declarations[104] and recommendations,[105] inter-institutional agreements, and resolutions adopted by other institutions than the EP is less clear. While the ECJ has held that Council resolutions are not legally binding in and of themselves,[106] it is not unlikely that the Court will give these measures some 'legal bite' by applying to them the doctrine of legitimate expectation. Finally, individuals cannot as a matter of English law have a reasonable expectation that administrative discretion will be exercised in accordance with a ratified, but unincorporated, international agreement.[107]

Oral statements generally carry less weight than written statements.[108] They are difficult to prove,[109] and often considered unlawful because the representing officer was not properly delegated the power to decide on the matter.[110] Expectations created by very precise oral assurances have, nonetheless, been upheld as legitimate in a few important cases.[111]

Conduct, such as the consistent and prolonged treatment of a person in a particular way, can create a reasonable expectation that the treatment will be continued until further notice.[112] Thus, in the important case of *Unilever* the Court of Appeal held that the Inland Revenue could not, without prior warning, discontinue a practice, consistently applied for about twenty-five years, of accepting annual tax refund claims after the expiry of a statutory time limit.

[102] Cases 87 and130/77, 22/83 and 9–10/84 *Salerno v Commission* [1985] ECR 2523 para 59.

[103] For recent discussion of 'soft' EC law, see F. Beveridge and S. Nott, 'A Hard Look at Soft Law', in P. P. Craig and C. Harlow (eds.), *Lawmaking in the European Union* (The Hague, 1998), 285.

[104] Compare Cases 143/83 *Commission v Denmark* [1985] ECR 427, 436 (unilateral declaration by minority of the Members States); C-292/89 *R v IAT, ex p Antonissen* [1991] ECR I-745, 778 (joint majority of Council and Commission declaration).

[105] See Case C-322/88 *Grimaldi v Fonds des maladies professionnelles* [1989] ECR 4407.

[106] Case C-4/96 *NIFPO v Department of Agriculture for Northern Ireland* [1998] ECR I-681 para 31. See also Cases 9/73 *Schlüter v Hauptzollamt Lörrach* [1973] ECR 1135, 1160; 59/75 *Mangera* [1976] ECR 91, 102; Schermers and Waelbroeck, above n. 74, 305–6. Compare G. Wellens and G. Borchardt, 'Soft Law in European Community Law' (1989) ELR 267, 312; J. Klabbers, 'Informal Instruments before the European Court of Justice' (1994) CMLRev 997, 1005–8.

[107] *Chundawadra v Immigration Appeal Tribunal* [1988] Imm AR 161; *R v Home Secretary, ex p Brind* [1991] 1 AC 696; *R v DPP, ex p Kebilene* The Times 31/3–99. See also *Thomas v Baptiste* The Times 23/3–99, but compare *R v Home Secretary, ex p Ahmed* [1998] INLR 570 (citing with approval *Minister for Education and Ethnic Affairs v Teoh* (1995) 128 ALR 353). See for discussion M. Hunt, *Using Human Rights Law in English Courts* (Oxford, 1997), 242–59.

[108] AG Van Gerven [1990] ECR I-3847 para 16.

[109] e.g. *Kuku v Home Secretary* [1990] Imm AR 27; *R v Shropshire CC, ex p Jones* (1997) 9 Admin LR 625; *R v Newport CBC, ex p Avery* [1999] JPL 452; Cases T-163/89 *Sebastiani v EP* [1991] ECR II-715 para 36–37; T-18/90 *Jongen v Commission* [1991] ECR II-187 para 35–36; T-30/90 *Zoder v EP* [1991] ECR II-207 para 25; T-22/92 *Weißenfels v EP* [1993] ECR II-1095 para 92.

[110] See section 6.

[111] Cases T-66/96 and 221/97 *Mellett v ECJ* [1998] ECR-SC II-1305; *R v Home Secretary, ex p Oloniluyi* [1989] COD 275; *Lewis v DPP* [1998] COD 98. See text at footnote 126. For *procedural* legitimate expectations based on oral assurances, see *A-G of Hong Kong v Ng Yuen Shiu* [1983] 2 AC 629.

[112] This is different from where a *general* policy is adopted and subsequently changed, see section 4.

Although the Revenue had neither followed any deliberate general policy, nor made an explicitly clear and unambiguous representation, its sudden change of conduct was an unfair and unreasonable breach of the applicant's reasonable expectations.[113] Consistent treatment of an individual is, and should be, distinguished from favourable treatment on one or a few occasions. For example, in *Efisol* the CFI held that a company which was awarded a 'quota' for the importation of certain chemicals suspected of depleting the ozone layer had no legitimate expectation, simply by virtue of this quota, of subsequently being awarded final import licences. An expectation could only arise if the Commission had specifically promised to grant the licences, or if it was guilty of unreasonable delay.[114]

It is not easy for silence, inaction, or delay alone to give rise to a legally protected expectation.[115] For example, when in *Keung* an immigrant's passport was accepted by mistake at the border, the applicant did not, some months later, have a reasonable expectation that he would be allowed to stay in the territory indefinitely.[116] This decision is in line with EC cases which held that inaction following an application for a decision cannot, in and of itself, generate a reasonable expectation of a favourable outcome even if the administration exceeds a statutory time limit.[117] Moreover, neither negotiations, however lengthy and intensive,[118] nor advice granted to an applicant on how to improve an application create reasonable expectations of a favourable outcome.[119]

Lengthy delay in a procedure leading to an *unfavourable* measure may, however, create a reasonable expectation if the delay is not attributable to the affected person. Thus, in *Kahn* it was said that if the authorities take no action towards an illegal immigrant for a period of over four years after his presence has come to their notice, a reasonable expectation might be created that he will not be deported.[120] The ECJ came to a similar result in the case of *RSV*. The Court found that a period of twenty-six months, which elapsed between the notification of a state aid to a ship yard and the Commission's decision that this

[113] *R v IRC, ex p Unilever* [1996] STC 681. For a procedural legitimate expectation based on practice, see *CCSU v Minister for the Civil Service* [1985] AC 374.

[114] Case T-336/94 *Efisol v Commission* [1996] ECR II-1343 para 32–36.

[115] *Khan v Home Secretary* [1987] Imm AR 543.

[116] *Keung v Home Secretary* [1992] Imm AR 201. See also *Nkiti v Immigration Officer, Gatwick* [1989] Imm AR 585; *R v Home Secretary, ex p Ansari*, 16/1–97.

[117] Cases T-123/89 *Chomel v Commission* [1990] ECR II-131; C-258–259/90 *Naviera Laida v Commission* [1992] ECR I-2901. See also Cases 92/85 *Hamai v ECJ* [1986] ECR 3157 para 8–9; T-23/90 *Peugeot v Commission* [1991] ECR II-653 para 47; T-5/93 *Tremblay v Commission* [1995] ECR II-185 para 76–80; T-44/93 *Saby v Commission* [1995] ECR-SC II-541 para 50–52.

[118] Cases C-249/87 *Mulfinger v Commission* [1989] ECR 4127 para 17–18. Compare Case 81/72 *Commission v Council* [1973] ECR 575.

[119] Case T-465/93 *Murgia Messapica v Commission* [1994] ECR II-361.

[120] *Khan v Home Secretary* [1987] Imm AR 543 (*obiter dictum*). See also *R v Home Secretary, ex p Sinclair* [1992] Imm AR 293. Compare *R v Secretary of State for Foreign and Commonwealth Affairs, ex p Samuel* The Times 17/8–89; *Musah v Home Secretary* [1995] Imm AR 236.

aid must be recovered by the Member State, amounted to a breach of legitimate expectations, given that similar aid had been approved in five previous years and that it did not require deep research for the Commission to make a determination.[121]

Where there is an explicit statement, its *wording* is obviously of crucial importance. Only very precisely worded representations will in practice create legitimate expectations and claims are frequently dismissed by the English[122] and the Community courts[123] on a construction of the relevant phrases. Indeed, litigants have so far only successfully relied on precise assurances before the Community courts in three,[124] and before the English courts in a small handful of, cases.[125] A few examples will illustrate this.

Immigrants who spend time in Britain on fixed time visas are often refused re-entry on return from short stays abroad because their visas automatically expire on leaving Britain. In the *Oloniluyi* case it was accepted that an immigrant caught by this rule had a legitimate expectation of being allowed re-entry as a result of, firstly, a stamp in her passport stating that she was 'exempt from requiring a visa' and, secondly, an oral assurance from an immigration officer that she would have 'no trouble in returning to the United Kingdom as long as

[121] Case 223/85 *RSV v Commission* [1987] ECR 4617. See also Cases T-194/97 and 83/98 *Branco v Commission*, 20/1–2000 para 89–91. Compare Cases 67/84 *Sideradria v Commission* [1985] ECR 3983 para 21; 8/83 *Bertoli v Commission* [1984] ECR 1649 para 21; 121/86 *Epiceiriseon v Council* [1989] ECR 3191; C-317/92 *Commission v Germany* [1994] ECR I-2039; T-142/97 *Branco v Commission* [1998] ECR II-3567 para 94–101; T-180–181/96 *Mediocurso v Commission* [1998] ECR II-3477 para 61–67; T-305–307/94, 313–316/94, 318/94, 325/94, 328–329/94 and 335/94 *Limburgse v Commission*, 20/4–99 para 121–135; T-182/96 *Partex v Commission*, 16/9–99 para 177–189.

[122] e.g. *Yakub v Chief Immigration Officer, Heathrow* [1988] Imm AR 177; *R v Secretary of State for Trade and Industry, ex p Lonrho Plc* [1989] 1 WLR 525; *Singh v Home Secretary* [1990] Imm AR 124; *R v Home Secretary, ex p Hammersmith and Fulham LBC* [1991] 1 AC 521; *Patel v Home Secretary* [1993] Imm AR 392; *Odishu v Home Secretary* [1994] Imm AR 475; *R v Home Secretary, ex p Clay*, 26/6–96; *R v BBC, ex p Kelly* [1996] COD 58; *R v Sevenoaks DC, ex p Wickham* [1998] JPL 1145.

[123] e.g. Cases 71/74 *Frubo v Commission* [1975] ECR 563; 303 and 312/81 *Klöckner-Werke v Commission* [1983] ECR 1507; 20–21/83 *Vlachos v ECJ* [1984] ECR 4149; 310/85 *Deufil v Commission* [1987] ECR 901; 265/85 *Van den Bergh en Jurgens v Commission* [1987] ECR 1155; 424–425/85 *Frico v VIV* [1987] ECR 2755; 111/86 *Delauche v Commission* [1987] ECR 5345; 181/87 *Leonard v Commission* [1988] ECR 3823; T-156/89 *Mordt v ECJ* [1991] ECR II-407; T-18/90 *Jongen v Commission* [1991] ECR II-187; C-400/92 *Germany v Commission* [1994] ECR I-4701; T-2/93 *Air France v Commission* [1994] ECR II-323; T-493/93 *Hansa-Fisch v Commission* [1995] ECR II-575; T-571/93 *Lefebvre v Commission* [1995] ECR II-2379; T-195/95 *Guerin Automobiles v Commission* [1996] ECR II-171; T-213/95 and 18/96 *SCK v Commission* [1997] ECR II-1739; T-92/96 *Monaco v EP* [1997] ECR-SC II-573; T-105/96 *Pharos v Commission* [1998] ECR II-285 para 64–66; T-113/96 *Dubois SA v Council and Commission* [1998] ECR II-125; T-46/98 and T-151/98 *CEMR v Commission*, 3/2–2000 para 78–82.

[124] Cases 144/82 *Detti v ECJ* [1983] ECR 2439; T-587/93 *Ortega Urretavizcaya v Commission* [1996] ECR-SC IA-349/II-1027; T-66/96 and 221/97 *Mellett v ECJ* [1998] ECR-SC II-1305.

[125] *R v Brent LBC, ex p MacDonagh* [1990] COD 3; *R v Northamptonshire CC, ex p Commission for the New Towns* [1992] COD 123; *R v CEC, ex p Kay* [1996] STC 1500; *R v Devon Health Authority, ex p Coughlan* [1999] Lloyd's LR Medical 306.

[she] came back before the [day] . . . [her] leave expired'.[126] However, in later cases the Court of Appeal held that the stamp alone did not give rise to any legitimate expectation although it appeared 'almost calculated to mislead'.[127] One judge even said that the expectation depended upon 'a lawyer's proper reading of the stamps irrespective of the fact that a lay person might have come to the wrong conclusion'.[128]

This restrictive approach is not limited to the field of immigration where the English courts have, due to a very heavy case-load, an incentive to discourage applications for judicial review.[129] The Community case law is equally strict. For example, in *ENU* a company, which had difficulties in disposing of excess uranium stemming from its production, sought to rely on the Commission's statements that it would 'give priority to finding a satisfactory solution to its problem', and that it 'shared the view that . . . supply policy should in future include "special action" to enable' cases such as ENU's to be resolved. The CFI found that these statements were not a specific assurance that the Commission would oblige other European companies to purchase ENU's uranium at the price it demanded.[130]

It is also clear from the case law that representations and assurances which are qualified or conditional will not create legitimate expectations. For example, in the case of *MFK* Lloyds of London had, on a number of occasions, consulted the Inland Revenue about the tax implications of a planned system of dollar-bonds. On one occasion the Revenue wrote that preferential treatment would be given, adding that 'any . . . comment is entirely without prejudice to the facts'. This vague formulation was, in the court's opinion, sufficient to qualify the representation so that no reasonable expectation arose.[131] Again, the situation is very similar in EC law. The CFI reaffirmed in *Langnese-Iglo* that a 'comfort letter', by which the Commission informally accepted the lawfulness of an agreement notified to it under Art 81 EC, did not create a legitimate expectation that the Commission would not reopen the matter, as it had reserved its right to do so 'in the light of appreciable changes of law or fact'.[132]

[126] *R v Home Secretary, ex p Oloniluyi* [1989] COD 275. Compare *R v Home Secretary, ex p Mowla* [1992] 1 WLR 70, 88; *R v Local Government Commission, ex p Cambridgeshire DC* [1995] COD 149, 150.

[127] *R v Home Secretary, ex p Islam* [1990] Imm AR 220; *R v Home Secretary, ex p Mowla* [1992] 1 WLR 70. See also *R v Home Secretary, ex p Katoorah* [1996] Imm AR 595.

[128] *R v Home Secretary, ex p Mowla* [1992] 1 WLR 70, 84–5 (Glidewell LJ). See also *R v Home Secretary, ex p Bhatti* [1989] Imm AR 189; *Miah v Home Secretary* [1991] Imm AR 581; *Jaramilo-Silva v Home Secretary* [1994] Imm AR 352.

[129] See L. Bridges, G. Mezaros and M. Sunkin, *Judicial Review in Perspective*, 2nd edn. (London, 1995), 31.

[130] Cases T-458 and 523/93 *ENU v Commission* [1995] ECR II-2459.

[131] *R v IRC, ex p MFK Underwriting Agencies Ltd* [1990] 1 WLR 1545. See also *R v London Borough of Ealing, ex p Denny* (1994) 26 HLR 424; *R v DPP, ex p Burke* [1997] COD 169.

[132] Case T-7/93 *Langnese-Iglo v Commission* [1995] ECR II-1533 para 35–41. See also Case T-229/94 *Deutsche Bahn v Commission* [1997] ECR II-1689; T-182/96 *Partex v Commission*, 16/9–99 para 193; D. Stevens, 'The "Comfort Letter": Old Problems, New Developments' (1994) ECLR 81.

What, then, is a sufficiently precise assurance? The recent case of Ms *Urretavizcaya* provides a rare example.[133] The applicant had been admitted to a reserve list of research assistants following a competition for 'positions in salary grade C3, B5 and B3'. She was offered, by letter, a position 'in grade B3', took it up and received a grade B3 salary for six months. When she asked for a written copy of her contract, the Commission decided to place her in the lower grade B5 and reduced her salary accordingly. The CFI held that the letter amounted to a precise assurance, the correctness of which the applicant had had no reason to doubt. Consequently, it annulled the grading decision and awarded damages equivalent to the difference between the B5 and B3 salaries.

II The Recipient's Situation

A specific, precise, unambiguous, and unqualified representation normally creates a reasonable expectation that the authority will act as it has represented. This presumption may, however, may be rebutted on three different grounds both in English and EC law.

First, the court may find that the individual's statements or conduct reveal that he did not actually (subjectively) hold any expectation, either due to a particularly cautious interpretation of the representation,[134] or simple unawareness of its existence.[135] For example, in *Peugeot* the CFI found that a letter from the applicant company to the Commission revealed that it already knew the views of the Commission officials, and it could therefore not claim a legitimate expectation of different treatment.[136]

While the requirement of subjectively held expectations is sound in principle,[137] the courts should be careful not to disadvantage the cautious or well-educated by inferring too readily that an applicant's *prima facie* reasonable expectations are not actually held. Moreover, if a representation is of general application, such as a circular or policy statement, the rationale for holding the authorities to it is not restricted to legal certainty, it includes formal equality.[138] There should therefore be no requirement of subjective expectations in such cases.[139]

[133] Case T-587/93 *Ortega Urretavizcaya v Commission* [1996] ECR-SC IA-349/II-1027. See also footnotes 124–5.

[134] *Jaramilo-Silva v Home Secretary* [1994] Imm AR 352, 356–7; *R v Devon CC, ex p Baker* [1995] 1 All ER 73, 89–90; *Boyle v Secretary of State for the Environment*, 31/3–99.

[135] *Lloyd v McMahon* [1987] AC 625, 696, 714; *R v Home Secretary, ex p Akyol* [1990] Imm AR 571; *R v Ministry of Defence, ex p Walker* The Times 11/2–99. Compare *Hughes v Department of Health and Social Security* [1985] AC 776, 788.

[136] Case T-23/90 *Peugeot v Commission* [1991] ECR II-653 para 48. See also Cases 169/73 *Compagnie Continentale France v Council* [1975] ECR 117 para 23; T-141/94 *Thyssen Stahl v Commission*, 11/3–99 para 510; T-46/98 and T-151/98 *CEMR v Commission*, 3/2–2000 para 78–79.

[137] See Forsyth, above n. 4, 376.

[138] See Ch. 1.2.B.

[139] *R v Secretary of State for Wales, ex p Emery* (1998) 96 LGR 83 citing De Smith 426. Similarly P. A. MacPherson, 'The Legitimate Expectation Doctrine and Its Application to Administrative Policy' (1995–6) CJALP 141, 173; Singh and Steyn, above n. 4, 19–20.

Second, expectations based on administrative advice or assurances obtained by fraud or deception are not reasonable.[140] It is common ground in English law that a person seeking a ruling or assurance must 'lay all cards face up on the table'.[141] That is, he must disclose all relevant facts and possibly even draw attention to relevant legal issues which are not self-evidently in play.[142] The latter requirement is problematic as it may force the applicant to seek legal assistance, and it should apply only to professional operators with adequate resources.[143] The disclosure requirement is, as are other aspects of the expectations principle, applied quite strictly in practice. Thus, in the *MFK* case the Inland Revenue gave, on one occasion, an unqualified assurance about the taxation of a system of dollar-bonds. However, the applicant had not made clear that a general ruling was being sought and the Revenue officer assumed that his assurance related to one issue of bonds only. Consequently, although no deception or fraud was alleged, the applicant's alleged expectation was not upheld.

The notion of reasonableness also tends to prevent individuals and undertakings from using administrative representations as a shield against criminal behaviour, such as violations of EC steel production regulations and competition law.[144] Moreover, while the expectation of an economic profit may be legitimate, at least in EC law,[145] the courts are unwilling to protect traders who seeks to profit from the exploitation of Community schemes in a way which is contrary to their purpose.[146] While one can understand these rulings, it may be noted that protection should not be denied simply because the authority, or the court, disapproves of a person's business tactics or personal morality.[147]

Third, an expectation is only reasonable if it was, given the person's experience and the regulatory context, unforeseeable that the administration would go back on its representation.[148] An individual can therefore not claim a reasonable expectation if he was warned specifically that a particular assurance or statement would not be adhered to.[149] For example, in *Willsman* the applicant had no legitimate expectation that he could withhold payment of tax after receiving a letter stating 'you must not withhold payment pending the outcome of your

[140] Cases C-96/89 *Commission v Netherlands* [1991] ECR I-2461 para 30; C-285/95 *Kol v Land Berlin* [1997] ECR I-3069 para 28. See also *McPhee v North Lanarkshire Council* (1998) SLT 1317.

[141] *R v IRC, ex p MFK Underwriting Agencies Ltd* [1990] 1 WLR 1545, 1569; *Matrix Securities Ltd v IRC* [1994] 1 WLR 334.

[142] *Matrix Securities Ltd v IRC* [1994] 1 WLR 334.

[143] See Sandler, above n. 4, 281.

[144] e.g. Cases 1252/79 *Lucchini v Commission* [1980] ECR 3753 para 9; 67/84 *Sideradria v Commission* [1985] ECR 3983 para 21; T-141/94 *Thyssen Stahl v Commission*, 11/3–99 para 554.

[145] Case 74/74 *CNTA v Commission* [1975] ECR 533.

[146] Cases 2/75 *EVGF v Mackprang* [1975] ECR 607; 96/77 *Bauche v Administration des Douanes* [1978] ECR 383; C-337/88 *SAFA* [1990] ECR I-1.

[147] See De Smith 429.

[148] Case C-250/91 *Hewlett Packard v Directeur General des Douanes* [1993] ECR I-1819 para 28.

[149] Cases 95–98/74, 15 and 100/75 *CAC v Commission* and *Council* [1975] ECR 1615 para 30; 235/82 *Ferriere San Carlo v Commission* [1983] ECR 3949 para 11–13; C-22/90 *France v Commission* [1991] ECR I-5285; T-451/93 *San Marco Impex Italiana v Commission* [1994] ECR II-1061 para 74; T-129/96 *Preussag Stahl v Commission* [1998] ECR II-609 para 79–83; T-141/94 *Thyssen Stahl v Commission*, 11/3–99 para 511.

. . . application since payment is required as demanded.' Two earlier reminders, which stated that 'queries or claims [will be] sort[ed] out before legal action [is taken] for recovery of unpaid . . . tax' were thus cancelled by the last letter.[150]

The notion of foreseeability is extremely important in Community law, because most litigants are professional traders and civil servants, and both of these groups may be expected to show considerable diligence in their dealings with the administration.[151] Traders must be 'prudent, discriminating, and well-informed'[152] and therefore aware that densely regulated policy areas, such as the Common Agricultural and Fisheries Policy and the steel sector, are inherently subject to frequent changes.[153] An administrative measure may, especially in such areas, be considered foreseeable if it could be predicted that a change would occur in some form; every detail of the change does not have to be foreseeable.[154] Professional economic operators must therefore be aware of the content of the Official Journal,[155] including proposals for legislation and communications by the Commission,[156] as well as general and specialized papers[157] and even of negotiations in the Council of Ministers about imminent changes of relevant trade rules and policies (*sic*).[158] It follows that a trader cannot base expectations upon a general tariff publication from a national customs authority when the true position can be ascertained from the Official Journal.[159]

Expectations claims are also often rejected because a measure was, in the Community judicature's view, foreseeable in the light of general economic developments and market trends.[160] For example, in *Frico* the Commission had

[150] *R v Bristol City Magistrates' Court, ex p Willsman* [1991] RA 292. See also *R v Department of Trade and Industry, ex p Blenheim* [1992] COD 453; *Musah v Home Secretary* [1995] Imm AR 236; *R v Home Secretary, ex p Dey* [1996] Imm AR 521.

[151] The trader's size and 'substantial economic importance' may be relevant in this connection. See Case T-243/94 *British Steel v Commission* [1997] ECR I-1887 para 78.

[152] Cases 78/77 *Lührs v Hauptzollamt Hamburg-Jonas* [1978] ECR 169 para 6; 265/85 *Van den Bergh en Jurgens v Commission* [1987] ECR 1155 para 44.

[153] Cases C-350/88 *Delacre v Commission* [1990] ECR I-395 para 33–34; T-489/93 *Unifruit Hellas* [1994] ECR II-1201.

[154] See AG Jacobs [1993] ECR I-4775. See also AG Mayras [1978] ECR 57 stating that the decision must come as lightning from a blue sky to be considered unforeseeable.

[155] Case C-80/89 *Behn v Hauptzollamt Itzehoe* [1990] ECR I-2659 para 13. See also Cases 90/77 *Stimming v Commission* [1978] ECR 995; 26/81 *Oleifici Mediteranei v EEC* [1982] ECR 3057; 52/81 *Faust v Commission* [1982] ECR 3745; 84/81 *Staple Dairy Products* [1982] ECR 1763; 235/82 *Ferriere San Carlo v Commission* [1983] ECR 3949.

[156] Cases C-13–16/92 *Driessen v Minister van Verkeer* [1993] ECR I-4751 para 31–34; C-22/94 *Irish Farmers Association* [1997] ECR I-1809 para 23.

[157] Cases 95–98/74, 15 and 100/75 *CAC v Commission* and *Council* [1975] ECR 1615 para 30; 97/76 *Merkur v Commission* [1977] ECR 1063 para 6; Case 338/85 *Pardini v Ministero del Commercio* [1988] ECR 2041 para 24–25

[158] Case 281/82 *Unifrex v Commission* [1984] ECR 1969 para 26.

[159] Case C-80/89 *Behn v Hauptzollamt Itzehoe* [1990] ECR I-2659 para 13.

[160] Cases 78/77 *Lührs v Hauptzollamt Hamburg-Jonas* [1978] ECR 169; 146/77 *British Beef v IBAP* [1978] ECR 1347; 127/78 *Spitta v Hauptzollamt-Frankfurt* [1979] ECR 171; 265/85 *Van den Bergh en Jurgens v Commission* [1987] ECR 1155.

stated publicly (in an answer to a question in the EP) that it did 'not envisage differentiating [butter storage] aid on the basis of interest rates current in the Member States'. The ECJ found that the Commission was, nonetheless, entitled to differentiate the aid some months later when large stocks started accumulating in states with low interest rates. For the storage companies should have been aware of this market development and predicted the Commission's action.[161]

As these decisions illustrate, the European courts' view of what professional traders and Community employees should be able to foresee is very strict.[162] While this view may be suitable for the largest and most well-informed economic operators, many smaller and less experienced operators are, as a result of increasing European integration, involved in cross-border trade. There is arguably room for a more flexible and liberal approach towards such operators and private individuals who rely upon statements from the Community administration.[163]

(B) Reasonable and Legitimate Expectations: Balancing and Judicial Deference

Public authorities must, under both English and EC law, consider reasonable expectations and weigh them against the reasons of public policy in favour of a decision which will disappoint such expectations. If the individual's expectation carries greater weight, it is legitimate and should be respected by the administration. In practice, however, expectations claims are rarely upheld by the courts. This is so for two reasons.

Expectations are, first, unlikely to be upheld unless the applicant can show some reliance and detriment.[164] This requirement has in English law been taken over from the private law doctrine of estoppel by representation.[165] In EC law, reliance is not an absolute condition for the protection of legitimate expectations, but it is a very important consideration in the courts' balancing of pub-

[161] Cases 424–425/85 *Frico v VIV* [1987] ECR 2755 para 32–33.

[162] For the Courts' approach in staff cases, see Cases 3/83 *Abrias v Commission* [1985] ECR 1995; T-576–582/93 *Browet v Commission* [1994] ECR-SC II-619.

[163] Similarly Sharpston, above n. 73, 158–9.

[164] *Khan v Home Secretary* [1987] Imm AR 543; *R v Home Secretary, ex p Oloniluyi* [1989] COD 275; *R v Secretary of State for the Environment, ex p NALGO* (1993) 5 Admin LR 785, 283; *R v Department of Trade and Industry, ex p Blenheim* [1992] COD 453, 454; *R v Jockey Club, ex p RAM Racecourses* [1993] 2 All ER 223, 236–7; *Jaramilo-Silva v Home Secretary* [1994] Imm AR 352, 357; *R v Lloyd's of London, ex p Briggs* (1993) 5 Admin LR 698, 710; *Matrix Securities Ltd v IRC* [1994] 1 WLR 334, 336; *R v IRC, ex p Warburg* [1994] STC 518; *R v The Law Society, ex p Mortgage Express*, 17/12–96; *R v Beatrix Potter School, ex p Kanner* [1997] ELR 468; *R v CEC, ex p Littlewoods Ltd* [1997] STC 317, 325; *R v Devon Health Authority, ex p Coughlan* [1999] Lloyd's LR Medical 306, 323; *R v Horseferry Road Magistrates' Court, ex p DPP* [1999] COD 441, 442. However, reliance is not a requirement in *procedural* expectations cases. See Ch. 2 at footnote 171.

[165] *Norfolk CC v Secretary of State for the Environment* [1973] 3 All ER 673, 677. See further Wilken and Villiers, above n. 2, 154–65, 267–78.

lic and private interests.[166] The requirement of reliance should be maintained because, it is thought, fairness only requires substantive, as opposed to procedural, protection of representations if the affected person suffers some harm. However, the courts should not take a narrow view of what constitutes harm or detriment. The 'moral harm' and upset caused by frustrated plans may in some instances be as important as actual financial loss,[167] and trust in government may require informal promises to be kept independently of financial detriment. It is also important to realize that the requirement of reliance should only apply to *individualized* representations (Situation 2). General representations are binding in individual cases on grounds of equal treatment,[168] and individuals should therefore be able to invoke them without showing reliance (Situation 3).[169]

The second reason why expectations claims are rarely upheld in English and EC law has to do with the intensity of judicial review. It was explained above that the hitherto traditional English position was that the courts would only interfere with an administrative decision, which disappointed a reasonable expectation, if that decision was 'unreasonable' or an 'abuse of power'.[170] That is, the English courts showed great deference towards the administration's balancing of individual and public interests. The Community courts never stated explicitly that they will only intervene if the decision to disappoint an expectation is unreasonable, abusive, or manifestly erroneous. It has therefore been suggested that EC law protects expectations to a considerably greater extent than English law.[171] The difference between the two legal systems is, however, smaller than the judicial rhetoric suggests. On the one hand, a comprehensive survey of the Community case law reveals that in practice the Community courts will only interfere if there is at least a significant imbalance between the interests at stake. On the other hand, English law has recently moved towards a more intensive review in expectations cases concerning representations addressed to one person or a limited class of persons.[172] The position in EC and English law is aptly illustrated by the following decisions, which also show that the courts' application of the principle of legitimate expectations is not as consistent as one might wish.

In the *Coughlan* case the Court of Appeal upheld a promise, given by a local authority to a disabled woman, about the health care she could expect to receive. The woman had agreed to move from a hospital, where she had lived for some years after a serious traffic accident had left her severely disabled, to a special housing unit on the assurance that this unit would be her 'home for

[166] See AG Trabucchi [1975] ECR 777; Sharpston, above n. 73, 158; J. Temple Lang, 'Legal Certainty and Legitimate Expectations as General Principles of Law', Paper presented at the Conference on General Principles of Community Law, Malmö 27–28 Aug. 1999, 15.

[167] See *R v Beatrix Potter School, ex p Kanner* [1997] ELR 468.

[168] See Ch. 1.2.B.

[169] See Cane, above n. 15, 144–5.

[170] See section 2.A.

[171] See Forsyth, above n. 4, 380–1.

[172] See section 2.A.

life'.[173] The Court found that the authority could not go back on this precise and unqualified representation, which the applicant had relied on, and which directly affected her 'right to a home' under Art 8 of the ECHR. Although the authority had been conscious of the promise, and of reasonable expectations created by it, and weighed those against the financial and practical arguments in favour of closing the unit, a fair balance had in the court's view not been struck. The CFI reached a similar result in *Urretavizcaya*. This case, which was discussed above,[174] upheld the expectations created by an assurance about the salary, which an EC employee would receive. As in *Coughlan*, the assurance was very specific and clear and the only interest which would be affected was the (Community) budget. Neither the institution's ability to adapt its general staff policy nor the interests of colleagues were at stake.[175]

These two decisions may be contrasted with *Kanner* and *Finsider*.[176] In the former case it was considered lawful to withdraw an offer of a place in a school made to Ms Kanner. A clear express promise had been made and there was some detriment due to the upset of the family and the expense of buying a school uniform. Nevertheless, the Divisional Court found that it was not *Wednesbury* unreasonable to go back on it. The reason for this was not spelled out quite clearly, but the court appears to have taken into account that it would have created some administrative difficulties and affected other parents, who had also applied for places, if the promise was upheld.[177] This is a restrictive application of the principle of legitimate expectations. It is difficult to accept the view that the school would not be able to absorb one extra pupil, and that it would therefore have a direct and detrimental effect upon the situation of other applicants if the promise made to Ms Kanner had been upheld.

The potential conflict between equal treatment and legitimate expectations, which seems to have influenced the court in *Kanner*, also played an important role in the EC case of *Finsider*. A steel company had obtained a Commission 'expert opinion' on its plans to invest in a new steel mill,[178] which expressed 'a favourable opinion on the realization of those investments'. Some months later, however, the Commission introduced stricter steel production quotas and Finsider's investment turned out to be unprofitable. The ECJ rejected the company's claim for breach of legitimate expectations. Although the Commission was 'well placed' to assess market developments, and although it had led Finsider to 'entertain certain expectations regarding the profitability of the investment', the Commission could not have foreseen that stricter quotas would

[173] *R v Devon Health Authority, ex p Coughlan* [1999] Lloyd's LR Medical 306.

[174] See text at footnote 133.

[175] See also Cases T-46/89 *Pitrone v Commission* [1990] ECR II-577; T-66/96 and 221/97 *Mellett v ECJ* [1998] ECR-SC II-1305.

[176] *R v Beatrix Potter School, ex p Kanner* [1997] ELR 468; Cases 63 and 147/84 *Finsider v Commission* [1985] ECR 2857.

[177] Note that the court approached this fact situation in terms of 'representations' although the offer may have amounted to a final determination.

[178] See Art 54(4) ECSC.

be required to cope with a worsening of the steel sector crisis. This reasoning is unsatisfactory. Surely, if the market developments were unforeseeable to the Commission's experts, then they were also unforeseeable to Finsider. The real reason for the decision appears to be that in the ECJ's view the Community interest in effective regulation of the steel sector outweighed Finsider's reasonable expectation. This is, again, a strict result. Finsider should arguably have been granted some form of exception from the new quotas during a transitional period. The adverse effect, which this might have had on Finsider's competitors, would be indirect, temporary, and spread in small proportions upon a large number of undertakings.

(C) Statutory Exceptions in French Law

The basic rule of French law is, as explained above, that individualized representations are not binding upon public authorities.[179] This may cause considerable hardship and undermine trust in government and statutory provisions have, therefore, been introduced in areas where particularly important economic interests are affected by administrative action; namely tax and land planning.

Art L80B of the *Code Fiscal* was enacted in 1987 to protect 'the confidence of the tax payer' (*la confiance du contributable*).[180] This rule provides that tax authorities are bound by an advance ruling about the liability to tax if the ruling is in the form of a written answer to a specific request for tax assessment of a factual situation or transaction and signed by a competent tax officer (*contrôleur*).[181] The request must be followed by correct and complete information,[182] and it only binds the authorities as regards the requesting physical or legal person.[183] If the applicant's factual situation changes in a relevant way, or he fails to comply with conditions imposed by the authority, then the ruling ceases to be binding.[184] Moreover, in the absence of an Art L80B ruling, the authorities are not bound by the way an applicant's transactions have been assessed in previous years.[185]

179 See section 2.B.

180 See *JC* Procédures Fiscales, Fasc 170–174; F. Douet, *Contribution à l'étude de la sécurité juridique en droit fiscal interne français* (Paris, 1997), 278–86.

181 CE 21/3–83 X DF 1983 no 48 comm 2204; CAA Nancy 12/10–95 *Dengreville* DF 1996 no 15 comm 510 (oral information is not binding). Failure to respond to a request for a tax ruling within three months may constitute an implicit tax ruling subject to Art L80B(2).

182 CE 15/5–68 X Rec 309 (concerning Art L80A but applicable by analogy).

183 CAA Bordeaux 28/6–94 *Dolmon* DF 1994 no 51 comm 2226; CAA Nancy 1/12–94 *Becquet de Mégill* DF 1995 no 30 comm 1602. Compare Cass Comm 29/11–94 *Société AXX Finance* JCP 1995 I 3825 (tax ruling to seller of real estate binds also towards the buyer).

184 CAA Paris 16/11–93 *Société Kraftverkehr* DF 1994 no 29 comm 1627.

185 CE 19/12–69 *X* DF 1970 no 6 comm 183; CAA Bordeaux 19/5–93 *Villessot* DF 1994 no 12 comm 575; CAA Paris 15/12–94 *SA Hamberger* DF 1995 no 41 comm 1901.

This provision resembles closely the position which flows from leading English cases like *MFK* and *Matrix-Churchill*.[186] However, the French statutory system is 'objective' in the sense that taxpayers do not have to prove the existence of subjectively held expectations. It is therefore less flexible, but also more clear and certain than the English principle of legitimate expectations.

Developers and landowners often request informal advice from planning authorities about existing building restrictions, the prospects of obtaining planning permission, etc. On general principle, such advice is not binding, but the *Code de l'urbanisme* makes it possible to obtain a binding 'certificate of information' *(certificat d'urbanisme)*.[187] This document lists existing planning restrictions on land and buildings[188] and is binding upon the planning authority for a period of one year. If the authorities certify that no restrictions apply, planning permission cannot be denied on grounds of subsequent changes in planning policy and planning legislation.[189]

This system of *certificat d'urbanisme* goes some way to protect legal certainty and expectations in the planning context, but it is far from perfect. A certificate which has been granted erroneously may be considered unlawful on the grounds of error of fact (*erreur de fait*), in which case it is not binding.[190] As the French courts take a broad view of *erreur de fait* in planning cases,[191] the authorities are often in a position to refuse planning permission although a favourable certificate has been granted.[192] Moreover, the certificate procedure is relatively slow[193] and it requires the developer to present an elaborate proposal to obtain a precise answer.[194] Therefore, although the certificate system is widely used, developers often have to rely on non-binding information and advice (*lettres de renseignement*) obtained outside the system.[195]

It emerges that French law and English law have, as in the tax field, reached rather similar solutions to a similar problem.[196] Both legal systems accept that

[186] See section 3.A.

[187] Art L410–1 *Code de l'urbanisme*. See generally E. Fatôme and M. le Lefondré, *Le Certificat d'urbanisme* (Paris, 1983); *JC* Fasc 445–60.

[188] This was until 1971 the certificate's only function. Consequently, the courts considered it a non-binding representation (which could however form the basis of liability in case of grave errors). See CE 10/7–64 *Duffaut* JCP 1964 II 13796; CE 14/10–77 *Le Bélier* DA 1977 no 376.

[189] The certificate does not protect the developer against changes in legislation unrelated to planning. See TA Nice 19/11–91 *Lancry-Laval* Gaz Pal 1992 II 136; *JC* Fasc 445–60 no 58–9, 122ff.

[190] CE 30/3–77 *Fiamma* DA 1977 no 165; CE 11/10–89 *Clery* AJDA 1990, 14; CE 4/11–94 *SCI 'Le Parc de Vaugien'* RFDA 1995, 231.

[191] See CE 17/6–77 *Cochet* Rec 281; CE 17/2–78 *SA Logeais-Jamin* Rec 86; CE 21/5–86 *Dalbray* DA 1986 no 369; CE 26/7–96 *Commune de Cagnes-sur-Mer* no 136.798.

[192] See *JC* Fasc 445–60 no 61, 132.

[193] The certificate must, in principle, be granted within two months, but this time limit is exceeded in as much as 50–60 per cent of all cases. See A. Lanza, 'Le certificat d'urbanisme', AJDA 1984, 294, 298; *JC* Fasc 445–60 no 45.

[194] See TA Nice 12/4–90 *Accardo* JCP 1991 II 195; *JC* Fasc 445–60 no 128. See also Lanza, above n. 193, 294–5 listing the many documents an applicant must submit.

[195] See *JC* Fasc 445–60 no 86–88.

[196] See *Western Fish Products v Penwith DC* [1981] 2 All ER 204 and section 6.

planning authorities should be bound by specific, lawful, and factually correct planning advice, but the courts are very reluctant to extend this binding effect to unlawful and erroneous advice due to the risk that neighbours and the wider public interest will be harmed as a result.[197]

4 Departure from General Representations in Particular Instances (Situation 3)

Discretionary administrative decision-making is to a very large extent carried out in accordance with pre-formulated policies. Still, decisions are occasionally made out of line with policy. This may happen either by mistake, because the policy is ignored or misunderstood, or deliberately, because countervailing public policy considerations are seen to justify a departure from policy.

There are, as explained in Chapter 1, two compelling reasons to limit the administration's freedom to depart from policy. First, to depart from a policy may disappoint the expectations of those who planned and relied upon it. Second, there is a strong egalitarian argument against treating one person differently from others subject to an existing policy. These two different rationales play different roles in English, French, and EC law. While the French courts only cite the principle of equal treatment to justify restrictions upon departure from policy, one finds scattered references to both equality (often called 'consistency') and expectations in English and EC case law.[198] Ideally, the courts should acknowledge the relevance of both rationales and, thereby, also the need for greater individual protection against departures from policy (Situations 3) than against general changes of policy (Situation 4).

To what extent, then, are authorities bound to apply existing policy in individual cases? This depends first of all on whether one is dealing with a set of rules 'disguised' as a policy statement (A), or a 'true' statement of policy (B).

(A) Categorization of Policy as Rules

The administration will be bound by what may appear to be a statement of policy if the courts decide to categorize it as a set of 'real' and legally binding

[197] However, an important difference remains in the greater availability of damages in French planning law. See Ch. 5.

[198] For references to the expectations rationale, see *R v Home Secretary, ex p Kahn* [1984] 1 WLR 1337; *R v DPP, ex p Duckenfield* [1999] 2 All ER 873; Case T-7/89 *Hercules Chemicals v Commission* [1991] ECR II-1711. For references to the equality rationale, see *R v IRC, ex p MFK Underwriting Agencies Ltd* [1990] 1 All ER 91, 107; *R v Home Secretary, ex p Urmaza* [1996] COD 479; Case 148/73 *Louwage v Commission* [1974] ECR 81 para 12. Some decisions even held policy binding without citing any rationale. e.g. *R v Chief Constable, ex p L* [1993] 1 All ER 756, 770; *R v DPP, ex p C* [1995] 1 Cr App Rep 136; *R v Commissioner of Police of the Metropolis, ex p P* (1996) 8 Admin LR 6; *Nicholson v Secretary of State for the Environment*, 31/7–97; *R v Governor of HM Prison Parkhurst*, 28/1–98.

rules.[199] The specificity and detail of the document tend to affect this categorisation.[200] Thus, in *Schofield* a detailed 'scheme' regulating the payment of criminal injuries compensation was considered a set of legally binding rules although it was based on the Crown prerogative rather than on a statutory power to make secondary legislation.[201] Similarly, in *CIRFS* the ECJ annulled the Commission's approval of a French state aid, because the approval derogated from a detailed and published Commission communication, known as a 'discipline', concerning state aid to the synthetic fibres industry. Although the Communication had no formal legal basis in the Treaty, it constituted 'a measure of general application [which] may not be impliedly amended by an individual decision'.[202]

(B) A Duty to Apply Policy in Particular Instances: The General Principle

It is now settled both in English, French, and EC law that a policy statement (which is not a binding rule in disguise), must be applied loyally in particular instances. The English courts' approach to this issue has developed over time,[203] but the recent case of *Gangadeen* has provided some clarification.[204] This decision concerned a policy statement setting out the criteria applicable to decisions about deportation of foreigners with children lawfully residing in Britain. The Court of Appeal accepted that 'the Home Secretary is in ordinary circumstances obliged to act in accordance with his declared policy' and cited previous

[199] See R. Baldwin, *Rules and Government* (Oxford, 1995), 87–8; Markus and Westgate, above n. 4, 155.

[200] See R. Baldwin and J. Houghton, 'Circular Arguments: The Status and Legitimacy of Administrative Rules' (1986) PL 239, 246. The relevant statute may also provide specifically that decision-makers must 'have regard to' or 'act under the general guidance of' policy documents imposed by central government or adopted by themselves: e.g. Housing Act 1996, s 182 (see *R v London Borough of Brent, ex p Macwan* (1994) 26 HLR 528); Local Authority Social Services Act 1970, s 7(1) (see *R v Islington LBC, ex p Rixon* [1997] ELR 66); National Health Service Act 1977, s 13(1) (see *R v North Derbyshire Health Authority, ex p Fisher* (1998) 10 Admin LR 27); Town and Country Planning Act 1990, s 54A (see *R v Leominster DC, ex p Pothecary* (1998) 10 Admin LR 484).

[201] *R v Criminal Injuries Compensation Board, ex p Schofield* [1971] 1 WLR 926; *R v Criminal Injuries Compensation Board, ex p Ince* [1973] 1 WLR 1334. See also *Steed v Secretary of State for the Home Office*, 1/5–98.

[202] Case C-313/90 *CIRFS v Commission* [1993] ECR I-1125 para 32–52. See also Joined Cases T-369/94 and T84/95 *DIR International Film v Commission* [1998] ECR II-357 para 82, and compare Cases 310/85 *Deufil v Commission* [1987] ECR 901; C-400/92 *Germany v Commission* [1994] ECR I-4701; T-243/94 *British Steel v Commission* [1997] ECR II-1887.

[203] See S. M. Nott and P. H. Morgan, 'The Significance of Department of the Environment Circulars in the Planning Process' (1984) JPL 624, 628; G. Ganz, *Quasi Legislation: Recent Developments in Secondary Legislation* (London, 1987), 16–7; Markus and Westgate, above n. 4, 154.

[204] *R v Home Secretary, ex p Gangadeen* [1998] 1 FLR 762. See previously *Conteh v Home Secretary* [1992] Imm AR 594; *R v Home Secretary, ex p Iye* [1994] Imm AR 63, 66–7; *R v Home Secretary, ex p Amankwah* [1994] Imm AR 240; *R v Home Secretary, ex p Hastrup* [1996] Imm AR 616.

case law which had related this duty to protection of legitimate expectations and consistency (formal equality) in administration.[205]

In France, the duty to apply policy was established by the *Crédit foncier de France* decision from 1970. This decision accepted that the administration could exercise a discretionary power, to award grants from a national fund in respect of housing improvements, in accordance with general written policy guidelines (*directives*).[206] *Commissaire de Gouvernement* Bertrand explained in this connection that once such a policy was laid down, the general principle of equal treatment (*égalité de traitement*) required the administration to apply it to all applications unless the special circumstances of the case or an overriding public interest justified a different result.[207]

The leading EC case of *Louwage* drew implicitly on this French case law. When the Commission refused two employees certain allowances contrary to its own staff remuneration policy set out in an 'internal directive' circulated to all employees, the ECJ found for the applicants stating that:

> Although an internal directive has not the character of a rule of law which the administration is always bound to observe, it nevertheless sets forth a rule of conduct indicating the practice to be followed, from which the administration may not depart without giving the reasons which have led it to do so, since otherwise the principles of equality of treatment would be infringed.[208]

The principle adopted in *Gangadeen*, *Crédit foncier de France*, and *Louwage* is, despite the different rationale cited by the courts, similar in three important respects. First, an existing policy (*directive*) cannot be ignored; it is a mandatory consideration in relation to the class of persons which fall within its scope.[209] The policy must be considered, given some weight by

[205] See for similar dicta *R v Home Secretary, ex p McInerny*, 25/7–95; *R v Home Secretary, ex p Stafford* [1998] 3 WLR 372, 378.

[206] CE 11/12–70 *Crédit foncier de France* Rec 750 confirmed by CE 29/6–73 *Société Gea* Rec 453; CE 3/11–76 *Aufaure* no 00.838; CE 18/11–77 *SA Marchand* Rec 442; CE 14/12–88 *SA Gibert Marine* AJDA 1989, 266; CE 18/10–91 *Union nationale de la propriété immobilière* Rec 338; CE 29/7–94 *Gentilhomme* Rec 371; CE 28/7–95 *Haguet* DA 1995 no 556. See generally P. Delvolvé, 'La notion de directive', AJDA 1974, 461; J. Boulouis, 'Sur une catégorie nouvelle d'actes juridiques: les "directives"', in *Recueil d'études en hommage à Charles Eisenmann* (Paris, 1975), 192; C. Pavlopoulos, *La directive en droit administratif* (Paris, 1978); M. Cliquennois, 'Que reste-t-il des directives? A propos du vingtième anniversaire de l'arrêt "Crédit foncier de France"', AJDA 1992, 3.

[207] *Crédit foncier de France*, *op cit*, 756–7. See also Braibant *conclusions* CE 12/12–72 *Robinet* D 1975, 216–7; TA Besançon 7/2–73 *Ballaud* AJDA 1973, 590; Stahl *conclusions* CE 12/12–97 *ONIFLHOR* DA 1998 chroniques no 4, 8.

[208] Case 148/73 *Louwage v Commission* [1974] ECR 81 para 12. See also Case 105/75 *Giuffrida v Commission* [1976] ECR 1395 para 17 (similar result based on the principle of 'proper administration').

[209] The scope of a policy may, however, be interpreted quite narrowly. e.g. *R v IRC, ex p Camacq Co* [1989] STC 785; *R v Jockey Club, ex p RAM Racecourses* [1993] 2 All ER 223; *R v Home Secretary, ex p Shahed* [1995] Imm AR 303; *R v Home Secretary, ex p Katoorah* [1996] Imm AR 595; Cases T-576–582/93 *Browet v Commission* [1994] ECR-SC II-619; T-244/94 *British Steel v Commission* [1998] ECR II-1887; CE 22/1–93 *Sabiani* no 89.078; CAA Bordeaux 15/1–91 *Arnal* DF 1992 no 19 comm 990.

the decision-maker, and balanced against the public interest in a departure.[210] Thus, in the case of *P* a juvenile offender had been cautioned by the police although he had not, as required by a prosecution policy circular, confessed to the crime. As it appeared that the question of departure from policy had not been considered, and no justification was offered, the court annulled the cautioning decision without further ado.[211]

Second, if the administration purports to follow a policy, it must not misconstrue its wording or purpose.[212] The courts will, in all three jurisdictions, construe policies, especially where they are 'couched in ordinary' language and 'predicated upon legal categories'.[213] However, the courts may show some deference towards the decision-maker's interpretation if a policy document contains vague and open-ended terms.[214]

Third, the duty to consider policy, apply it correctly, and justify departure is subject to judicial review and decisions have, at least in English and EC law, been struck down for failing to comply with one or more of these requirements. It is not, and should not be, an excuse that the decision-maker *inadvertently* forgot to consider or misconstrued policy.[215] What, then, if a policy has been correctly understood and considered, and a justification is offered for departure? How carefully will the courts review this justification and, therefore, the balancing of individual and public interests? A comparison of decided cases

[210] Similarly *Bristol DC v Clark* [1975] 3 All ER 978, 981–2 (public housing); *R v Bolton MBC, ex p Kirkman* [1998] JPL 787 (planning); *R v Brent LBC, ex p MacDonagh* [1990] COD 3 (eviction of squatters); *R v DPP, ex p Burke* [1997] COD 169 (prosecution); *R v North Derbyshire Health Authority, ex p Fisher* (1998) 10 Admin LR 27, 32, 42–3 (NHS policy).

[211] *R v Commissioner of Police of the Metropolis, ex p P* (1996) 8 Admin LR 6. See also *R v Chief Constable, ex p L* [1993] 1 All ER 756, 770; *R v DPP, ex p C* [1995] 1 Cr App Rep 136; *R v DPP, ex p Duckenfield* [1999] 2 All ER 873. For successful challenges of departure without any justification being offered in EC law, see Cases 80–83/81 and 182–185/81 *Adam v Commission* [1984] ECR 3411; 129 and 274/81 *Lux v Court of Auditors* [1984] ECR 4127; T-33/91*Willams v Court of Auditors* [1992] ECR II-2499; T-92/96 *Monaco v EP* [1997] ECR-SC II-573. Compare Cases 190/81 *Blomefield v Commission* [1983] ECR 3981; T-134/96 *Smets v Commission* [1997] ECR II-2333 (no departure proven on the facts).

[212] *R v Derbyshire CC, ex p Woods* [1998] Env LR 277, 290 (planning, confirming *Gransden v Secretary of State for the Environment* [1986] JPL 519); *R v Secretary of State for the Environment, ex p West Oxfordshire DC* (1993) 25 HLR 417 (public housing); *R v North Derbyshire Health Authority, ex p Fisher* (1998) 10 Admin LR 27, 42 (NHS).

[213] *R v Home Secretary, ex p Urmaza* [1996] COD 479; Case C-164/98P *DIR International Film v Commission,* 27/1–2000 para 22–27. See also *R v Criminal Injuries Compensation Board, ex p Schofield* [1971] 1 WLR 926; *R v Secretary of State for the Home Office, ex p Lancashire Police Authority* [1992] COD 161; *R v Home Secretary, ex p Northumbria Police Authority* (1993) 5 Admin LR 489; *R v Home Secretary, ex p Pierson* [1997] 3 WLR 492, 501, 508, 515.

[214] *Virgin Cinema Properties v Secretary of State for the Environment* The Independent 20/10–97; *R v Chief Probations Officer for the West Midlands, ex p Ludhera* [1999] COD 101. See further J. Maurici, 'The Meaning of Policy: A Question for the Court?' (1998) JR 85, 91.

[215] *Niarchos v Secretary of State for the Environment* (1978) 35 P and CR 259, 264; *R v Commissioner of Police of the Metropolis, ex p P* (1996) 8 Admin LR 6; *R v North Derbyshire Health Authority, ex p Fisher* (1998) 10 Admin LR 27, 32; *R v DPP, ex p Duckenfield* [1999] 2 All ER 873, 877.

suggests that there is little difference between the three jurisdictions at this stage.

The position in English law has traditionally been that the courts will only interfere if the balancing is *Wednesbury* unreasonable and a suggestion, made by Sedley J in *Urmaza*,[216] that departures from policy should be reviewed more carefully was explicitly rejected in *Gangadeen*.[217] It has, however, subsequently been accepted in *Coughlan* that a more intensive review than mere *Wednesbury* applies in cases concerned with expectations based on individualized representations. It would be entirely logical for the English courts to extend the *Coughlan* approach to departure cases. For the normative justification for protection against departure from policy is as strong, and possibly even stronger, than the justification for protection of expectations created by individualized assurances.[218]

The French courts also show considerable deference towards the administration's balancing of private and public interests. They will only interfere if the administration made a manifest error (*erreur manifest)*; that is if there was a very serious imbalance, or lack of proportion, between the individual and public interest at stake.[219] Indeed, to this author's knowledge the French courts have never found that the administration made such an error since *Crédit foncier de France* was decided in 1970.[220]

The Community judicature's standard of review in departure cases is difficult to ascertain precisely, because no justification for departure was offered by the Community administration in the cases decided so far. It was seen above that the Community courts show some deference in cases concerning departure from individualized assurances and promises: they will only intervene if there is a significant imbalance between the private and public interests at stake.[221] It may be assumed that the Community judicature will apply a similar, or a slightly more intensive, standard of review in relation to departure from policy.

[216] See *R v Home Secretary, ex p Urmaza* [1996] COD 479.

[217] *R v Home Secretary, ex p Gangadeen* [1998] 1 FLR 762, 770 confirming *Wycombe BC v Secretary of State for the Environment* [1988] JPL 111, 112–13; *R v Home Secretary, ex p Hastrup* [1996] Imm AR 616; *R v DPP, ex p Burke* [1997] COD 169. See B. Schwehr, 'A Study in Fairness in the Field of Community Care' (1997) JSWFL 247, 250.

[218] See Ch. 1.2.B.

[219] CE 18/11–77 *SA Marchand* Rec 442; CE 23/5–80 *Agence nationale pour l'amélioration de l'habitat* Rec 238; TA Nice 26/10–89 *Maestri* Rec 434. French authors state that the balancing is subject to 'minimal' or 'restrained' judicial control. See A. de Laubadère, J. C. Venezia, and Y. Gaudemet, *Traité de droit administratif*, vol. i, 14th edn. (Paris, 1996) 702.

[220] See Cliquennois, above n. 206, 7. A survey of over 100 decisions reported on Lexis revealed only three cases in which *directives* have been invoked successfully before the CE and CAA, and all of these concerned procedural rather than substantive guidelines. See TA Besançon 7/2–73 *Ballaud* AJDA 1973, 590; CE 5/12–80 *Syndicat des Importateurs de Chariots de Manutention* Rec 461; CAA Nancy 9/4–91 *Adnet* DF 1992 no 7 comm 314.

[221] See section 3.A.

(C) The Scope of the Duty to Apply Policy: 'Circulaires' *and* 'Directives'

The notion of 'policy' which must be applied loyally is fairly wide in English and EC law. A written statement which sets out an interpretation of statutory provisions, a policy for application of discretion, or a prevailing practice is *prima facie* binding whatever its precise form or designation.[222] By comparison, the scope of the duty to apply policy is more limited in French law. A distinction is drawn in French law between two types of policy documents; *directives* and *circulaires*.[223] While a *directive* sets out general guidelines and criteria to be applied in the exercise of discretionary powers, a *circulaire* interprets and comments on precise legislative provisions.[224] This distinction is problematic because many administrative documents are in practice not labelled accordingly. What is in substance a *directive* may be entitled administrative instruction (*instruction*),[225] note of information (*note de service*)[226] or even *circulaire*.[227] The case law also does not shed much light on the distinction, as the courts often fail to explain whether a particular document is in substance a *directive* or a *circulaire*.[228]

Though difficult to apply, the distinction between *directives* and *circulaires* is very important because the latter are not subject to the principle laid down in *Crédit foncier.* The 'logic' of this is as follows. According to traditional French case law there are two types of *circulaires*.[229] One type adds to or departs from the legislative provisions it purports to interpret (*circulaire réglementaire*). Such a *circulaire* is unlawful and, for that reason, not binding on the administration.[230] Another type of *circulaire* interprets the relevant provisions without adding to or departing from them (*circulaire interprétative*). While such a *circulaire* is lawful, the courts consistently held that it has no legally binding

[222] The Community courts use the terms internal instruction, internal measure, and internal directive synonymously. See Case T-134/96 *Smets v Commission* [1997] ECR II-2333. For application of the *Louwage* case law to documents entitled decision, procedure, memorandum, and Guide to Staff Reports, see respectively Cases C-58/94 *Netherlands v Council* [1996] ECR I-2169 para 37–38; 181–184/86 *Del Plato v Commission* [1987] ECR 4991; 282/81 *Ragusa v Commission* [1983] ECR 1245 para 18; T-33/91*Willams v Court of Auditors* [1992] ECR II-2499 para 66. Compare, for internal recommendations, Cases 40/86 *Kolivas v Commission* [1987] ECR 2643; T-26/91 *Kupka-Floridi v ECOSOC* [1992] ECR II-1615 para 25.

[223] See generally on *circulaires* Y. Gaudemet, 'Remarques à propos des circulaires administratives', in *Mélanges Stassinopoulos* (Paris, 1974); *LGA* 514; *Circulaire 'sur les circulaires'* of 15/6–87, D 1987, 231.

[224] See Cliquennois, above n. 206, 5.

[225] CE 20/1–71 *Union départementale des sociétés mutualistes du Jura* Rec 45; CAA Paris 5/11–96 *Société Foncina* no 95PA03514.

[226] CE 29/7–94 *Gentilhomme* Rec 371; CE 28/7–95 *Haguet* DA 1995 no 556.

[227] Braibant *conclusions* 12/12–72 *Robinet* D 1975, 216–7; CE 18/11–77 *SA Marchand* Rec 442; CE 26/6–85 *ATDPPE* Rec 207; CE 12/12–97 *ONIFLHOR* DA 1998 chroniques no 4.

[228] e.g. CE 18/11–87 *Gisti* Rec 528; CE 28/11–97 *Arnal* no 125.920.

[229] See *LGA* 507, 512.

[230] A survey of unpublished case law reveals that *circulaires* are often held unlawful on this ground, e.g. CE 4/11–88 *Benes* no 61.185; CE 30/11–90 *Vidal* no 114.914; CE 27/9–91 *Boude* no 86.540; CE 12/5–97 *Besnard* no 140.910.

effects,[231] and an individual can therefore not invoke it to challenge a decision, which is based on a different interpretation of the relevant provision.[232]

The French Decree of 18 November 1983 purported to simplify this case law and improve legal certainty by stating (in Art 1) that lawful *circulaires* bind the administration in particular instances just like *directives*. However, this decree has not changed the law in practice.[233] Although *circulaires* have been enforced by some lower administrative courts,[234] the CE always refused to follow their example.[235] The reason for this defiance is, first, an unwillingness on behalf of the CE to accept that a profound change in administrative principles was implemented by administrative decree and not by statute.[236] Second, the French constitution confers rule-making powers upon the administration on specific subject matters,[237] but ministers do not have inherent (prerogative) rule-making powers in other areas.[238] The CE takes the view that granting *circulaires* the same (limited) binding force as *directives* would effectively grant ministers such powers and thereby upset the constitutional division of powers.[239]

The exclusion of *circulaires* from the general duty to apply policy reduces the protection of equality and legitimate expectations to a considerable extent in practice. For while *directives* are used by the French administration in a number of areas, such as state subsidies, social welfare, and town planning,[240] far more documents entitled 'circulaire', 'instruction' or 'note' are published every year. Some of these documents may be *directives* in substance, but the courts very rarely look behind the title to the substance of the document,[241]and there is evidence that the courts will rather categorize a policy statement as a non-binding

[231] CE 29/1–54 *Notre-Dame du Kreisker* Rec 64.

[232] The applicant may obviously argue that the interpretation applied to his case is unlawful on traditional grounds of statutory construction, but he cannot invoke the *circulaire* in support of such a claim.

[233] See *LGA* 514; Chapus 476; *JC* Fasc 107–30 no 23–24.

[234] TA Nice 11/6–87 *Syndicat commerçants non sédentaires des Alpes-Maritimes* AJDA 1988, 538; TA Marseille 11/12–87 *Bernardi* Rec 494; TA Clermont-Ferrand 3/4–90 *Gand* AJDA 1990, 643; CAA Paris 28/9–95 *Benferhat* no 94PA01762.

[235] For a few notable examples, see CE 19/6–85 *Commune de Bouguenais* Rec 104; CE 20/3–89 *SCI de Periaz* DA 1989 no 208; CE 19/6–92 *Département Puy-de-Dôme* Rec 237; CE 25/4–94 *Ministère d'éducation nationale* Rec 189; CE 21/11–94 *Albayrak* RFDA 1995, 100; CE 6/5–96 *Association Aquitaine* Rec 144; CE 9/10–96 *Moyo* DA 1997 no 12.

[236] Art L80A of the *Code Fiscal* contains a *statutory* provision which obliges tax authorities to apply prevailing practice and policy, whatever its form, in particular instances, and this provision is regularly applied by the French courts. See, e.g. CAA Nantes 10/11–94 *Chapelle* DF 1995 no 13 comm 634 and further Douet, above n. 180, 206–34.

[237] Art 34 and 37 of the French Constitution. These articles provide that the basic rules of public law must be made by Parliamentary *loi*, rather than by administrative decree. See J. S. Bell, *French Constitutional Law* (Oxford, 1992), 88 ff.

[238] CE 7/2–36 *Jamart* Rec 172.

[239] See Douet, above n. 178, 174–5; Woehrling, above n. 19, 15.

[240] See Cliquennois, above n. 206, 6–7.

[241] This author's survey of over 100 judgments, in which Art 1 of the 1983 Decree was mentioned, revealed only a few decisions which questioned the administration's categorization of a document as a *circulaire*.

circulaire than as a *directive* if the correct categorization is in any way in doubt.[242]

(D) Other Requirements: Publication and 'Internal Documents'

The duty to apply policy only applies to published, as opposed to purely 'internal' documents.[243] This rule applies in English, French, and EC law, but while there are no strict requirements as to the form of publication in English and EC law,[244] a French *directive* is only binding if it has been published in the *Journal Officiel* or an official ministerial *Bulletin*.[245] Individuals cannot rely upon policy set out in French ministerial answers to parliamentary questions,[246] press releases, informative leaflets, or the section of the *Journal Officiel* entitled 'internal documentation'.[247]

The requirement of publication, as a precondition for the duty to apply policy in particular instances, is problematic for several reasons.[248] First, it may be fortuitous whether a particular statement is binding because internal rules and policies are not systematically published.[249] Even in France, where the administration is required by law to publish all *directives* and *circulaires*,[250] publication is forgotten or omitted from time to time.[251] Second, it clearly does not encourage open government that the administration can exclude judicial review by keeping policies secret. Third, individuals may not realize that policies published as 'internal documentation' are subject to special rules and can therefore not be relied on safely.[252] Finally, and most importantly, policy statements often 'codify' already existing practice.[253] It is, as will be explained below, accepted that the administration has a *prima facie* duty to apply practice

[242] Compare the conclusion of the *Commissaire de Gouvernement* with the CE's judgment in CE 4/11–77 *Moussa* Rec 417; CE 12/12–97 *ONIFLHOR* DA 1998 chroniques no 4, 8; CE 5/10–98 *Djoussou* DA 1999 no 2. See also Cliquennois, above n. 206, 9–10.

[243] *R v Home Secretary, ex p Hastrup* [1996] Imm AR 616. Similarly *R v IRC, ex p MFK Underwriting Agencies Ltd* [1990] 1 All ER 91, 107; *R v Home Secretary, ex p Amankwah* [1994] Imm AR 240; *Home Secretary v Abdi* [1996] Imm AR 148; CE 31/5–89 *Castellani* no 91.681; CAA Nantes 24/11–93 *Prono* no 92NT00504; CE 17/10–97 *Majorel* no 148.660; Cases 343/81 *Michael v Commission* [1983] ECR 4023 para 13; T-63/89 *Latham v Commission* [1991] ECR II-19 para 25; T-155/94 *Climax Paper Converters v Council* [1996] ECR II-873 para 115.

[244] See text at footnotes 94–106.

[245] Art 1 Decree of 28/11–83. CE 17/10–97 *Majorel* no 148.660. See also CE 31/5–89 *Castellani* no 91.681; CAA Nancy 23/2–95 *Steinmetz* no 93NC00840; CAA Nantes 24/11–93 *Prono* no 92NT00504; CAA Lyon 9/7–92 *Torres* no 91LY00241. Compare Cliquennois, above n. 206, 11.

[246] CE 16/2–94 *SARL Arley* Rec 766; CAA Nantes 30/12–97 *Société France Habitation* no 94NT00825.

[247] CAA Nantes 24/11–93 *Prono* no 92NT00504.

[248] See Baldwin, above n. 199, 114; D. Woodhouse, *In Pursuit of Good Administration: Ministers, Civil Servants and Judges* (Oxford, 1997), 171.

[249] For discussion of publication in one area of EC law, see A. Evans, *EC Law of State Aid* (Oxford, 1997), 409–13.

[250] Art 9, Law of 17/6–78.

[251] See footnote 245.

[252] See Douet, above n. 180, 198–9.

[253] Cases 25/83 *Buick v Commission* [1984] ECR 1773; 7/86 *Vincent v EP* [1987] ECR 2473, 2477.

in particular instances. Unpublished policy documents which reflect prevailing practice ought therefore logically to be subject to the same principle.

(E) Departure from Practice

The duty to apply policy in individual cases also applies to unwritten, but settled, administrative practice. While in French law this duty flows solely from the principle of equal treatment, the English and the Community courts have referred to both equality[254] and legitimate expectations.[255] The leading French case of *Contremoulin* and the EC case of *Ferriere San Carlo* neatly illustrate the operation of these principles. [256]

In *Contremoulin* the CE decided that the applicant was entitled to be granted a place for his child in a school near his place of work in accordance with an existing practice, which some of his colleagues had already benefited from, of granting places to workers living far away from their homes. In the absence of particular circumstances, or an overriding public interest, the principle of equal treatment demanded a loyal application of the practice.[257] The *Ferriere San Carlo* case concerned a fine imposed by the Commission for the applicant's steel deliveries in excess of a quarterly quota. This fine apparently derogated from a two-year-old practice of permitting stocks to be run down even if this meant that the quota would be exceeded, and the ECJ held that the Commission had violated the applicant's legitimate expectations as it had not even considered whether the practice actually covered the situation.[258]

The practical impact of the duty to follow practice in particular instances is, however, limited by three factors. First, it may be difficult to prove the existence of a practice, which has not been 'codified' by a written policy statement.[259] Second, there is some uncertainty about when a practice becomes sufficiently 'settled'.[260] While a practice applied consistently for as long as twenty-five to

[254] e.g. *North Wiltshire DC v Secretary of State for the Environment* [1992] 3 PLR 113, 122.

[255] *CCSU v Minister for the Civil Service* [1985] AC 374; *R v IRC, ex p Camacq Co* [1989] STC 785.

[256] Case 344/85 *Ferriere San Carlo v Commission* [1987] ECR 4435; CE 10/7–95 *Contremoulin* AJDA 1995, 925.

[257] See also CE 24/4–64 *Villard* Rec 256; CE 15/10–69 *Association 'Caen-Demain'* Rec 435; CE 19/2–93 *SARL Gilda* no 103.047. Compare CE 3/12–20 *Duquesnoy* Rec 1034; CE 21/5–20 *Jacquot* Rec 543; CE 13/3–64 *Dubreuil* RDP 1965, 11. See further P. Amselek, 'Le rôle de la pratique dans la formation du droit', RDP 1983, 1471; G. Teboul, *Usages et coutume dans la jurisprudence administrative* (Paris, 1989), 137–41; Kessler *conclusions* CE 7/2–94 *Duchêne* Rec 55.

[258] The Commission had 'on principle' refused to consider this possibility when asked to do so by the applicant. Compare Case T-141/94 *Thyssen Stahl v Commission*, 11/3–99 para 507–511.

[259] e.g. *Samir v Home Secretary* [1993] Imm AR 551; *Patel v Home Secretary* [1993] Imm AR 392; *R v IRC, ex p Warburg* [1994] STC 518; Case 92/85 *Hamai v ECJ* [1986] ECR 3157 para 8–9.

[260] See *R v Home Secretary, ex p Bennett* The Times 18/8–86; *R v Brent LBC, ex p Gunning* (1985) 84 LGR 168; *R v Gwent CC, ex p Bryant* [1988] COD; *R v Secretary of State for the Environment, ex p Kent* [1988] JPL 706; *R v British Coal Corporation, ex p Vardy* [1993] ICR 720, 758.

thirty-five years is clearly settled,[261] an individual will not normally have a legitimate expectation of obtaining a beneficial decision simply because it has on a few previous occasions been awarded to him[262] or another person in similar circumstances.[263] Third, the courts will presumably only interfere if the administration has ignored the practice completely, as was the situation in *Contremoulin* and *Ferriere San Carlo*, or if the justification offered for departing from practice is *Wednesbury* unreasonable or manifestly erroneous (*erreur manifest*).

5 Departure from General Representations on the Grounds of a Shift in Policy (Situation 4)

It is a well-recognized principle, in English, French, and EC law that authorities have the power to change their policies from time to time. Without such a power, authorities would not be able to act effectively in the public interest. Individuals can therefore not legitimately expect that a favourable policy or practice will be maintained, and the mere fact that a person is disadvantaged by a change normally does not give rise to any cause for complaint.[264]

However, as explained in Chapter 1, effective government in the public interest must be reconciled with fairness, certainty, and trust in administration all of which require respect for legitimate expectations. A general change of policy may, as a departure from policy in a particular instance, disappoint the expectations and reliance of individuals who have acted upon the initial policy; especially if the change is implemented without prior warning. There is, therefore, a compelling argument for imposing certain restrictions upon the *way in which* the power to change policy can be used. Authorities should consider the effect of policy changes upon the expectations of those affected and balance such expectations against the policy arguments in favour of the change. Advance notice and transitional provisions, or exceptions, should then be granted to

[261] See text at footnote 113.

[262] e.g. *R v North East Thames Health Authority, ex p de Groot* [1988] COD 25; *R v Birmingham CC, ex p Sheptonhurst* [1990] 1 All ER 1026; Cases 16–19/59 *Geitling v High Authority* [1960] ECR 45, 64 and 67/63 *SOREMA v High Authority* [1964] ECR 321, 352; C-69/89 *Nakajima v Council* [1991] ECR II-2069 para 119–120; T-20/91 *Holtbecker v Commission* [1992] ECR II-2599 para 53; C-258–259/90 *Naviera Laida v Commission* [1992] ECR I-2901; T-498/93 *Dornonville v Commission* [1994] ECR-SC II-813 para 46; T-134/96 *Smets v Commission* [1997] ECR II-2333.

[263] *Yakub v Chief Immigration Officer, Heathrow* [1988] Imm AR 177. Compare *R v Director General of Electricity Supply, ex p Scottish Power*, 3/2–97.

[264] *Hughes v Department of Health and Social Security* [1985] AC 776, 778; Cases 19/61 *Mannesman v High Authority* [1962] ECR 717, 752 (coal and steel policy); 52/81 *Faust v Commission* [1982] ECR 3745, 3762 (CAP and import restrictions); C-216/87 *R v Ministry of Agriculture, ex p Jaderow* [1989] ECR 4509 (fisheries policy); C-280/93 *Germany v Council* [1994] ECR I-4973 para 80 (*ibid*); C-69/89 *Nakajima v Council* [1991] ECR II-2069 para 119–120 (anti-dumping policy); T-134/96 *Smets v Commission* [1997] ECR II-2333 (staff remuneration policy).

ensure that expectations are upheld to the extent that this does not defy the purpose of the change of policy. In this way, legitimate expectations may be upheld by focusing on the *temporal dimension* of policy changes without questioning the power to change policies as such.

This argument has not so far found favour with the French courts.[265] Indeed, according to the principle of 'mutability' (*mutabilité*), the administration's power to change policy is virtually absolute.[266] General rules and policy may always be changed with prospective and immediate effect.[267] Nobody has the 'right to the maintenance of general rules and policies' since general rules and policies 'do not create rights for the future', and the courts therefore will not insist on the adoption of transitional measures or exceptions to protect expectations and reliance.[268] Thus, in the leading case of *Syndicat national de la meunerie à seigle* the administration had, in 1947, fixed certain criteria for regulation of retail prices of rye and declared that these criteria would apply until 1952. However, a less favourable policy was adopted in 1950 with effect for that year's harvest. The CE held, on reasons given by *Commissaire de Gouvernement* Donnedieu de Vabres that the administration's discretionary power to change rules and policy is not and could not be limited. The fact that some producers had apparently relied financially upon the existing policy was on this view irrelevant.[269]

The English courts have in recent years accepted that the power to change policies is not absolute. The administration must give 'adequate [and] clear advance notification to those likely to be affected by' a change,[270] as it may otherwise be considered an abuse of power or *Wednesbury* unreasonable having regard to 'the nature and extent of the alteration and the length of notice'.[271] In

[265] It has been presented to the CE, notably by Genevois in *conclusions* CE 19/5–83 *Club sportif de la Fève* AJDA 1983, 426, 429.

[266] See J. Carbajo, *L'application dans le temps des décisions administratives exécutoires* (Paris, 1980) 108–50; J. Petit, 'Contribution à l'étude des conflits de lois dans le temps en droit public interne', Doctoral thesis (Paris II 1993), 348–410, 629 ff. The principle of *mutabilité* is contrasted with that of *non-rétroactivité*, according to which administrative decisions and rules must not be retroactive. See P. Delvolvé, 'Le principe de non-rétroactivité dans la jurisprudence économique du Conseil d'État', in *Mélanges Marcel Waline*, vol. ii (Paris, 1974), 355, and 'Acte administratif', in F. Gazier, R. Drago and A. Dupie (eds.), *Encyclopédie Dalloz: Répertoire de contentieux administratif* (Paris, 1996), no 542f.

[267] Indeed, there is a presumption that a new general regulation applies to existing circumstances. See CE 28/6–46 *Société Le Polo* Rec 184; Gentot *conclusions* CE 16/6–72 *SCI du moulin de Segères* AJDA 1973, 85; CE 27/5–87 *SNPSGA* Rec 181; CE 23/12–88 *Aitelhadj* Rec 461; CE 28/7–89 *Biscay* Rec 167.

[268] Genevois *conclusions* CE 19/5–83 *Club sportif de la Fève* AJDA 1983, 426, 429. An exception to the principle of *mutabilité* is made where a change in general rules interferes with existing contractual obligations, but it is not applicable to changes in policy. See Delvolvé, above n. 266, no 542, 547–8.

[269] CE 25/6–54 *Syndicat national de la meunerie à seigle* D 1955, 50 subsequently confirmed on several occasions, e.g. CE 23/10–74 *Valet* Rec 500.

[270] *R v Ministry of Defence, ex p Walker* The Times 11/2–99.

[271] *R v Joint Committee on Higher Medical Training, ex p Goldstein* (1993) 11 BMLR 10.

practice, however, it is very difficult to establish that a change of policy, or its application to particular individuals, is unreasonable, and the English courts have so far been reluctant to engage in more intensive review.[272] The case of *Hargreaves* is a pertinent example.[273] In this instance, the Home Secretary had changed policy on prisoners' home leave with immediate effect in the light of concerns over crimes committed by prisoners on leave. This change, which had a severely traumatizing effect on some of the thousands of prisoners it affected, was made despite evidence that a large proportion of the relevant crimes were not attributable to home leave. It was argued to the court that home leave facilitates societal reintegration and rehabilitation, and that a better screening process could have solved the problems without restricting the freedom of all prisoners. Still, the court found that the Minister had not acted unreasonably.[274]

The English courts' deferential approach may be contrasted with the Community judicature's approach in the cases of *CNTA* and *Mulder*.[275] In *CNTA* a trading company had concluded export contracts in reliance on a general regulation, which provided for the payment of monetary compensation amounts (MCA). It had obliged itself to carry out the contracts by obtaining an export permit, which pre-fixed the MCA, and it had lodged a security with the authorities to guarantee its compliance with this obligation. The ECJ held that the entitlement to MCA was conditional upon completion of the export. Consequently, the licence was not a final and irrevocable decision, which created vested rights for CNTA. However, the Court found that CNTA had a legitimate expectation that the Commission would not change its policy and abolish these amounts with effect for its existing contract.[276]

The *Mulder* case also concerned the EC Common Agricultural Policy.[277] Milk farmers had been encouraged and agreed to cease production for a five-year period during which they received an EC premium. During this period the EC milk quota system was changed so that allocation of production quotas became dependent on production in previous years. This effectively prevented

[272] A more intensive balancing approach was applied in *R v Devon Health Authority, ex p Coughlan* [1999] Lloyd's LR Medical 306, but it was accepted that this approach is mostly applicable to instances where the representation is individualized and the expectation is therefore confined to one person or a few people (para 59, 71). In other words, the *Coughlan* approach applies to what is here called Situation 2 and not Situation 4.

[273] *R v Home Secretary, ex p Hargreaves* [1997] 1 WLR 906. For other decisions holding changes of policy lawful, see *Findlay v Home Secretary* [1985] AC 318, 338; *R v Torbay BC, ex p Cleasby* [1991] COD 142; *R v Panel on Take-overs and Mergers, ex p Fayed* [1992] BCC 524; *Ali v Home Secretary* [1994] Imm AR 489; *R v Ministry of Defence, ex p Walker* The Times 11/2–99; *R v Independent Television Commission, ex p Flextech Plc* [1999] COD 109. Compare *R v Department of Trade and Industry, ex p Blenheim* [1992] COD 453; *R v Shropshire CC, ex p Jones* (1997) 9 Admin LR 625.

[274] See also critical comments by Forsyth (1997), above n. 4, and Foster, above n. 4.

[275] For more detailed treatment of legitimate expectations and immediate application of policy, see Schwarze 1130–45; Tridimas, above n. 73, 180–5.

[276] Case 74/74 *CNTA v Commission* [1975] ECR 533.

[277] Cases 120/86 *Mulder (I) v Minister van Landbouw* [1988] ECR 2321.

farmers who had ceased production from returning to their profession. The ECJ held, in *Mulder*, that although farmers could not expect to return to milk production on exactly the same terms as before, they could legitimately expect not to be excluded specifically by virtue of the obligation they had undertaken. Thus, the Court acknowledged the important Community interest in regulation of the milk sector, which had been plagued by over-production, but found that this did not justify the immediate and full application of the new policy to those who had taken part in the scheme. The Council responded by awarding the affected farmers a special quota of 60 per cent of the quantity they had marketed in the year before they ceased production, but the ECJ found, in *Spagl*, that this was insufficient, and a higher quota was subsequently awarded by a Council regulation.[278]

A direct comparison of *Mulder* and *Hargreaves* leaves the impression that EC law imposes considerably greater constraints upon policy changes than English law.[279] While the English courts will only interfere with manifestly unreasonable changes in policy, the Community courts will intervene if there is a significant imbalance between the justification for the change and the affected persons' interests. This difference is real and important, but a survey of the Community case law reveals that the applicants' success in *CNTA* and *Mulder* is a rare occurrence.[280] Policy changes are frequently considered foreseeable in the light of market developments or statements from the administration, and the Community courts do not often find a significant imbalance between the public and private interests at stake.[281] The main exception is where, as in *CNTA* and *Mulder*, the person undertook binding legal obligations towards the authorities in such a way that he is affected specifically and more gravely by the change than others.[282] Conversely, a change in policy which affects existing contractual relations between individuals does not, in and of itself, violate the Community principle of legitimate expectations.[283]

[278] Case C-189/89 *Spagl v Hauptzollamt Rosenheim* [1990] ECR I-4539. Certain aspects of these arrangements were subsequently annulled. See Cases C-264/90 *Wehrs v Hauptzollamt Lüneburg* [1992] ECR I-6285; C-21/92 *Kamp v Hauptzollamt Wuppertal* [1994] ECR 1619.

[279] See Forsyth, above n. 4, 380–1.

[280] See however the generous result in the staff Case 127/80 *Grogan v Commission* [1982] ECR 869. This case should—as noted by Tridimas, above n. 73, 196–7—be treated as an aberration.

[281] See e.g. Cases C-133, 300 and 362/93 *Crispoltoni (II) v Fattoria Autonoma Tabacchi* [1994] ECR I-4863; T-521/93 *Atlanta v Council* [1996] ECR II-1707; C-138/95P *Campo Ebro Industrial v Council* [1997] ECR I-2027; C-284/94 *Spain v Council* [1998] ECR I-7309; T-125/96 *Boehringer v Council*, 1/12–99. See similarly Mackenzie Stuart, above n. 73, 59; Sharpston, above n. 73, 158.

[282] A different situation occurs where secondary legislation imposes a specific duty upon the Commission, over and above the general principle of legitimate expectations, to take into account existing contracts and goods in transit. Compare Cases C-152/88 *Sofriimport v Commission* [1990] ECR I-2477; C-51/95P *Unifruit Hellas v Commission* [1997] ECR I-727.

[283] e.g. Cases 1/73 *Westzucker v Einfuhr- and Vorratstelle für Zucker* [1973] ECR 723; 84/78 *Tomadini v Amministrazione delle Finanze* [1979] ECR 1801; 112/80 *Dürbeck v Hauptzollamt-Frankfurt* [1981] ECR 1095; 52/81 *Faust v Commission* [1982] ECR 3745.

The reluctance in English law, and to a lesser extent EC law, to interfere with general changes of policy contrasts with the courts' greater willingness to uphold expectations created by specific administrative assurances.[284] Why this difference? The answer is, first, that while policies are generally known to be impermanent, specific assurances more easily convey an objectively reasonable impression of finality or promise. Second, to restrict the temporal application of a policy may affect important public interests, and it will inevitably limit the decision-maker's discretion to some extent. Holding a public body to its assurance in a particular instance will typically have less effect on the public interest and the decision-maker's freedom of action.[285] However, the courts should be wary of drawing too rigid distinctions between these two categories.[286] On the one hand, what appears to be a general change of policy may in fact impact severely on a limited class of persons who have planned and relied upon previous policy.[287] Such action can be just as unfair as a decision to go back on a specific assurance. On the other hand, it is somehow paradoxical to deny judicial protection when a change of policy disappoints the expectations of a very large number of persons. The courts should not shy away from checking that the application of policy to individuals who have been led to expect something different is fair, and they should insist on the adoption of appropriate transitional measures.[288]

6 Legitimate Expectations and Unlawful Representations

(A) The General Principle

The conflict between the principles of legality and legal certainty which arises when public authorities make, and subsequently revoke, unlawful decisions was examined in Chapter 3. It was seen that there are important differences between English, French, and EC law, for while English public authorities are almost entirely free to revoke unlawful decisions, revocation is in French and EC law subject to fairly strict time limits.

A conflict between legality and certainty also occurs when authorities make unlawful informal representations which they subsequently seek to resile from. To what extent, if at all, can individuals hold authorities to unlawful represen-

[284] See section 3.

[285] See also *R v Secretary of State for the Environment, ex p NALGO* (1993) 5 Admin LR 785 (legitimate expectations claims will more rarely succeed against general secondary legislation than individualized decisions).

[286] See T. R. S. Allan, *Law, Liberty, and Justice: The Legal Foundations of British Constitutionalism* (Oxford, 1993), 175–6, 201.

[287] e.g. *R v Secretary of State for Health, ex p US Tobacco International Inc* [1992] QB 353; Case T-92/96 *Monaco v EP* [1997] ECR-SC II-573.

[288] See *R v Devon Health Authority, ex p Coughlan* [1999] Lloyd's LR Medical 306, 327–8.

tations? There is, in this context, little difference between English, French, and EC law. The general rule is that unlawful representations are *not* binding, and they can neither give rise to an estoppel by representation[289] or a legitimate expectation.[290] This rule applies even if the administration made a very precise and unqualified assurance. For example, in *Pauvert* the applicant had been offered, at an interview and in writing, a job as a chauffeur. However, according to the vacancy notice the job required 'fifteen years of work experience as a chauffeur', and of the applicant's fifteen years of experience only ten were as a chauffeur. In these circumstances, the Court of Auditors was not bound by its job offer. A formal decision to promote the applicant had not been made and he had, in the ECJ's opinion, no legitimate expectation as he did not satisfy the legal conditions and should have known the nature and length of his own work experience.[291] Similarly, in the leading French case of *Société des huileries de Chauny*, the CE held that the Minister of Finance was not, and could not be, bound by a written assurance to French oil traders that a price regulation would remain in force, since that assurance fettered the Minister's discretionary power to regulate prices and was therefore unlawful.[292]

(B) Exceptions

An individual who relies upon an unlawful representation in good faith about its lawfulness may suffer great hardship when the administration subsequently goes back on it. There is, therefore, an argument for limiting the principle of legality to promote fairness, legal certainty, and trust in government. This argument has not been accepted in French law and EC law. A distinction is drawn between administrative decisions, which become irrevocable after a certain time, and informal representations which are in theory never binding.[293] The protection against individual hardship is slightly more developed in English law, because it is accepted that *ultra vires* statements may create an estoppel by representations in two special situations.[294]

First, the English administration may be bound by statements made by its officers in excess of delegated powers.[295] In EC law, the absence of formal

[289] See footnote 11.

[290] *R v Gaming Board, ex p Kingsley* [1996] COD 241, 242; *R v CEC, ex p Littlewoods Ltd* [1997] STC 317, 325; *R v Criminal Injuries Compensation Board, ex p Keane* [1998] COD 128; Cases 112/77 *Töpfer v Commission* [1978] ECR 1019; 188/82 *Thyssen v Commission* [1983] ECR 3721 para 11; C-301/90 *Commission v Council* [1992] ECR I-221 para 27; C-313/90 *CIRFS v Commission* [1993] ECR I-1125 para 45; C-31–44/91 *Lageder v Amministrazione delle Finanze* [1993] ECR I-1761 para 33–36; T-2/93 *Air France v Commission* [1994] ECR II-323 para 101; T-22/99 *Rose v Commission*, 22/2–2000 para 36–41.

[291] Case 228/84 *Pauvert v Court of Auditors* [1985] ECR 1969.

[292] CE 24/4–64 *Société des huileries de Chauny* Rec 249.

[293] See AG Warner [1980] ECR 3121; Schwarze 1091, 1093 who are critical.

[294] For a more detailed analysis, see Ch. 3.5.B.

[295] *Western Fish Products v Penwith DC* [1981] 2 All ER 204.

delegation makes the official's representation unlawful and unable to found legitimate expectations.[296] Thus, in *Frubo* the Director-General for competition informed a company that, in his view, an agreement notified under Art 81(1) EC would qualify for an exception under Art 81(3) in the light of certain amendments proposed by Frubo. This did not arouse a legitimate expectation, as the Director was not 'authorised [by the Commission] to enter into . . . a commitment'.[297]

Second, while English officials may, at least in some cases, waive procedural formalities, this has never been accepted in EC law. For example, in *Burban* the applicant had allegedly been informed during a telephone conversation with the Head of the EP's Staff Management Service that written proof of qualifications should not be submitted with an application for participation in a job competition. The ECJ held that 'erroneous information given by an official who has no authority to change [the] provisions [of the notice of competition] cannot . . . enable or . . . oblige [the administration] to act contrary to that notice'.

The only concession to individual's legal certainty in EC law occurs in cases concerning fines imposed by the Commission on companies for violations of EC law.[298] Specific and misleading assurances made by Commission officials may lead to mitigation of such fines, as in *Thyssen* where a senior Commission official's alleged assurance that a company would be allowed to exceed a steel production quota to supply a particular customer swayed the ECJ to reduce the fine, imposed in spite of this assurance, to a token 5 ECU.[299]

As a final note, it may be added that French statutory tax law provides an interesting exception to the principle that unlawful assurances are not binding.[300] French tax authorities have a general power to revise and increase tax liability, normally for a period of three years after the end of the tax year.[301] Art L80A of the *Code Fiscal*, which was adopted to reduce the legal uncertainty caused by this power, stipulates that tax authorities are bound by the interpretation, policy, or practice (*doctrine*), which was prevailing on the day it made a decision about liability to tax. Thus, while tax authorities can change policy and interpretation of tax rules with prospective effect, already assessed tax lia-

[296] For the Community procedure of delegation (*habilitation*), see Case C-137/92P *Commission v BASF* [1994] ECR I-2555.

[297] Case 71/74 *Frubo v Commission* [1975] ECR 563, 582. See also Cases 21/64 *Figli v High Authority* [1965] ECR 214, 258; 188/82 *Thyssen v Commission* [1983] ECR 3721 para 11.

[298] In what appears to be an exercise in double standards, the ECJ has accepted that unlawful advice about the interpretation of EC law may create legitimate expectations in favour of Member States who incur expenses on behalf of the Community structural funds. See Case 133/84 *UK v Commission* [1986] ECR 1257. Compare Cases 347/85 *UK and Ireland v Commission* [1988] ECR 1749; C-238/96 *Ireland v Commission* [1998] ECR I-5810 para 93–110. See also Temple Lang, above n. 166, 11.

[299] See also Case 78/83 *USINOR v Commission* [1984] ECR 4177 (75% reduction). Compare Case T-229/94 *Deutsche Bahn v Commission* [1997] ECR II-1689.

[300] See *JC* Procédures Fiscales Fasc 170–174; Douet, above n. 180, 206–34.

[301] This is known as the *droit de reprise*.

bilities cannot be revised in the light of such changes.[302] This rule applies even if the original interpretation or policy was unlawful, and there are no strict requirements as to the publication, designation, or form of the policy as long as the individual can show that it prevailed at the time.[303] This legislative provision is remarkable because it acknowledges, rightly, that the legal certainty and expectations of tax payers should in some instances prevail over the principle of legality. The public interest is not seriously harmed if, as a result of an unlawful practice or policy, a person escapes tax liability. The cost is born by the taxpaying community as a whole, and third parties will rarely be directly affected to any significant extent.[304]

7 Comparison and Suggestions for Reform

(A) Comparative Summary

The detailed comparative study of English, French, and EC law has revealed that the difference between the English principle of legitimate expectations, as an aspect of *Wednesbury* unreasonableness, and the EC law principle of substantive legitimate expectations is smaller than the judicial rhetoric suggests. In both legal systems, the principles are limited in three respects.

First, the concept of objectively reasonable expectations is narrow. The individual must show that the administration gave a *lawful,* specific and unqualified assurance (Situation 2), or that it departed from a published policy (or settled practice) applicable to the relevant class of persons (Situations 3–4). It must also be shown that the change was unforeseeable to a well-informed and cautious person. English and EC law are in this respect quite similar.

Second, the concept of legitimate expectations is also narrow, because the courts show deference towards the administration's balancing of expectations and countervailing public policy considerations. Here, however, there is an important difference between English and Community law. The English courts are, as the *Hargreaves* case reveals,[305] very reluctant to interfere where legitimate expectations are disappointed as a result of general changes of policy (Situation 4), and it remains to be seen whether the more intensive standard of review adopted in *Coughlan* will be extended to these types of situations.[306] It is possible to hypothesize that, presented with the facts of cases like *CNTA* and

[302] Procedural matters, such as time limits and recovery of tax, are not covered by the provision. See CE 22/6–77 *Société lyonnaise de construction* Rec 752; CE 24/4–81 *SARL Tranchant Frères* DF 1983 no 5 comm 149.

[303] *Doctrine* may be proven by reference to, e.g. ministerial decisions (CE 30/6–72 X Rec 500, CE 26/10–77 X Rec 402) and answers to parliamentary questions (CE 29/4–77 *SA Economiques Troyens* Rec 195).

[304] See Woehrling, above n. 19, 16.

[305] *R v Home Secretary, ex p Hargreaves* [1997] 1 WLR 906.

[306] See footnote 272.

Mulder, the English courts would have come to a similar conclusion as that arrived at by the ECJ, albeit on traditional *Wednesbury* grounds.[307] However, as the case of *Spagl* reveals, the Community principle of legitimate expectations goes further than *Wednesbury*.[308] The Community courts will restrict the application of a policy change if there is a *significant imbalance* between the interests of those affected and the policy considerations in favour of the change.

Third, the protection of expectations created by *unlawful* representations is virtually non-existent in English, French, and EC law. The principle of legality is generally seen to override the concerns for fairness, certainty, and trust in administration. Only in English law is it accepted that an estoppel may arise in special circumstances.

These three limitations on the principle of legitimate expectations in English and EC law reduce the actual protection of expectations to some considerable extent. The difference between, on the one hand, English and EC law and, on the other hand, French law is therefore less dramatic than the total absence of a principle of legitimate expectations in French law might suggest. Moreover, the French courts have utilized the principle of equal treatment to 'fill the gap' in relation to departure from policy in particular instances (Situation 3). This being said, the French cases of *Bouveret* and *Syndicat national de la meunerie à seigle*[309] show that the absence of substantive legitimate expectations does occasionally lead to outcomes which are difficult to accept in terms of fairness, certainty, and trust in administration.

(B) Suggestions for Reform I: Lawful Representations

It is submitted that the traditional English position, according to which the courts will only intervene if the administration ignores legitimate expectations or acts wholly unreasonably, is unsatisfactory. This is so for two main reasons.[310] First, fairness, legal certainty, and trust in administration suggest that legitimate expectations should enjoy a higher level of protection. To maintain that the disappointment of a reasonable expectation is lawful so long as it is not irrational, perverse, or unreasonable comes perilously close, in cases of any complexity, to allowing administrators to ignore expectations altogether.[311] Second, the concept of reasonableness is inherently elastic. It does not provide

[307] See Forsyth, above n. 4, 380–1.

[308] Case C-189/89 *Spagl v Hauptzollamt Rosenheim* [1990] ECR I-4539.

[309] CE 18/10–57 *Bouveret* Rec 542; CE 25/6–54 *Syndicat national de la meunerie à seigle* D 1955, 50.

[310] See Jowell and Lester, above n. 3; Forsyth, above n. 4; Craig (1992, 1996), above n. 4. Compare Walker, above n. 3, 573–4.

[311] See *R v Devon Health Authority, ex p Coughlan* [1999] Lloyd's LR Medical 306, 324; T. R. S. Allan, 'Fairness, Equality, Rationality: Constitutional Theory and Judicial Review', in C. Forsyth and I. Hare (eds.), *The Golden Metwand and the Crooked Cord: Essays in Honour of Sir William Wade* (Oxford, 1998), 15, 27; Craig 620.

useful guidance to administrators in their day-to-day work, or a precise standard of judicial review.[312] The adoption of a more precise and coherent principle would increase certainty and consistency in the application of administrative law both at the level of administration and judicial review.[313] This effect would be enhanced because the many semantic confusions in the present case law would be cleared up.

How might the law be changed to meet these concerns? There appear to be three options.[314] The first option is to use the stricter variant of *Wednesbury* review, sometimes known as 'super-*Wednesbury*', which has—even before the Human Rights Act 1998—been applied in cases concerning interference with human rights, to review interference with legitimate expectations.[315] While this would certainly enhance the protection of legitimate expectations, it is not an appropriate solution. There is, as argued in Chapter 1, a solid justification for protecting expectations in administrative law, but it is readily apparent that expectations are not normatively equal to human rights. They should therefore not be subject to exactly the same standard of review.

The second option is to change the general nature of the *Wednesbury* test itself. In *ITF* Lord Cooke said that the traditional formulation is both exaggerated and tautologous. The test of review should, he argued, not be whether an administrative decision is 'so unreasonable that no reasonable authority could ever have come to it', but rather 'whether the decision in question was one which a reasonable authority could reach'.[316] This change of emphasis would provide a more intensive and adequate standard of review, and it would have the added advantage of creating a neat symmetry between public law principles and the tort of negligence as it is now applied to discretionary decision-making.[317] However, the notion of 'reasonableness' is little more precise or coherent than 'unreasonableness'. Lord Cooke's idea is therefore not a sufficient reform,

[312] See M. Kerry, 'Administrative Law and Judicial Review' (1986) Public Administration 163; D. Feldman, 'Judicial Review: a Way of Controlling Government?' (1988) Public Administration 21, 22–6; S. James, 'The Political and Administrative Consequences of Judicial Review' (1996) Public Administration 613, 624–5.

[313] See Baldwin and Horne, above n. 4, 710–11; Jowell and Lester, above n. 3, 381; Gordon and Ward, above n. 4,1664; Forsyth, above n. 4, 384.

[314] It is now generally accepted that the question cannot be answered by adherence to, or an adaptation of, private law concepts such as the principle of estoppel by representation. For the issues of fairness, trust, and government in the public interest which arise in public law are too different from the private law context in which estoppel principles developed. See *R v Independent Television Commission, ex p TSW* [1996] EMLR 291; *R v IRC, ex p Unilever* [1996] STC 681, 695; De Smith 564.

[315] See footnote 40.

[316] *R v Chief Constable of Sussex, ex p International Trader's Ferry* [1998] 3 WLR 1260, 1289. See also *R v Parliamentary Commissioner for Administration, ex p Balchin* [1997] COD 146.

[317] In *Barrett v Enfield LBC* [1999] 3 All ER 193 the House of Lords adopted a standard of reasonableness, rather than *Wednesbury* unreasonableness, as the touchstone of public law negligence liability. See P. P. Craig and D. Fairgrieve, 'Barrett, Negligence and Discretionary Powers' (1999) PL 626, 647–9.

something more is required to clarify precisely in what circumstances a 'reasonable' authority will be entitled to disappoint expectations.

The third option, suggested by Paul Craig, is to replace *Wednesbury* with the principle of proportionality.[318] When faced with a conflict between reasonable expectations and an administrative decision purporting to achieve some objective, the court would check whether that action was necessary and suited to attain the objective, and whether it imposed excessive burdens upon the individual.[319] The adoption of proportionality as a general principle of judicial review has considerable merit.[320] First, the notion of proportionality is more precise, structured and coherent than the traditional *Wednesbury* test. Consistency and certainty in the application of law would accordingly be enhanced by its adoption.[321] Second, when applying the proportionality test, administrators and courts would have to identify competing interests and balance them against each other. This structures the decision-making process and facilitates the granting of reasons for decisions.[322] Reasons make the value-judgments inherent in discretionary decision-making more transparent, and this may in turn reduce the perception of judicial bias in favour of certain ideologies and classes of society or, at least, facilitate debate about the appropriateness of judicial values.[323] Third, it is well-known that the English courts occasionally strike decisions down which are not 'so unreasonable that no reasonable authority could ever have come to' them.[324] *Wednesbury* is in such cases a veil behind which the reality of judicial review hides.[325] To adopt a principle of proportionality would therefore add realism and intellectual honesty to English law.[326]

[318] P. P. Craig, 'Substantive Legitimate Expectations and the Principles of Judicial Review', in M. Andenas (ed.), *English Public Law and the Common Law of Europe* (London, 1998), 23; 'Unreasonableness and Proportionality in UK Law', in E. Ellis (ed.), *The Principle of Proportionality in the Laws of the EU*, (Oxford, 1999), 85.

[319] Ibid. 43.

[320] See J. L. Jowell and A. Lester, above n. 3; 'Proportionality: Neither Novel nor Dangerous', in J. L. Jowell and D. Oliver (eds.), *New Directions in Judicial Review* (London, 1988); De Smith 593–606; G. Wong: 'Towards the Nutcracker Principle: Reconsidering the Objections to Proportionality' (2000) PL 92. Compare S. Boyron, 'Proportionality in English Administrative Law: A Faulty Translation?' (1992) OJLS 237; J. Laws, 'Wednesbury', in C. Forsyth and I. Hare (eds.), *The Golden Metwand and the Crooked Cord: Essays in Honour of Sir William Wade* (Oxford, 1998), 185. See also G. de Búrca, 'Proportionality and Wednesbury Unreasonableness' (1997) EPL 561.

[321] Although proportionality is also flexible and thus liable to be applied with different degrees of intensity depending upon the values of the judge who applies it and the subject-matter of the case. See G. de Búrca, 'The Principle of Proportionality and its Application in Community Law' (1993) YEL 105 and E. Ellis, 'The Concept of Proportionality in European Community Sex Discrimination Law' in E. Ellis (ed.), *The Principle of Proportionality in the Laws of the EU* (Oxford, 1999).

[322] See Feldman, above n. 312, 27.

[323] On the alleged bias in favour of individualistic and conservative values in the British courts, see J. A. G. Griffith, *The Politics of the Judiciary*, 5th edn. (London, 1997).

[324] For a few prominent examples, see *Hall v Shoreham-by-Sea UBC* [1964] 1 WLR 240; *Secretary of State for Science and Education v Tameside MBC* [1977] AC 1014; *R v IRC, ex p Unilever* [1996] STC 681.

[325] See more generally for this view A. Hutchinson, 'The Rise and Ruse of Administrative Law and Scholarship' (1985) MLR 293, 313.

[326] See Jowell and Lester, above n. 3, 372; Craig 582–3.

Society, including for this purpose Parliament and the administration,[327] is arguably ready for such honesty after many years of judicial activity in the field of public law; the perceived need to cloak review in the rhetoric of manifest unreasonableness is no longer pertinent.[328] Finally, the courts must apply the principle of proportionality in cases which fall within the scope of EC law,[329] and some form of proportionality analysis will also have to be applied under section 6 of the Human Rights Act 1998.[330] The application of the principle of proportionality in purely domestic cases would therefore simplify, and make more comprehensible, the structure of English administrative law.

The future of proportionality as the general standard of judicial review in English law is, however, far from certain. The courts might find it prudent to pause and think further about two issues. First, how would the notion of proportionality impact on the policy-making process within the administration itself? Proportionality rests on what might be described as a legalistic concept of administration. It emphasizes caution and the use of cost-benefit analysis of alternative policy options. While that may seem a perfectly sensible way of proceeding to most lawyers,[331] social scientists might question whether that approach is realistic or appropriate in all contexts.[332] Second, it is generally recognized that proportionality provides a stricter standard of review than traditional *Wednesbury* unreasonableness, and that it enables the courts to undertake very detailed and intensive scrutiny.[333] It may be, as influential commentators assure us, that the English courts would apply the principle of proportionality with restraint, making use of the inherent flexibility of that

[327] For discussion of administrative reactions to judicial review, see C. Harlow, 'Administrative Reaction to Judicial Review' (1976) PL 116; G. Zellick, 'Government Beyond Law' (1985) PL 283; Kerry, above n. 312; James, above n. 312; S. Halliday, 'The Influence of Judicial Review on Bureaucratic Decision-Making' (2000) PL 110.

[328] It may be added that judicial attempts to hide behind the language of *Wednesbury* are unlikely to be successful given that judicial activism has become a pet subject of academics and journalist alike.

[329] Cases 5/88 *Wachauf v Germany* [1989] ECR 2609; C-260/89 *ERT* [1991] ECR I-2925. See P. P. Craig and G. De Búrca, *EU Law: Text and Materials*, 2nd edn. (Oxford, 1998), 317–31.

[330] See D. Feldman, 'Proportionality and the Human Rights Act', in E. Ellis (ed.), *The Principle of Proportionality in the Laws of the EU* (Oxford, 1999), 117.

[331] See J. L. Jowell, 'Is Proportionality an Alien Concept?' (1996) EPL 401, 410.

[332] See C. Lindblom, 'The Science of Muddling Through' (1959) Public Administration Review 79; J. G. March, H. A. Simon, and H. Guetzkow, *Organisations*, 2nd edn. (London, 1993) who emphasize that policy-making takes place under conditions of bounded rationality.

[333] See e.g. N. Emiliou, *The Principle of Proportionality in European Law* (The Hague, 1996), 272; N. Fennelly, 'Legal Interpenetration—Towards Freedom of Movement of Principles', in M. Andenas (ed.), *English Public Law and the Common Law of Europe* (London, 1998), 7, 18; M. Ross, 'Behind Proportionality: The Cultural and Constitutional Context', ibid. 83, 91; F. G. Jacobs, 'Recent Developments in the Principle of Proportionality in EC Law', in E. Ellis (ed.), *The Principle of Proportionality in the Laws of the EU* (Oxford, 1999), 1, 20; N. Green, 'Proportionality and the Supremacy of Parliament in the UK', ibid. 145, 153; T. Tridimas, 'Proportionality in Community Law: Searching for the Appropriate Standard of Scrutiny', ibid. 65, 69, 84; Feldman, above n. 330, 127–9. Compare Lord Hoffmann, 'A Sense of Proportion', in Andenas op cit. 148; 'The Influence of the European Principles of Proportionality', in Ellis op cit. 107.

principle to avert the risk of excessive interference with administrative autonomy.[334] But the House of Lords might prefer to wait and see how the principle of proportionality works out in EC law and human rights cases before it completely abandons the orthodoxy of *Wednesbury*.[335]

Moreover, even if proportionality is adopted as the *general* principle of judicial review in English law, it is by no means certain that it should be applied in legitimate expectations cases. On the one hand, it may be recalled that breach of legitimate expectations has already developed into a distinct species of unlawfulness, which is subject to a detailed case law. There is a risk of confusion between that important case law and other areas of review if the same principle is applied across the board, and it may therefore be preferable to develop a specific test of review for expectations cases. On the other hand, it is settled case law that the administration must take account of reasonable expectations and balance them against countervailing policy considerations. The question is how closely the courts should review that balancing exercise. Using proportionality—with its three tiers of suitability, necessity, and overall balance—to answer that question seems unnecessarily complex, and no other legal system known to this author has directly linked the principles of proportionality and legitimate expectations in this way.

It is, therefore, desirable to develop a test of review which (*a*) prescribes a more appropriate threshold for judicial interference than traditional *Wednesbury* unreasonableness, (*b*) is specifically tailored to legitimate expectations cases, and (*c*) is conceptually less complex than the principle of proportionality. It is submitted that the courts could develop such a test by drawing upon the recent *Coughlan* case and the study of EC law. In *Coughlan* it was accepted that the principle of legitimate expectations is conceptually distinct from the principle of *Wednesbury* unreasonableness, and that once it is established that a person holds a reasonable expectation, then the court will have the task of weighing the requirements of substantive fairness against any overriding interest relied upon for taking an action which will disappoint the expectation.[336] This balancing approach provides a good starting point for legal reform because it is capable of giving more protection to legitimate expectations than the traditional *Wednesbury* test. It meets the requirements of fairness, legal certainty, and trust in administration. However, the balancing approach set out in *Coughlan* is somewhat lacking in precision; to say that the administration's balancing of expectations was 'unfair' or an 'abuse of power' does not tell one at which point the court will intervene.[337] EC law provides an important lesson in this context. We have seen that the EC judicature will only intervene if there

[334] See e.g. De Smith 606.
[335] See the reservations expressed in *R v Home Secretary, ex p Brind* [1991] 1 AC 696, 767.
[336] *R v Devon Health Authority, ex p Coughlan* [1999] Lloyd's LR Medical 306, 322, 326.
[337] See Bamforth, above n. 5; Craig (1998), above n. 4, 39.

is a *significant imbalance* in favour of the individual's expectations. A similar test should, it is submitted, be adopted in English law.[338]

This test benefits from essentially the same advantages as proportionality: although the notion of significant imbalance is flexible to some extent, it is more precise, structured, and coherent than both the traditional *Wednesbury* test and the notion of substantive fairness in and of itself. It therefore adds consistency and certainty to the law, whilst facilitating the granting of reasons. What are, then, the objections to the adoption of a principle of legitimate expectations subject to a test of significant imbalance for judicial intervention? Seven objections have been advanced in the theory; namely that it would fetter discretionary powers (i), harm third parties (ii), make unrealistic demands of administrators (iii), exceed the bounds of legitimate judicial review (iv), create adjudicatory difficulties for the courts (v–vi), and increase the, allegedly undesirable, difference between private and public law (vii). It is important to consider these objections, although they are all, for reasons explained below, unconvincing.

(i) *Fettering of discretion*: The first objection to substantive protection of legitimate expectations, over and above *Wednesbury* unreasonableness, is that it would restrict or 'fetter' the discretionary powers of public authorities. For by upholding the expectation of an individual (or a section of society) in a particular instance, the administration is prevented from using its power effectively in the wider public interest.[339] This objection fails for two reasons.

First, discretionary powers are never entirely unfettered in practice. Every exercise of administrative power limits to some extent the way in which that power can subsequently be used, and decision-makers are, as socio-legal research has shown, subject to numerous financial, social, and practical constraints.[340] The danger to the public interest of restrictions imposed by legal principles, such as legitimate expectations, must be assessed relatively to these practical restrictions.

Second, and more importantly, it was seen above that the EC doctrine of legitimate expectations has neither fettered the Community institutions' discretionary powers, nor shifted the economic risk of societal change from economic operators to the Community institutions. The principle only led the Community courts to limit administrative power to the extent justified by the requirements of fairness, legal certainty, and trust in administration. While the

338 The notions of fairness and significant imbalance are already part of English private law concerning unnegotiated terms in consumer contracts. See SI 1994 no 3159 discussed by R. Goode, 'International Restatements of Contract and English Contract Law' (1997) Uniform LR 231.

339 *Findlay v Home Secretary* [1985] AC 318, 338. See similarly Peiris, above n. 17, 80; France, above n. 17, 142; Wade 375; Cranston, above n. 17, 57; Poole, above n. 5, 431–2; Beloff, above n. 17, 8.27.

340 See K. Hawkins, 'The Use of Legal Discretion: Perspectives From Law and Social Science', in K. Hawkins (ed.), *The Uses of Discretion* (Oxford, 1992), 11, 38; Craig 523–5.

Community administration has been left free to change policies in tune with changing societal demands, certain *temporal* restrictions have been imposed on the way new policies are implemented. The adoption of a significant imbalance test in English law would similarly leave administrative flexibility largely intact.[341]

(ii) *Harm to third parties*: A second objection to the principle of substantive legitimate expectations is that third parties, who may not be heard, might be harmed if expectations are upheld. If, for example, the expectation of a property owner, who has received advice about a planning matter, is upheld, then the interests of his neighbours may be harmed.[342] This objection also fails for three reasons.

First, third-party interests are not directly affected in all cases. For example, to uphold a representation about the taxation of an individual is not likely to have direct adverse consequences for third parties.[343] The only interest affected is the Treasury and thus, in an indirect way, the whole taxpaying community.

Second, the effect on third parties is part of the circumstances which the authority, and the reviewing court, must take into account in the balancing process.[344] The possibility of harm to third parties is, therefore, not a convincing objection to the recognition of substantive legitimate expectations as such, but an important consideration when deciding upon their ambit.

Third, the procedural difficulty of ensuring that third parties are heard may be solved by an extension of the principles of procedural fairness. It should be incumbent upon an authority which purports to uphold an expectation to consider possible harm to third parties and grant them a say in the process. This is particularly important and practically feasible if a few identifiable persons, such as neighbours in planning cases, will be harmed directly.

(iii) *A lack of realism?* The principle of substantive legitimate expectations might also be criticized on the grounds that it makes excessive demands of administrators.[345] Public authorities have limited resources,[346] legal training has traditionally played a limited role in British central governmental departments,[347] and case workers in some local authorities have been found to operate

[341] See similarly Craig, above n. 4, 310; Allan, above n. 311, 32.

[342] *Western Fish Products v Penwith DC* [1981] 2 All ER 204, 221. Similarly Wade 374; Poole, above n. 5, 435.

[343] See also *Robertson v Minister of Pensions* [1949] 1 KB 227 (a representation concerning a pension).

[344] See Craig 648.

[345] See G. Richardson and M. Sunkin, 'Judicial Review: Questions of Impact' (1996) PL 79, 101 citing M. Shapiro for the general point that courts' conception of rational decision-making may not always fit an untidy reality.

[346] See footnote 332.

[347] See M. Kerr, 'Administrative law and the Administrator' (1983) Management in Government 168; L. Blom-Cooper, 'Lawyers and Public Administrators, Separate and Unequal' (1984) PL 215; G. Drewry, 'Public Lawyers and Public Administrators: Prospects for an Alliance?' (1986) Public Administration 173. Principles of judicial review are also virtually absent from British textbooks on public administration. See Cranston, above n. 17, 64, 74.

largely in ignorance of modern administrative law.[348] Is it realistic to require financially and legally 'starved' decision-makers to recognize and balance expectations against other considerations?[349] There are two responses to this question.

First, it may simply be irrelevant whether the principle of legitimate expectation is difficult to comply with in practice, because principles of judicial review are intended to *improve* decision-making processes. On this view, the courts should make legitimate expectations one of the 'hot topics' which will make all administrators think twice and force government to provide legal training. There is some evidence that judicial review already has this effect. Administrators' general knowledge of administrative law appears to have increased in recent years,[350] lawyers are closer to the policy-making process than before,[351] and more funds are set aside for training programmes.[352]

Second, the principle of legitimate expectations arguably does not ask the impossible of decision-makers. The notion of expectations is, as seen above, part of procedural fairness and *Wednesbury* unreasonableness, and administrators must therefore already now be aware of expectations created by their own conduct. There is no evidence that this has caused any real problems in practice.[353] Consider also the four types of situations in which expectations issues arise: a decision-maker who seeks to revoke a favourable decision or resile from a specific assurance is very unlikely to overlook the fact that this may affect the addressee's situation and expectations (Situations 1–2). If one officer's assurance is overlooked by another, the affected person should be able to request a review of the decision.[354] Expectations considerations are also readily recognizable when a decision is made which departs from existing policy. For departures are normally subject to deeper consideration than decisions which apply policy, and if the policy has simply been overlooked the affected person may ask for a review (Situation 3). Finally, it is far from unrealistic to require general

[348] See I. Loveland, *Housing Homeless Persons* (Oxford, 1995). See also Baldwin and Horne, above n. 4, 708; Richardson and Sunkin, above n. 345, 97.

[349] See James, above n. 312, 629–31 who is sceptical.

[350] The distribution in Whitehall of the two leaflets by the Treasury Solicitor's Department, *Judge Over Your Shoulder* and *Ombudsman in Your Files* and increased legal training are important aspects of this increased awareness. See A. Barker, 'The Impact of Judicial Review: Perspectives from Whitehall and the Courts' (1996) PL 612, 613–6; James, above n. 312, 620–2; Richardson and Sunkin, above n. 345, 95; A. H. Hammond, 'Judicial Review: the Continuing Interplay between Law and Policy' (1998) PL 34, 40–1. Compare Halliday, above n. 327, 122.

[351] See Barker, above n. 350, 614; Richardson and Sunkin, above n. 345, 97.

[352] The British government set aside £4.5 million in 1999–2000 for training of administrators. See G. Slapper, 'Modernising Justice' (1999) Student LR 31, 35, and the Civil Service College prospectus 1994–5 cited by James, above n. 312, 622.

[353] See Bradley, above n. 28, 5 reporting that the Department of the Environment complied effectively with the limited principle of estoppel by representation introduced by the planning case of *Lever Finance v Westminster City LBC* [1971] 1 QB 222.

[354] There is also an argument for the assignment of advisory functions to particular officials and recording of advice. See Bradley, above n. 28, 19.

policy-making to take account of expectations, as policy is normally made by senior officials and subject to, if not comprehensive rationality, quite detailed consideration (Situation 4).[355]

(iv) *The constitutional role of the judge*: It is trite that judges must not substitute their judgment for that of the administration; judicial review is concerned with the lawfulness and not the merits of administrative action. In Britain, this requirement of judicial restraint is intimately linked with the theory of *ultra vires*, and it finds its expression in the limits of traditional *Wednesbury* review. Some commentators object to substantive legitimate expectations for fear that this principle would lead the courts to be much more concerned with the merits of administrative decision-making and thus exceed the bounds of legitimate judicial action.[356] This argument fails for two different reasons.

First, the study of EC law has shown that the principle of legitimate expectations does not lead to substitution of judgment.[357] It is possible to limit intervention to situations of *significant imbalance* between expectations and countervailing policy considerations. Community law also shows that even when the court finds that an imbalance exists, and an administrative decision is set aside, the court does not have to replace it with a decision of its own. The unlawful decision may be remitted to the administration, which has then a (more limited) discretionary choice about how to 're-balance' the interests.[358] Thus, while the adoption of a significant imbalance test in English law would represent a small shift towards more detailed consideration of the merits, that shift would, even within the existing *ultra vires* theory, be fully justified by the gain in fairness, certainty, and trust in administration.[359]

Second, the orthodoxy of *ultra vires* and its insistence upon judicial restraint hardly provides a cogent theory of modern public law.[360] While detailed consider-

[355] Recent British case law suggests that senior policy-makers routinely consider transitional measures aimed at protecting expectations. See e.g. *R v Ministry of Agriculture, Fisheries and Foods, ex p Hamble Fisheries* [1995] 2 All ER 714; *R v Home Secretary, ex p Hargreaves* [1997] 1 WLR 906.

[356] See Cranston, above n. 17, 58; Allison, above n. 17, 175. See also Laws, above n. 320, 196 arguing more generally for a *uniform* principle of judicial review (*Wednesbury* unreasonableness) applied with varying intensity.

[357] See similarly Forsyth, above n. 4, 240–1, 375; Singh and Steyn, above n. 4, 19.

[358] e.g. Cases 120/86 *Mulder (I) v Minister van Landbouw* [1988] ECR 2321 (review of initial decision); C-189/89 *Spagl v Hauptzollamt Rosenheim* [1990] ECR I-4539 (review of the 're-balanced' decision).

[359] See G. Slynn, '"But in England There is No. . ."', in *Festschrift für Wolfgang Zeidler* (Berlin, 1987), 397, 401; Allan, above n. 4; Foster, above n. 4, 733.

[360] See D. Oliver, 'Is the *Ultra Vires* Rule the Basis of Judicial Review?' (1987) PL 543; J. Laws, 'Judicial Remedies and the Constitution' (1994) MLR 213; Lord Woolf, above n. 5, 65–7; P. P. Craig, '*Ultra Vires* and the Foundations of Judicial Review' (1998) CLJ 63. This is not to deny that the theory is convenient, or that it may serve a 'decorative' function. See C. F. Forsyth, 'Of Fig Leaves and Fairy Tales: the Ultra Vires Doctrine, the Sovereignty of Parliament and Judicial Review' (1996) CLJ 122; Laws, above n. 320, 193; Allan, above n. 311, 20, 23.

ation of constitutional fundamentals is beyond the scope of this book, it may be noted that the political accountability of the administration has been weakened by an erosion of ministerial responsibility to Parliament; by the transfer of powers to the EC; and by privatization of tasks now outside direct ministerial control.[361] These developments call for other sources of accountability, including judicial review of administrative action.[362] The courts have already responded to the weakness of political accountability, and thus the ailing *ultra vires* theory, by engaging in intensive review of administrative action in cases concerning violation of human rights,[363] and that development will naturally be reinforced by the Human Rights Act 1998. Expectations cases have a strong claim also to benefit from more bold judicial scrutiny than traditional *Wednesbury.*

(v) *Judicial competence*: British judicial review judges are recruited from the Bar and therefore by training and experience more familiar with 'legal' issues of interpretation and precedent than with 'political' balancing of conflicting policy considerations. It has, on this basis, been doubted whether the judiciary is well placed to apply substantive principles of law in which balancing plays an important role.[364] The recruitment and training of judges are important issues, and there may well be room for improvement.[365] However, they are not convincing objections to the adoption of a significant imbalance principle of legitimate expectations in English law.

First, the judicial awareness of administrative and political practice is probably greater than some critics of judicial review will have it.[366] The establishment of the Crown Office List in 1981 has contributed greatly in this

[361] See I. Harden and N. Lewis, *The Noble Lie: The British Constitution and the Rule of Law* (London, 1986), chs. 4–5; Laws, above n. 360, 223; C. Harlow, 'A Special Relationship?', in I. Loveland (ed.), *A Special Relationship? American Influences on Public Law in the UK* (Oxford, 1995), 79, 95. The use of 'Next Step Agencies' has similar effects upon accountability. See R. Baldwin, 'Ministerial Responsibility and Government by Agency' (1988) MLR 622.

[362] For similar views, see R. M. Dworkin, *Political Judges and the Rule of Law* (London, 1980), 291; Harden and Lewis, above n. 361, ch. 9; R. Rawlings, 'Courts and Interests', in I. Loveland (ed.), *A Special Relationship? American Influences on Public Law in the UK* (Oxford, 1995), 99, 113; James, above n. 312, 627; M. Radford, 'Mitigating the Democratic Deficit? Judicial Review and Ministerial Accountability', in P. Leyland and T. Woods (eds.), *Administrative Law Facing the Future: Old Constraints and New Horizons* (London, 1997), 35.

[363] See Allan, above n. 311, 28 and cases cited in footnote 40.

[364] See *R v Home Secretary, ex p Brind* [1991] 1 AC 696, 767. See also J. D. B Mitchell, 'The Causes and Effects of the Absence of a System of Public Law in the United Kingdom' (1965) PL 95, 118; M. Loughlin, 'Innovation Financing in Local Government: The Limits of Legal Instrumentalism—Part 2' (1991) PL 568, 590; Cranston, above n. 17, 63; R. Cotterel, *Law's Community: Legal Theory in Sociological Perspective* (Oxford, 1995), 176.

[365] See D. Pannick, 'The Law Lords and the Needs of Contemporary Society' (1982) Political Quarterly 318, 328 and the proposals by Lord Woolf, *Protection of the Public—A New Challenge* (London, 1990), 18–19, 81, 115–20; *Access to Justice: Final Report to the Lord Chancellor on the Civil Justice System in England and Wales* (London, 1996), 251.

[366] See C. Harlow, 'Droit Privé—*English Style*' (1997) OJLS 517, 520. Compare Richardson and Sunkin, above n. 345, 80–5 noting that there is scant empirical evidence on the extent of judges' administrative expertise.

respect,[367] and judges gain valuable experience in their work as chairmen of judicial inquiries into matters of the administration.[368]

Second, although judges are not trained in practical administration, as is the case in France, they are both capable of and experienced at balancing conflicting interests. For balancing is part and parcel of the task of judicial review itself.[369] In cases which fall within the scope of EC law, English judges must apply the Community law principles of substantive legitimate expectations and proportionality. This requires them to balance, and there is no evidence that this causes any real difficulty.[370] Balancing of competing considerations is also evident in cases concerning human rights, and the frequency of these cases are likely to increase with the entry into force of the Human Rights Act 1998. Moreover, when a judge considers whether to grant or withhold a discretionary remedy sought in a judicial review case, he will have to 'strike a balance between the conflicting public interests that arise'.[371]

Third, it is commonly acknowledged that the English courts vary the intensity of review under the *Wednesbury* formula in the light of the subject matter of the case.[372] The courts will, for example show more deference towards the administration's action if highly technical issues arise from the actions of expert administrators,[373] than if human rights are affected in addition to legitimate expectations.[374] In this way the relative expertise of specialist administrators and generalist judges is reflected in the degree of judicial scrutiny. The proposed test of 'significant imbalance' is flexible enough to enable the courts to continue this commendable variation of the degree of judicial scrutiny.

(vi) *Polycentrism and the adversarial process*: There is a certain tension between the procedural and evidentiary constraints upon judicial adjudication and the

[367] Some judges on the List have gained experience as Treasury Counsel.

[368] See Woolf, above n. 40, 586.

[369] See Cane, above n. 15, 228; Craig 647.

[370] e.g. *R v Secretary of State for Health, ex p Eastside Cheese Co* (1999) 11 Admin LR 254; *R v Chief Constable of Sussex, ex p International Trader's Ferry* [1998] 3 WLR 1260. See also De Búrca, above n. 320; Craig 589–90.

[371] *R v Governors of Bacon's School, ex p ILEA* [1990] COD 414. The issue of withholding remedies arises in about 6 per cent of all judicial review cases. See A. P. Le Sueur, 'Justifying Judicial Caution: Jurisdiction, Justiciability and Policy', in B. Hadfield (ed.), *Judicial Review: A Thematic Approach* (Dublin, 1995), 228, 232.

[372] See Laws, above n. 320.

[373] See *R v Secretary of State for the Environment, ex p Hammersmith and Fulham LBC* [1991] 1 AC 521; *R v Cambridge Health Authority, ex p B* [1995] 2 All ER 129, 135–6. See also Loughlin, above n. 364, 590–5; M. Hopper, 'Financial Services Regulation and Judicial Review', in J. Black, P. Muchlinski and P. Walker (eds.), *Commercial Regulation and Judicial Review* (Oxford, 1998), 84–5 for discussion of deference in review of local government finance, utilities, and financial regulation.

[374] See e.g. *R v Devon Health Authority, ex p Coughlan* [1999] Lloyd's LR Medical 306 where the applicant's right to a home was affected. See also Craig (1998), above n. 4, 40–4.

polycentric nature of the principle of substantive legitimate expectations.[375] British judicial review takes the form of adversarial disputes between two parties, where the court decides the case on the (predominantly written) evidence presented by the parties.[376] The English High Court has, unlike the CE and the Community courts, no power to investigate facts, call expert witnesses,[377] or consult third parties[378] of its own motion.[379] Nor does it benefit from the investigative input and independent advice of a *Commissaire de Gouvernement* or an Advocate General. However, to uphold a plaintiff's expectation as legitimate may have repercussions which go beyond the two parties. As the parties cannot always be relied upon to present the court with the data relevant to consider these wider repercussions, it may have difficulty balancing expectations against other considerations in an informed way. For example, the court might not be presented with relevant information about the interests of neighbours in a case between a planning authority and a landowner who relies on an assurance by the authority that a development may proceed without planning permission.[380] Important as it is, the polycentrism argument should not prevent the adoption of a distinct principle of substantive legitimate expectations. This is so for two reasons.

First, most judgments have implications for later cases and third parties simply by virtue of their precedential value.[381] Taken to its full conclusion, the polycentrism argument therefore suggests that courts should rarely, if ever, be involved in judicial review. But that is surely not a desirable result. Polycentrism

[375] See M. Purdue, above n. 17, 193; Allison 222; and generally on polycentrism L. L. Fuller, 'The Forms and Limits of Adjudication' (1978) Harvard LR 353; A. Chayes, 'The Role of the Judge in Public Law Litigation' (1976) Harvard LR 1281; J. W. F. Allison, 'Fuller's Analysis of Polycentric Disputes and the Limits of Adjudication' (1994) CLJ 367.

[376] Cross-examination of witnesses is possible but rarely allowed in practice. See Order 53 r 8 cf Order 38 r 2(3) and *O'Reilly v Mackman* [1983] 2 AC 237; *R v Medicines Control Agency, ex p Pharma Nord Ltd* [1997] COD 439; *R v Radio Authority, ex p Wildman* [1999] COD 255. Nor can the court, independently of the parties, order oral evidence or cross-examination if it considers the written evidence insufficient; *R v CEC, ex p. Lunn Poly*, 2/4–98.

[377] The CE and the ECJ can carry out site visits and order expert briefs, but the ECJ rarely uses these powers. See Art R158–171 *Code des tribunaux administratifs et des cours administratives d'appel*, Art 45(2) Rules of Procedure of the ECJ; and J. S. Bell, 'Reflections on the Procedure of the Conseil d'État', in G. Hand and J. McBride (eds.), *Droit sans frontières: Essays in Honour of L. Neville Brown* (Birmingham, 1991), 211, 212–16; D. Lasok, *The European Court of Justice: Practice and Procedure*, 2nd edn. (London, 1994), 397–403.

[378] This contrasts with the ECJ's practice of consulting the Community institution and the Member States. See T. Koopmans, 'Judicial Activism and Procedural Law' (1993) European Review of Private Law 67, 80–1. The CE also has the power to consult, but this power is used very rarely. See Bell, above n. 377, 216.

[379] Indeed, the prevailing judicial attitude is that 'under public law, it is not the role of the courts to find the facts.' See Lord Woolf, 'Public Law–Private Law: Why the Divide?' (1986) PL 220, 225. Consequently, the courts are generally unwilling to order discovery of documents (Order 53 r 8). See *R v Chief Constable of the Warwickshire Constabulary, ex p Fitzpatrick* [1998] 1 All ER 65 confirming *R v Secretary of State for the Environment, ex p Islington LBC* [1992] COD 67.

[380] See *Western Fish Products v Penwith DC* [1981] 2 All ER 204, 221.

[381] See M. Cappelletti, *The Judicial Process in Comparative Perspective* (Oxford, 1989), 25.

is, at most, a cogent argument against judicial review in *particularly* complex cases where many different policy arguments have to be weighed against a person's expectations.[382] The adjudicatory difficulties which arise in such cases can to some extent be reflected in the intensity of review. The courts may, as pointed out above, show greater deference in highly technical and particularly polycentric disputes.[383]

Second, adjudicatory problems problem should arguably be solved by procedural reform rather than by the retarded development of fair principles of substantive administrative law.[384] Important procedural reforms have already taken place.[385] The English courts are increasingly minded to allow third parties to join review cases and provide evidence,[386] and litigants are increasingly making use of statistical material to inform the court's judgment.[387] Other reforms are likely to occur in the near or intermediate future. The Freedom of Information Act will increase litigants' general access to public documents and that will in turn increase the information available in judicial review litigation.[388] Moreover, the restrictions on discovery have been loosened in cases involving breach of EC law rights,[389] and a similarly liberal attitude will be required for the courts to undertake their responsibilities under the Human Rights Act 1998.[390] This generous approach to procedure in cases with a European dimension may have a spill-over impact on purely domestic judicial review cases. Two other reforms, both of which deserve careful consideration, are the creation of a British equivalent to the EC Advocate General and the French *Commissaire de Gouvernement*,[391] and the creation of a judicial power

[382] See Allison 194–7.

[383] In other words, the well-established principle of justiciability will, to some extent, continue to limit the reach of judicial review. See A. P. Le Sueur, above n. 371; Craig (1999), above n. 318, 103.

[384] See G. Gerapetritis, *Proportionality in Administrative Law: Judicial Review in France, Greece, England and in the European Community* (Athens, 1997), 265.

[385] See M. Loughlin, *Legality and Locality: the Role of Law in Central-Local Government Relations* (Oxford, 1996), 403–7 arguing that a 'public law model' of adjudication is replacing the traditional private law model, and D. Feldman, above n. 330, 130 arguing that the Divisional Court is 'well able . . . to inquire into and assess government policy'. See also Richardson and Sunkin, above n. 345, 87.

[386] Order 53 r 9(1) and Order 16 r 6(2)(b), e.g. *Leyland Cars v Vyas* [1979] 3 WLR 762; *R v Coventry Airport, ex p Phoenix Aviation,* [1995] 3 All ER 47; *R v Bow Street Metropolitan Stipendiary Magistrate, ex p Pinochet* [1999] 2 WLR 827; *R v Devon Health Authority, ex p Coughlan* [1999] Lloyd's LR Medical 306. See also C. Harlow and R. Rawlings, *Pressure Through Law* (London, 1992) 194–5; Justice and Public Law Project: *Interventions in Public Interest Cases* (London, 1996); M. Fordham, *Judicial Review Handbook*, 2nd edn. (London, 1997), 23.1.6–23.1.10.

[387] See C. Harlow, above n. 366, 522.

[388] For a discussion of the problems caused by inaccessibility of public information, see R. Rawlings, above n. 362, 105.

[389] e.g. *R v Secretary of State for Transport, ex p. Factortame Ltd* [1999] 3 WLR 1062 discussed by Feldman, above n. 330,159–63.

[390] See Feldman, above n. 330, 161.

[391] See J. A. G. Griffith, 'Judicial Decision Making in Public Law' (1985) PL 564, 582; Lord Woolf, above n. 365, 109–13.

to order expert evidence and consultation with affected authorities, interest groups, and third parties.[392]

(vii) *The public–private divide*: The seventh, and last, objection to the proposed principle of legitimate expectations stems from a criticism of the distinction between public law and private law.[393] John Allison has argued that British legal and political theory lacks a clear conception of 'the state', and that distinct public law principles will therefore not work properly in English law.[394] This analysis is interesting but, with respect, unconvincing.[395]

On the one hand, the fact that the exact scope of public law is to some extent unclear and contentious is hardly a cogent reason not to apply fair substantive principles of law to those bodies that can be ascribed to the 'public' sphere without real difficulty.[396] The need to keep the regulatory powers of the state in check should not be forgotten, whatever the conceptual difficulties involved. Moreover, the presence of a strong state tradition in French legal theory has not provided cut-and-dried solutions when the courts have had to decide on the scope of administrative law in the wake of increasing privatization.[397] It is therefore difficult to see why the absence of a state tradition in Britain poses a particular and grave problem for the development of a distinct administrative law.

On the other hand, the conception of the state which exists in English legal theory is arguably not much less clear or developed than that found in most other countries.[398] Since medieval times, English law has known a concept of 'the Crown'[399] which is functionally equivalent to the concept of 'the state' which one finds in French and other Continental legal theory.[400] And while there has been no *institutional* private–public distinction in the form of separate administrative courts in Britain, a *procedural* divide has existed for

[392] See D. Pannick, above n. 365, 328; R. Baldwin and C. McCrudden, *Regulation and Public Law* (London, 1987), 67.

[393] Most commentators do not challenge the merits of substantive administrative law, but the procedural exclusivity which arose after the introduction of the Application for Judicial Review procedure (RSC Order 53, Supreme Court Act 1981) and the case of *O'Reilly v Mackman* [1983] 2 AC 237. See W. H. R. Wade, 'Public Law, Private Law and Judicial Review' (1983) LQR 166; P. Cane, 'Public Law and Private Law: A Study of the Analysis and Use of a Legal Concept', in J. Eekelaar and J. Bell (eds.), *Oxford Essays in Jurisprudence* (Oxford, 1987), 57.

[394] Allison ch. 5.

[395] The denial of a separate public law suggests that public authorities should be subject to ordinary principles of estoppel by representation (Allison 131), but this is an unacceptable position (as Allison seems to concede at 182).

[396] For discussion of public law and powerful private bodies, see G. Borrie, 'The Regulation of Public and Private Power' (1989) PL 552; P. P. Craig, 'Public Law and Private Power', in *The Province of Administrative Law* (Oxford, 1997), 196.

[397] See Brown and Bell ch. 6.

[398] Allison 81–7 concedes that a reasonably clear public–private divide developed in the early 20th cent.

[399] See Allison 70.

[400] See J. S. Bell, 'English Law and French Law—Not So Different?' (1995) CLP 63, 72, 77–8.

centuries because the prerogative remedies applied only to inferior tribunals and other public bodies.[401] Public authorities (and certain other powerful organizations like trade unions) have also for many years been subject to different *substantive* principles, some more generous and some more restrictive, than ordinary individuals.[402] In any event, the courts have in recent years incrementally developed a concept of 'the state' (as distinct from the Crown) when deciding what bodies are subject to the judicial review procedure,[403] to vertical direct effect of EC directives,[404] and to specific public law principles of negligence liability.[405] The Human Rights Act 1998 is likely to stimulate this conceptual development because its rules apply only to 'public authorities'.[406]

Thus, it may be concluded that there are strong arguments in favour of, and no really convincing objections to, the adoption in English law of a distinct principle of substantive legitimate expectations subject to a significant imbalance test for judicial intervention.

(C) Suggestions for Reform II: Unlawful Representations

Our discussion has, so far, been concerned with expectations based on lawful (*intra vires*) administrative representations. The question remains whether the principle of legitimate expectations should also be applied to unlawful (*ultra vires*) representations. It is submitted that it should for the following reasons.

The general rule, which applies in all the legal systems known to this author, is that the administration is not bound by unlawful acts and conduct. This rule, which protects the legality of administrative action, is a sound starting point for consideration of the legal effects of unlawful representations. However, it is necessary to push the analysis further. For although legality in administration is extremely important, it should not *always* be allowed to trump considerations of individual fairness and trust in administration. Administrators ought to balance, in the particular circumstances of each case, the individual's expectations and reliance against the public interest in seeing legality respected. The courts should check this balancing and intervene whenever there is a significant imbalance between the relevant interests.

[401] See Harlow, above n. 366, 521.

[402] This is true even if the courts were not thinking in the 16th–19th cents. in hard and fast categories of public and private. See H. W. Arthurs, '*Without the Law*': *Administrative Justice and Legal Pluralism in Nineteenth Century England* (Toronto, 1985).

[403] See Order 53 r 1 and Lord Woolf, 'Judicial Review: A Possible Programme for Reform' (1992) PL 221, 231–2.

[404] Case C-188/89 *Foster v British Gas Plc* [1990] ECR I-3313.

[405] See Ch. 5.

[406] S 6(1).

This flexible approach has at least one major advantage. Administrative mistakes are a fact of life. To uphold an unlawful representation, on the grounds of legitimate expectations, spreads the loss suffered by the affected individual as a result of such a mistake in minute portions upon the whole community. This will, at least in some instances, be a more fair and desirable outcome than leaving the loss with the individual.

What are the objections to this proposal? A number of practical and conceptual objections were considered in Chapter 3, where it was argued that revocation of unlawful formal *decisions* should be subject to a balancing principle of legitimate expectations. We have seen that the courts generally take the view that informal representations should be treated differently; that they cannot create legally protected expectations. This view does not withstand examination. It is true that informal advice is not always subject to formal procedures in the same way as formal decisions, and the risk that unlawful advice is granted inadvertently is therefore greater. However, this does not mean that unlawful representations should *never* be upheld. Administrators should be required to stand by their representations in those instances where the affected person could reasonably expect the representation to be lawful and where upholding it would not cause *significant* harm to third parties or the wider public interest compared to the individual's interest.

Such instances will admittedly be rare in practice. Expectations induced by unlawful representations are likely to be upheld much less readily than expectations created by lawful action, because the principle of legality is part and parcel of the balancing of public and private interests. A person seeking to hold an authority to an unlawful representation would, therefore, be expected to show considerable detrimental reliance in addition to a reasonable expectation that the representation was lawful. An example may illustrate the point made. Imagine that a person, who is seeking to open a pharmacy in a village, is advised erroneously about a statutory time limit for applying for a tax exemption applicable in the first year of trading; that the advice is in writing, clear, and unqualified; that there is no other pharmacy in the vicinity; and that denying the tax exemption will seriously jeopardize the viability of the pharmacy owner's investment. To uphold the owner's reasonable expectation of receiving the exemption would, in these circumstances, not fetter the tax authority's discretionary powers, nor would it directly cause harm to any third parties. Indeed, the opening of a pharmacy may be in the interest of the people living in the area, and the owner obtains a benefit, which he would have had a statutory entitlement to had he not relied on the erroneous advice. Moreover, the financial consequences of the error are spread upon the taxpaying community rather than left with the individual who acted in trust upon the administration's advice.

Now it might be objected that the award of compensation or damages for the loss caused by reliance upon administrative representations (and decisions) would be preferable to substantive protection of legitimate expectations both in situations as that just mentioned and more generally.[407] There will be a discussion of this issue, concerning the relationship between substantive principles and compensatory remedies, in the following two chapters.

[407] See Wade 375–8.

Chapter 5

Compensatory Protection of Legitimate Expectations (I): Revocation of Decisions

1 Introduction

The administration has, as seen in previous chapters, extensive inherent and statutory powers to depart from its own informal representations and to revoke formal decisions. The exercise of these powers may not only cause disappointment of legitimate expectations: individuals who rely upon administrative decisions and representation may also suffer consequential physical injury, property damage, and economic loss. In this and the following chapter I will examine to what extent individuals can recover such loss through principles of administrative damages liability, statutory compensation schemes, and *ex gratia* payments. In other words, how do compensatory remedies in English,[1] French,[2] and EC law[3] complement the procedural and substantive principles examined in previous chapters and thus contribute to meeting the requirements of fairness and trust in the relationship between citizens and the administration?

The scope of the discussion is strictly limited. No attempt will be made to analyse the historic peculiarities of Crown liability in English law,[4] and attention will be focused on the liability of administrative bodies rather than individual officers.[5] Space and time also precludes detailed study of liability in

[1] See generally C. Harlow, *Compensation and Government Torts* (London, 1982); S. Arrowsmith, *Civil Liability and Public Authorities* (South Humberside, 1992); De Smith chapter 19; J. Morrell and R. Foster, *Local Authority Liability* (Bristol, 1998); B. S. Markesinis, J.-B. Auby, D. C. Coester-Waltjen, and S. F. Deakin, *Tortious Liability of Statutory Bodies: A Comparative and Economic Analysis of Five English Cases* (Oxford, 1999).

[2] See generally C. Harlow, 'Fault Liability in French and English Law' (1976) MLR 516, 'Remedies in French Law' (1977) PL 227; M. Deguergue, *Jurisprudence et doctrine dans l'élaboration du droit de la responsabilité administrative* (Paris, 1994); F. Gazier, R. Drago (eds.), *Encyclopédie Dalloz: Répertoire de la responsabilité de la puissance publique* (Paris, 1996); Chapus 1129–1290; *JC* Fasc 700, 806 ff.; Brown and Bell ch. 8.

[3] See generally H. G. Schermers, T. Heukels, and P. Mead (eds.), *Non-Contractual Liability of the European Communities* (The Hague, 1988); Schwarze 505–45; T. Heukels and A. McDonnell (eds.), *The Action for Damages in Community Law* (The Hague, 1997); F. Fines, *Étude de la responsabilité extracontractuelle de la Communauté Économique Européenne* (Paris, 1997); P. P. Craig and G. De Búrca, *EU Law: Text and Materials*, 2nd edn. (Oxford, 1998) ch. 12.

[4] See Wade 819–45.

[5] The following questions will therefore not be discussed: the delimitation of acts imputable to public authorities and 'private' acts of employees, concurrent liability of officers and authorities (*cumul*), and individual employees' contribution towards damages imposed on authorities.

national law for breach of EC law,[6] the impact of the ECHR upon national law,[7] and procedural issues such as the division between public and private law jurisdictions.[8]

The material will be structured as follows. After a brief comparative overview (section 2), this chapter deals first with compensation for lawful revocation of lawful decisions (section 3), and then with unlawful revocation of lawful decisions and (lawful) 'revocation' of unlawful decisions (section 4). Preliminary conclusions are drawn, and suggestions for reform presented, at the end of sections four and five. Chapter 6 deals with liability for loss caused by informal administrative representations.

2 Administrative Liability in English, French, and EC Law: A Comparative Overview

Anyone who takes a cursory look at administrative liability in English, French, and EC law will be struck by a number of institutional, conceptual, and substantive differences. A more careful study reveals, however, that some of these differences are less marked than they appear.[9]

In institutional terms, while French legal and revolutionary history led to the development of a separate system of administrative courts,[10] administrative liability was always subject to the jurisdiction of the ordinary courts in Britain and in the EC. This institutional difference is significant, primarily because the French public law courts are subject to different procedures and recruit differ-

[6] See *R v Secretary of State for Transport, ex p. Factortame Ltd* [1999] 3 WLR 1062; CE 30/10–96 *SA Cabinet Revert* Rec 397 and discussion by C. Harlow, 'Francovich and the Problem of the Disobedient State' (1996) ELJ 199; A. Barav, 'Damages in Domestic Courts', in Heukels and McDonnell, above n. 3; J. Convery, 'State liability in the United Kingdom after Brasserie du Pêcheur' (1997) CMLRev 603; P. P. Craig, 'Once More unto the Breach: The Community, the State and Damages Liability' (1997) LQR 67; C. Lewis, 'Damages and the Right to an Effective Remedy for Breach of European Community Law', in C. Forsyth and I. Hare (eds.), *The Golden Metwand and the Crooked Cord, Essays in Honour of Sir William Wade* (Oxford, 1998), 319.

[7] See J. Wright, 'Local Authorities, the Duty of Care and the European Convention on Human Rights' (1998) OJLS 1; Lord Hoffmann, 'Human Rights and the House of Lords' (1999) MLR 159.

[8] For treatment of this topic in French law, see Brown and Bell ch. 6.

[9] See notably D. Lévy, *La responsabilité de la puissance publique et de ses agents en Angleterre* (Paris, 1957); J. S. Bell, 'The Law of England and Wales', in J. S. Bell and A. W. Bradley (eds.), *Governmental Liability: A Comparative Study*, UKCLS Vol 13, (London, 1991), 17. For general comparative overviews of public law liability, see H. Mosler (ed.), *Liability of the State for Illegal Conduct of its Organs*, Heidelberg Colloquium Max Planck Institut 1964, (Cologne, 1967); Council of Europe: *La responsabilité de l'État et des collectivités publiques régionales et locales pour les dommages causés par leurs agents et leurs services administratifs*, Actes du 9. colloque de droit européen, Université Complutense, Madrid 2–4 October 1979, (Strasbourg, 1980); Fines, above n. 3, 109–203.

[10] A constitutional revision in 1870 repealed the immunity granted to officials by Art 75 of the 1800 constitution, and the Law of 24/5–1872 gave the CE's decisions upon suits against the administration the force of judgments. See Allison 171–3.

ent types of judges than the ordinary English courts.[11] However, the differences have reduced in recent years. On the one hand, the English courts have developed a specialist *de facto* administrative division (the Crown Office List) which deals with judicial review cases and damages suits linked with such proceedings.[12] On the other hand, certain damages claims, which are 'administrative' in nature, are subject to the jurisdiction of the civil courts in France, notably suits against judges and other persons acting in a judicial capacity, school teachers employed in public sector, social security bodies, and the police in its crime investigating capacity (*police judiciare*).[13]

In conceptual terms, English law differs from French and EC law by being a law of torts rather than a law of tort. The common law has traditionally been concerned with interference with rights or interests each corresponding to a separate tort, such as the tort of trespass protecting the person and the tort of defamation protecting reputation. Actions against public authorities must always be put within the corners of one of the existing torts. French law has been more concerned with what constitutes faulty conduct, leaving the question of protected interests a subordinate place in the law of delict.[14] Consequently, French law developed a comprehensive principle of liability for fault, which is supplemented by a more limited principle of no-fault liability. EC law follows the French rather than the English pattern. The resulting difference between separate torts and general principles of liability is still important today. The English tort of negligence expanded throughout the twentieth century and this tends to disguise the traditional common law orientation because the tort of negligence is overtly concerned with faulty conduct. However, the scope of negligence in public law has been restricted considerably in recent years, and negligence cases are generally decided in an 'incremental' way which looks more to precedent than to a comprehensive concept of fault.[15]

Central to English law is the idea, developed by Professor Dicey, that public authorities are and should be subject to ordinary tort law.[16] By contrast, French administrative liability is, according to the famous *Blanco* case from 1873, subject to an 'autonomous' body of law which is separate from the private law of delict.[17] Dicey emphasized this difference and asserted the superiority of the English model.[18] It is now widely accepted that Dicey overstated the

[11] See Brown and Bell 59–121.

[12] RSC Order 53, r 7(1). Note however that most damages claims are still transferred out of the Crown List (and begun as writ actions before the ordinary High Court) after the public law issue is decided. See C. Harlow and R. Rawlings, *Law and Administration*, 2nd edn. (London, 1997), 619.

[13] See Brown and Bell 136–48 and, for explanation of the distinction between *police administrative* and *police judiciare*, ch. 3 n. 156.

[14] See Harlow, above n. 1, 40.

[15] *Murphy v Brentwood DC* [1991] AC 398; *X v Bedfordshire CC* [1995] 2 AC 633, 751; *Barrett v Enfield CC* [1999] 3 All ER 193, 208.

[16] A. W. Dicey, *Introduction to the Study of the Law of the Constitution*, 10th edn. (London, 1959),193–4, 202.

[17] TC 28/2–1873 *Blanco* Rec 707 confirming CE 6/12–1855 *Rothschild* Rec 705.

[18] Dicey, above n. 16, 387–90.

difference,[19] notably because the English Crown was immune to liability suits until 1947.[20] Later developments have confirmed that the difference between the two models is not great. The French public and private liability principles have gradually converged throughout the twentieth century.[21] Remaining differences relate primarily to specifically governmental tasks which have no parallel in private law, such as regulatory action and discretionary decision-making in licensing and welfare. These specifically governmental tasks are, however, also subject to special rules in English law. Thus it appears that both legal systems are developing 'autonomous' liability rules for specifically administrative *tasks* rather than for administrative *bodies*.[22] The difference between the English and the French model is, therefore, to some extent conceptual rather than substantive. The French see the specificity of liability for administrative decision-making as symptomatic of the autonomy of administrative liability as such, while the English see such specificity as a limited and special derogation from the ordinary law of tort.

English administrative liability is vicarious in nature, while French and EC law liability is corporate.[23] That is, English public bodies are held liable through the tortious acts of their employees, while French and EC bodies are directly liable as legal entities for 'system faults' (*fautes de service*). This difference is neither absolute nor very important in practice.[24] French liability is not purely corporate because a French official who makes a very serious mistake, or acts maliciously, may be sued directly in the civil courts for his *faute personelle*.[25] And English liability is not purely vicarious since public authorities may be directly liable for breach both of statutory duties which are laid upon them *as authorities*, and for common law duties such as the ordinary duties of property owners.[26]

[19] See H. W. Arthurs, 'Rethinking Administrative Law: A Slightly Dicey Business' (1979) Osgoode LJ 1, *"Without the Law": Administrative Justice and Legal Pluralism in Nineteenth Century England* (Toronto, 1985).

[20] The Crown Proceedings Act 1947 equated the liability of the Crown in tort with that of 'a private person of full age and capacity'. See Wade 820 ff.

[21] Compare R. Chapus, *Responsabilité publique et responsabilité privée* (Paris, 1957); R. Drago in *Encyclopédie Dalloz*, above n. 2, ch. 5; J.-Y. Vincent *JC* Fasc 842 no 18 (arguing that there is little or no difference) with the more recent view that certain practically important differences still remain Chapus 1330–1; J. Moreau *JC* Fasc 700 no 14; M. Paillet *JC* Fasc 818 no 4.

[22] This is arguably a sound development in view of the increasing contracting-out and privatization of traditionally public tasks. See C. Harlow, 'State Liability: Problem Without Solution' (1995–6) NJCL 67, 73.

[23] See Dicey, above n. 16, 404–5; Harlow, above n. 2, 516; M. Paillet in *JC* Fasc 818 no 3.

[24] An English administrative body will in theory not be liable if an official is vested by statute with a power to make decisions or take actions over which the administrative body has no control (the 'independent discretion rule'). However, public bodies and their insurers do not plead this in practice due to the unjust results for the officer and the plaintiff alike. See Arrowsmith, above n. 1, 139.

[25] TC 30/7–1873 *Pelletier* D 1874 III 3. These suits are rare in practice, see Chapus 1271–81.

[26] See Harlow, above n. 22, 71.

At the level of substantive principles of liability, one finds a number of apparent differences between, on the one hand, French law and, on the other hand, English and EC law. Two features of liability for unlawful decision-making are particularly striking from a comparative point of view.

First, unlawfulness is equated with fault in French law (*illegalité = faute*). A decision which is unlawful, in the sense that it may be annulled in judicial review proceedings, always constitutes a service fault (*faute de service*) which is capable of making the administration liable in damages.[27] By contrast, not all unlawful (*ultra vires*) decisions can give rise to liability in English law. A case must always be put into a recognized tort, and in the most common tort (negligence) liability only arises if the decision was vitiated by a substantive, as opposed to procedural, and particularly serious form of illegality.[28] The relation between fault liability and unlawfulness is not entirely clear in EC law, but there are signs that the Community judicature will equate unlawfulness with fault as in French law.[29]

Second, while the English courts are concerned with *whether* the administration owes a duty of care towards particular individuals, rather than with the applicable standard of care, the French and the EC courts assume that the administration has a general duty to administer competently, the issue being *what* this standard requires in the circumstances. These are conceptually very different ways of delimiting the scope of administrative liability. It will be considered below whether, and to what extent, English law may draw lessons from the Continental approach to this issue.[30]

The principles of liability for lawful administrative decisions (no-fault liability) also look strikingly different in French and English law. The French courts have developed two interesting and intimately linked general principles of liability for risks (*théorie de risque*)[31] and breach of equality before public burdens (*égalité devant les charges publiques*).[32] The former provides that when a risk caused by a dangerous activity undertaken by the administration in the public interest materializes, causing abnormal harm to certain individuals, the loss should borne by society via an award of damages against the administration. The latter provides more generally that any decision or action taken in the public interest, which causes abnormal and grave harm to a limited class of persons, must be followed by compensation.[33] Their application in French law may be illustrated by the leading case of *Couitéas* from 1923. Mr Couitéas' land on French territory in Tunisia had effectively been occupied by local tribesmen. He

[27] CE 26/1–73 *Driancourt* Rec 78.

[28] *X v Bedfordshire CC* [1995] 2 AC 633; *Barrett v Enfield CC* [1999] 3 All ER 193.

[29] Cases C-55/90 *Cato v Commission* [1992] ECR I-2533 para 18.

[30] See section 5.

[31] CE 28/3–19 *Regnault-Desroziers* RDP 1919, 239.

[32] CE 30/11–23 *Couitéas* Rec 789.

[33] The principle of equality before public burdens is expressed in a general form in Article 13 of the Declaration of the Rights of Man of 1789, but it is uncertain whether the modern liability doctrine can be derived from Article 13. See J. S. Bell, *French Constitutional Law* (Oxford, 1992), 66, 214–15.

obtained an order from a French court for the eviction of the tribesmen, but the authorities refused to execute it on the grounds that this would trigger a civil war. In this special situation, the CE ruled that Mr Couitéas had suffered a grave and special loss in the public interest for which he should be compensated. The no-fault principle established in this case has subsequently been applied in numerous similar situations, for example, where the police refuse to evict tenants or to clear strikers' blockades of traffic installations.[34]

The no-fault liability principles have no equivalent in English law.[35] This may be explained from two perspectives. On the one hand, the difference between English and French law reflects differences in political ideology.[36] The English approach to tort liability is broadly speaking utilitarian—a sacrifice is allowed for the greater good and the loss lies where it falls. French law is influenced by a more 'collectivist', or—if one prefers—socialist, ideology which assumes that pursuit of the greater good requires the compensation of those who are injured by such pursuits. As the French put it, the risk of harm caused by administrative action should be 'socialized' through the provision of compensation.[37] On the other hand, the difference between English and French law in this area reflects that the French and the English hold different views about the proper role of law in society.[38] The typical French response to a policy problem, such as compensation for loss caused by lawful administrative action, is to devise legal rules. Thus, the courts developed the risk and equality liability doctrines to solve this problem. In Britain the role of formal legal rules, and tort law in particular, is perceived as less natural or useful. Thus, the courts have shied away from developing risk or equality based liability. It has instead been left to administrative authorities to award equitable (*ex gratia*) compensation on an *ad hoc* basis to alleviate severe hardship.

Finally, it is important to note that English, French, and EC law largely agree that the primary purpose of administrative liability is to redress wrongs by compensating actual losses. Deterrence of administrative bodies and individuals is at most an ancillary purpose.[39] This is evident from the facts that exemplary (or

[34] e.g. CE 3/7–59 *Sablayrolles* Rec 425; CE 22/6–84 *Société Sealink UK* Rec 246; CE 22/6–84 *Société Jokelson et Handsteam* Rec 247.

[35] The position in EC law is less clear, see section 3.C.

[36] See G. Monti, '*Osman* v. *UK*—Transforming English Negligence Law into French Administrative Law?' (1999) ICLQ 757.

[37] See Harlow and Rawlings, above n. 12, ch. 3 drawing on the writings of Léon Duguit.

[38] See J. S. Bell, 'English Law and French Law—Not So Different?' (1995) CLP 63, 89–97.

[39] See in English law I. Englard, *The Philosophy of Tort Law* (Aldershot, 1993), 7 ff.; De Smith 757; R. F. V. Heuston and R. A. Buckley, *Salmond and Heuston on the Law of Torts*, 21st edn. (London, 1996) 23, but compare Harlow, above n. 22, 73–4. See in French law M.-A. Latournerie, 'The Law of France', in J. S. Bell and A. W. Bradley (eds.), *Governmental Liability: A Comparative Study*, UKCLS vol 13 (London, 1991), 198; Lochak, 'Réflexion sur les fonctions sociales de la responsabilité administrative', in J. Chevallier (ed.), *Le droit administratif en mutation* (Paris, 1993). Deterrence arguably plays a greater role in relation to the EC law principles of state liability for non-implementation of EC law. See Harlow, above n. 6, 204–10.

punitive) damages are very rarely awarded against public authorities,[40] and that public authorities are allowed to take out legal liability insurance. Moreover, while a financial loss which is caused in a manner insulting to the pride or dignity of a person can lead to aggravated damages, such damages are still compensatory rather than deterrent in nature.[41] Given this important similarity, it would not be very surprising to find that the legal systems do, despite different rules and different political moralities, reach similar outcomes in practice. It is to this issue that we now turn.

3 Compensation for Loss Caused by Lawful Decisions

It was seen in Chapter 3 that the administration is often able to revoke lawful decisions to the disadvantage of the persons who benefit from them: the French and English administrations have inherent powers to revoke certain discretionary decisions, and many statutes also grant the administration plenty of flexibility to revoke decisions. An individual who has relied financially upon a decision may suffer a loss when the administration exercises such revocation powers, particularly if he was not given adequate notice in advance of the decision. In this section I will consider to what extent principles of damages liability, statutory compensation, and *ex gratia* payments cover such loss caused by lawful revocation of lawful decisions.[42]

(A) English Law

According to Professor Dicey's highly influential theory of the Rule of Law, the administration is, and should be, liable in damages when it acts *outside,* but not *inside,* its powers.[43] In accordance with this view, compensation for loss caused by the lawful revocation of lawful decisions is virtually non-existent in English law.[44] The position may be set out in three points.

First, to decide lawfully (*intra vires*) is a defence to some torts, like nuisance and false imprisonment. An individual cannot claim damages for what is the 'inevitable' consequence of the exercise of statutory powers.[45] Thus, while a decision to revoke a parole licence is a *prima facie* tortious act because it

[40] Exemplary damages are unknown in French administrative law. They may be available in the English tort of misfeasance in public office (see footnote 176), but this tort is hardly ever applied, and they are unavailable in the tort of negligence (*Cassell and Co v Broome* [1972] AC 1027).

[41] *Cassell v Broome* [1972] AC 1027, 1085.

[42] A different problem arises when a lawful decision is revoked contrary to general principles of finality or irrevocability. This problem, which may be termed 'unlawful revocation of a lawful decision' is discussed in section 4.

[43] Dicey, above n. 16, 193–4.

[44] See Arrowsmith, above n. 1, 241; Wade 763.

[45] *Geddis v Proprietors of Bann Reservoir* (1878) 3 AC 430, 455–6; *Hague v Deputy Governor of Parkhurst Prison* [1992] 1 AC 58.

deprives a person of his liberty, the Criminal Justice Act 1991 gives the authorities a power to make this decision and provides a shield against the tort (of false imprisonment).[46] At the same time, lawful (*intra vires*) decisions do not give rise to liability in other torts, like negligence and misfeasance in public office. The administration does not breach its duty of care by making decisions within its powers.[47]

Second, there is no developed risk or 'equality of burdens' principle in English law. The English courts have granted damages for the consequences of a lawful decision on one occasion. In *Burmah Oil* the British army had destroyed valuable oil installations in Burma to prevent them from falling into the hands of the enemy. The House of Lords granted damages in addition to an *ex gratia* payment, which had been offered by the British government.[48] This was, however, a unique case. The court's reasoning turned upon the Scottish law concept of 'eminent domain' rather than on a general principle of reallocation of loss suffered in the public interest. Moreover, Parliament subsequently overruled the decision by retroactive legislation, thereby sending a clear signal that compensation for lawful administrative action should be left in the hands of the executive.[49]

Third, statutory provisions generally do not provide compensation for lawful revocation. Planning permissions cannot be revoked without compensation for expenses incurred in reliance on the permission.[50] However, this appears to be the only example in current English statute law; trading licences, tax rulings, seaworthiness certificates, and many other favourable decisions can be revoked without compensation.[51] Moreover, *ex gratia* payments are rarely, if ever, awarded to compensate loss caused by lawful administrative decision-making. Central and local authorities have the power to make *ex gratia* payments on an *ad hoc* basis (normally following a recommendation by the Parliamentary Commissioner for Administration or a Local Government Ombudsman) or on the basis of more formalized schemes governed by internal guidelines.[52] The literature concerning such payments does not reveal any examples of awards, and a recent attempt by the Parliamentary Commissioner for Administration to secure compensation for lawful, but seriously delayed, use of planning powers in connection with the Channel Tunnel project was resisted by the government.[53]

[46] S 34(4)b.

[47] *Dorset Yacht Co v Home Office* [1970] AC 1004, 1031; *X v Bedfordshire CC* [1995] 2 AC 633, 736; *Barrett v Enfield CC* [1999] 3 All ER 193, 209.

[48] *Burmah Oil v Lord Advocate* [1965] AC 75.

[49] See Harlow and Rawlings, above n. 12, 49–52.

[50] Town and Country Act 1990, s 107.

[51] See ch. 3 n. 2.

[52] See Harlow, above n. 1, 128 ff.; Arrowsmith, above n. 1, 244–50; Harlow and Rawlings, above n. 12, 606–10; D. Woodhouse, *In Pursuit of Good Administration: Ministers, Civil Servants and Judges* (Oxford, 1997), 72–80; M. Amos, 'The Parliamentary Commissioner for Administration, Redress and Damages for Wrongful Administrative Action' (2000) PL 21.

[53] See G. Drewry, 'The Ombudsman, Parochial Stopgap or Global Panacea?', in P. Leyland and T. Woods (eds.), *Administrative Law Facing the Future: Old Constraints and New Horizons* (London, 1997), 83, 101.

(B) French Law

Compensation for lawful administrative action is, according to traditional wisdom, far more readily available in French than in English law because the French courts can award damages on the basis of no-fault liability.[54] However, a critical reading of the case law reveals a rather different picture. The French position may be summarized as follows.[55]

First, a lawful decision does not constitute a *faute de service* (a negligent act),[56] because the administration does not breach an obligation incumbent upon it (i.e. it does not fall below the standard of care) by acting lawfully.[57] For example, a licensee has no remedy based on the principle of liability for *faute de service* if his licence is revoked in accordance with the principle that *autorisations d'occupation du domaine public* and *autorisations de police* do not 'create rights'.[58]

Second, the no-fault liability principle of equality before public burdens (*égalité devant les charges publiques*) is extremely narrow.[59] The equality principle is in theory of general application; it is not limited to the classic situation where the police refuses to execute a court order or remove strikers. The administration may therefore in theory be liable if the conditions laid down in the case law are fulfilled, that is, if a lawful decision (revocation) causes a loss which is abnormal (of a certain gravity) and special (the plaintiff being part of a limited class of victims).[60] However, a survey of recent case law reveals that the conditions for no-fault liability are very strict in practice. The leading *Rigal* case is a pertinent example.[61] A private radiologist's licence to utilize a caesium source for medical treatment, from which he had benefited for around ten years, was revoked in the light of concerns over the efficiency and side effects of low

[54] The CE has also once imposed liability for the lawful but sudden revocation of a quarry licence on the basis of the private law theory of 'abuse of rights' (CE 22/11–29 *Compagnie des Mines de Siguiri* S (1930) III 17) but this theory has not been applied in subsequent cases. Liability would today be imposed on the basis of fault, since the sudden revocation of a valuable licence might be in breach of the principle of proportionality. See L. Richer, *La faute du service public dans la jurisprudence du Conseil d'État* (Paris, 1978), 24–6; Deguergue, above n. 3, 605–8.

[55] See generally P. Delvolvé, *Le principe de l'égalité devant les charges publiques* (Paris, 1969); P. Amselek, 'La responsabilité sans faute des personnes publiques d'après la jurisprudence administrative', in *Mélanges Eisenmann* (Paris, 1975); R. Errera, 'The Scope and Meaning of No-Fault Liability in French Administrative Law' (1986) CLP 157; E. K. Banakas, 'Public Authority Liability for Pure Economic Loss: A Comparative Study of English, French and German Law', in *Afieroma Eton Andrea A. Gaze* (Athens, 1994); Chapus 1227–70.

[56] Genevois *conclusions* CE 19/6–81 *Carliez* AJDA 1981, 105; CE 26/6–70 *Bartoli* Rec 442; CE 29/9–82 *Vernet* Rec 320.

[57] See Paillet *JC* Fasc 818 no 93.

[58] CE 29/3–68 *Michelin* Rec 217; CE 1/2–80 *Rigal* AJDA 1981, 44. See R. Chapus, *Droit administratif général*, vol. ii, 11th edn. (Paris, 1998), 494–501.

[59] The principle of no-fault liability for risks (*risque*) is not applied to the foreseeable consequences of lawful decisions. It concerns accidental consequences of physical activities. See e.g. CE 3/11–97 *Hôpital Joseph-Imbert D'Arles* Rec 412 and Chapus 1253.

[60] CE 30/11–23 *Couietas* Rec 789.

[61] CE 1/2–80 *Rigal* AJDA 1981, 44.

intensity radioactive treatments. Consequently, Mr Rigal had to invest in new and expensive apparatus or close his clinic. The CE found that the administration had acted lawfully, as the licence was an *autorisation de police* which could be revoked prospectively in the interest of public health even in the absence of an explicit statutory revocation power. Fault liability was therefore excluded. The Conseil d'État's *Commissaire de Gouvernement* argued, however, that damages should be awarded on the basis of the equality principle, since the Ministry's new policy affected only about 30 of the 180 private radiologists in France all of whom had suffered a serious loss in the public interest.[62] The CE was not impressed; it rejected Mr Rigal's case without mentioning the question of no-fault liability.[63]

The restrictive approach taken in the *Rigal* case is evident in numerous other decisions, all of which rejected liability for lawful revocation of licences and other favourable decisions.[64] Thus, in a recent case the owner of a discotheque, which was situated in a natural cave, sought to recover damages of 870,000 francs caused by a closure order made on public safety grounds. He argued that his business had been shut down in the general public interest, and that this constituted a special and abnormal loss violating the principle of equality before public burdens. The CE rejected the claim on the basis that owner had wilfully accepted the risk that the place might be closed in case of natural changes in the cave.[65] In other words, society should not be made to bear the normal and reasonably foreseeable business risk, which the owner had chosen to take.

These decisions show that no-fault liability is of limited significance as a source of compensation in revocation situations. There is, in fact, only one known example of a successful claim for compensation based on no-fault liability in a revocation situation.[66] This claim was made in the *Villa Jacob* case from 1989. Archaeological remains were discovered on a building site and the authorities demanded a modification of the development. Consequently, the company had to obtain a second planning permission and this caused serious

[62] The precise amount of loss was not clear, and the matter was complicated by the fact that thirty of eighty public hospitals were also affected.

[63] This must, in the light of French judicial style and the fact that the *Commissaire de Gouvernement*'s conclusions were published, be interpreted as a clear rejection of his suggestion.

[64] e.g. CE 22/11–61 *Ville d'Agen* Rec 668; CE 3/3–65 *Coudert* AJDA 1965, 487; CE 7/10–66 *Asope* Rec 523; CE 30/10–70 *Minot* no 75.343; CE 26/2–71 *Roze* no 73.120; CE 16/4–82 *Cheriet* no 29.435; CE 6/2–81 *Compagnie française de raffinage* Rec 62 and CE 6/12–85 *Gaz de France* Rec 361; CE 16/5–80 *Syndicat intercommunal des eaux de Casserousse* no 7.794; CE 18/6–82 *Barbe* RDP 1983, 520; CE 6/6–84 *Malvaux* no 41.365; CE 27/4–84 *Corap* no 40.980; CE 7/12–84 *Fons-Sicart* no 20.047; CE 10/6–88 *Ministre du redéploiement industriel* Rec 571; CE 25/11–88 *SARL 'La Flèche d'argent'* no 71.513; CE 1/7–91 *Auzolles* no 81.562; CE 11/12–91*'Styx FM'* no 103.881; CE 16/6–95 *Achache* D 1995, 179.

[65] CE 10/7–96 *Meunier* Rec 289. See also CE 16/11–98 *Sille* DA 1998 no 23 and I. Mariani-Benigni, 'L'"exception de risque accepté' dans le contentieux administratif de la responsabilité', RDP 1997, 841.

[66] This author surveyed some 250 published and unpublished decisions involving damages claims for revocation of decisions.

delay. Compensation for delays caused by 'excavations' was prescribed by the relevant statute, but it was unclear whether this also included delay in situations where no excavations had actually taken place. The CE found that while there was no right to statutory compensation, the company's loss was abnormal and special and it awarded damages on this ground.[67] This was, it is submitted, a special case which is unlikely to be relevant in other contexts. It concerned an interference with a highly valued and constitutionally recognized interest, namely property, and the statutory compensation provisions indicated Parliament's intention that archaeological preservation should not be pursued to the detriment of individual property owners. Moreover, there was an obvious risk that owners would fail to report archaeological finds, as Villa Jacob had duly done, if compensation for resulting delays was denied. The recent *Garcia* case confirms that *Villa Jacob* is not of general precedential value. Mr Garcia had been granted a building permission which was revoked (before building works had commenced) on the grounds that the house would constitute a health risk. The CAA of Lyon found the revocation lawful in substance and held explicitly that the authorities 'cannot be liable for a breach of equality before public burdens' in these circumstances.[68]

Third, statutory compensation is available to the same limited extent as in English law, that is, only for revocation of planning permissions. Unlike English local authorities, French planning authorities do not have a general statutory power to revoke individual planning permissions and there is, therefore, no provision equivalent to s 107 of the Town and Country Planning Act 1990. Compensation is, however, provided in situations where general planning restrictions interfere with existing (lawful) building permissions.[69] For example, the beneficiary of a building permission which is not yet fully utilized will be entitled to compensation if the area in which he was entitled to build is subsequently declared *zone inconstructible*.[70] Expenses incurred in reliance on the permission will normally be indemnified,[71] but compensation for lost profits is very rarely awarded.[72]

It was mentioned above that in English law *ex gratia* payments are rarely awarded for loss caused by lawful decisions. In France, liability proceedings cannot be commenced without a preliminary claim for payment addressed to the

[67] CE 20/1–89 *SCI Villa Jacob* Rec 23. Compare CE 11/3–87 *Weisbach* D 1988, 55.

[68] CAA Lyon 17/10–90 *Garcia* no 89LY00768. However, the court added that by leaving Mr Garcia's building permission in force for about six months after a report had revealed that the permission was granted by mistake, the administration was liable in fault for unreasonable delay. See also CE 16/10–96 *Vuillecard* no 116.867 and compare CE 19/2–88 *Société Robatel* D 1988, 365.

[69] *Code de l'urbanisme* Art L160–5. See Chapus 1142–3.

[70] An area in which new buildings must not be erected.

[71] CE 4/3–77 *SA Simotel* Rec 122. Compare CE 4/3–77 *Consorts Guillerot* AJDA 1977, 319.

[72] Pure economic loss, including loss of profit, is in principle recoverable in French law, but the requirements of causation and damage are applied strictly to such claims under Art L160–5. e.g. CE 10/6–88 *SA Bonnargent-Goyon* Rec 238; CE 7/3–90 *Bore de Loisy* Rec 983.

(allegedly) responsible administrative body, and there is therefore always an opportunity to consider an *ex gratia* payment.[73] However, while claims are normally met if the administration considers itself legally responsible,[74] *ex gratia* payments are apparently quite rare.[75] This is so partly for practical, and partly for ideological reasons. Administrative litigation is seen as the normal method of dispute-resolution because it is relatively accessible and cheap in France, and because French public lawyers generally prefer formal legal rules to *ad hoc* discretionary solutions.[76] *Ex gratia* payments are also restricted by the CE, which held the administration should never be condemned to pay a sum which is not legally owed,[77] and by the *Cour des Comptes*[78] which is critical of 'unnecessary' out-of-court settlements.[79] Moreover, while the French ombudsman (*Médiateur*) can recommend the payment of compensation on purely 'equitable' grounds this power is exercised extremely cautiously.[80] It follows that to the extent *ex gratia* payments actually occur, they are hardly a source of compensation in revocation situations.

(C) EC Law

Lawful and favourable decisions are generally irrevocable under the EC law principle of vested rights.[81] An EC institution will therefore only be in a position to revoke a lawful and favourable decision by reference to a specific statutory revocation provision. If, by applying such a provision, the institution inflicts a loss upon an individual, the individual will not be able to obtain compensation. That is so for three reasons.

First, an EC institution is only liable in fault if its decision is 'illegal', i.e. unlawful in the sense that it could be annulled in judicial review proceedings.[82] The revocation of a decision in accordance with a revocation provision obviously does not fulfil this requirement. The same applies where a decision falls

[73] On the requirement of a *décision préalable* and exhaustion of appeals, see R. Chapus, *Droit du contentieux administratif*, 6th edn. (Paris, 1996), 328–49.

[74] Some commentators claim, however, that the French administration is inclined to litigate if there is any doubt about responsibility, rely on technical defences, and appeal in many cases. See R. Amson and D. Lindon, 'Un Ombudsman en France', JCP 1970, 2322, 2453.

[75] The author is indebted to Professor Etienne Picard and advocate Arial Dahan for information on this issue. See also C. Harlow, 'Administrative Liability: A Comparative Study of French and English Law', Ph.D. thesis (London School of Economics, 1979), 280–1 citing interviews with French officials and the President of the *Commission du Rapport* of the CE.

[76] An attempt was made in 1980 to encourage informal pre-litigation settlements by the setting up of regional appeal committees competent to 'advise' aggrieved individuals whose requests for compensation had been rejected, but it failed due to a lack of interest. Later attempts to introduce 'conciliation' procedures also failed due to the resistance of the CE. See Chapus, above n. 73, 330–1, 344–6.

[77] CE 19/3–71 *Mergus* 235.

[78] This is the budget watchdog which checks all governmental payments. See J. Raynaud, *La Cour des Comptes* (Paris, 1980).

[79] See Harlow, above n. 75, 280.

[80] See http://www.mediateur-de-la-republique.fr/pres/index.htm; Chapus 426–30.

[81] See Ch. 3.2.C.

[82] Case 4/69 *Lütticke v Commission* [1971] ECR 325 para 10.

outside the principle of irrevocability, for example, because it is conditional. Thus, in *Azienda Agricola* the Commission had reduced a financial grant on the ground that the recipient had failed to complete certain works for which the money had been awarded. The CFI rejected the applicants' claim that the revocation was substantively and procedurally flawed, and held that the Commission was therefore not liable in damages for the applicant's alleged reliance loss.[83]

Second, the Community courts never explicitly acknowledged a principle of no-fault liability.[84] The ECJ accepted in the *Boer Buizen* case that the Commission may have 'a certain responsibility' towards undertakings suffering disproportionate burdens as a result of Community measures, but the Court found that on the facts no such burden had been imposed.[85] In the *Biovilac* case the ECJ held that *if* a no-fault liability principle existed in EC law, it would be subject to strict conditions.[86] Thus, the CFI held in *Dorsch Consult* that no-fault liability would only arise if (i) the decision affects a particular circle of persons in a disproportionate manner by comparison with others (unusual damage) and (ii) exceeds the limits of the economic risks inherent in operating in the sector concerned (special damage), without (iii) the measure that gave rise to the alleged damage being justified by a general (economic) interest.[87]

A European no-fault principle along these lines would be even narrower than the French principle of equality before public burdens. The third requirement, in particular, restricts the principle considerably and actually negates the very purpose of no-fault liability, which is to ensure compensation to particular individuals who suffer grave harm *in the public interest*. Consequently, if the Community courts acknowledge a principle of no-fault liability, it is unlikely to protect individuals against the consequences of lawful revocation of decisions. This conclusion is also valid if the Courts would require 'only' unusual and special damage, because these requirements are likely to be

[83] Case T-218/95 *Le Canne v Commission* [1997] ECR II-2055 para 82–83. See also Case 92/75 *Roy v Commission* [1976] ECR 343.

[84] See H. J. Bronkhorst, 'The Valid Legislative Act as a Cause of Liability of the Communities', in T. Heukels and A. McDonnell (eds.), *The Action for Damages in Community Law* (The Hague, 1997); Fines, above n. 3, 389–99. Commentators and AGs disagree on the merits of such a principle. For critical comment, see AG Roemer [1973] ECR 1273; AG Reischl [1977] ECR 665; AG Verloren van Themaat [1982] ECR 3089; Schwarze 532; Craig and De Búrca, above n. 3, 536. Compare AG Mayras [1972] ECR 422–3; AG Trabuchi [1975] ECR 141; AG Lenz [1987] ECR 1069.

[85] Case 81/86 *De Boer Buizen* [1987] ECR 3677.

[86] Case 59/83 *Biovilac v EEC* [1984] ECR 4057 para 28 confirming Case 267/82 *Développement SA v Commission* [1986] ECR 1907 para 33. Similarly Cases T-113/96 *Dubois SA v Council and Commission* [1998] ECR II-125 para 42. See previously Cases 9 and 11/71 *Compagnie d'Approvisionnement v Commission* [1972] ECR 391 para 46; 54–60/76 *Compagnie Industrielle v Council* [1977] ECR 645 para 19.

[87] Case T-184/95 *Dorsch Consult Ingenieurgesellschaft v Council and Commission* [1998] ECR II-667 para 80.

interpreted in the light of national laws, notably the restrictive French case law discussed above.[88]

Third, there are to this author's knowledge no provisions of secondary EC law which provide compensation for revocation of decisions,[89] and the Community institutions hardly ever make use of their budgetary authority to make *ex gratia* payments.[90]

(D) Preliminary Conclusion

It emerges that the English, French, and Community courts, while applying different concepts and principles, actually reach rather similar results in practice. Damages liability is *very* rarely imposed in response to lawful revocation of administrative decisions, statutory compensation is almost non-existent, and *ex gratia* payments appear to be exceptional.

This finding must be understood in the light of the procedural and substantive principles examined in previous chapters: it was seen that while the English and French administrations have extensive inherent powers to revoke lawful and favourable discretionary decisions, the EC administration must rely upon specific statutory provisions because the EC principle of vested rights prohibits the revocation of all favourable and lawful decisions.[91] These extensive powers, vested in the English and French administration to the potential detriment of individual's legitimate expectations and legal certainty, are not complemented or 'balanced' by compensatory remedies. The upshot is that EC law provides significantly more protection of individual's substantive legitimate expectations and reliance than either of the two national legal systems.

The absence of no-fault compensation in English law is, in this light, rather unsatisfactory.[92] Clearly, compensation for lawful administrative action cannot be made too readily available. For if an individual could claim compensation every time a lawful decision affects him adversely, decision-making would be impossible and the very aim of the decision would be undermined if that aim was to effect an economic redistribution. Moreover, as the CFI pointed out in *Dorsch Consult*, the taxpaying community should not, through the award of damages or compensation, bear ordinary business risks on behalf of economic

[88] The Court would also take into account no-fault liability in other Member States, notably the German principle of *Sönderopfer*. However, this principle is not significantly wider than the French doctrine, see F. Schockweiler, C. Wivénes, and J.-M. Godart, 'Le régime de la responsabilité extracontractuelle du fait d'actes juridiques dans la Communauté européenne', RTDE 1990, 27.

[89] This author surveyed all existing general EC measures which refer to 'revocation' and related terms in the Celex database. For the absence of compensation for lawful revocation of EC tender procedures, see Case T-13/96 *TEAM v Commission* [1998] ECR II-4073 para 68–71.

[90] See the Community Budget Part A, line 2341 concerning payments made 'for reasons of equity' (OJ [1998] L44/1, 415). According to Mr Peter Oliver of the Commission's Legal Service, *ex gratia* compensation has been awarded by the Commission in only one or two exceptional cases in the last decade. In 1998 no payments were made by any of the EC institutions under heading 2341.

[91] See Ch. 3.2.C.

[92] See similarly Brown and Bell 194.

operators.[93] However, it is submitted that some form of compensation should, as in France, be available when the revocation of a favourable decision causes what Carol Harlow calls 'disproportionate or abnormal' loss. To be a bit more precise, compensations should be granted if, and only if, grave harm is caused to a strictly limited class of persons in the wider public interest.[94]

The question, then, is how this might be implemented. The English courts are very unlikely to be willing to develop a general principle of no-fault liability,[95] and a detailed discussion of this possibility is therefore unnecessary for present purposes.[96] Suffice it to say that, in the light of the French experience, there is a danger that such a principle would be little more than an exercise in symbolic reassurance. This is not to say, however, that nothing can be done. A more limited proposal, which relies upon legislators and administrators, might be as follows.

First, specific legislative compensation provisions tailored to the problems of different policy areas should be adopted. The English Town and Country Planning Act 1990, which deals with revocation of planning permissions, might be used as a model for such provisions. Section 107 of this Act provides full compensation for expenses, but not for financial loss (loss of profit expected as a result of the development), whenever a planning authority uses its power to revoke a building permission. It is possible that less complete compensation will be sufficient in other areas. A trader whose licence is revoked because part of an old market place is to be used for a hospital should not be indemnified fully for his lost profits. But if fairness, certainty, and trust in administration is to be taken seriously, the trader must be given some opportunity to voice his interests, a reasonable period to redirect his business, *and* some measure of economic assistance to assist him in doing so.

Second, a principle of compensation for grave and abnormal loss should be introduced into administrative *practice*.[97] The Treasury guidelines, which currently restrict *ex gratia* payments severely, should be reconsidered. Decision-makers should be educated about, and encouraged to follow, a concept of fair and good administration embracing a principle of compensation. The difficulty of turning round ingrained administrative practices is obvious. However, it is

[93] See footnote 87.

[94] For similar proposals in American and Canadian theory, see D. Rosenberg, 'The Causal Connection in Mass Expose Cases: A Public Law Vision of the Tort System' (1984) Harvard LR 851; D. Cohen and J. C. Smith, 'Entitlement and the Body Politic: Rethinking Negligence in Public Law' (1986) Canadian Bar Review 1.

[95] Harlow's comment to that effect applies with even greater force today. See Harlow, above n. 1, 110.

[96] See generally P. P. Craig, 'Compensation in Public Law' (1980) LQR 413; Harlow, above n. 1, 102–15; Arrowsmith, above n. 1, 245–7; J. W. F. Allison, 'The Procedural Reason for Judicial Restraint' (1994) PL 452, 452–9; Harlow and Rawlings, above n. 12, 622. Compare H. Street, *Governmental Liability: A Comparative Study* (Cambridge, 1953), 78; JUSTICE—All Souls Review Committee, *Administrative Justice: Some Necessary Reforms* (Oxford, 1988) 248–351, 362.

[97] See C. Harlow, 'Back to Basics: Reinventing Administrative Law' (1997) PL 245, 256.

submitted that institutional attitudes and 'working rules' can be changed by training and revised guidelines.[98] Increasing familiarity with compensation issues, if and when new legislative compensation provisions come into force, will facilitate this change.

4 Compensation for Loss Caused by Unlawful Decisions

It was examined above to what extent individuals can recover loss suffered as a result of lawful administrative decisions. However, administrative decisions are not always made in accordance with the law; unlawful decisions are a fact of life even in the most well functioning administration. In this section, we shall see how loss caused by unlawful decisions is compensated in English, French, and EC law by principles of damages liability, statutory compensation schemes, and *ex gratia* payments.

One may distinguish between two types of situations in which unlawful decisions cause loss to individuals. First, the administration can make a favourable and *lawful* decision which it subsequently revokes in a way which violates the general principle of irrevocability. This is unlawful revocation of a lawful decision. Second, the administration can make a favourable and *unlawful* decision which it subsequently revokes by a lawful decision which 'regularizes' the situation. This is lawful revocation (or replacement) of an unlawful decision.[99]

The person benefiting from the initial decision may, in both of these scenarios, suffer disappointed expectations and, if he relied upon the initial decision in the belief that it was a lawful and final determination,[100] also suffer personal injury, property damage, and economic loss. For example, a ship's seaworthiness certificate may, and should, be revoked if it is discovered that the ship has been approved although its hull violates important safety regulations. The question is whether the owner is, or should be, able to recover his potentially devastating loss from the administration. In other words, should the risk of mistaken decisions be borne by the individual or should it be spread among the taxpaying community via an award of damages or compensation?

(A) English Law

Modern English case law is imbued with the view that damages liability is an improper response to the problems caused by unlawful administrative decision-

[98] Police practices have been transformed with some, if not total, success by such initiatives over the last 15 years. See A. Sanders and R. Young, *Criminal Justice,* 2nd edn. (London, 1998).

[99] As explained in Ch. 3.5.C.I such 'regularization' must be carried out within two months in French law and within a reasonable period in EC law. If these conditions are not complied with, the administration's action may be called an unlawful revocation of an unlawful decision.

[100] Individuals are, as pointed out in Ch. 1, rarely well placed to discover that an administrative decision is unlawful.

making. Several complex assumptions underpin this view.[101] The courts fear that liability will lead officials to approach their duties in an over-cautious manner (the chilling effect), that great volumes of—mostly hopeless—litigation will be created (the floodgates effect), that the courts are not able to set appropriate standards of care for difficult decisions and should not get involved in second-guessing such decisions (the justiciability issue), and that damages actions will erode more suitable administrative remedies.[102] More generally, the British courts are alive to the view that recovery of pure economic loss[103] may give rise to an indeterminate and potentially vast liability, which will put a strain on public authorities' resources.[104] The scope of administrative tort liability has, in the light of these concerns, been limited to the point where the risk of unlawful decisions tends to fall on the affected individual.[105] Three basic principles lead to this result.

First, the fact that a decision is unlawful, i.e. that it has been or could be annulled by judicial review, does not give rise to a *prima facie* right to damages. The case must be fitted into a recognized tort protecting a recognized right or interest.[106] Three torts are of particular relevance for present purposes, namely breach of statutory duty, negligence, and misfeasance in public office. While the former tort is in theory strict, the two latter torts only lie if the decision was vitiated by a particularly serious type of unlawfulness or made with malicious intent.

Second, it is not everybody who can rely on a tort against a public authority to obtain damages for unlawful decision-making. Breach of statutory duty only lies if a construction of the statute shows that the duty was created for the benefit of the person affected by the unlawful decision, and negligence only lies if the decision-maker owed a duty of care towards that person. These requirements are rarely satisfied.

Third, not all types of loss can be recovered in the three torts referred to above. While property damage and personal injury is covered, lost profits and other pure economic loss can normally not be recovered in the tort of negligence.[107] This restriction is of paramount importance in cases involving, for example, unlawfully denied or revoked licences, financial aid, and welfare benefits.

[101] Needless to say, different judges share these assumptions to varying degrees.

[102] For an articulation of these arguments, see *Dorset Yacht Co v Home Office* [1970] AC 1004; *Hill v Chief Constable of West Yorkshire* [1989] AC 53; *X v Bedfordshire CC* [1995] 2 AC 633; *W v The Home Office* [1997] Imm AR 302; *Phelps v Hillingdon LBC* [1999] 1 All ER 421, 441–2. Compare *Barrett v Enfield CC* [1999] 3 All ER 193, 208–9, 228.

[103] i.e. a financial loss which is not causally consequent upon physical injury to the plaintiff's own person or property.

[104] See *Stovin v Wise* [1996] AC 923, 952.

[105] *R v Ealing London BC, ex p Parkinson* (1996) 8 Admin LR 281, 285.

[106] *X v Bedfordshire CC* [1995] 2 AC 633, 730; *Malone v Metropolitan Police Commissioner* [1979] 2 WLR 700.

[107] The exception being loss caused by negligent representations, see Ch. 6.

The *Reeman* case is a recent example of these principles in practice.[108] Mr and Mrs Reeman invested their savings in the purchase of a vessel which had been approved as seaworthy by the Department of Transport. It later emerged that the vessel's hull violated important safety regulations and the seaworthiness certificate was revoked. This caused the Reemans a devastating loss which they sought to recover from the Department. The Court of Appeal dismissed their claim on three grounds. The fact that the ship had been unlawfully approved did not in itself give rise to a right to damages, the authority did not owe a duty of care in negligence towards purchasers of vessels, and the loss suffered was purely economic and would therefore not be compensated. Let us, with this example in mind, examine a bit more closely the torts of (I) breach of statutory duty, (II) negligence, and (III) misfeasance before making some comments on (IV) causation and (V) contributory negligence.

I Breach of Statutory Duty

A public authority which deprives a person of a benefit, which it is under a statutory duty to provide, may in theory be liable in damages for breach of this duty.[109] In practice, however, things look different because most public administration is carried out under statutory powers rather than duties,[110] and because the tort is limited in the following three ways.

First, the courts will construe the statute to determine whether Parliament intended the duty to be enforceable in tort.[111] The duty must be for the benefit of a limited class of individuals, rather than for the public at large, and intended to protect that class against the type of loss suffered.[112] This construction is inherently difficult,[113] some would say impossible,[114] because Parliament often has not considered the question of damages liability at all.[115] The construction is therefore influenced by policy considerations, and the prevailing judicial view is that damages liability is not good policy.[116] Second, the courts are unlikely to find an enforceable duty if the administration is required to make discretionary choices to fulfil it,[117] or if the statute provides appeals procedures or other

[108] *Reeman v Department of Transport* [1997] 2 Lloyd's Rep 648. Compare *Perrett v Collins* [1998] 2 Lloyds LR 255.

[109] See generally K. Stanton, *Breach of Statutory Duty in Tort* (London, 1986); Arrowsmith, above n. 1, 197 ff.; B. S. Markesinis and S. F. Deakin, *Tort Law*, 4th edn. (Oxford, 1999), 336–53.

[110] See Wade 245. Liability for the exercise of powers is *at least* as limited as breach of statutory duty, see the discussion of negligence below.

[111] *Stovin v Wise* [1996] AC 923, 952–3.

[112] *X v Bedfordshire CC* [1995] 2 AC 633; *O'Rourke v Camden LBC* [1997] 3 WLR 86. The possibility of enforcement of a 'public right', mentioned in *Lonrho v Shell Petroleum (No 2)* [1982] AC 173, was criticized and not applied in later case law. See Arrowsmith, above n. 1, 203.

[113] *Solomons v Gertzenstein* [1954] 2 QB 243, 266; *R v Knowsley BC, ex p Maguire* [1992] COD 499.

[114] *Ex p Island Records* [1978] Ch 122, 134.

[115] Statutes rarely state *explicitly* that the duties they impose are actionable, but see Local Government Act 1988, s 19(7).

[116] See Arrowsmith, above n. 1, 202–3.

[117] *Wyatt v Hillingdon LBC* (1978) 77 LGR 727, 733; *T v Surrey CC* [1994] 4 All ER 577, 597; *X v Bedfordshire CC* [1995] 2 AC 633, 736; *O'Rourke v Camden LBC* [1997] 3 WLR 86.

means of enforcement.[118] Third, a statutory duty which is, exceptionally, actionable may be interpreted as a duty to 'take all reasonable steps'. That is, an element of fault is injected although breach of duty is in principle a strict tort.[119]

These three restrictions produce a strong *de facto* presumption against the availability of damages for breach of statutory duty, notably in relation to licensing, social welfare, and financial aid.[120] For example, the recent and significant *O'Rourke* decision held that the duty to provide housing for certain categories of homeless persons is not actionable. The reason is that the Housing Act is a scheme of social welfare intended for the benefit of society in general, as well as the homeless, the implementation of which depends largely on the housing authority's judgment and discretion. A housing authority is therefore not liable if it withdraws, on unlawful grounds, public housing from a homeless person.[121] This decision is in line with previous decisions like *Booth* and *Maguire* which held that duties (or powers) to provide industrial grants and taxi licences are not actionable.[122]

II The Tort of Negligence

Negligence[123] resembles the general principle of fault liability in French and EC law in the sense that it covers all activities, including decision-making by public authorities,[124] which fall below a judge-made standard of reasonable (*bonus pater*) conduct. Negligence liability presupposes that the decision-maker owes

[118] Ibid. Breach of statutory duty may also be excluded if other torts provide adequate compensation, see *Phillips v Britannia Hygiene Laundry Co* [1923] 2 KB 832.

[119] *Read v Croydon Corporation* [1938] 4 All ER 631; *Jayne v National Coal Board* [1963] 2 All ER 220; *Ministry of Housing and Local Government v Sharp* [1970] 2 QB 223. See Arrowsmith, above n. 1, 198–9.

[120] See footnote 117 and A. Mason, 'Negligence and the Liability of Public Authorities' (1998) Edinburgh LR 3, 7. Compare Arrowsmith, above n. 1, 203 referring, prior to *X* and *O'Rourke*, to a 'weak presumption'.

[121] *O'Rourke v Camden LBC* [1997] 3 WLR 86 overruling *Thornton v Kirklees MBC* [1979] QB 626; *R v London Borough of Lambeth, ex p Barnes* [1993] COD 50.

[122] *Booth and Co (International) v National Enterprise Board* [1978] 3 All ER 624, 635–6; *R v Knowsley BC, ex p Maguire* [1992] COD 499. See also *Calveley v Chief Constable of Merseyside* [1989] AC 1128; *Hague v Deputy Governor of Parkhurst Prison* [1992] 1 AC 58; *Olotu v Home Office* [1997] 1 All ER 385; *Clunis v Camden and Islington Health Authority* [1998] 3 All ER 180.

[123] See generally P. P. Craig, 'Negligence in the Exercise of a Statutory Power' (1978) LQR 428; Arrowsmith, above n. 1, 168–96; Morrell and Foster, above n. 1; Markesinis and Deakin, above n. 109, 360–72; D. Brodie, 'Public Authorities and the Duty of Care' (1996) JR 127, 'Public Authorities—Negligence Actions—Control Devices' (1998) Legal Studies 1; J. Convery, 'Public or Private? Duty of Care in a Statutory Framework: *Stovin v Wise* in the House of Lords' (1997) MLR 559; M. Andenas and D. Fairgrieve, 'Sufficiently Serious? Judicial Restraint in Tortious Liability of Public Authorities and the European Influence, in M. Andenas (ed.), *English Public Law and the Common Law of Europe* (London, 1998); P. P. Craig and D. Fairgrieve, 'Barrett, Negligence and Discretionary Powers' (1999) PL 626; Craig chapter 26.

[124] This was accepted in *British Cast Plate Manufacturers v Meredith* (1792) 4 TR 794, confirmed by *Mersey Docks v Gibbs* (1864–66) 11 HLC 686; *Geddis v Proprietors of Bann Reservoir* (1878) 3 AC 430, 455–6. See Craig, above n. 123, 428–31.

a duty of care to the plaintiff (i), which is breached (ii), and that the unlawfulness caused the loss (iii).[125] These conditions have in recent years been interpreted restrictively in cases concerning unlawful decision-making by public authorities.[126]

(i) *The existence of a duty of care*: Whether a public authority owes a duty of care depends upon a number of factors. There must be sufficient proximity between the decision-maker and the plaintiff. This is determined by an overall assessment of their relationship, an essential aspect of which is whether the decision-maker was able to foresee that his decision would cause somebody in the plaintiff's situation a loss.[127] The fact that there is a geographical proximity between, for example, a local authority and a welfare client living in its area is neither necessary nor sufficient.[128] Moreover, it must be 'just, fair and reasonable' to impose a duty in the circumstances. These criteria are at once complex, overlapping, and imprecise thus leaving the courts plenty of room to limit the scope of negligence in accordance with the judicially dominant view that liability has virtually no role in administrative law.[129]

To determine more precisely whether it is 'just, fair and reasonable' to impose a duty of care, the courts will look closely at precedent[130] and the statute under which the decision was made.[131] It speaks against liability if the statute prescribes consultation of the affected person as part of the decision-making process;[132] if there are alternative means of challenging the decision, such as a statutory appeal system;[133] if the decision is deemed to be 'final' or 'not subject to review';[134] and if the statute provides for some form of economic compensation.[135] However, the mere fact that the decision may be challenged by judicial

[125] *Caparo Industries Plc v Dickman* [1990] 2 AC 605.

[126] For discussion of policy factors restricting negligence in private law, see B. S. Markesinis, *Foreign Law and Comparative Methodology* (Oxford, 1997), 228–53.

[127] *Caparo Industries Plc v Dickman* [1990] 2 AC 633; *X v Bedfordshire CC* [1995] 2 AC 633.

[128] See Heuston and Buckley, above n. 39, 203.

[129] See Mason, above n. 120, 10 and for judicial acknowledgment of the point made *Welton v North Cornwall DC* [1997] 1 WLR 570.

[130] The courts will develop new categories of negligence 'incrementally and by analogy with established categories'. See *Murphy v Brentwood DC* [1991] AC 398; *X v Bedfordshire CC* [1995] 2 AC 633, 751; *Barrett v Enfield CC* [1999] 3 All ER 193, 204. See for discussion of this approach J. Stapleton, 'The Condition of the Law of Tort', in P. Birks (ed.), *The Frontiers of Liability* (Oxford, 1994); K. Stanton, 'Incremental Approaches to the Duty of Care', in N. J. Mullan (ed.), *Torts in the Nineties* (North Ryde, Australia, 1997), 34.

[131] *X v Bedfordshire CC* [1995] 2 AC 633, 739; *Stovin v Wise* [1996] AC 923, 952–3.

[132] *Gupta v London Borough of Brent,* 25/10–93; *X v Bedfordshire CC* [1995] 2 AC 633, 750; *Phelps v Hillingdon LBC* [1999] 1 All ER 421, 441.

[133] *Jones v Department of Employment* [1988] 2 WLR 493, 509–10; *Hill v Chief Constable of West Yorkshire* [1989] AC 53, 59; *Gupta v London Borough of Brent,* 25/10–93; *T v Surrey CC* [1994] 4 All ER 577, 599; *X v Bedfordshire CC* [1995] 2 AC 633, 751; *Harris v Evans* [1998] 1 WLR 1285, 1297–8; *Phelps v Hillingdon LBC* [1999] 1 All ER 421, 441–2.

[134] *Jones v Department of Employment* [1988] 2 WLR 493.

[135] *Hill v Chief Constable of West Yorkshire* [1989] AC 53; *Elguzoli-Daf v Commissioner of Police of the Metropolis* [1995] 2 WLR 173; *W v Essex CC* [1998] 3 WLR 534.

review is not, and should not be, sufficient to exclude the possibility of a duty of care in negligence.[136] There are obvious parallels between this 'construction approach' to the duty of care problem and the tort of breach of statutory duty. The two torts have to a large extent been harmonized into one strictly confined tort; damages will only exceptionally be awarded in negligence if there is no actionable statutory duty and that is, as explained above, extremely rare.[137] It is, moreover, clear that negligence claims for careless exercise of discretionary powers are limited to instances where the public body's action caused additional harm to that which would have occurred if the body had not acted at all.[138]

The tort of negligence is further restricted by what is known as the 'policy-operational' distinction.[139] This complex distinction can be roughly stated as follows. A decision involves 'policy' if it is made subject to a discretionary power and the decision-maker has balanced competing public and private interest. For example, matters of social policy, allocation of finite resources, and the balancing of desirable social aims against the risk to the public interest in so doing.[140] A decision which merely implements a policy is 'operational'. There is no clear-cut line between policy and operational decisions,[141] but it is evident that many decisions in fields such as town planning,[142] trade licensing,[143] welfare,[144] and financial aid contain a significant element of policy. The policy-operational distinction was criticized in *Stovin v Wise* as an inadequate tool for determining the extent of a duty of care.[145] However, there is a tension in *Stovin* in so far as the judgment did not state an alternative test for the ambit of the law of negligence and proceeded to apply criteria which are very similar to those underlying that distinction.[146] In any event, Lord Hoffmann concluded

[136] *West Wiltshire DC v Garland* [1995] 2 WLR 439, 447. Similarly J. Stapleton, 'Duty of Care, Peripheral Parties and Alternative Opportunities for Deterrence' (1995) LQR 301, 319–21. The possibility of appeal to the Parliamentary Commissioner for Administration may also be insufficient to exclude a duty of care. See *Barrett v Enfield CC* [1999] 3 All ER 193, 228.

[137] *Stovin v Wise* [1996] AC 923, 953. See similarly P. Cane, 'Suing Public Authorities in Tort' (1996) LQR 13, 16; Wright, above n. 7, 4; Markesinis and Deakin, above n. 123, 373.

[138] *Stovin v Wise* [1996] AC 923, 949. See Craig 853.

[139] Introduced into English law by *Anns v Merton LBC* [1978] AC 728, 754. See Craig, above n. 123; S. H. Bailey and M. J. Bowman, 'The Policy/Operational Dichotomy—A Cuckoo in the Nest' (1986) CLJ 430; Arrowsmith, above n. 1, 169–75; R. Bailey-Harris and M Harris, 'The Immunity of Local Authorities in Child Protection Functions—Is the Door Now Ajar?' (1998) CFLQ 227, 229–32.

[140] *X v Bedfordshire CC* [1995] 2 AC 633, 737 approving *Rowling v Takaro Properties Ltd* [1988] AC 473.

[141] *Dorset Yacht Co v Home Office* [1970] AC 728, 754; *Barrett v Enfield CC* [1999] 3 All ER 193, 211.

[142] *Strable v Dartford BC* [1984] JPL 329, 330; *Ryeford Homes v Sevenoaks DC* [1990] JPL 36.

[143] See Arrowsmith, above n. 1, 176, 184.

[144] *Jones v Department of Employment* [1988] 2 WLR 493.

[145] *Stovin v Wise* [1996] AC 923, 951. See also critical *W v Essex CC* [1998] 3 WLR 534, 547, but compare *Barrett v Enfield LBC* [1998] QB 367, 378.

[146] Lord Keith relied upon *Hill v Chief Constable of West Yorkshire* [1989] AC 53, but that decision appears to have applied the policy-operational distinction under another name. See Andenas and Fairgrieve, above n. 123, 293.

that there is a presumption against the availability of damages for unlawful discretionary decisions and that exceptions to this presumption are likely to be rare.[147] More recently, it was accepted in *Barrett* that the policy-operational distinction is a 'guide' in deciding whether the particular issue is justiciable and therefore capable of giving rise to a common law duty of care.[148]

The modern approach to 'just, fair, and reasonable' and justiciability means that public authorities rarely owe a duty of care towards persons affected by unlawful administrative decisions. A few recent examples will suffice to illustrate this.[149] The cases of *Gupta* and *Harris* found that planning authorities and Health and Safety Executive officers were not liable for unlawfully ordering the closure of hotels and bungee jumping facilities, as they do not owe a duty of care towards the individuals affected by their decisions.[150] *Reeman* held, as explained above, that the Department of Transport is not liable towards buyers of vessels who rely on the correctness of a seaworthiness certificate,[151] and *W v Essex CC* held that immigration officials are not liable for decisions about asylum seekers' leave to enter Britain and about their temporary detention.[152] Finally, a Scottish case has held that a Traffic Commissioner owed no duty of care towards a bus driver whose driver's licence had been revoked on incorrect medical grounds.[153]

(ii) *The requirement of gross unlawfulness*: English law does not equate unlawfulness with negligence (fault). The mere fact that an administrative act is unlawful, and may be annulled in a judicial review action, does not prove that the decision-maker acted negligently.[154] The well-known case of *X v Bedfordshire CC* laid down the rule that only decisions vitiated by *Wednesbury* unreasonableness (i.e. decisions 'so unreasonable that no reasonable authority could have reached them') are capable of giving rise to a claim in negligence.[155] Unreasonableness is a very grave form of unlawfulness, which constitutes a 'very substantial hurdle' for the plaintiff.[156] While it may be considered

[147] Exceptions are most likely to occur where the harm suffered by the individual is grave, e.g. *Reffell v Surrey CC* [1964] 1 WLR 358; *Knight v Home Office* [1990] 3 All ER 237.

[148] *Barrett v Enfield CC* [1999] 3 All ER 193, 211 drawing upon *Rowling v Takaro Properties Ltd* [1988] AC 473.

[149] See also *Thorne v University of London* [1966] 2 QB 237; *Wood v The Law Society* The Times 30/7–93; *Elguzoli-Daf v Commissioner of Police of the Metropolis* [1995] 2 WLR 173.

[150] *Gupta v London Borough of Brent*, 25/10–93; *Harris v Evans* [1998] 1 WLR 1285, 1298. On planning authorities, see also *Strable v Dartford BC* [1984] JPL 329; *Ryeford Homes v Sevenoaks DC* [1990] JPL 36; *Lam v Brennan* [1997] 3 PLR 22. Compare *Welton v North Cornwall DC* [1997] 1 WLR 570 (this case is discussed in chapter 6).

[151] *Reeman v Department of Transport* [1997] 2 Lloyd's Rep 648.

[152] *W v The Home Office* [1997] Imm AR 302.

[153] *Johnstone v Traffic Commissioner* (1990) SLT 409.

[154] *Partridge v GMC* (1890) 25 QBD 90; *Abbott v Sullivan* [1952] 1 KB 189, 251–2; *Dunlop v Woollahra MC* [1982] AC 158, 172.

[155] *X v Bedfordshire CC* [1995] 2 AC 633, 736, 761; *Stovin v Wise* [1996] AC 923, 953. Compare *W v Essex CC* [1998] 3 All ER 111, 142.

[156] *Barrett v Enfield LBC* [1998] QB 367, 375–6.

unreasonable to make decisions on no evidence,[157] it is probably not negligent unintentionally[158] to take into account irrelevant considerations,[159] to make errors of primary fact or law,[160] or to violate the principles of procedural fairness.[161] The difficulty of showing unreasonableness is exacerbated by two factors. One is that many negligence claims have tended to proceed as strike-out actions without detailed evidence.[162] Another is that the court adjudicating upon a negligence claim is not bound by a previous judicial review decision. Thus, when determining a damages claim in the *Maguire* case, the judge reassessed the reasonableness of a refusal to award a taxi licence and came to the opposite result of the judge which had originally reviewed it.[163]

It emerges that, due to the strictly limited duty of care and the requirement of *Wednesbury* unreasonableness, all but a grossly delinquent authority is effectively accorded an immunity for the negligent exercise of a statutory discretion. The tort of negligence provides virtually no protection against unlawful revocation of favourable decisions and therefore no protection of individuals' legitimate expectations and reliance upon such decisions.

Judicial attitudes may, however, be changing in the light of academic criticism[164] and the ECtHR's ruling in *Osman* that the existence of a *de facto* immunity from negligence actions is incompatible with the right to a fair trial.[165] In the recent case of *Barrett,* the House of Lords accepted that *X v Bedfordshire CC* restricted liability too much, and that it is preferable for the courts to 'apply directly the common law concept of negligence' rather than the public law concept of *Wednesbury* as a precondition for negligence liability.[166] *Barrett* appears to represent a shift away from the strict delimitation of duty of care towards a fuller consideration of breach of duty in individual cases.[167] However, it is far

[157] See Craig, above n. 123, 449; *Johnstone v Traffic Commissioner* (1990) SLT 409, 413.

[158] The decision-maker may be liable for misfeasance in public office if he knew that he was acting unlawfully. See section 4.A.III.

[159] See De Smith 762.

[160] *Rowling v Takaro Properties Ltd* [1988] AC 473, 502.

[161] *Dunlop v Woollahra MC* [1982] AC 158, 172; *R v Deputy Chief Constable of Thames Valley Police, ex p Cotton* [1989] COD 318, 320. See De Smith 762; Cane, above n. 137, 16–7.

[162] Negligence actions are often struck out as disclosing no reasonable cause of action under RSC Order 18 r 19. See e.g. *E v Dorset CC* [1995] 2 AC 685, 693; *Bennett v DPP* (1998) 10 Admin LR 245. While *Barrett v Enfield CC* [1999] 3 All ER 193 held that actions should not be struck out on grounds of just, fair and reasonable, a claim was subsequently struck out on grounds of proximity in *Palmer v Tees Health Authority* The Times 6/7–99 and *Gallagher v Berrow Wood School Ltd*, 7/10–99. Compare *Farah v British Airways Plc* The Times 26/1–2000.

[163] *R v Knowsley BC, ex p Maguire* [1992] COD 499.

[164] See JUSTICE—All Souls, above n. 96, 361–364; De Smith 791–5; Cane, above n. 137; Brodie, above n. 123; Andenas and Fairgrieve, above n. 123; Mason, above n. 120; Wright, above n. 7; Markesinis, Auby, Coester-Waltjen and Deakin, above n. 1.

[165] Art 6 ECHR, *Osman v UK* (1999) 11 Admin LR 200. The case of *X v Bedfordshire CC* is now pending before the ECtHR, and it seems likely that it will follow the lead from *Osman*.

[166] *Barrett v Enfield CC* [1999] 3 All ER 193, 211, 225. This presupposes, of course, that the matter is justiciable in the first place.

[167] See Craig and Fairgrieve, above n. 123. For a more pessimistic prognosis, see Markesinis, Auby, Coester-Waltjen and Deakin, above n. 1, 43.

from clear *what is* as a matter of common law a negligent breach of duty in the context of discretionary decision-making.[168] There are dicta in *Barrett* which suggest that *Wednesbury* unreasonableness, or a very similar concept, will remain part of public law negligence actions, although it will apply at the breach level rather than at the duty level.[169] It is hoped that the House of Lords will soon provide a further clarification and liberalization of this developing area of law.[170]

III Misfeasance in Public Office

While the existence of the tort of misfeasance[171] is beyond doubt,[172] its scope is strictly limited. Misfeasance applies if, and only if, there were a 'deliberate and dishonest abuse of power' by the decision-making body.[173] Thus, although the affected person does not need to prove that the decision violated a specific right or a duty,[174] and although pure economic loss[175] and possibly also exemplary damages may be granted,[176] nobody has yet, as far as can be ascertained from published material, relied successfully on this tort in a British court.[177] The House of Lords will have the opportunity, in the appeal of *Three Rivers*, to redefine the scope of misfeasance, but there are reasons to think that misfeasance will remain a tort of little practical relevance.[178]

IV Causation

Damages liability presupposes, in all legal systems, a causal connection between the unlawful act and the loss.[179] Although causation does not play a great prac-

[168] Lord Hutton may have meant to refer to 'the standard of the ordinary skilled man exercising . . . that skill' (*Bolam v Friern Hospital* [1957] 1 WLR 582, 586), but the question is then *how* this standard applies to public bodies. For an explicit reference to this standard, see *Gower v Bromley LBC* The Times 20/10–99.

[169] *Barrett v Enfield CC* [1999] 3 All ER 193, 209–11, 230.

[170] See further section 5.

[171] See generally Arrowsmith, above n. 1, 226–34; Craig 875–80. See also J. McBride, 'Damages as a Remedy for Unlawful Administrative Action' (1979) CLJ 323; R. C. Evans, 'Damages for Unlawful Administrative Action: The Remedy for Misfeasance in Public Office' (1982) ICLQ 640; Harlow, above n. 1, 58–68; C. Hadjiemmanuil, 'Civil Liability of Regulatory Authorities after the *Three Rivers* Case' (1997) PL 32; D. Elvin, 'Misfeasance in Public Office' (1998) JR 26.

[172] *Dunlop v Woollahra MC* [1982] AC 158; *Bourgoin SA v Ministry of Agriculture, Fisheries and Food* [1986] QB 716; *Jones v Swansea CC* [1990] 1 WLR 54; *Racz v Home Secretary* [1994] 2 AC 45; *Three Rivers DC v Governor and Company of the Bank of England (No 3)* [2000] 2 WLR 15.

[173] *Three Rivers DC v Governor and Company of the Bank of England (No 3)* [2000] 2 WLR 15.

[174] *Three Rivers DC v Governor and Company of the Bank of England (No 3)* [1996] 3 All ER 558, 583–4.

[175] See Arrowsmith, above n. 1, 228–9.

[176] *Rookes v Barnard* [1964] AC 1129, 1236; *Arora v Bradford CC* [1991] IRLR 165, 169. See Arrowsmith, above n. 1, 165; P. Cane, *An Introduction to Administrative Law*, 3rd edn. (Oxford, 1996), 255–6. Compare De Smith 789–90 and see further Law Commission Report no 132.

[177] e.g. *Jones v Swansea CC* [1990] 1 WLR 54; *Lam v Brennan* [1997] 3 PLR 22; *Bennett v DPP* (1998) 10 Admin LR 245. Morrell and Foster, above n. 1, 21 note that successful claims are 'rare'.

[178] See Craig 880.

[179] For comparative discussion, see A. M. Honoré, 'Causation and Remoteness of Damage', *International Encyclopaedia of Comparative Law*, vol. xi, ch. 7 (New York, 1971); F. H. Lawson and B. S. Markesinis, *Tortious Liability for Unintentional Harm in the Common Law and the Civil Law*, Vol I-II, (Cambridge, 1982), 118–26.

tical role in English public law cases, because the duty of care is so narrowly defined, it is very important from a comparative point of view. One may distinguish between two aspects of causation. First, the unlawful decision must actually be *a* cause of the loss; i.e. there must be causation in fact. This is determined by the classic 'but-for' (*sine qua non*) test.[180] Second, the damage must not be too remote a consequence of the unlawful decision. The test which applies within the English tort of negligence is whether it was foreseeable to the reasonable man (decision-maker) that his unlawful decision would cause the kind of damage that it did.[181]

A particular causation problem arises where a benefit has been deprived unlawfully, for example, due to a procedural error or an irrelevant consideration. Would the person have been awarded (or allowed to maintain) the benefit had it not been for the unlawfulness? The unlawfulness only *caused* the person a loss if this question is answered in the affirmative. There are three possible solutions to this problem.[182] The court may await the outcome of a renewed application;[183] it may award damages proportionate to the lost chance of obtaining the benefit; or it may assess for itself whether it is likely on the balance of probabilities that the decision would in any event have been made. The first solution is often impractical and there is a risk that the decision-maker will repeat the unlawful decision to avoid liability. The second solution is presently unavailable due to the absence of liability for loss of a chance in English tort law.[184] The third solution is also problematic. To assess what the decision-maker would have done but for the unlawful element comes close to substitution of judgment.[185] The English courts are very reluctant to do this, and causation analysis therefore tends to lead to the rejection of damages claim, either on the ground that the court cannot ascertain whether the unlawfulness caused the plaintiff's loss, or on the rather unconvincing ground that the plaintiff could and should simply have ignored the unlawful decision.[186]

[180] See J. A. Jolowicz and W. V. H. Rogers, *Winfield and Jolowicz on Tort*, 15th edn. (London, 1998), 199.

[181] *The Wagon Mound (No 1)* [1961] AC 388; *The Wagon Mound (No 2)* [1967] 1 AC 617. It is not proposed to discuss to what extent this test applies to the torts of misfeasance and breach of statutory duty. See J. Cartwright, 'Remoteness of Damage in Contract and Tort: A Reconsideration' (1996) CLJ 488, 496–504; Markesinis and Deakin, above n. 109, 191–202.

[182] See G. Ganz, G. Ganz, 'The Limits of Judicial Control over the Exercise of Discretion' (1964) PL 367; McBride, above n. 171, 334–40; De Smith 776–7.

[183] e.g. *R v Knowsley BC, ex p Maguire* [1992] COD 499.

[184] Liability for loss of chance is applied in contract, see *Chaplin v Hicks* [1911] 2 KB 786. Whether this principle is applicable in tort was left open in *Hotson v East Berkshire Health Authority* [1987] AC 750. For a recent argument in favour of liability for loss of chance, see Jansen (1999). Compare McBride, above n. 171, 336; Arrowsmith, above n. 1, 32.

[185] See Craig, above n. 96, 439; De Smith 776. Compare Arrowsmith, above n. 1, 31.

[186] *O'Connor v Isaacs* [1956] 2 QB 288; *Dunlop v Woollahra MC* [1982] AC 158. See the convincing critique by McBride, above n. 171, 337–40.

V Contributory Fault

The liability of a public authority may be reduced by the plaintiff's own contributory negligence (fault).[187] This possibility has rarely been considered in modern English case law because the duty of care is so narrowly defined. In contrast, the importance of contributory fault is, as explained below, great in French and EC law.

The survey of English tort law demonstrates that the level of formalized compensatory protection against unlawful revocation is very low. Individuals are generally unlikely to obtain damages and statutory compensation schemes are patchy. There are, of course, other ways of seeking redress. Central and local government has the power to make *ex gratia* payments, but such payments are according to published Treasury guidelines only made in 'genuinely exceptional' circumstances.[188] The Parliamentary Commissioner for Administration (PCA) or a Local Government Ombudsman (LGO) can also recommend financial remedies when injustice has been caused by maladministration.[189] Compensation has, for example, been secured by the PCA to truck drivers whose heavy vehicle licences had been unlawfully revoked.[190]

The ombudsman system has procedural advantages in terms of cost and informality,[191] but it is limited in several respects and therefore not an adequate alternative to liability in tort:[192] certain areas are outside the remit of the ombudsmen, and complaints about central government must pass through members of Parliament some of whom may be reluctant to refer cases to the Parliamentary Commissioner.[193] The ombudsmen's recommendations are also not widely circulated to decision-makers.[194] Public authorities are therefore unlikely to award compensation unless the aggrieved individual goes through the complaints procedure,[195] and this may both deter victims and strain the ombudsmen's capacity.[196] Moreover, the quantum of compensation awarded is generally modest; it does not cover future loss; and central and local authorities

[187] Law Reform (Contributory Negligence Act) 1945.

[188] First Report of the Select Committee on the Parliamentary Commissioner for Administration, *Maladministration and Redress,* HC 112 (1994). See also Woodhouse, above n. 52, 77–8.

[189] Local Government Act 1974, s 31(3). See literature cited in footnote 52.

[190] C373/92 reported in *Annual Report* 1993 (HC 290). See also C588/92 reported in *Annual Report 1994* (HC 307).

[191] Speed used to be another advantage of the Ombudsman system, but the Parliamentary Commissioner's average throughput time now exceeds eighty-eight weeks. See P. Giddings, 'The Parliamentary Ombudsman: A Successful Alternative?', in D. Oliver and G. Drewry (eds.), *The Law and Parliament* (London, 1999), 125, 134.

[192] See A. W. Bradley, 'Administrative Justice and the Binding Effect of Official Acts' (1981) CLP 1, 10–11; Wright, above n. 7, 26; Craig and Fairgrieve, above n. 123.

[193] Some MPs never refer complaints to the Parliamentary Commissioner. See Giddings, above n. 191, 130–2.

[194] See Woodhouse, above n. 52, 73–4.

[195] See Wade 94.

[196] The Parliamentary Commissioner's case law has expanded rapidly in recent years. See *Annual Report 1996* (HC 386), 37; Amos, above n. 52, 25–6.

have on occasion been reluctant to comply with recommendations for payment of compensation.[197]

(B) French Law

The French judiciary's basic assumptions about administrative liability appear to differ markedly from those of their English colleagues. In France, this area of law is influenced by an egalitarian ideology which sees the 'socialization' of risk through damages liability and statutory compensation schemes as both practical and economically sound.[198] One does not find in judgments, opinions of the CE's Commissaires de Gouvernement, or extra-judicial writings much reference to the risk that liability may have a chilling effect, open the flood-gates, force the courts into non-justiciable areas, or undermine alternative complaints procedure and remedies. French administrative judges are more inclined to think that liability improves the quality of decision-making, that its ambit can be controlled without denying that the state owes a duty of care towards its citizens, and that administrative discretion can be reviewed without usurpation of administrative functions. Moreover, the CE has until very recently lacked mandatory remedies, and damages liability has been used as an alternative means of securing effective compliance with the principle of legality.[199]

It is, on this basis, unsurprising to find that the principles of French law concerning liability for unlawful decisions differ from the principles of English law in three important respects. First, unlawfulness is equated with fault in French law (*illégalité = faute*). An administrative decision which has been or could be annulled in judicial review proceedings always constitutes a 'service fault' (*faute de service*) on the basis of which the administration *may* be liable in damages. It is in principle irrelevant whether the unlawfulness is procedural or substantive in nature; it may, for example, consist in an error of law, a failure to give reasons, an error of primary fact, or an irrelevant consideration.[200] Thus, in *Ordonneau* the president of the commission responsible for competition matters in France obtained damages for lost salary because the administration had

[197] See P. M. Brown, 'The Ombudsmen, Remedies for Misinformation', in *Administrative Law and Government Action*, G. Richardson and H. Genn (eds.), (Oxford, 1994), 333–5 (reporting compliance problems in up to 24 per cent of cases concerned with misleading advice); Woodhouse, above n. 52, 74–6; Drewry, above n. 53, 102–3. Compare *Annual Report 1998* (HC 845) para 1.4; Giddings, above n. 191, 128 (reporting 'near 100 per cent' compliance with the Parliamentary Commissioner's recommendations).

[198] See text above at footnote 36.

[199] It is perhaps more correct to state that the CE deprived itself of mandatory remedies, see CE 27/1–1893 *Le Loir* Rec 136; CE 4/11–83 *Noulard* Rec 451. Injunctions were, however, introduced in 1995 (Art L8, *Code des tribunaux administratifs et des cours d'appel administratives*) The CE's unwillingness to address injunctions to the administration may derive from its historical evolution as an advisory body. See Harlow, above n. 6, 206.

[200] CE 26/1–73 *Driancourt* Rec 78; confirmed by CE 28/3–80 *Yverneau* RDP 1980, 1744; CE 27/5–87 *Legoff* AJDA 1987, 694; CE 9/6–95 *Lesprit* AJDA 1995, 745. See Deguergue, above n. 3, 185–95.

erred in law when it compulsorily retired him pursuant to provisions which were not applicable to the special post of president.[201]

Second, the administration owes a duty to decide lawfully towards *all* physical and legal persons. That is, the requirement of a duty of care does not limit the scope of liability as in English law.[202] The French courts have, for example, imposed fault liability on the police for its failure to prevent accidents and crimes,[203] on social services for the acts of foster parents who injured children in care,[204] and on road services for failing to ensure lighting of obstacles[205] and for failing to remove illegally parked vehicles.[206]

Third, there are fewer restrictions on the type of loss which may be recovered in French law. A person harmed by an unlawful decision may recover pure economic loss and 'moral loss' as well as physical injury and property damage.[207]

It follows from these principles that the administration is, in principle, liable in fault if it revokes a lawful decision which has created rights for the affected person. Thus, in *Dumas* a public institute for continuing education sought to revoke a decision to employ a teacher on the basis of which he had resigned from his previous position. The CE held that although an employment contract had not been signed, the institute's action violated the principle that favourable decisions create rights. It had therefore acted unlawfully and it was held liable in fault for Mr Dumas's lost income and inconvenience.[208] The administration may also be liable for revoking a lawful decision which has not created rights, such as a licence, if the revocation is procedurally or substantively flawed. For example, in the *Neuvecelle* case a licence to operate a childrens' sanatorium was revoked without consultation of the owner amidst allegations of poor maintenance of its buildings and children suffering injuries while in residence. It was later shown that most of these allegations were unfounded. The CE found that the revocation was vitiated by factual and procedural errors and therefore faulty, and that the owner was entitled to the profits lost during the period of closure. It made no difference to this liability that the licence was an *autorisation de police*, which could at any stage have been revoked if this was in the interest of public health. [209]

[201] CE 7/7–89 *Ordonneau* Rec 161.

[202] See Fines, above n. 3, 192.

[203] CE 29/7–58 *Ville de Perpignan* Rec 213; CE 26/6–85 *Garagnon* Rec 254.

[204] CE 23/9–87 *Ouaras* Rec 290.

[205] CE 8/5–63 *Commune de Maison Lafitte* DA 1963 no 215.

[206] CE 20/10–72 *Marambert* AJDA 1972, 597.

[207] See Harlow, above n. 2, 241; Fines, above n. 3, 199.

[208] CE 25/1–89 *Dumas* no 66.207. For other examples of liability for violation of *droits acquis*, see CE 31/1–36 *Bouzy* Rec 142; CE 27/4–45 *Brousser* Rec 82; CE 20/1–60 *Zagame* Rec 35; CAA Nantes 11/6–92 *SARL Centre dramatique national de Rennes* Rec 1288; CAA Paris 18/7–95 *SARL Siey-BWA* Rec 1024; CAA Nantes 8/11–95 *Commune de Faye-d'Anjou* AJDA 1996, 331.

[209] CE 19/5–76 *SA du Château de Neuvecelle* RDP 1976, 1385 (the profit loss was reduced by 1/3 because the authority would have been entitled to take certain measures in view of the true allegations). See for related examples CE 4/12–1879 *A* D 1880 III 41 (discussed by Dicey, above n. 16, 410); CE 1/12–48 *JICF* Rec 449; CE 19/12–52 *Saurel* RDP 1953, 719; CE 15/4–75 *'La Comédie de Bourges'* Rec 231; CE 3/12–82 *Société continentale de promotion immobilière* Rec 409.

The comments above might suggest to the reader that damages for unlawful decisions are far more readily available in French than in English law.[210] That is, however, true only to a certain extent. The French courts are well aware of the policy arguments against administrative liability, in particular the risk of bankrupting public authorities and of unduly inhibiting their exercise of discretionary powers. While these considerations are rarely spelled out, they certainly play an important role in practice.[211] Indeed, the French courts have developed what Geneviève Viney has called 'a number of indirect and quasi-occult methods' to control the ambit of liability.[212] One may identify five such methods: variation of the concept of legality by so-called 'substitution of motives'(I); a requirement of gross fault (*faute lourde*) for certain types of decisions (II); strict application of the concepts of 'direct' causation (III), 'certain' damage (IV), and contributory fault (V).

I Variation of the Concept of Legality

There are two procedural routes by which damages for unlawful decisions may be obtained in France. The plaintiff may either seek judicial review of the decision and apply for damages in a separate action or he may join the two actions. In joined actions, which are the most common,[213] the legality and liability issues are decided by the same panel of judges.[214] They will therefore rule on the lawfulness of the decision in full cognisance of the liability consequences their ruling will entail. If policy reasons militate against an award of damages, the court may, typically without spelling out these reasons, hold a *prima facie* unlawful decision lawful by applying a technique known as substitution of motives and legal basis (*substitution de motifs et base légale*).[215] This technique has two permutations.

First, a reviewing court will normally reject as 'ineffective' arguments (*moyens inopérant*) seeking to establish that a decision is unlawful if it was made subject to a statutory duty (*compétence liée*).[216] The unlawfulness may relate to personal incompetence, procedural irregularity, error of law, error of

[210] See JUSTICE—All Souls, above n. 96, 360; Allison 180–1.

[211] Policy arguments are largely ignored in the French public law literature. See however Chapus, above n. 73, 484; Mariani-Benigni, above n. 65, 848, 876–7.

[212] G. Viney, 'Modération et limitation des réponsabilité et des indemnisations', in J. Spier (ed.), *The Limit of Liability: Keeping the Floodgates Shut* (The Hague 1996), 127–8.

[213] Whereas in Britain legality and liability issues are typically split between the Crown List and the High Court's list of cases begun by writ. See footnote 12.

[214] In separate actions liability will be decided either by the same judges or by colleagues from within the same administrative court.

[215] See B. Pacteau, *Excès de pouvoir et motifs de l'acte administratif* (Paris, 1977), 89–107; Chapus, above n. 73, 653–61, 790–4; J.-M. Peyrical, 'Le juge administratif et la sauvegarde des actes de l'administration', AJDA 1996, 22.

[216] CE 4/12–59 *Geoffroy* Rec 654; CE 19/5–83 *Bertin* Rec 208 CE 3/2–99 *Montaignac* AJDA 1999, 631 with case note at 468. See J.-M. Auby, 'Les Moyens inopérants dans la jurisprudence administrative', AJDA 1966, 5.

fact, and even misuse of power (*détournement de pouvoir*).[217] Second, the court may uphold a decision based on a discretionary power (*pouvoir discretionnaire*) which was not actually applicable in the circumstances if, in the court's view, the decision could have been made under another statutory provision or an inherent (prerogative) power. The court will then 'substitute the legal basis' (*substitution de base légale*).[218] A discretionary decision made on the basis of incorrect facts or irrelevant considerations may also be upheld if the court considers that an identical decision would have been made on the basis of the correct facts and lawful considerations (*substitution de motifs*).[219]

The rationale for this 'substitution' technique is according to French writers that it is wasteful to annul a decision if the administration must (or may) subsequently adopt a similar decision.[220] Thus, the substitution technique fulfils a function similar to the power, vested in English courts, to withhold discretionary public law remedies.[221] However, while an English court will declare an *ultra vires* decision unlawful and *then* withhold the remedy sought, a French court applying the substitution technique will actually declare the decision lawful. The upshot is that the French applicant loses his chance of obtaining damages for faulty decision-making, and it is thought that this is an important reason why the French courts resort to substitution.

There are no precise criteria for what unlawful decisions will be upheld by substitution, but the courts are reluctant to uphold *prima facie* unlawful decisions which are based on wide discretionary powers.[222] There may be two explanations for this. One explanation is that it is difficult to ascertain whether a discretionary decision would actually have been made on alternative grounds than the unlawful grounds initially relied on, and that by making this determination the court comes extremely close to substitution of judgment. Another explanation is that judicial review of discretionary decisions, by principles such as 'manifest error of appreciation', is inherently flexible. Liability may therefore be controlled by a covert variation of these principles rather than by the overt application of the substitution technique.[223]

A survey of the case law reveals that the substitution technique is not infrequently applied in cases concerning unlawful revocation. A few examples will suffice for present purposes. The *Gillet* case concerned the revocation of a building permission which had been granted by an officer in excess of his delegated

[217] See Genevois *conclusions* CE 19/6–81 *Carliez* AJDA 1981, 105 with examples.

[218] CE 24/7–87 *Damman* Rec 892; CE 15/4–92 *Polat* Rec 981; CE 17/1–97 *Association "Vivre a Couret"* no 120.228.

[219] In situations of mixed lawful and unlawful considerations the court may 'neutralize' the latter (*neutralisation des motifs*). See CE 12/1–68 *Perrot* Rec 36; Peyrical, above n. 215, 23–8.

[220] See Peyrical, above n. 215, 29.

[221] See Bingham LJ, 'Should Public Law Remedies be Discretionary?' (1991) PL 64.

[222] See Peyrical, above n. 215, 29–31; *JC* Fasc 1152 no 128–130.

[223] No attempt can be made, within the confines of this book, to prove the existence of such variation.

competence. The builder's damages claim was dismissed on the basis of somewhat contorted judicial reasoning. The CE held that the permission was unlawful and that the authority was under a duty to revoke it. Consequently, the authority had not acted unlawfully and was not liable. Thus, the court used the doctrine of ineffective arguments (*moyens inopérant*) to dismiss liability for the revocation while failing to explain why the authority was not liable for making the unlawful permission in the first place.[224] A similar result was reached by a different reasoning in the *Coopération laitière* case. This case concerned an order that certain milk producers deliver their produce to specified dairy plants. The order was revoked, to the detriment of the dairy plants, on the ground that it had proved unworkable in practice. The dairy plants showed that this ground had no basis in reality, but the CE upheld the revocation and rejected their claim for lost profits. The court held that the decision-maker had not had the power to make the order in the first place and it substituted this reason for the efficiency consideration initially relied on (*substitution de motifs*).[225]

The *Gillet* and *Coopération laitière* cases both concerned unlawful decisions which were subsequently revoked or replaced by lawful decisions. The substitution technique is applied less frequently in cases concerning unlawful revocation of lawful decisions. This is unsurprising because the person who has been unlawfully deprived of a (lawfully awarded) benefit is typically more deserving than the person who has been awarded a benefit by an unlawful decision. The *Desamis* case is a leading example. It concerned a discretionary decision to revoke a bar licence on the grounds that the owner had been drinking with the customers. A first instance court found this allegation unfounded and annulled the revocation. On appeal to the CE the minister argued that the owner was also guilty of other offences and that the revocation should be upheld by substitution. The CE rejected this argument on the basis that the power to revoke lawfully awarded bar licences was discretionary. The court could not ascertain precisely whether the alternative violations, even if proven, would have led to revocation and it would therefore not apply the substitution doctrine.[226]

II The Requirement of Gross Fault

Administrative liability is limited to some extent by what may be called fault-grading.[227] Tasks which are 'particularly difficult' only give rise to liability if the

[224] CE 12/5–76 *Gillet* RDP 1977, 229 See also CE 17/1–69 *Bagot* no 71.559; CE 23/5–80 *Nivault* RDP 1981, 792; CE 2/10–87 *Castel* RFDA 1988, 869; CE 27/9–93 *SCI Les balcons du Lac* no 124.633.

[225] CE 6/11–59 *Coopération laitière de Belfort* Rec 581. See also CE 13/2–52 *Costa* Rec 104; CE 14/5–75 *Ayache* no 88.216. Compare CE 17/10–62 *Pernaud* Rec 545.

[226] CE 8/1–71 *Desamis* AJDA 1971, 297. See also CE 11/6–93 *Société Landrieu* Rec 173; CE 17/9–99 *Société Cannon Immobilière* AJDA 1999, 1038. Compare CE 5/11–86 *Le Ng* D 1987 SC 188 (procedurally flawed revocation under statutory duty, *moyen inopérant*).

[227] The seminal case is CE 10/2–05 *Tomaso Gréco* Rec 139. See generally Harlow, above n. 2, 518–26; J. F. Couzinet, 'La notion de faute lourde administrative', RDP 1977, 283; Chapus 1198–218; F. Raynaud and P. Fombeur, 'Chronique générale de jurisprudence administrative', AJDA 1998, 403, 418–24.

authority was guilty of 'gross fault' (*faute lourde*). That is, a lower level of care is required in view of the difficulty of the task.

The concept of 'difficult' tasks has vague contours. Its scope is determined as much by the historically deep-rooted idea that 'the public power' (*la puissance publique*) is immune to law suits as by modern conceptions of the role of liability in public law.[228] Difficult tasks should not be confused with the broad concept of policy decisions in English law.[229] In fact, it is normally not considered difficult to make administrative decisions in French law. Even discretionary decisions which entail the balancing of competing interests, such as planning permissions and decisions to ban cinema films on grounds of public morality, are not considered 'difficult'.[230] It is decisions and physical actions taken 'in the field'—such as fire fighting, the removal of strikers, and traffic control—rather than decision-making 'in the office' which is considered difficult and therefore subject to the requirement of *faute lourde*.[231] The upshot is that it is normally easier to establish fault in the making of an administrative decision than in its practical implementation. This has the opposite effect of the policy-operational dichotomy in English law, which makes the administration less liable for decision-making than for implementation.[232]

The importance of fault-grading has decreased in the last thirty years.[233] A requirement of 'exceptionally gross fault', which had been applied in certain contexts, was abandoned in the 1960s, and the scope of gross fault has been restricted very considerably.[234] Today fault-grading only applies to two types of decisions of relevance for present purposes.

First, decision-making by state tax authorities (*services fiscaux*) on matters of direct taxation is in principle subject to gross fault liability.[235] However, simple fault applies if the particular decision did not pose any special difficulties, such as routine computerized calculation and recovery[236] and application of clearly worded non-discretionary rules to a set of facts.[237] The requirement of gross fault in tax law reflects the old notion of immunity of central public power and an acceptance by the courts that tax authorities are

[228] See Chapus 1210–13.

[229] See footnote 139.

[230] e.g. CE 17/6–83 *SCI Italie-Vandrezane* Rec 267; CE 22/3–66 *Société les Films Marceau* AJDA 1966, 254.

[231] See Chapus 1207. However, certain dangerous police activities, like the use of firearms to stop a suspect, may be subject to no-fault liability. In this way, the courts protect innocent victims without attempting to assess whether the police acted negligently. See Brown and Bell 196.

[232] See section 4.A.

[233] See C. Geuttier, *La responsabilité administrative* (Paris, 1996), 108–13.

[234] For recent examples of this tendency , see CE 10/4–92 *Epoux V* Rec 171; CE 21/6–97 *Theux* RFDA 1998, 8; CE 13/3–98 *Améron* AJDA 1998, 418.

[235] CE 21/12–62 *Husson-Chiffre* Rec 710; CE 26/3–82 *SA Etablissement Bienvenu* D 1983 IR 319. See J. F. Touchard, 'A propos de la responsabilité pour faute de l'administration fiscale', RDP 1992, 785; T.-X. Girardot and F. Raynaud, 'Chronique générale de jurisprudence administrative française' AJDA 1998, 97, 112–17. Indirect taxation is, however, subject to the jurisdiction of the civil law courts. See Brown and Bell 145.

[236] CE 27/7–90 *Bourgeois* Rec 242.

[237] CE 29/12–97 *Commune d'Arceuil* AJDA 1998, 180.

understaffed and likely to be swamped by damages claims if subject to the strict principle of simple fault (*illégalité = faute*).

Second, ministers are in French law empowered to exercise control over decisions by local authorities, including *communes* and *départements,* and a number of bodies providing public services such as the national bank (*Banque de France*), railways (*SNCF*), universities, state schools, hospitals, and health insurance schemes (*caisses de sécurité sociale*).[238] A decision made by one of these bodies, which appears to be unlawful, may be suspended and referred by the minister to an administrative court for review.[239] Ministerial decisions made within this system of administrative control, known as *tutelle*, are subject to gross fault liability.[240] The main reasons for this are, first, that strict ministerial liability would deflect responsibility from the controlled to the controller and, second, that the courts are reluctant to impose a duty upon the minister to prevent harm to third parties.

It is not entirely clear what constitutes gross fault.[241] The courts take into account a number of elements including the statutory context, the nature of the damage caused, and whether the administration erred repeatedly or only once.[242] In the context of discretionary decision-making, it is certainly a gross fault to act arbitrarily or with malicious intent, but the courts normally categorize less serious illegalities as simple faults.[243] Thus, the CE found in *Markovitch* that a minister was not grossly at fault when he set aside the appointment of a director of a social security body on the basis of a legislative provision which had not yet entered into force.[244] In *Gérard* a driving licence was suspended pending criminal proceedings for drink driving. The fact that the criminal court did not find the allegation proved did not mean that the suspension had been grossly faulty.[245] In *Verdier* the CE held that a decision to authorize the redundancy of a private employee for economic reasons was manifestly erroneous (*erreur manifest d'appréciation*) because the employee's position had actually been filled by another person. Nevertheless, the decision-maker's error did not constitute a gross fault.[246] These decisions show that

[238] This power is granted by Law of 2/3–82 and a number of more specific statutes. See Chapus 374–99.

[239] In practice, this power is exercised by the prefects (*préfets*) on behalf of ministers and the procedure is accordingly known as *déféré préfectoral.*

[240] CE 10/7–57 *Ministre du travail* Rec 467; CE 2/7–79 *Triolle* Rec 873; CE 29/4–87 *Ministre de l'Intérieur* Rec 161. Compare CE 9/4–93 *G, D and B* Rec 110; CE 25/3–94 *Commune de Kintzheim* Rec 162; CAA Marseille 21/1–99 *Ministre de l'Intérieur* RFDA 1999, 1032.

[241] See Chapus 1199 stating that 'nothing is more fluid than the concept of gross fault'.

[242] See M. Paillet, *La responsabilité administrative* (Paris, 1996), 127.

[243] See M. Paillet *JC* Fasc 820 no 36.

[244] CE 27/10–71 *Markovitch* Rec 640. See also CE 23/2–77 *Verheyde* no 00.794.

[245] CE 7/7–71 *Gérard* Rec 513. Note that gross fault was exceptionally applied to a decision, which was not made 'in action' because it was made on the basis of a provision on short-term suspension for reasons of urgency. Similarly CAA Nantes 19/5–94 *Rouzin* Rec 1177.

[246] CE 28/7–89 *Verdier* no 69.858.

errors of law and primary fact are not normally considered gross faults, and the *Verdier* case suggests that even manifestly erroneous (unreasonable) decisions may be considered simply faulty.

It emerges that the fault-grading technique is still of some practical importance in revocation situations.[247] Gross fault must still be shown in the practically significant areas of tax and ministerial *tutelle*, and it is clearly very difficult for litigants to prove it in practice. [248]

III Causation

The requirement of causation plays a very important role as a limitation upon liability in French law.[249] As in English law, the causation requirement has two limbs. There must be causation in fact (*causalité matérielle*), which is determined by the 'but-for' test, and the damage must not be too remote a consequence of the unlawful decision, i.e. the causal link must be 'direct' (*causalité directe*). To draw the line between 'direct' and 'indirect' causes, the French courts apply a theory of adequate cause (*causalité adéquate*).[250] According to this theory, the causal link is direct if in the normal run of things it was probable that the unlawful decision would cause the damage.[251] The court will make an *ex post facto* assessment of probabilities of different courses of events rather than, as an English court, ask whether the damage was foreseeable at the time the decision was made.

The classic causation problem in relation to unlawful decisions is, as explained above, whether the unlawfulness—for example an irrelevant consideration or a failure to grant a hearing—actually caused the plaintiff a loss or, in other words, whether it is likely that the decision would have been made in the absence of the unlawfulness. The French courts are, unlike the English courts, not afraid to determine this question for themselves.[252] In practice, however, the causation assessment often leads to the dismissal of the plaintiff's claim. This is particularly so if the decision violated procedural rules, such as

[247] Similarly Banakas, above n. 56, 59. Compare Harlow, above n. 2, 516, 521–2.

[248] See however the successful claim in CAA Nancy 9/3–94 *Broutard* Rec 1179.

[249] See Guettier, above n. 233, 126; Viney, above n. 212, 131 and more generally J.-P. Tagourdeau, 'Le caractère certain et direct du préjudice en matière de responsabilité extra-contractuelle de la puissance administrative', AJDA 1974, 508 ; P. Vialle, 'Lien de causalité et dommage direct dans la responsabilité administrative', RDP 1974, 1243; Chapus 1145–53.

[250] Galmot *conclusions* CE 14/10–66 *Marais* D 1966, 636–7; Grevisse *conclusions* CE 19/12–69 *Établissement Delannoy* RDP 1970, 787. Similarly Tagourdeau, above n. 249, 513–14; Banakas, above n. 56, 59. For comparative discussion of *causa adequata*, see Honoré, above n. 179, 49–55.

[251] The courts have rejected the causation concept of equivalent conditions (*équivalence des conditions*) which effectively equates causation in fact with causation in law. Compare Vialle, above n. 249, 1267 ff. for the view, not shared by other theory, that the CE applies none of these theories but rather a theory of direct consequence (or proximity) according to which legal causation depends upon the fault being *temporally* closer to the loss than other contributing facts.

[252] Actions for damages are in France *contentieux de pleine juridiction*. This means that the court is competent to go beyond simple review. See Brown and Bell 178.

the prohibition against delegation[253] or the right to hearing and reasons.[254] Dismissal of civil servants[255] and revocation of licences without a hearing are core examples. Thus, in the *Dame Deux* case a licence to carry out certain medical treatments at the expense of the national medical insurance was revoked without a hearing. The decision was appealed to a special commission which overruled it for this reason. However, a subsequent damages claim failed because the owner had actually failed to comply with legal requirements to examine patients daily and to keep proper records. The CE found that this failure, rather than the procedural error, was the real and direct cause of the owner's loss of livelihood.[256]

Damages claims based on substantive unlawfulness are also regularly dismissed on grounds of causation. For example, in *Pratt-Flottes* a closure order had been made against a sanatorium because a boy called Moussa had died while in residence. This was shown to be factually incorrect and the CE annulled the decision. But liability was dismissed because other children had in fact suffered injuries or died. The order was therefore justified in substance and not the cause of the loss suffered by the owner of the sanatorium.[257]

These cases demonstrate that public authorities will often escape liability because 'direct causation' is difficult to prove. The French causation case law may be criticized.[258] First, the CE's judgments often fail to explain all relevant facts and to justify why a particular cause is considered too indirect. This leads to a lack of transparency which is exacerbated by the fact that a conceptual distinction between the requirements of direct causation and 'certain' damage is not maintained.[259] The courts may be suspected of deliberately omitting clear reasoning to hide the fact that the causation test is used to limit administrative liability in the light of unarticulated policy considerations. Second, the courts' independent causation assessment leads, like the substitution of motives technique, to some evaluation of the merits and substitution of judgment.[260] This is problematic even though judges in the higher French courts have considerable practical experience with administration and access to a rich file compiled by

[253] CE 28/11–80 *Domergue* no 16.618.

[254] See Richer, above n. 54, 29; J. Moreau, 'Les conséquences des illégalités procédurales en droit administratif français' (1993) ERPL Ed spécial 85, 91–2; M. Paillet *JC* Fasc 818 no 130, Fasc 870 no 76–80.

[255] e.g. CE 9/1–59 *Dumas* Rec 31; CE 2/10–70 *Chastang* Rec 1198; CE 18/6–86 *Krier* Rec 166; CE 29/10–86 *Bonneau* Rec 248; CAA Nancy 28/7–95 *Centre hospitalier de Roubaix* no 44.577.

[256] CE 22/1–69 *Deux* Rec 956. See also CE 11/10–61 *Clémant* Rec 559; CE 19/6–81 *Carliez* AJDA 1981, 103.

[257] CE 15/7–64 *Prat-Flottes* Rec 438. See also CE 8/3–63 *Massad* Rec 143; CE 19/5–76 *SA du Château de Neuvecelle* RDP 1976, 1385; CE 13/6–80 *Haeuw* Rec 628; CE 22/1–93 *Société de Sannois-Ermont-Franconville* D 1994 SC 66; CAA Paris 10/2–94 *SA Ballande* Rec 1182; CAA Paris 29/9–95 *Graillet* Rec 1032.

[258] See J. Moreau, 'L'influence du développement de la construction européenne sur le droit français de la responsabilité de la puissance publique', in *Mélanges J. Boulouis* (Paris, 1991), 419.

[259] See Tagourdeau, above n. 249, 517–18.

[260] See, commenting on this problem in the English context, Bingham, above n. 221, 72–3.

the instructing judge.[261] Moreover, by almost routinely refusing liability for breach of procedural requirements the French courts underestimate the important connection between procedure and substance. It is often difficult, if not impossible, to say for certain whether a hearing or reasons would have prompted a different outcome, and there is evidently a risk that the courts' attitude will encourage unwanted administrative practices.[262] This may in turn perpetuate the unfairness caused by a decision which violates basic procedural requirements, and ultimately undermines public confidence in the administration.[263]

IV The Requirement of Actual and Certain Damage

There are no general restrictions in French law on the type of loss which may be recovered in liability actions. The administrative courts may, unlike in the English tort of negligence, award damages for 'moral' and pure economic loss caused by unlawful decision-making.[264] However, the plaintiff must always show that his loss is 'actual and certain' (*dommage certain*) rather than hypothetical or a mere possibility (*dommage incertain* or *éventuel*).[265] Liability claims are often dismissed on this ground. This is particularly so in two types of situations.

First, the requirement of certain damage restricts administrative liability towards persons who are not immediately protected by the relevant legislation. For example, the loss caused by the failure of a regulatory body to prevent harm to third parties will often be dismissed as too uncertain or indirect.[266] While the English courts hold that regulatory agencies owe no duty of care towards third parties,[267] the French courts accept the possibility of liability, but limit it quite severely in practice by a combination of fault-grading, strict causation and certainty of damage.[268]

Second, the availability of damages for loss of profit (*manque a gagner*), is restricted to some extent by the requirement of certain damage.[269] While it is

[261] See Brown and Bell 79–88, 94–101.

[262] Similarly, discussing this issue in judicial review, D. H. Clark, 'Natural Justice: Substance and Shadow' (1975) PL 27; T. R. S. Allan, *Law, Liberty, and Justice: The Legal Foundations of British Constitutionalism* (Oxford, 1993), 202.

[263] *John v Rees* [1970] Ch 345, 402.

[264] See footnote 207.

[265] See generally F. Sallet, *La perte de chance dans la jurisprudence administrative relative à la responsabilité de la puissance publique* (Paris, 1994); Chapus 1137–45.

[266] e.g. CE 24/3–86 *Thiémard* Rec 179 (mining activities); CE 29/3–46 *Caisse départemental d'assistance sociale de Meurthe-et-Moselle* Rec 100 (municipal banks); CE 24/1–64 *André* Rec 329; CAA Paris 30/3–99 *El Shikh* AJDA 1999, 951 (banks and building societies); and footnote 240.

[267] *Yuen Kun Yeu v A-G of Hong Kong* [1988] AC 175; *Philcox v Civil Aviation Authority* The Times 8/6–95.

[268] See Lawson and Markesinis, above n. 179, 97–8, 119–20; J. S. Bell, 'Administrative Liability in French Law' (1996) EPL 337, 339–40.

[269] A survey of some 220 decisions mentioning *manque a gagner* shows that successful claims for lost profits are rare. See similarly Latournerie, above n. 39, 220; P. Cadenat, 'Chronique de jurisprudence des cours administratives d'appel', AJDA 1997, 275, 285–6.

relatively straightforward to prove that a decision caused property damage or personal injury, loss of profit is more problematic because it concerns future events. A profit will only be considered sufficiently certain if there is 'a very serious chance' that it would have been earned in the absence of the unlawful decision.[270] In this way, the requirement of certain damage, often combined with 'direct' causation in the courts' reasoning, works as a control-device in the same way as the rule of English law preventing recovery of pure economic loss in negligence.[271] This is practically very important for revocation of favourable decisions, such as planning permissions and licences, as the following examples illustrate.

A person who is awarded an unlawful planning permission or licence, which is later revoked or replaced by a less favourable licence, will normally be able to recover expenses incurred in reliance on the permission, such as payments to an architect and construction works.[272] For example, in the *Italie-Vandrezane* case a development company recovered over 148 million francs for expenses it had incurred in reliance on a permission to erect an office tower in central Paris which had been granted in violation of certain planning provisions.[273] However, loss of profits caused by the inability to complete a planned development is rarely awarded.[274] This also applies in other contexts, such as licensing. Thus, in the *Pernaud* case the beneficiary of a pharmacy licence, which had been awarded by an incompetent officer and revoked shortly after sales had commenced, obtained damages for his purchase of medicine and business premises. The licence could lawfully have been awarded by the mayor, and the requirement of causation in fact (*causalité materielle*) was therefore satisfied. However, the claim for lost profits was rejected as the shop had only been open for a few days and profits were therefore too uncertain.[275]

The French case law is considerably more liberal in relation to loss caused by the unlawful revocation of lawfully awarded licences.[276] For example, in the

[270] CE 27/5–87 *Legoff* AJDA 1987, 694. See Tagourdeau, above n. 249, 519–24; Chapus 1137–8.

[271] See Lawson and Markesinis, above n. 179, 69–70; Banakas, above n. 56, 58.

[272] The same applies where a lawfully awarded planning permission is subsequently revoked, e.g. CE 25/6–71 *Bruchet* Rec 488; CE 28/7–93 *Roux* no 87.047; CE 4/12–74 *Corniche* no 93.953.

[273] CE 17/6–83 *SCI Italie-Vandrezane* Rec 267. See also CE 6/10–82 *Crédit Lyonnais* DA 1982 no 372; CE 9/12–88 *SCI L'Ollivette* no 77.247.

[274] CE 7/1–70 *Rosier* Rec 9; CE 12/11–75 *Résidence du Pays d'Oc* Rec 1263 CE 24/3–78 *Société Urba-Foret* no 5.290; CE 21/9–90 *SCI le Trait d'Union* no 90.313. The same applies where planning permission is unlawfully refused. e.g. CE 30/3–66 *Ravinetto* Rec 247; CE 24/4–70 *Consorts Chodron de Courcel* Rec 278; CE 7/3–90 *Bore de Loisy* Rec 983; CE 22/1–93 *Société de Sannois-Ermont-Franconville* D 1994 SC 66; CE 16/11–98 *Sille* DA 1998 no 23. Compare CE 23/12–81 *Stinco* Rec 488; CE 11/3–83 *'CEFIC'* D 1984 IR 344; CE 12/12–84 *Socomi* RDP 1985, 1395. See also J.-B. Auby, 'Responsabilité en matière d'urbanisme', in F. Gazier, R. Drago (eds.), *Encyclopédie Dalloz: Répertoire de la responsabilité de la puissance publique* (Paris, 1996).

[275] Instead the profits made while the shop was open were deducted from the amount payable for expenses, CE 17/10–62 *Pernaud* Rec 545.

[276] The reader is reminded that lawfully awarded licences may often be revoked *lawfully* under the doctrine of *autorisations de police*, in which case the licensee is not entitled to damages or compensation. See section 3.B.

Roussillon case the mayor of the town of Bollene revoked in 1978 a decision which allowed taxi owners to utilize more than one vehicle. Consequently, Mr Roussillon was unable to use one of his two taxis until 1985 when the CE finally annulled the revocation on the grounds that a 'one taxi per licensee' policy did not serve a relevant purpose. Damages of 227,000 francs were awarded for lost profit, a substantial amount of money though the reported facts do not reveal whether it covered the full loss.[277]

'Certain loss' is, like 'direct causation', a flexible concept which leaves the courts considerable freedom to take into account policy consideration. The test is in comparison with English law fairly strict, and it is clear that causation works as an effective control device on French administrative liability. However, it is equally clear that causation is a more flexible and subtle control device than the duty of care concept in English law. French law leaves individuals harmed by unlawful revocation of licences and other beneficial decisions a window of opportunity which has been firmly shut by the English courts.

V Contributory Fault

The French courts generally expect individuals dealing with the administration to act with considerable prudence.[278] A failure in this respect will cause damages to be reduced on grounds of contributory fault. Reductions of between 25 and 75 per cent are often made,[279] either on the grounds that the plaintiff knew[280] or ought to have known[281] that a permission he had obtained was unlawful or that he otherwise acted in a faulty manner.[282] For example, in *Société European Homes* the applicant had obtained planning permission to erect a block of flats on land which the local authorities had offered to sell. The permission was subsequently revoked, as it violated certain planning provisions, and the company lost about 3 million francs on a bank loan and over 10 million

[277] CE 5/11–90 *Roussillon* no 86.418. See also CE 19/5–76 *SA du Château de Neuvecelle* RDP 1976, 1385; CE 10/2–75 *Commune de Curvalle* no 91.153; CE 3/12–82 *Société continentale de promotion immobilière* Rec 409; CE 20/11–85 *Palma* no 38.667; CE 20/11–89 *Fougère* no 59.857; CE 24/10–90 *Le Grand Large* no 52.874. For award of profit loss for unlawful refusal to grant licences, see CE 17/5–60 *Heitz* Rec 370; CE 6/6–69 *Ducret* Rec 954.

[278] See generally J. Moreau, *L'influence de la situation et du comportement de la victime sur la responsabilité administrative* (Paris, 1957), *JC* Fasc 700 no 164; 870 no 99ff; J. P. Payre, 'Faute et fait de la victime dans le contentieux de la responsabilité administrative extra-contractuelle', AJDA 1980, 398 ; Chapus 1153–9.

[279] See Harlow (1977), above n. 2, 242; Payre, above n. 278, 403.

[280] e.g. CE 3/11–72 *Maury* D 1973, 761 (25 per cent reduction); CE 12/11–75 *Résidence du pays d'Oc* Rec 1263 (50 per cent); CE 23/6–76 *Société Construction immobilière Rhodanienne* Rec 1111 (25 per cent); CAA Paris 18/4–95 *Boulley* no 93PA00511 (50 per cent).

[281] e.g. CE 21/9–90 *SCI Hameau de Beauvoir* no 67.776 (25 per cent reduction). Compare CE 14/3–90 *Plat* Petites Affiches 3/7–91, 18.

[282] Damages claims may be dismissed entirely on the ground that the plaintiff accepted the risk that the decision on which he relied might be unlawful, see CE 31/1–42 *Bergs* Rec 27. However, a survey of cases reported in the Lexis database reveals that the CE and the CAA have not explicitly referred to 'acceptance of risk' in cases about revocation of unlawful decisions since 1964. For acceptance of risk in other areas, see Mariani-Benigni, above n. 65 and text at footnote 65.

francs of expected profits. The claim for loss of profit was dismissed entirely on the rather surprising ground that the company could not claim a profit which it would have derived from an unlawful construction.[283] The reliance loss was reduced by 25 per cent, as the CE found that the company had acted with imprudence by applying for the permission before finally signing the land purchase contract.[284] The court's approach is, as in several related cases, quite strict. It is difficult to see why an early application should be considered a significant contributory fault given the notorious slowness of French planning procedures.[285]

It emerges that French public authorities are far from always liable for unlawful decisions. The practical impact of the broad principle of administrative fault (*illégalité = faute*) is limited to a considerable extent by a pragmatic and strict application of substitution of motives, fault-grading, causation, damage, and contributory fault. Clearly, the French courts are sensitive to the policy considerations which have led the English courts to limit liability in recent years.[286] The French judiciary's tendency to limit liability in practice is not explainable by the existence of alternative sources of compensation. Statutory compensation for revocation of favourable decisions is virtually unheard of in France, and *ex gratia* compensation does not play any significant role in practice.[287] It follows that, at least in some contexts, outcomes are quite similar to English law.

(C) EC Law

The basic EC law principles of liability for unlawful decisions resemble French, rather than English, law in three respects. First, the Community courts assume that the institutions have a general duty to decide lawfully towards all physical and legal persons.[288] That is, the duty of care concept is not used to limit liability in EC law. Second, there are no strict limitations on the types of loss which may be recovered in EC law. Damages may be awarded for physical injury, property damage, 'moral' loss such as inconvenience, and even pure economic loss.[289] Third, the Community courts have adopted the principle of

283 This amounts to saying that loss of profit can *never* be claimed for revocation of unlawful decisions, a proposition which is not supported by previous case law.

284 CE 15/3–89 *Société European Homes* no 66.906.

285 On this topic, see Études du Conseil d'État: *Urbanisme—pour un droit plus efficace* (Paris, 1992).

286 For similar findings in studies of the French private law of delict, see Viney, above n. 212; Markesinis, above n. 126, 223–53.

287 See section 3.B.

288 e.g. Case 27/76 *United Brands v Commission* [1978] ECR 207, 305–6, 345 (The ECJ implied that the Commission owes a duty towards companies in its discretionary decision-making in competition matters)

289 e.g. Cases 54–60/74 *Kampfmeyer v Commission and Council* [1976] ECR 711; T-73/89 *Barbi v Commission* [1990] ECR II-619.

illégalité = faute.[290] The fact that a decision was or could be annulled in judicial review proceedings is normally sufficient to establish that the administration was at fault.[291] While liability for legislative measures[292] which involve the exercise of discretionary powers only applies if there is a 'sufficiently serious breach of a superior rule of law for the protection of the individual',[293] liability for individualized decision-making is not subject to this requirement.[294] According to a settled formula, liability for decisions is only conditional upon 'proof by the applicant of the unlawfulness of the alleged conduct of the Community institution concerned, the reality of the damage and the existence of a causal link between that conduct and the alleged damage.'[295] The nature of the illegality is in principle irrelevant, and damages have in some staff cases[296] been awarded for unfavourable decisions made on the basis of erroneous facts[297] and improper procedures.[298]

The operation of these principles is neatly illustrated by the case of *Algera*, the only known example of a successful damages claim in a revocation situation.[299] In this case, the Common Assembly had appointed Ms Algera and assigned her to a certain salary bracket, but subsequently revoked the appointment. The ECJ found that the bracketing, but not appointment, was unlawful and it therefore annulled the revocation of the latter. Ms Algera was then awarded damages for the inconvenience caused by the unlawful revocation of her appointment. The Court did not question whether the Assembly owed a

[290] See T. Tridimas, *The General Principles of EC Law* (Oxford, 1999), 314.

[291] The Community courts use the terms illegality, unlawfulness, and fault interchangeably. See e.g. Cases 59/83 *Biovilac v EEC* [1984] ECR 4057; T-108/94 *Candiotte v Council* [1996] ECR II-87 para 54; C-395/95P *Geotronics SA v Commission* [1997] ECR I-2271 para 46, 57.

[292] A measure is 'legislative' if in substance it applies to generalized circumstances and a 'decision' if it applies to individualized circumstance, the title or form of the measure is irrelevant See Cases T-481 and 484/93 *Vereinging Van Exporteurs in Levende Varkens v Commission* [1995] ECR II-2941 para 86–88; C-390/95P *Antillean Rice Mills v Commission* [1999] ECR I-769 para 56–60; AG Fennelly, Opinion in Case C-352/98P, of 27/1–2000, para 27–33. See also A. Arnull, 'Liability for Legislative Acts under Article 215(2) EC', in T. Heukels and A. McDonnell (eds.), *The Action for Damages in Community Law* (The Hague, 1997), 131–5.

[293] Cases 5/71 *Zuckerfabrik Schöppenstedt v Council* [1971] ECR 975; C-152/88 *Sofriimport v Commission* [1990] ECR I-2477. See Arnull, above n. 292, 136–9; Craig, above n. 6.

[294] Cases T-226/94 *Paul Dischamp SA v Commission* [1996] ECR II-575 para 39; T-481 and 484/93 *Vereinging Van Exporteurs in Levende Varkens v Commission* [1995] ECR II-2941 para 80–82; T-113/96 *Dubois SA v Council and Commission* [1998] ECR II-125 para 54–59.

[295] e.g. C-55/90 *Cato v Commission* [1992] ECR I-2533 para 18; C-136/92P *Commission v Lualdi* [1994] ECR I-1981 para 42; T-107/96 *Pantochim v Commission* [1998] ECR II-311 para 48.

[296] Staff cases are subject to similar principles as those developed under Art 288, see AG Lenz [1994] ECR I-1991. For the possibility of liability for misuse of power, error of fact, irrelevant considerations, and breach of legitimate expectations outside the staff context, see Cases C-370/89 *Etroy v EIB* [1993] ECR I-2583 para 27–36; T-230/94 *Farrugia v Commission* [1996] ECR II-195 para 42; T-336/94 *Efisol v Commission* [1996] ECR II-1343 para 30–31.

[297] Case 68/63 *Luhleich v Commission* [1965] ECR 727. See also Case T-73/89 *Barbi v Commission* [1990] ECR II-619.

[298] Case 110/63 *Willame v Commission* [1965] ECR 649.

[299] Cases 7/56 and 3–7/57 *Algera v Common Assembly* [1957] ECR 39. A survey of about 350 ECJ and CFI decisions referring to Art 288 (previously Art 215) EC revealed no other examples.

duty of care, or whether its failure to respect the employee's vested rights was 'serious'. The fact that the Assembly made an unlawful decision was sufficient, in and of itself, to establish fault and liability for consequential loss.[300]

It was seen above that the French courts limit liability in practice by a number of techniques. These techniques also play an important role in EC law. Therefore, to determine the extent to which EC law actually protects individuals' expectations and reliance upon administrative decisions, it is necessary to consider variation of the concept of unlawfulness (I), 'direct' causation (II), 'certain' damage (III), and contributory fault (IV).

I Variation of the Concept of Legality

It was explained above that the French courts limit liability by a variation of the concept of legality. In some cases, open-ended principles of review may be applied 'flexibly' to avoid the imposition of liability. In other cases, the French courts resort to substitution of legal basis and of motives to 'repair' *prima facie* unlawful decisions.[301]

The Community courts also rely on these techniques, albeit to a lesser extent than the French courts. It is likely, though difficult to prove, that open-ended principles of review like proportionality are applied in a 'flexible' way to limit the consequences of the strict principle of *illégalité = faute*.[302] It is also interesting to note that a doctrine of substitution of legal basis has developed in recent Community case law.[303] In *Gunzler Aluminium* the Commission had decided, on a request from the German authorities, that a trading company was liable to pay certain import duties. The Commission incorrectly assumed that the duties had already been paid and it therefore applied Regulation No 1430/79 on remission of duties rather than Regulation No 1697/79 on the post-clearance recovery of duties. The CFI found this to be an error of law. However, it held that 'the two sets of rules pursue the same aim, namely to limit the post-clearance payment of import and export duties to cases where such payment is justified and compatible with the protection of legitimate expectations'. Moreover, the facts which had justified the decision under Regulation 1430/79 would also justify a decision under Regulation 1697/79. Consequently, the 'error was of a purely formal nature as it did not . . . have any decisive influence as to the outcome' and there was accordingly 'no need to annul the contested decision on the ground that the Commission relied on the wrong legal basis'.

While this case shows that the Community courts may substitute one legal basis for another, and thereby limit liability for error of law, they have so far

300 The Assembly had agreed to pay outstanding salary, so there was no claim for lost income, but the Court awarded a small sum for inconvenience. The Court did not consider whether the unlawful bracketing decision, which was revoked within a reasonable period, could also give rise to a claim in damages.

301 See section 4.B.I.

302 No attempt can be made, within the confines of this book, to prove the existence of 'hidden' variation of principles of proportionality and the like in EC law.

303 Case T-75/95 *Gunzler Aluminium v Commission* [1996] ECR II-497 para 55.

been reluctant to substitute irrelevant considerations or 'motives' with relevant and lawful ones. Thus, in the recent *Farrugia* case, the applicant had applied for an EC scholarship to study abroad. His application was rejected on the factually erroneous ground that he was not a British national. In this situation a French court might find that the scholarship *could* equally have been dismissed on some other lawful ground and uphold the refusal by substitution of motives. The CFI, however, examined only whether the refusal *had actually* been made on some other lawful ground in addition to nationality. As it found that nationality was indeed the only reason relied on, it annulled the refusal.[304]

II Causation

The Community causation requirement has two limbs: causation in fact and remoteness.[305] Causation in fact is, as in English and French law, determined by the but-for test.[306] Remoteness is more complicated because the ECJ has failed to state clearly which test it applies. Some commentators argue that the Court applies a test equivalent to the French concept of *cause adéquate*,[307] others that it applies the German concept of 'sufficient cause'.[308] Recent case law suggests, however, that a unique Community concept of causation is developing. Thus, the CFI has held that damage must be 'an objectively foreseeable consequence in the normal course of events'.[309] This statement combines the 'foreseeability' analysis applied in English law with the 'normality' analysis inherent in the French adequate cause theory. It must be read in conjunction with previous case law suggesting that the unlawful decision which is alleged to have caused the plaintiff a loss must be the 'direct, immediate and exclusive cause' of that loss.[310]

The EC law requirement of causation is responsible for the failure of many damages claims in practice, both in cases concerning legislative acts,[311] and administrative decisions.[312] The Community courts will, when faced with an

[304] Case T-230/94 *Farrugia v Commission* [1996] ECR II-195 para 31–36. The applicant's claim for damages was dismissed on other grounds, see text at footnote 314.

[305] See generally A. G. Toth, 'The Concepts of Damage and Causality as Elements of Non-Contractual Liability', in T. Heukels and A. McDonnell (eds.), *The Action for Damages in Community Law* (The Hague, 1997) 191–8; Fines, above n. 3, 400–9.

[306] e.g. Cases T-168/94 *Blackspur v Council and Commission* [1995] ECR II-2627; T-213/95 and 18/96 *SCK v Commission* [1997] ECR II-1739

[307] See AG de Lamothe [1971] ECR 346; Fines, above n. 3, 401.

[308] See Schwarze 517.

[309] Case T-184/95 *Dorsch Consult Ingenieurgesellschaft v Council and Commission* [1998] ECR II-667 para 72.

[310] e.g. Cases 64/76, 113/76, 167/78 239/78, 27–28/79 and 45/79 *Dumortier Frères v Council* [1979] ECR 3091 para 21; C-363–364/88 *Finsider v Commission* [1992] ECR I-359 para 25; T-175/94 *International Procurement Services v Commission* [1996] ECR II-729 para 55; T-7/96 *Perillo v Commission* [1997] ECR II-1061 para 41. See also Toth, above n. 305, 192.

[311] See Toth, above n. 305; Fines, above n. 3, 402 with examples.

[312] See footnote 306 and Cases 150/77 *Bertrand v Ott* [1978] ECR 1431; T-54/96 *Oleifici Italiani v Commission* [1998] ECR II-3377 para 67; T-13/96 *TEAM v Commission* [1998] ECR II-4073 para 60.

unlawful decision which has allegedly caused a loss, examine the whole file and determine whether the administration could, and would on the balance of probabilities, have made the same decision even if it had not made any legal errors. This assessment may lead to the dismissal of the applicant's claim, both where the decision was procedurally and substantively flawed.

Thus, in *Compagnia Italiana Alcool* the ECJ held that the Commission's refusal to grant a tender to an Italian company was insufficiently motivated, but rejected a claim for damages on the ground that, if the decision had been properly motivated, the net outcome would have been the same. That is, the company's loss of a profitable contract was caused by the Commission's lawful decision not to award the contract rather than by the unlawful lack of reasons.[313] In the *Farrugia* case discussed above the Commission had rejected a scholarship application on the basis of an incorrect view of the applicant's nationality.[314] The CFI found that the application did not satisfy other legal requirements necessary for it to be treated on its merits. Consequently, it was not established that the applicant had a 'strong chance' of being granted the benefit, and the loss was therefore deemed 'uncertain'. This case exemplifies that the Community courts find it difficult to distinguish clearly between the concepts of certain damage and direct causation. It would arguably have been preferable for the Court to hold in *Farrugia* that the error of fact did not in fact cause the applicant's loss of a scholarship because his application did not fulfil the basic requirements.

These cases may be contrasted with the interesting *Moritz* case in which a senior Commission civil servant was awarded damages for a decision which had refused him promotion.[315] Applicants for the vacant position had been assessed on the basis of periodic performance reports, but the report covering the last two years of Mr Moritz's service was missing because his superior had delayed writing it. The Commission argued against liability, as it could not be established whether Mr Moritz would actually have been awarded the position if the report had been available. The CFI held, however, that as the Commission was undeniably guilty of maladministration by delaying the report, and as the appointing committee had not been aware of the full facts contained in the (favourable) report, the delay had indeed caused some damage. Still, the CFI did not award full damages equivalent to the salary increase which Mr Moritz would have obtained. It awarded *ex aequo et bono* a sum of BFR 150,000 taking into account that the applicant's age effectively prevented him from 'trying again later'. Thus, instead of asking the classical but-for question (would the applicant have obtained the benefit had it not been for the illegality), the Court

[313] Case C-358/90 *Compagnia Italiana Alcool v Commission* [1992] ECR I-2457. See also Case T-390/94 *Schröder v Commission* [1997] ECR II-501 para 65–66.

[314] Case T-230/94 *Farrugia v Commission* [1996] ECR II-195 para 43–45. See also Case T-478/93 *Wafer Zoo v Commission* [1995] ECR II-482.

[315] Case T-20/89RV *Moritz v Commission* [1993] ECR II-1423.

actually awarded damages for the applicant's loss of a *chance* to obtain a certain benefit.

The *Moritz* case shows that the Community courts may take a flexible approach to causation issues, but it remains to be seen whether a fully-fledged doctrine of liability for loss of chance will develop.[316] This would be an interesting, but complex, conceptual development, which would take EC law beyond the position in English law.

III Actual and Certain Damage

There are no strict limitations on the type of loss which may be recovered in EC law. Damages may be awarded for personal injury,[317] property damage, pure economic loss,[318] and 'moral loss' in the form of inconvenience, uncertainty, and damage to reputation.[319] This wide definition of indemnifiable loss is in line with French law and it is, therefore, not surprising to find that the Community courts require fairly strict proof of 'actual and certain' damage.[320]

Actual damage refers to the fact that a loss must be proven by the applicant and can only be recovered if it has not been passed on to some other party or otherwise been compensated.[321] Liability claims will be dismissed if, for example, a company has unlawfully been forced to make unlawful fiscal payments which it has subsequently passed on to its customers.[322] The same applies if a person, who has been prevented from exercising a profession[323] or taking up an employment position[324] by the unlawful acts of a Community institution, has had alternative income.

Certain damage refers to the fact that the damages must either have materialized or be imminent and foreseeable with 'sufficient degree of certainty'.[325] For example, in *Dorsch* a German company sought to recover

[316] The practice of awarding damages for loss of chance in staff cases was approved by the ECJ in Case C-259/96P *Council v Nil* [1998] ECR I-2915 para 28–29. Compare the less generous Case T-158/89 *Hecken v ECOSOC* [1991] ECR II-1341 para 37.

[317] Case 9/69 *Sayag v Leduc* [1969] ECR 337.

[318] Cases 54–60/74 *Kampfmeyer v Commission and Council* [1976] ECR 711.

[319] Cases 7/56 and 3–7/57 *Algera v Common Assembly* [1957] ECR 39; 182/80 *Gauff v Commission* [1982] ECR 799; T-73/89 *Barbi v Commission* [1990] ECR II-619; T-203/96 *Embassy Limousines v EP* [1998] ECR II-4239. However, as these cases reveal, the quantum of damages awarded for moral loss is normally small.

[320] Liability for legislative acts is subject to the added requirement of 'specific' damage, see Cases C-104/89 and 37/90 *Mulder (II) v Council and Commission* [1992] ECR I-3061, 3132. See also Arnull, above n. 292, 146–8; Toth, above n. 305, 179–91.

[321] The burden of proof is rather strict, see Cases 26/74 *Roquette Frères v Commission* [1976] ECR 677 para 22; T-54/96 *Oleifici Italiani v Commission* [1998] ECR II-3377 para 68–69; C-401/96P *Somaco v Commission* [1998] ECR I-2587 para 71.

[322] Cases 241–242 and 245–250/78 *DGV Deutsche Getreideverweitung v Council and Commission* [1979] ECR 3017 para 14.

[323] e.g. Cases C-104/89 and 37/90 *Mulder (II) v Council and Commission* [1992] ECR I-3061 para 33.

[324] e.g. Case 110/63 *Willame v Commission* [1965] ECR 649.

[325] Cases 54–60/74 *Kampfmeyer v Commission and Council* [1976] ECR 711 para 6. See Fines, above n. 3, 412–17.

damages from the EC when, during the Gulf War, the Iraqi authorities suspended payments of debts to foreign companies in the light of UN and EC sanctions. There was no real doubt about the causal link, because the Iraqi statute which had suspended the payments referred to the sanctions, albeit in convoluted diplomatic language. The CFI found, however, that the loss was not yet certain. Since Dorsch had for diplomatic reasons not formally requested payment, there was no formal refusal to pay, and the sum might therefore in the CFI's view be paid later when sanctions were lifted.[326]

As in French law, the requirement of certain damage limits the availability of compensation for loss of profits to a considerable extent. For loss of profit is concerned with future events which may be difficult to prove. The *TEAM* case is a pertinent example.[327] The applicant undertaking sought to recover expenses it had incurred by taking part in a public tender procedure for modernization of a railway junction in Warsaw, which had been annulled by the Commission, and also to obtain damages for profits it expected to make on the project. The CFI dismissed both claims. The expenses were not a sufficiently direct consequence of the Commission's decision to annul the procedure, but rather the result of the Polish government's decision to abandon the project without requesting that another tendering procedure be carried out. The expected profit loss was 'not real and existing, but future and hypothetical'. For even though an evaluation committee had, in the annulled tendering procedure, recommended acceptance of *TEAM's* bid, it could 'not have been certain of securing the contract, since the contracting authority is not bound by the evaluation committee's proposal but has a broad discretion.'[328]

IV Contributory Fault

It was mentioned above that the French courts take a strict view of contributory fault and often reduce damages claims on this ground. A similar pattern is emerging in the Community case law although, so far, most cases have concerned legislative acts,[329] breach of secrecy,[330] incorrect advice or misrepresentation,[331] and physical actions[332] rather than administrative decisions. Damages will generally be reduced if the plaintiff did not act as a 'prudent and experienced person'. For example, liability for unreasonable delay may be

[326] Case T-184/95 *Dorsch Consult Ingenieurgesellschaft v Council and Commission* [1998] ECR II-667.

[327] Case T-13/96 *TEAM v Commission* [1998] ECR II-4073 para 76.

[328] Advocate General Jacobs has now endorsed the CFI's judgment, see Opinion in Case C-13/99P of 17/2–2000.

[329] e.g. Cases 36/62 *Acières du Temple v High Authority* [1963] ECR 289, 296–298; 26/81 *Oleifici Mediterranei v EEC* [1982] ECR 3057, 3079–80.

[330] Cases 145/83 *Adams v Commission* [1985] ECR 3539; 222/84 *Sommerlatte v Commission* [1986] ECR 1805; T-36/89 *Nijman v Commission* [1991] ECR II-699; C-293/95P *Odigitria v Council and Commission* [1996] ECR I-6129 (confirming T-572/93 *Odigitria v Council and Commission*).

[331] See Ch. 6.

[332] Case C-308/87 *Grifoni v Commission* [1990] ECR I-1203.

reduced if the applicant failed to supply all relevant information[333] or did not remind the institution that it had failed to act.[334] The *Kampfmeyer* case illustrates the ECJ's strict approach. The applicant was one of several traders who sought to import maize from France to Germany and thereby benefit from a zero rate levy temporarily applicable in Germany. The German authorities refused, contrary to Community law, applications for import licences and the Commission initially confirmed this unlawful refusal. While holding the Commission liable in principle, the ECJ reduced damages very considerably. Traders who had concluded contracts by the time they applied for licences were awarded damages equivalent to only 10 per cent of their lost profits due to the 'speculative nature' of the transactions. Traders who had not concluded contracts were awarded no damages at all, as their loss of expected profits was deemed too uncertain. This case shows how contributory fault may, combined with the requirement of certain damage, limit the Community's liability for economic loss to a considerable extent.[335]

The EC law principles of liability for unlawful decisions are, after more than 30 years of judicial activity, far from fully developed. The role of substitution of legal basis, the relation between direct causation and certain damage, and liability for loss of chance are issues which remain unclear. The lack of clarity is, of course, partly due to the fact that the case law is not very rich because the EC institutions only exercise direct administrative powers in limited fields such as staff, competition, public procurement, and structural funds. However, the Community courts' terse style of reasoning also plays a part in the relatively slow development of this area of law. Damages claims are often dismissed by the Community courts on the ground of causation or damage without consideration of other conditions for liability, and this reduces greatly the extent to which each case contributes to the development and clarification of Art 288.

So far, the EC law principles of liability for unlawful decision-making have developed along the lines of French rather than English law. The concepts and basic principles are very similar and the same techniques are utilized to limit the liability of the institutions. However, the Community judicature may have taken these limitation techniques too far. Since the birth of the EEC in 1957 only two known damages claims have actually succeeded outside the staff context,[336] and the case law gives the impression that the Community courts provide indi-

[333] Case T-514/93 *Cobrecaf v Commission* [1995] ECR II-624.

[334] Case 58/75 *Sergy v Commission* [1976] ECR 1139, 1162.

[335] Cases 54–60/74 *Kampfmeyer v Commission and Council* [1976] ECR 711. See also Cases 74/74 *CNTA v Commission* [1975] ECR 533; T-514/93 *Cobrecaf v Commission* [1995] ECR II-624.

[336] Cases 145/83 *Adams v Commission* [1985] ECR 3539; T-514/93 *Cobrecaf v Commission* [1995] ECR II-624. For staff cases see notably Cases 7/56 and 3–7/57 *Algera v Common Assembly* [1957] ECR 39; 68/63 *Luhleich v Commission* [1965] ECR 727; T-20/89RV *Moritz v Commission* [1993] ECR II-1423.

viduals who suffer loss when administrative decisions are revoked limited legal protection.[337] This is problematic; in particular when it is remembered that alternative sources of protection are not available through statutory schemes or *ex gratia* compensation.[338]

5 Preliminary Conclusion and Suggestions for Reform

The comparative study of the principles which govern liability for unlawful decision-making has revealed that the important differences between English, French, and EC law as regards conceptualization and basic principles do not lead to very different outcomes.[339] The courts are aware of the need to keep 'the flood-gates' of liability shut, and loss caused by reliance upon administrative decisions is therefore available only to a limited extent. The legal techniques utilized to limit liability for unlawful acts do however differ markedly. While the English courts delimit liability strictly as a matter of general principle, in particular by the notion of duty of care, the French and the Community courts control liability on a case-by-case basis by a flexible application of the principles of legality, direct causation, certain damage, and contributory fault.

What, then, are the differences in terms of outcomes? The overall impression is that the level of compensatory protection is significantly, but not dramatically, higher in French and EC law than in English law. This materializes in three different ways. First, the French principle of unlawfulness = fault, which also applies in EC law, creates a presumption in favour of liability which makes it considerably easier to 'get a case off the ground' than in English law. The French and the Community courts always have the *option* of awarding damages to an individual who has suffered a loss by reliance upon an unlawful decision. The English courts hardly have this option, because the duty of care concept is extremely narrow and *Wednesbury* unreasonableness is in most instances a condition precedent for showing negligence.

Second, while the French and the Community courts apply the requirements of causation, damage, and contributory fault strictly, the result is very often a *reduction* of the plaintiff's claim by 25–75 per cent rather than its dismissal, the greatest restrictions normally occurring in relation to claims for loss of profit. Consequently, the amount of damages awarded in France may not always cover the full loss as a British lawyer would understand it.[340]

[337] Fines, above n. 3, 419 concludes in a similar vein on the basis of a comprehensive survey of EC case law.

[338] See section 3.C.

[339] Compare Allison 180–1 emphasizing the difference between French and English liability principles.

[340] However, the level of compensation is not 'grossly inadequate' as claimed by D. M. Provine, 'Courts in the Political Process in France', in H. Jacob (ed.), *Courts, Law, and Politics in Comparative Perspective* (New Haven, 1996), 177, 188. See also Markesinis, Auby, Coester-Waltjen and Deakin, above n. 1, 110–12.

Third, English law leaves the risk of unlawful decisions entirely with licensees, recipients of welfare benefits, and economic aid because pure economic loss is not covered by the ordinary tort of negligence.[341] By way of contrast, in French and EC law, licensees and the like are compensated for reliance loss[342] and, less often, for loss of profit caused by unlawful revocation or denial of favourable decisions.[343]

These three findings must be read in the light of the procedural and substantive principles examined in previous chapters. In French and EC law, the pecuniary remedies provide an important *supplement* to the basic protection of legal certainty and legitimate expectations provided by principles of finality (or irrevocability) of administrative decision. The English courts, however, are rather insensitive to the connection between substantive principles and compensatory remedies. For although English administrative authorities have *wider* inherent powers to revoke unlawful decisions than their French and EC counterparts, they are *less* liable to compensate individuals who suffer loss as a result hereof. Thus, English law promotes legality and administrative flexibility at the cost of individuals' legitimate expectations and legal certainty. This state of affairs is unsatisfactory. A rethinking of the *de facto* immunity of public authorities in English tort law, taking into account the expectations of individuals, is indispensable.[344] The need for reform is further underlined by the fact that the ECtHR has found English tort law wanting, and that under the Human Rights Act 1998 the English courts will be bound to take into account the jurisprudence of the Strasbourg institutions.[345]

How, more precisely, should English tort law should be reformed to meet these concerns? That is a question with wide-ranging implications which cannot be explored fully within the confines of this book. It will suffice for present purposes to consider two options for reform. First, English law could adopt the strict French liability principle, which opens a *prima facie* right to damages whenever an institution makes an unlawful (*ultra vires*) decision.[346] The English courts are clearly not likely to go down this path. Nor would this be the best solution.[347] Decision-making may necessitate the gathering of complex factual data and construction of provisions which may be open to more than one interpretation as well as difficult discretionary balancing operations. It would be too onerous to impose liability whenever an institution errs in one of these aspects

[341] e.g. *Partridge v GMC* (1890) 25 QBD 90; *R v Knowsley BC, ex p Maguire* [1992] COD 499; *Reeman v Department of Transport* [1997] 2 Lloyd's Rep 648.

[342] e.g. CE 17/6–83 *SCI Italie-Vandrezane* Rec 267, CE 17/10–62 *Pernaud* Rec 545.

[343] e.g. CE 19/5–76 *SA du Château de Neuvecelle* RDP 1976, 1385; CE 3/12–82 *Société continentale de promotion immobilière* Rec 409; CE 5/11–90 *Roussillon* no 86.418.

[344] See Markesinis, Auby, Coester-Waltjen and Deakin, above n. 1, 114–15 and footnote 164.

[345] Human Rights Act 1998, s. 2. See for discussion Lord Hoffmann, above n. 7; Craig 869–72.

[346] For a proposal along these lines, see *Justice*, above n. 96, para 11.83.

[347] See Markesinis, Auby, Coester-Waltjen and Deakin, above n. 1. See also AG Trabucchi [1975] ECR 560; AG Darmon [1992] ECR I-2533 for discussion of this issue in EC law.

of decision-making. Indeed, the French case law strongly suggests that the courts would feel 'forced' to adopt a restrictive and in some instances strained interpretation of the concepts of causation and damage if such a liability rule were adopted. There is also a risk that a strict liability would inhibit the development of principles of judicial review, because findings of unlawfulness in decision-making would carry direct financial implications for public authorities.

Second, there is more force in Paul Craig's suggestion that English law should draw upon the principles of state liability for violation of EC law obligations.[348] Under those principles, liability applies to decisions which amount to a 'sufficiently serious breach' of law.[349] Whether a breach is 'sufficiently serious' is decided by reference to a range of criteria, including the clarity of the rule breached, the amount of discretion, and whether the breach was intentional or involuntary. In conceptual terms, the serious breach test differs from the present law of negligence in that it limits liability by reference to the *level of care* required, combined with the classic requirements of causation and damage, rather than by the almost complete exclusion of a *duty of care*.[350] In practical terms, the test would allow some pecuniary protection of those who suffer through unlawful decision-making, whilst acknowledging the very real difficulties which decision-makers face in their daily work, the need to protect the scarce resources of public defendants, and the courts' desire not to interfere with non-justiciable issues.

The suggestion for a sufficiently serious breach test in English law has been criticized by John Allison. He notes, first, that the sufficiently serious breach test is based on a deterrence rationale; it aims to enhance the effectiveness of EC law. The test is therefore inappropriate in a domestic context, as English tort law is more concerned with redress of loss—and respect for the administration's ability to act in the public interest—than with deterrence. This argument confuses the rationale with the rule itself. The sufficiently serious breach test is sufficiently flexible to allow the English courts to mould it to the concerns and rationales of English tort law.

A second argument against the proposed test is that it necessitates a judicial balancing exercise of numerous variables which is incompatible with existing institutional and procedural arrangements: on the one hand English judges are not by training skilled at balancing variables; on the other hand the balancing is inhibited by the adversarial judicial process. These contentions were

[348] P. P. Craig, 'Once More unto the Breach: The Community, the State and Damages Liability' (1997) LQR 67, 'The Domestic Liability of Public Authorities in Damages: Lessons from the European Community?', in J. Beatson and T. Tridimas (eds.), *New Directions in European Public Law* (Oxford, 1998), 75. See also Andenas and Fairgrieve, above n. 123; Mason, above n. 120.

[349] Cases C-46 and 48/93 *Brasserie du Pêcheur and Factortame (III)* [1996] ECR I-1029.

[350] For earlier suggestions along these lines, see D. Howarth, 'My Brother's Keeper? Liability for Acts of Third Parties' (1994) Legal Studies 88, 92; Wright, above n. 7, 9.

examined critically above in our discussion of substantive legitimate expectations.[351] It was argued in that context that English judges are indeed capable of balancing conflicting variables on a case-by-case basis and that the solution to adjudicatory difficulties lies in reform of procedural rules rather in the ossification of the existing and unsatisfactory principles of administrative law. It might be added at this point that the judiciary has already proven its ability to handle the sufficiently serious breach test in cases concerning violations of EC law.[352]

Finally, Allison asserts that the sufficiently serious breach test would not work due to the absence in English law of a clear public–private divide. That argument is also unconvincing in my view. It is difficult to see how the need to distinguish between public and private bodies (or tasks) under the serious breach test is any greater than under the existing principles of negligence liability.[353] That test would, if anything, reduce the public–private divide by replacing the existing limitation on negligence liability, based on the public law concept of *Wednesbury* unreasonableness, with a concept which is specific to the law of tort.[354]

The recent case of *Barrett* represents a welcome, but small, step away from the strict delimitation of duty of care and thus a move in the direction of a sufficiently serious breach test.[355] This case clearly deserves further elaboration. It may however be doubted whether the courts are willing to carry out wide-ranging reform of this area of law.[356] If this is true, there is a strong case for legislative action. The insertion of section 6 in The Human Rights Act 1998, which provides for liability for administrative acts incompatible with the rights of the ECHR, shows that Parliament is not unable or unwilling to adjust the boundaries of the law of tort. Still, as much as section 6 is likely to become an important remedy in practice, it is too limited in scope to resolve all problems of governmental liability. To achieve a fair and comprehensive system of administrative liability in English law, it seems necessary to consider the adoption of a more general legislative provision providing redress for unlawful administrative action amounting to a sufficiently serious breach of law.[357]

[351] See Ch. 4.7.B.

[352] *R v Secretary of State for Transport, ex p Factortame Ltd* [1999] 3 WLR 1062.

[353] See also Ch. 4.7.B where it is argued that the public–private divide is not much less clear in Britain than in other European legal systems.

[354] See Andenas and Fairgrieve, above n. 348, 326.

[355] See text at footnote 164–170.

[356] See JUSTICE—All Souls, above n. 96, 361; De Smith 793; Amos, above n. 52, 29.

[357] Compensation under such a statute might draw upon a special fund, see De Smith 794.

Chapter 6

Compensatory Protection of Legitimate Expectations (II): Informal Representations

1 Introduction

Individuals who rely on administrative representations may suffer a loss if the administration departs from what it has represented. In this chapter, I will analyse to what extent English,[1] French,[2] and EC law provide redress for such loss. The aim is to determine how compensatory remedies complement procedural and substantive principles of administrative law in protecting legitimate expectations, and to draw some conclusions about the future development of English law in this area. The chapter will be structured in the following fashion.

First, the general principles of English, French, and EC law will be set out. Attention will be focused on administrative damages liability, though there will also be some comments on *ex gratia* compensation.[3] A distinction will be drawn between two types of situations. In the first situation, the administration makes a misrepresentation of law, fact, or intent which it subsequently resiles from. Here the question is whether the risk of administrative error should fall on the individual or the administration itself (section 2). In the second situation, the administration makes a correct representation, which it subsequently resiles from in the light of a reassessment of the applicant's case or a general change in administrative policy. Here the question is whether the economic risk of policy changes should fall on those who relied on the existing policy or on the administration (section 3).[4] There will then be a discussion of the requirements which limit the scope of liability, namely reasonable reliance (section 4), causation, remoteness, and damage (section 5). Finally, the outcome of the

[1] See generally P. P. Craig, 'Negligent Misstatements, Negligent Acts and Economic Loss' (1976) LQR 213; J. A. Jolowicz and W. V. H. Rogers, *Winfield and Jolowicz on Tort*, 15th edn. (London, 1998), 365–85; J. Morrell and R. Foster, *Local Authority Liability* (Bristol, 1998), 171–96.

[2] See generally M. Di Malta, 'Les renseignements administratifs', D 1964 chron 33, 225; J.-M. André, 'La responsabilité de la puissance publique du fait des diverses formes d'engagements non contractuels de l'administration', AJDA 1976, 20; Y. Weber, 'Promesses, renseignements, retards', in F. Gazier, R. Drago (eds.), *Encyclopédie Dalloz: Répertoire de la responsabilité de la puissance publique* (Paris, 1992); O. Fickler-Despres, 'Les promesses de l'administration', JCP 1998 I no 104.

[3] Statutory compensation for loss caused by administrative representations is extremely limited. See however Local Land Charges Act 1975, s 10.

[4] If a final administrative decision causes a loss due to an incorrect statement made by another authority or officer to the decision-maker, rather than to the plaintiff, then the liability of both authorities depends on the principles of unlawful decision-making discussed in Ch. 5. See *Harris v Evans* [1998] 1 WLR 1285, 1301; *W v Essex CC* [1998] 3 All ER 111, 138.

comparative survey will be summed up, and some limited proposals for reform will be presented (section 6).

2 Damages Liability for Misrepresentations

It is well-established in English, French, and EC law that the administration may be liable for damage caused by the misrepresentations of its own officers.[5] The principles governing this liability may be summarized as follows.

(A) English Law

Negligence liability for damage caused by misstatements was firmly established in English private law by the landmark decision of *Hedley Byrne v Heller*.[6] Under the principle established by that case, subsequently extended to cover also negligent provision of services, a person who makes an incorrect statement of fact, law, or intent is liable for damage—including pure economic loss—suffered by a recipient of the statement if, firstly, the representor wilfully assumed responsibility for its correctness,[7] secondly, the recipient acted in reasonable reliance upon this assumption of responsibility and, thirdly, the representor knew that the statement would be communicated to, and acted upon, by the recipient for a specific purpose.[8] If these conditions are fulfilled, it is in theory unnecessary to show that the imposition of liability is just, fair, and reasonable.[9] It is also irrelevant why the representor made a mistake; the fact that it may have been difficult to ascertain the truth does not exonerate him from liability. The representor's ability to provide accurate information is only relevant in so far as the courts are more likely to find an assumption of responsibility if he was in the profession of giving advice or at least held himself out as having special knowledge.[10]

There can be no doubt that public authorities have special knowledge, and it is clear that they are subject to the *Hedley Byrne* principle. However, the appli-

[5] This chapter is not concerned with the personal liability of individual officers. For *responsabilité pour faute personnelle* in French law, see CE 12/6–53 *Caisse nationale de marchés de l'État* Rec 28.

[6] *Hedley Byrne v Heller* [1964] AC 465 subsequently confirmed in *Caparo Industries Plc v Dickman* [1990] 2 AC 605; *Williams v Natural Life Health Foods Ltd* [1998] 1 WLR 830.

[7] This depends upon the court's objective assessment, the representor's subjective state of mind is not decisive, *Williams v Natural Life Health Foods Ltd* [1998] 1 WLR 830, 835. The assumption of responsibility concept has been criticized (Craig, above n. 1, 216; K. Barker, 'Unreliable Assumptions in the Modern Law of Negligence' (1993) LQR 461; B. Hepple, 'The Search for Coherence' (1997) CLP 67, 88), but reaffirmed in *Smith v Bush* [1990] 1 AC 831, 846; *Henderson v Merett Syndicates Ltd* [1994] 3 WLR 761, 774; *Williams v Natural Life Health Foods Ltd* [1998] 1 WLR 830, 837.

[8] *Caparo Industries Plc v Dickman* [1990] 2 AC 605, 638.

[9] *Henderson v Merett Syndicates* [1995] AC 145, 181; *Williams v Natural Life Health Foods Ltd* [1998] 1 WLR 830, 834.

[10] *Spring v Guardian Assurance Plc* [1995] 2 AC 296, 318.

cation of that principle is limited to special situations[11] because cases concerning misrepresentations are to some extent informed by the policy considerations which led to a restriction of negligence liability for discretionary decision-making.[12] Provision of advice to individuals is often part and parcel of the statutory functions which the administration must fulfil, and the English courts are reluctant to impose liability for statements made in the course of and in accordance with such functions for fear that it will adversely affect their exercise, cause a flood of claims, and erode alternative remedies.[13] This is aptly illustrated by two recent cases.

In *Welton v North Cornwall DC* an environmental health officer had advised the owner of a guest house that considerable modifications of his kitchen were required to comply with the health and safety regulations, and that a closure order would be issued if building works were not undertaken promptly. It later emerged that this statement was out of line with both the relevant legislation and administrative policy, and that at least 90 per cent of the then completed modifications were in fact unnecessary. The local food authority was held liable for the expenses on the basis of an assumption of responsibility by the officer.[14] However, the Court of Appeal emphasized that liability would not have arisen for an erroneous statement made in the course of 'offering . . . an advisory service', as this might inhibit the exercise of statutory functions. There were special circumstances in this case, because the officer's statements involved 'the imposition . . . outwith the legislation of detailed requirements enforced by threats of closure and close supervision'.[15]

Special circumstances were also found to justify liability in the recent case of *W v Essex CC*.[16] A local authority had given specific assurances to foster parents that a boy placed in their care was not a suspected sex offender, although the authority was aware that the boy had abused his sister. When the boy subsequently abused the foster parents' four children, the Court of Appeal held that while the authority was not liable for the nervous shock suffered by the foster parents, it could be liable in negligence towards the children under the

[11] See De Smith 783. The case law is sparse and pragmatic to the point of incoherence. See J. Stapleton, 'Duty of Care and Economic Loss, A Wider Agenda' (1991) LQR 249, 295; Hepple, above n. 7, 70–2. Some decisions involving public authorities are of limited precedential value, e.g. *Ministry of Housing and Local Government v Sharp* [1970] 2 QB 223 (*Hedley Byrne* not considered in detail); *Coats Patons v Birmingham Corporation* (1971) 70 LGR 356 (conceded that *Hedley Byrne* applied), or irrelevant for present purposes, *Culford Metal Industries Ltd v Export Credits Guarantee Department* The Times 25/3–81; *AB v Tameside Health Authority* (1997) 8 Med LR 91.

[12] See Ch. 5.4.A.

[13] See Morrell and Foster, above n. 1, 4, 178, 188; R. Mullender, 'Negligent Misstatement, Threats, and the Scope of the *Hedley Byrne* Principle' (1999) MLR 425, 428. These policy considerations are, however, less forceful where the harm suffered is grave. See *Perrett v Collins* [1998] 2 Lloyds LR 255.

[14] *Welton v North Cornwall DC* [1997] 1 WLR 570.

[15] Ibid. 580–1. See also *Blake v The London Borough of Barking* [1996] NPC 134; *Harris v Evans* [1998] 1 WLR 1285, 1298, 1301; *W v Essex CC* [1998] 3 WLR 534, 547; *Haddow v Tendring DC*, 6/2–98.

[16] *W v Essex CC* [1998] 3 WLR 534. See case note by K. Oliphant (1998) CFLQ 303.

Hedley Byrne principle as it had assumed responsibility for the correctness of the assurance given to the parents. Thus, the suspicion that the relevant officer had deliberately misinformed the plaintiff and the grave loss which had been caused outweighed, to some extent, the court's concerns about the adverse effect of liability on the workings of welfare agencies.[17]

(B) French Law

It has been accepted in French law since the 1950s that the administration may be liable in fault (*faute de service*) for loss caused by the misrepresentations of its officers.[18] This liability has a wider scope than the English *Hedley Byrne* rule, and it is applied with less hesitation in practice.[19] The French courts do not take the view that liability will adversely affect the exercise of statutory functions, or that the practical difficulty of giving accurate advice is so great that liability must be limited to special situations. There is therefore no immunity in French law for statements made in accordance with statutory functions and no free-standing requirement of proximity or wilful assumption of responsibility.[20] The administration is *prima facie* liable in fault whenever one of its officers makes an incorrect representation of fact, law, or intent which is relied upon by a person acting without any fault of his or her own.[21]

[17] Ibid. 558–60. For another example of deliberate misinformation, see *Davy v Spelthorne BC* [1984] AC 262.

[18] CE 22/7–49 *Aubery* Rec 37; CE 21/12–51 *Feiz Karam* Rec 612; CE 25/6–54 *Otto* Rec 380; CE 18/10–57 *Bouveret* Rec 542. See previously rejecting liability CE 15/6–23 *Fellus* Rec 496; CE 22/5–39 *La Soie artificielle de Valenciennes* Rec 346 and, exceptionally, accepting liability CE 30/6–22 *Lamiable* S 1922, 25; CE 16/1–35 *Jacque* Rec 61.

[19] It has been suggested that the CE should in special circumstances impose liability even without fault under the principle of *égalité devant les charges publiques*. See Kahn *conclusions* CE 27/1–61 *Vannier* Rec 68-9; Ordonneau *conclusions* CE 29/6–62 *Société Manufacture des Machines du Haut-Rhin* Rec 436 ff.; André, above n. 2, 27. However, this form of no-fault liability has remained irrelevant for practical purposes. See CE 29/6–62 *Société Manufacture des Machines du Haut-Rhin* Rec 432; CE 13/3–85 *Société Barlocher* Rec 79; CE 19/2–88 *Société Robatel* D 1988, 365; CE 17/3–89 *Société Sodevam* AJDA 1989, 472; CAA Bordeaux 25/7–94 *Société Arboricole de l'Agenais* no 93BX00676 (confirmed by CE 6/6/-97 no 161.900); TA Paris 14/10–97 *Société Batignolle* DA 1998 no 118; CE 16/11–98 *Sille* DA 1998 no 23.

[20] Conversely, the rule used to be that public authorities are only liable for 'obligatory' statements. That is, a response to a question from an individual only caused liability if the authority was fulfilling a duty to answer based on statute or internal rules (*directives*). See CE 19/2–54 *Langlade* Rec 118; CE 23/10–57 *Cornialez* Rec 548; CE 10/7–64 *Duffaut* JCP 1964 II 13796; CE 23/3–66 *Boitard* Rec 222. This rule has not been cited in any recent judgments known to this author, and it appears to have been abandoned. Compare Weber, above n. 2, no 69–71; M. Deguergue, *Jurisprudence et doctrine dans l'élaboration du droit de la responsabilité administrative* (Paris, 1994), 179.

[21] That is, the standard of liability is simple fault (*faute simple*) rather than gross fault (*faute lourde*), see CE 16/1–35 *Jacque* Rec 61. The administration might even be liable without fault if the plaintiff suffered a loss while assisting the public services in the fulfilment of their duties (i.e. if he was a *collaborateur occasionnel*). See e.g. CE 31/3–99 *Hospices civils de Lyon* AJDA 1999, 528 and B. S. Markesinis; J.-B. Auby; D. C. Coester-Waltjen and S. F. Deakin, *Tortious Liability of Statutory Bodies: A Comparative and Economic Analysis of Five English Cases* (Oxford, 1999), 34–5.

The case of *Aubin* is a pertinent example.[22] Mr Aubin, who was living and working on either side of the French–Belgian border, had been advised by the French authorities to register for unemployment benefit in Belgium. When he did so, the French legislation precluded him from registering in France although it turned out that neither Belgian nor EC law entitled him to benefits in Belgium. The CE held the French authorities liable for Mr Aubin's lost unemployment benefits and for the inconvenience caused. The fact that the information had been granted as part of a general advisory service, and that the correct interpretation of the EC law rules was far from clear, did not prevent liability from arising.[23] This case reveals the potential breadth of liability for misrepresentations in French law. However, it will be seen below that the French courts limit the burden of liability to some extent by a strict application of the concepts of direct causation, certain damage, and contributory fault.[24]

(C) EC Law

The Community judicature has accepted that the Community administration is *prima facie* liable for loss caused by its own misrepresentations. Although the case law is sparse, it is clear that Community liability is not dependent upon an assumption of responsibility and that there is no general immunity for statements made in the course of statutory functions. For example, in *Houyoux* the ECJ awarded a Community employee damages for the loss of a rent allowance, which she had failed to apply for in time due to incorrect information in a leaflet produced, and sent to her, by the Commission's personnel department.[25]

The Community administration may, however, be exempt from liability if it was difficult to provide accurate information. This was established in the case of *Parise-Richez,* where a number of Community officials had received information, believed to be correct at the time, about their pension rights from a specifically designated information officer. The ECJ held that the officials could not recover the difference between the pension they had been led to expect and that actually paid after they had sought and obtained early retirement. For 'apart from the exceptional instance, the adoption [and communication] of an

[22] CE 20/1–88 *Aubin* RDP 1988, 903. See also CE 28/4–71 *Berger-Sabatel* Rec 313; CE 1/12–72 *Texierp* Rec 1222; CE 30/10–81 *Bonhoure* Rec 902; CE 28/6–85 *Legendre* DA 1985 no 443; CE 3/3–89 *Société Sagatour* Rec 905; CAA Paris 2/10–90 *Société Internationale de télévision* Rec 970; CE 16/11–98 *Sille* DA 1998 no 23.

[23] The CE subsequently sought a preliminary ruling from the ECJ on their proper meaning. See also CE 20/2–74 *Sucrerie coopérative agricole de Vie-Sur-Aisne* Rec 121; CE 21/6–85 *Manzano* Rec 765.

[24] See section 5 and C. Blumann, *La renonciation en droit administratif français* (Paris, 1974), 277–9; André, above n. 2, 29; Weber, above n. 2, no 42.

[25] Cases 176–177/86 *Houyoux v Commission* [1987] ECR 4333. See also Cases 29, 31, 36, 39–47 and 50–51/63 *Usines de la Providence v High Authority* [1965] ECR 911.

incorrect interpretation [of legal provisions] does not constitute in itself a wrongful act'.[26]

(D) The Temporal Dimension of the Concept of Misrepresentation

The central question in cases concerning misrepresentations is whether the representation was correct or incorrect at the time it was made. If the representation was correct, then there is no misrepresentation and therefore no faulty or negligent act.[27] Thus, in *Roberts v Llanelli BC* the plaintiff was informed that Llanelli BC intended to expropriate a building from which he ran a sports club. It was later discovered that the building was protected, and no expropriation was carried out, but by then the trainers had left with most of the customers and the club had closed down. The Court of Appeal found that there was no misstatement: the Council had actually planned the expropriation and this plan had not been represented as unchangeable.[28] Similarly, in *Lafont* the CE held that a local planning authority was not liable for representing that a piece of land was *constructible* (not subject to planning restrictions) as the authority did not know, and could not have foreseen, that the land would shortly after be expropriated as part of a major development.[29]

The incorrectness of statements of intent can be difficult to prove, but liability may be imposed if the courts infer from subsequent action that the administration knew that it might change its mind. In *Davy v Spelthorne BC* a planning authority had assured a property owner of its intention to suspend an enforcement notice for a period of three years, and he therefore did not appeal against it. When the authority nonetheless took enforcement action just one month after the expiry of the time limit for appealing, the Court of Appeal inferred that the initial representation had been untrue, and it refused to strike out the plaintiff's claim against the authority.[30]

3 Damages Liability for Departure from Correct Representations

(A) English Law

The English *Hedley Byrne* principle is concerned with *mis*representations. A public authority which departs from an initially correct statement due to a sub-

[26] Cases 19–20, 25 and 30/69 *Richez-Parise v Commission* [1970] ECR 325 para 36 cited with approval in Cases 137/79 *Kohll v Commission* [1980] ECR 2601 para 14–15; T-123/89 *Chomel v Commission* [1990] ECR II-131 para 29. This statement has so far only been applied in staff cases, but it probably applies more generally. See T. Tridimas, *The General Principles of EC Law* (Oxford, 1999), 314.

[27] Harmful but correct information does not give rise to liability in the absence of defamation or a breach of secrecy, e.g. CE 3/6–53 *Société Carret* Rec 259; CAA Nantes 28/2–90 *Plunian* Rec 969.

[28] *Roberts v Llanelli BC*, 25/2–98.

[29] CE 14/3–86 *Lafont* Rec 74.

[30] *Davy v Spelthorne BC* [1984] AC 262.

sequent reassessment of the particular case or a general change in policy is not liable under this principle. Liability can only arise if the administration's decision to depart from its initial representation fulfils the strict conditions for negligence in discretionary decision-making. The administration will, therefore, only be liable if it owed a duty of care to the person who relied on the representation, and the decision to disappoint that expectation was *Wednesbury* unreasonable.[31] More specifically, it must be shown that the representation was sufficiently precise and unqualified to create a reasonable expectation, and that there was a very serious imbalance in the administration's balancing of this expectation against countervailing policy considerations.[32] These are high hurdles for the plaintiff to pass, and a claim of this nature does not appear ever to have succeeded in the English courts.[33]

(B) EC Law

Community law also conceptualizes the problem of loss caused by correct administrative representations as an aspect of fault liability for discretionary decision-making, and it also links this liability with the principle of legitimate expectations. The scope of liability is, however, wider in EC law than in English law: the duty of care concept does not restrict Community liability,[34] and the Community courts review the balancing of reasonable expectations and public policy more intensively than the English courts.[35] In practice, the Community courts have upheld damages claims on a number of occasions.[36]

For example, in the recent *Embassy Limousines* case the plaintiff company had been informed (correctly) by the EP that a formal decision to award it a contract for the supply of limousine services would be made, and that it should be ready to start delivering these services shortly.[37] Embassy Limousines immediately invested in chauffeurs and vehicles, but the EP subsequently changed its mind due to rumours in the press about the company's chauffeurs, and it awarded the contract elsewhere. The CFI found that the EP had violated the principle of legitimate expectations and it awarded the plaintiff damages for its now futile investments.

[31] See Ch. 5.4.A where the connection between negligence and *Wednesbury* unreasonableness is discussed in the light of *Barrett v Enfield CC* [1999] 3 All ER 193.

[32] See Ch. 4.2.A.

[33] For an unsuccessful claim, see *R v Knowsley BC, ex p Maguire* [1992] COD 499.

[34] See Ch. 5.7.A.

[35] Ibid.

[36] See notably Cases 74/74 *CNTA v Commission* [1975] ECR 533, [1976] ECR 797; C-104/89 and 37/90 *Mulder (II) v Council and Commission* [1992] ECR I-3061; T-195 and 202/94 *Quiller v Council and Commission* [1997] ECR II-2247; T-587/93 *Ortega Urretavizcaya v Commission* [1996] ECR-SC IA-349/II-1027 (discussed in Ch. 4.3.A.I). See also Cases 169/73 *Compagnie Continentale France v Council* [1975] ECR 117; 289/81 *Mavridis v EP* [1983] ECR 1731 para 25.

[37] Case T-203/96 *Embassy Limousines v EP* [1998] ECR II-4239.

(C) French Law

French administrative law differs from English and EC law in that it does not acknowledge the principle of legitimate expectations. The French administration is in theory free to depart from its own specific representations (Situation 2) and to change general policies (Situation 4).[38] However, the French courts acknowledge that individuals who rely on administrative policies and representations may suffer hardship, and that it would be unfair if the whole risk fell on them rather than on the administration. They have, therefore, accepted that the administration may be liable in fault if it states (correctly) that it will apply a certain policy, or take a certain course of action, but subsequently fails to do so. This is known as fault liability for breach of non-contractual promise (*promesse non-contractuelle*).[39] This liability resembles the Community law principle of fault liability for breach of legitimate expectations in two respects.[40]

First, the French administration is only liable if it made a clear and unqualified statement of intent (*promesse*) which would in EC law be able to found a reasonable expectation.[41] For example, in *Batignolle* the plaintiff company had been deeply involved in consultations and the preparation of plans for a large development project in Paris. When this project was abandoned for technical and financial reasons, the company sought to recover its expenses.[42] The *Tribunal Administratif* of Paris held that the planning authority was not liable, *inter alia* because no real promise had been made. The development plan had not been presented as final or unchangeable, and the company's involvement at the consultation stage did not in itself amount to a promise that its investment would be rewarded.[43]

Second, the French courts take into account, on the one hand, the affected person's situation and reliance and, on the other hand, the considerations of

[38] See Ch. 4.2.C.

[39] The rationale for this liability is somewhat uncertain. Some decisions suggest that it is faulty to fetter discretionary powers by promising to use them in a certain fashion (liability for unlawful promises), other decisions suggest that it is simply faulty for the administration not to act as it speaks (liability for breach of lawful promises). Compare CE 24/4–64 *Société des huileries de Chauny* Rec 249; CE 20/1–88 *Possado* no 80.059. It is submitted that it would be more satisfactory to base this liability on the notion of equality before public burdens.

[40] Liability for breach of non-contractual promise also has parallels in the principle of *fait du prince* which applies to contracts between individual and the administration. See Brown and Bell 207.

[41] A survey of more than 100 CE and CAA decisions on the Lexis database revealed that the notion of *promesse* is narrowly defined, e.g. CE 18/5–56 *Société Léon Claeys* AJDA 1956 II 260, 269; CE 16/11–60 *Société d'exploitation des chantiers d'Ajaccio* Rec 621; CE 17/3–89 *Société Sodevam* AJDA 1989, 472; CAA Bordeaux 25/7–94 *Société Arboricole de l'Agenais* no 93BX00676 (confirmed by CE 6/6/-97 no 161.900). Litigants often make spurious claims that promises were made, e.g. CE 23/3–66 *Boitard* Rec 222; CE 24/2–71 *Laraque* Rec 154; CE 16/11–79 *Commune de Sainte-Maure de Touraine* Rec 437; CE 25/1–84 *HLM d'Aix-en-Provence* no 41.619; CE 27/5–87 *Wisnewski* no 66.442.

[42] TA Paris 14/10–97 *Société Batignolle* DA 1998 no 118.

[43] The company's argument that it should in any event be compensated for a breach of 'the principle of legitimate expectations' was rejected as irrelevant.

public interest which led the administration to go back on its representation (*promesse*). Liability will not be imposed, or the awarded damages will be reduced significantly, if there were compelling reasons in favour of the administration's decision to disappoint those who relied upon a (correct) administrative representation. For example, in *Société Internationale de télévision* a minister had failed to honour a clear and unqualified promise to approve a broadcasting contract which had been negotiated between the plaintiff and a licensing authority. The court held that in the 'absence of a justification in the form of considerations of general interest', the minister's decision to delay approval constituted faulty conduct.[44] However, the French courts do not always admit openly to the fact that they balance the private and public interests on a case-by-case basis.[45] To achieve fair results in each case, the courts often resort to a hidden and pragmatic 'variation' of the concepts of administrative promise,[46] contributory fault,[47] direct causation, and certain damage. This technique may be illustrated by comparing two leading cases.[48]

In *Société Sagatour* a senior civil servant (*secrétaire général pour les affaires économiques de la Guadeloupe*) had assured a company in writing that the administration would provide 650,000 francs of financial aid towards the development of a golf course, and he had encouraged the company to pre-finance the project and commence building works as soon as possible. The money was never paid, for reasons the administration failed to explain to the court, and the state was held liable for the full amount plus additional expenses.[49] In this case, a precise and individualized assurance was breached without justification. Consequently, the CE accepted that a promise had been made and imposed full liability for the loss caused by the plaintiff's reliance.[50]

[44] CAA Paris 2/10–90 *Société Internationale de télévision* Rec 970.

[45] See however TA Paris 14/10–97 *Société Batignolle* DA 1998 no 118.

[46] Promises are in some cases categorized 'creatively' as statements of fact which were correct at the time they were made and therefore not faulty, e.g. CE 7/10–66 *Asope* Rec 523; CE 23/12–70 *Benoist* Rec 796; CE 14/3–86 *Lafont* Rec 74.

[47] Reductions of liability on grounds of contributory fault is statistically the rule rather than the exception in France, e.g. CE 4/10–67 *Syndicat intercommunal d' électrification de la région de Pont-Saint-Esprit* no 68.650 (25 per cent reduction); CE 28/4–71 *Montrand* AJDA 1971, 683; CE 13/11–74 *Coulibeuf* Rec 567 (33 per cent reduction); CE 12/3–54 *Weickert* Rec 152, CE 11/5–56 *Société Lesieur-Afrique* Rec 184; CE 9/7–80 *Zerlauth* no 10.620; CE 30/10–81 *Bonhoure* Rec 902; CE 28/6–85 *Legendre* DA 1985 no 443; CE 25/11–88 *Commune de Carry-Le-Rouet* no 89.106; CE 16/11–98 *Sille* DA 1998 no 23 (50 per cent reduction); CE 26/5–76 *Société Normande de Construction* no 97.511; CE 20/1–88 *Possado* no 80.059 (60 per cent reduction); CE 21/12–51 *Feiz Karam* Rec 612; CAA Bordeaux 13/11–95 *Compagnie des salins* Rec 1023 (66 per cent reduction); CE 9/7–75 *Felix-Faure* Rec 411; CE 12/10–84 *Société La Centrale de charcuterie alsacienne* Rec 327 (75 per cent reduction).

[48] See also section 5.

[49] CE 3/3–89 *Société Sagatour* Rec 905.

[50] See also for individualized promises CE 21/12–51 *Feiz Karam* Rec 612; CE 11/5–56 *Société Lesieur-Afrique* Rec 184; CE 4/10–67 *Syndicat intercommunal d' électrification de la région de Pont-Saint-Esprit* no 68.650; CE 13/11–74 *Coulibeuf* Rec 567; CE 26/5–76 *Société Normande de Construction* no 97.511; CE 20/1–88 *Possado* no 80.059.

In *Société des huileries de Chauny*, a leading precedent in this area, a senior civil servant and a minister had encouraged private companies to purchase a surplus of food oil from a nationalized company by writing to the companies that existing regulations 'protect against variations in the price' of the oil.[51] The CE held that by promising to leave the policy of fixed oil prices unchanged the minister had unlawfully fettered his discretion. The state administration was therefore *prima facie* liable in fault for the traders' loss which arose when the price was subsequently set free in the light of changing developments in the oil market. However, the court reduced the liability by half, as it found that the traders should have sought further verification of the minister's letter before purchasing the oil.[52] In this case, a specific promise was breached in the light of compelling public policy considerations, namely the consumers' interest in affordable foodstuff. The CE therefore applied the notion of contributory fault 'creatively' to share the risk of reliance between state and individuals.[53]

4 The Requirement of Reasonable Reliance

(A) Detrimental Reliance and Causation in Fact

Liability for misrepresentation is, in English law, conditional upon the plaintiff showing detrimental financial reliance.[54] While there is no exact equivalent in French and EC law, the requirement of causation leads to similar results in those jurisdictions.[55] For if the representation was not the basis on which the affected person took action, then it did not cause the relevant loss.[56] It follows that the administration is not liable for reliance on a statement if the recipient was warned that it was incorrect.[57] The absence in French and Community law of a free-standing requirement of financial detriment does, however, mean that damages can more easily be awarded for non-material damage such as inconvenience and anxiety. Thus, in *Ordoux* a civil servant was awarded 10,000 francs for the upset caused by incorrect information about the place he would be

[51] CE 24/4–64 *Société des huileries de Chauny* Rec 249.

[52] There is agreement in French theory that this was overly strict and out of line with existing case law. See case notes by M. Waline, RDP 1964, 799; M. Fromont, D 1964, 579.

[53] See also CE 16/11–98 *Sille* DA 1998 no 23.

[54] *Caparo Industries Plc v Dickman* [1990] 2 AC 605, 638. See also *Roberts v Llanelli BC*, 25/2–98.

[55] See Jolowicz and Rogers, above n. 1, 383–4 explaining reliance as an aspect of causation rather than a free-standing requirement of English law.

[56] CE 16/1–35 *Jacque* Rec 61; Cases 19–20, 25 and 30/69 *Richez-Parise v Commission* [1970] ECR 325. For illustrations of this issue in the employment law context, see CE 1/12–72 *Texierp* Rec 1222; CE 13/2–74 *Pierre* Rec 1149; CE 9/7–80 *Zerlauth* no 10.620; CE 28/10–83 *Giorgetti* no 37.070; CE 25/1–89 *Dumas* no 66.207; CE 12/2–90 *Clouet* Rec 970.

[57] CE 8/3–39 *Diaz* Rec 149; CAA Paris 5/11–91 *SCI Gaumont* no 89PA02370 (confirmed by CE 12/7–93 no 132.71); Case 169/73 *Compagnie Continentale France v Council* [1975] ECR 117; M. R. Brazier *et al*, *Clerk and Lindsell on Torts*, 17th edn. (London, 1995), no 7–77.

placed in France after a period of service abroad, although he had not relied financially on the information before it was rectified.[58]

(B) Reasonable Reliance: What Representations?

Administrative liability for misrepresentations (and in French law for breach of *promesse*) is subject to the recipient's own negligence or fault. In English law, the administration is only liable if the person's reliance was reasonable. In French and EC law, the person must have acted with sufficient diligence and care (*prudence*).[59] The notions of reasonable and prudent reliance are quite similar in practice, but while unreasonable reliance tends to exclude liability in English law,[60] the French courts prefer to reduce damages, typically by 25 to 75 per cent.[61]

To determine whether a person acted reasonably, the courts will take into account the form and content of the representation, the context in which it was made, and the knowledge of the recipient. Written statements carry considerable weight, especially if the information is current. The courts have found that individuals could reasonably rely on, for example, letters,[62] telexes,[63] published deliberations of local elected authorities,[64] informative leaflets,[65] and published circulars (*circulaires*).[66] Reliance on oral statements without verification has often been considered unreasonable in English cases,[67] and although the French courts have, on a number of occasions, awarded damages, they have typically been reduced by between one-third and three-quarters.[68] It is submitted that it should not always be considered unreasonable to rely on oral information, such

[58] CE 27/7–88 *Ordoux* Rec 304. See also CE 1/10–66 *Aubert* no 65.312.

[59] e.g. CE 16/11–98 *Sille* DA 1998 no 23; Case 169/73 *Compagnie Continentale France v Council* [1975] ECR 117.

[60] See Jolowicz and Rogers, above n. 1, 384.

[61] See footnote 47.

[62] e.g. *W v Essex CC* [1998] 3 WLR 534; CE 1/12–72 *Texierp* Rec 1222; Cases 29, 31, 36, 39–47 and 50–51/63 *Usines de la Providence v High Authority* [1965] ECR 911.

[63] CE 27/7–88 *Ordoux* Rec 304.

[64] CE 25/11–88 *Commune de Carry-Le-Rouet* no 89.106.

[65] TA Dijon 24/6–74 *Prévost* Rec 739.

[66] CAA Lyon 9/7–90 *Jigot* Rec 969 and (implicitly) CE 12/6–70 *Consorts Leclerc* RDP 1971, 761; CAA Bordeaux 25/7–94 *Société Arboricole de l'Agenais* no 93BX00676. See also Cases 176–177/86 *Houyoux v Commission* [1987] ECR 4333.

[67] *JFG Properties Ltd v Lambeth BC* (1986) 277 EG 648; *Tidman v Reading BC* [1994] 3 PLR 72, 92; *Roberts v Llanelli BC*, 25/2–98. Similarly Clerk and Lindsell, above n. 57, no 7–70–7–71; Morrell and Foster, above n. 1, 183. Compare *Chaudry v Prabhakar* [1988] 3 All ER 718 (conceded that advice given on social occasion fell under *Hedley Byrne*); *Lambert v West Devon BC* [1997] JPL 735.

[68] CE 25/6–54 *Otto* Rec 380; TA Lille 14/12–60 *Consorts Leroy* Rec 612; TA Dijon 10/1–66 *Charles* Rec 701. The problem of proof is considerable in such cases. See e.g. CE 20/1–61 *Baurin* Rec 48; CE 19/12–80 *Société d'études et de gestion des grandes surfaces* no 9.859; CAA Bordeaux 5/4–90 *Camps* Petites Affiches 3/7–91, 18; CE 7/10–91 *Proucelle* no 83.540; CE 4/3–92 *Amède* no 87.717; CE 26/6–92 *Beausse* no 72.164; CE 13/11–96 *Elections municipales de Guérande* no 179.972.

as statements made in a meeting or by telephone. This would especially apply if the transaction is not of great economic importance.

Reliance on mere silence or inaction is rarely considered reasonable.[69] In French law, there is a statutory provision to the effect that the administration's silence for a period of four months following an application amounts to a negative decision.[70] Applicants can therefore not reasonably expect that administrative silence will lead to a favourable decision.[71] The same applies if the grant of a favourable decision is subject to a procedure in more than one stage, and the applicant passes the first stage. Thus, when a weapons producer in the French *Haut-Rhin* district obtained a pre-permit to sell munitions production machinery to the Syrian government, the administration was not liable in fault for the producer's reliance and lost profits when it refused the final export licence in view of the Suez Crisis. The producer was aware of the statutory requirements, and as the administration had never promised to deliver a final permission, the reliance was deemed unreasonable (*imprudent*).[72]

It is well-established in English law that the recipient's reliance is more likely to be considered reasonable if the representation was an answer to a specific question than a statement for more general circulation.[73] Administrative liability is also imposed more frequently for individualized advice and assurances than for more general statements in French and EC law, but the administration has on occasion been held liable for general statements which had been sent in copy to an individual or published in an official journal.[74]

The wording of the representation must normally be clear and without any disclaimer of responsibility.[75] For example, in *Pinon* the CE refused to impose liability on a planning authority, although its director had stated that 'a favourable recommendation will be made if planning permission is sought', as this did not amount to a promise that permission would eventually be granted.[76] Conduct may, however, amount to an implicit representation on which individuals should be able to rely. This is well-established in French law, as the *Résidence Arcole* case illustrates. In this case, a company was informed

[69] CE 11/2–55 *Société fabriques réunies de lampes électriques* Rec 83; B. S. Markesinis and S. F. Deakin, *Tort Law*, 4th edn. (Oxford, 1999), 94.

[70] See Brown and Bell 165–6.

[71] CE 31/1–50 *Chabot* Rec 526.

[72] CE 29/6–62 *Société Manufacture des Machines du Haut-Rhin* Rec 432. See also CE 13/3–85 *Société Barlocher* Rec 79; CE 19/2–88 *Société Robatel* D 1988, 365; CE 26/6–89 *Commune de Blanc-Mesnil* Rec 905.

[73] *Caparo Industries Plc v Dickman* [1990] 2 AC 605, 620–1; *Possum v Diamond* [1996] 2 All ER 774. The author's survey of about 300 decisions which refer to 'Hedley Byrne' on the Lexis database has not revealed any examples of administrative liability for circulars and other general statements.

[74] e.g. CAA Lyon 9/7–90 *Gigot* Rec 969; Cases 176–177/86 *Houyoux v Commission* [1987] ECR 4333. See also CE 12/6–70 *Consorts Lecher* RDP 1971, 761; CAA Bordeaux 25/7–94 *Société Arboricole de l'Agenais* no 93BX00676 (implicitly accepting the possibility of liability for published circulars).

[75] *Hewings v Teignbridge DC*, 15/11–95 cited by Morrell and Foster, above n. 1, 187.

[76] CE 6/10–78 *SARL Le Grand Arc* no 5.119. See also CE 15/12–76 *Société de promotion, d'études et de recherches* Rec 1102; CE 6/10–82 *Baron* no 23.417; CE 12/2–86 *Gros-Flandre* no 49.452.

by a local authority that its application for a building permission had been recommended for approval by local and departmental planning committees, and it was asked to pay expenses related to parking facilities adjacent to the proposed building. When it later emerged that planning permission had not been, and would not be, granted, the CE imposed full liability on the authority for the expenses.[77]

The recipient's knowledge and experience also affects the assessment of reasonable reliance. Professional economic operators and civil servants are expected to be aware of the legislative framework, and in French law damages are often reduced on the grounds that such plaintiffs should have shown greater care in their dealings with the administration. For example, in *Monrand* the liability of a regional educational authority (*académie*) for incorrect information about pension rights was reduced by one third because the recipient, a director of a French school, could and should have enquired further.[78] Private individuals are generally treated more leniently. In *Prévost* the applicant, who was unemployed, had taken a job and moved to a different region on the basis of information in an administrative leaflet to the effect that he would receive a mobility bonus. However, the leaflet failed to mention the fact that jobs in the public sector were not subject to the bonus scheme. Although Mr Prévost had not sought verification of the content of the leaflet, his action was considered reasonable and liability was imposed for his expenses.[79]

(C) Reasonable Reliance: Whose Representations?

The requirement of reasonable reliance poses particular problems when individuals rely on statements about matters which are outside the authority of the representing body or officer.[80] The general rule in English and French law is that individuals, rather than the administration, bear the risk of reliance on such 'unofficial' statements.[81] While a public officer who is personally competent to decide, or specifically designated to advise on, a legal issue may create liability by his or her statements, this does not apply to employees whose tasks do not ordinarily include the giving of advice. Thus, in *Roberts v Llanelli BC* technical staff employed by a local authority had told the owner of a sports club of the authority's plans to expropriate the club house while visiting to measure its size. The Council was not liable for loss which occurred as a result of these comments, as they were not 'part of the task [the employees] were performing and

[77] CE 26/10–73 *SCI Résidence Arcole* Rec 601.
[78] CE 28/4–71 *Monrand* AJDA 1971, 683. See also CE 9/7–80 *Zerlauth* no 10.620.
[79] TA Dijon 24/6–74 *Prévost* Rec 739. Compare CE 30/10–81 *Bonhoure* Rec 902.
[80] The Community courts have not yet ruled on this issue.
[81] CE 23/10–57 *Corniallez* Rec 548; CE 11/2–55 *Société fabriques réunies de lampes électriques* Rec 83; CE 4/1–64 *Cavaudeau* AJDA 1964, 450; CE 9/1–70 *Laengy* Rec 13.

authorized to perform, but collateral matters or observations not intended or entitled to be relied on'.[82]

However, individuals cannot always know or verify whether an officer has authority to advise on behalf of the administration.[83] Liability may therefore be imposed for statements which are made by officers who appear to be acting lawfully and on behalf of the authority. This is well established in French law, where liability has on a number of occasions been imposed for statements by officers (and elected representatives) who exceeded their personal authority when giving advice.[84] For example, in the case of *Compagnie de salins* the mayor of a local authority (*commune*) had assured a company that certain planning restrictions would be lifted if it agreed to sell a piece of land to the *commune* at the symbolic price of one franc. The restrictions could in fact only be lifted by the full planning committee, and although the court found that the company was aware of this problem, the *commune* was held liable for a third of the company's loss when the committee refused to fulfil the mayor's promise.[85] There is also support in recent English case law for liability for statements by officers with apparent authority. In *Lambert v West Devon BC* a senior building control officer had informed the plaintiff by telephone that he could carry out building works on his property without additional planning permission. The Council was held liable for loss incurred in reliance on this statement although the officer, who was responsible for granting building regulation approval, had no power to grant planning consent.[86]

French law even admits the possibility of liability for statements made in excess of the authority of the relevant public body. Thus, in *Delcher* a municipal planning authority had granted a planning permission and provided (inaccurate) information about the level of an existing street. Although the construction and levelling of streets fell squarely within the competence of the Ministry of Reconstruction, the planning authority was held liable, since street levelling was a matter which planning authorities could reasonably be expected to deal with.[87]

5 The Requirements of Causation and Damage

The requirements of causation in fact, remoteness (*causalité directe*), and damage (*dommage certain*) are rarely examined in English *Hedley Byrne* cases due to the narrow scope of this tort in relation to public authorities. By way of

[82] *Roberts v Llanelli BC*, 25/2–98

[83] See the discussion in *JFG Properties Ltd v Lambeth BC* (1986) 277 EG 648, 650.

[84] CE 14/6–61 *Société European Metal Trading* Rec 392; CE 22/1–64 *Quenza* AJDA 1964, 450; CAA Paris 28/4–92 *Banque Socredo* Rec 514; CAA Bordeaux 13/11–95 *Compagnie des salins* Rec 1023.

[85] Ibid.

[86] *Lambert v West Devon BC* [1997] JPL 735.

[87] CE 10/3–65 *Delcher* Rec 869.

contrast, these requirements play a very important role in French and EC law. It was seen in Chapter 5 that these conditions limit liability for unlawful decision-making to a considerable extent. The same strict conditions apply to liability for informal representations, and it will therefore suffice to give a few examples at this juncture.[88]

The *Caladou* case is a classic example of the CE's hands-on approach to causation in fact. Mr Caladou had received incorrect information about a time limit and thereby lost his opportunity to apply for war damage compensation. The CE assessed Mr Caladou's application under the relevant provisions *do novo* and found that the claim would probably not have succeeded. Consequently, the incorrect advice had not in fact caused any loss, and the administration was not liable.[89] The ECJ relied on a similar reasoning in the case of *Parise-Richez* where it held that a number of staff members had not proven that their decisions to seek early retirement from the Commission were based on information about their pension rights which they had received from a Commission official.[90] The Court found that they would in any event have sought retirement, since none of them had sought to be reinstated in their old positions when they discovered that their pensions were smaller than initially advised.[91]

In English law, liability for misstatements presupposes that the representing authority knew that its statement would be communicated to the recipient, either specifically or as a member of an ascertainable class, and that the recipient would act upon it for a certain purpose.[92] This rule prevents a vast liability from arising in situations where a misstatement is communicated from one recipient to a number of others. There is no explicit requirement in French and EC law that the representing authority knew the recipient or the purpose for which the statement was to be used, but the notion of direct causation (*causalité directe*) limits the scope of liability in a similar fashion. Loss suffered by a person in reliance on a statement which was made for, and communicated to, another is normally considered too remote to cause liability.[93] Thus, in the leading French case of *Banque Bastide* a public authority had erroneously informed an applicant for war damage compensation that his claim had been accepted. By showing the administration's letter to the Banque Bastide, the applicant obtained a loan which he failed to pay back. The bank's loss was, according

[88] See further Weber, above n. 2, no 57; Fickler-Despres, above n. 2, 138.

[89] CE 18/11–60 *Caladou* AJDA 1960, 190. See also CE 20/2–74 *Sucrerie coopérative agricole de Vie-Sur-Aisne* Rec 121; CE 3/1–74 *Paya* no 92.956; CE 28/11–80 *Domergue* no 16.618. Compare CE 25/11–88 *Commune de Carry-Le-Rouet* no 89.106.

[90] Cases 19–20, 25 and 30/69 *Richez-Parise v Commission* [1970] ECR 325 para 43.

[91] Compare Case 23/69 *Fiehn v Commission* [1970] ECR 547.

[92] *Caparo Industries Plc v Dickman* [1990] 2 AC 605, 638.

[93] The Community courts have not yet ruled on this issue.

to the CE's unequivocal ruling, so indirect a consequence of the misrepresentation that the authority was not liable for it.[94]

The requirements of direct causation (*causalité directe*) and certain damage (*dommage certain*) overlap to some degree, and both are applied particularly strictly to claims for pure economic loss.[95] Indeed, French litigants' attempts to recover lost profits are practically always futile in cases concerning informal administrative representations.[96] For example, in *Le Mas des Aulnes* a land development company was awarded over one million francs for expenses incurred in reliance on a prefect's assurance that the state would purchase its land at market price if a proposed development was not approved by local planning authorities. However, the CE rejected as too uncertain a claim of several million francs of profits, which the development would allegedly have generated.[97]

6 Comparison and Suggestions for Reform

(A) Comparative Summary

The comparative study of the principles of damages liability for administrative representations has revealed significant differences between English, French, and EC law. Judicial views about the appropriateness of tort in the public law context differ considerably, and this affects the application of the liability principles in practice. Our findings may be set out in three points.

First, while the English courts remain reluctant to impose liability for misrepresentations made by authorities in the course of their statutory advisory functions, the French courts often award damages for loss caused by administrative misrepresentations (*renseignements erronés*) and breach of (correct) administrative assurances (*promesses non-contractuelles*). While the Community judicature took a cautious approach to liability for misrepresentations in *Parise-Richez*, it has developed a fairly generous approach to breach of legitimate expectations created by (correct) administrative assurances.

Second, the difference in terms of outcomes between English, French, and EC tort law is reduced to some extent by two factors. On the one hand, the French

[94] CE 17/4–53 *Banque Bastide* Rec 177. See also CE 26/1–39 *Deydier* Rec 546; CE 25/5–90 *Abadie* AJDA 1990, 825. Compare CE 13/4–83 *District de Forbach* Rec 147 (liability for statement directly to a bank).

[95] See Ch. 5.4.B.I and André, above n. 2, 29; Weber, above n. 2, no 57; Fickler-Despres, above n. 2, 138.

[96] e.g. CE 12/3–54 *Weickert* Rec 152; CE 24/4–64 *Société des huileries de Chauny* Rec 249; CE 7/4–65 *Société Air Couzinet Transoceanic* Rec 229; CE 26/10–73 *SCI Résidence Arcole* Rec 601; CE 16/3–77 *SA Beausite* no 97.644; CE 16/11–84 *Société Publimontre* no 40.662; CE 16/11–98 *Sille* DA 1998 no 23. Compare CE 11/5–56 *Société Lesieur-Afrique* Rec 184 (the only known award of profit loss by the CE).

[97] CE 25/3–91 *SARL Le Mas des Aulnes* no 66.578.

courts often limit the amount of damages awarded by a pragmatic and quite strict application of the notions of contributory fault, direct causation, and certain damage.[98] Thus, while English law places almost the entire risk of administrative error on individuals, French law normally provides redress at a level below what would be considered full compensation in England. On the other hand, the English Parliamentary Commissioner for Administration and the Local Government Ombudsmen provide a practically important source of compensation for victims of misleading or incorrect administrative advice.[99] The notion of maladministration, which is applied by the Ombudsmen as the basis of recommendations for compensation, resembles the *Hedley Byrne* rule to some extent. However, the types of loss or detriment, which will be considered by the Ombudsmen, is wider than in tort cases, and there is no immunity for statements made by officers as part of their normal statutory functions.[100] For example, in the *Snakebite* case the tax authorities were made to pay £30,000 compensation to a brewer who had started production of a potent alcoholic drink after being told wrongly that it would incur no extra VAT charges.[101]

The differences between English, French, and EC tort law must be understood in the light of our study of procedural and substantive principles in the previous chapters of this book. The greater availability of damages for misrepresentation and breach of non-contractual promises, in French law compared to English law, reflects the absence of comprehensive procedural and substantive protection of legitimate expectations in French law. The French judiciary has preferred to protect individuals who rely on administrative representations by compensating actual loss rather than by interfering directly with the process of administrative decision-making.[102] Overall, English and French law achieve a not very dissimilar level of protection of legitimate expectations, albeit by very different legal mechanisms.

A comparison of EC law with French and English law leaves the two latter jurisdictions in a somewhat unfavourable light. We have seen in Chapters 4 and 5 that the Community law principles of irrevocability and substantive legitimate

[98] Indeed, leading practitioners in the field of planning law claim that it is virtually impossible to obtain full compensation. The author is indebted to Professor Jean-Bernard Auby for this information.

[99] See A. R. Mowbray, 'A Right to Official Advice: The Parliamentary Commissioner's Perspective' (1990) PL 68; P. M. Brown, 'The Ombudsmen, Remedies for Misinformation', in G. Richardson and H. Genn (eds.), *Administrative Law and Government Action* (Oxford, 1994). The French ombudsman (*Médiateur*) also has the power to recommend compensation, but this does not appear to have had any real impact. See http: //www.mediateur-de-la-republique.fr/pres/index.htm; Chapus 426–30.

[100] See Mowbray, above n. 99, 79–84; Brown, above n. 99, 312–8; D. Woodhouse, *In Pursuit of Good Administration: Ministers, Civil Servants and Judges* (Oxford, 1997), 74–5.

[101] See E. Hoskins, 'Snakebite and Estoppel' (1987) VAT Intelligence 407. See also I. McLeod, 'Local Authorities, Estoppel and the Ombudsman' (1989) LGR 505, 507.

[102] This may reflect a more general and historically determined preference for compensatory remedies in French public law. See C. Harlow, 'Francovich and the Problem of the Disobedient State' (1996) ELJ 199, 206.

expectations are more comprehensive and more rigorously enforced than the equivalent principles in English and French law. In this and the previous chapter, we have seen that the Community law principles of liability for administrative representations are about as generous as those found in French law. The upshot is that EC law provides more overall protection of legitimate expectations than either of the two national legal systems.

(B) Suggestions for Reform

It is submitted that English law does not at present provide adequate protection of individuals who suffer loss by reliance on administrative misrepresentations. The English courts are, as explained in Chapter 4, extremely reluctant to admit that unlawful representations can create estoppel or substantive legitimate expectations. At the same time, individuals who rely on administrative misrepresentations in good faith find it difficult to obtain damages under the *Hedley Byrne* rule, and the Ombudsman system does not provide a really satisfactory alternative remedy.[103] The result is that the financial risk of administrative error often falls on individuals rather than on the administration itself. This state of affairs arguably falls short of the requirements of fairness, certainty, and trust in the relationship between the administration and individuals.

How, then, might English law be changed to provide better protection of those who rely on administrative misrepresentations? It is submitted that two complementary reforms will be necessary to achieve this.

First, the principle of substantive legitimate expectations should be extended to cover unlawful representations.[104] If a balancing of the private and public interests in a particular case shows that the harm to the public interest does not exceed the individual's expectations and reliance, then the administration should be held to its words.[105] This development would reduce the number of instances in which individuals suffer any financial loss. Still, it is inevitable that the effect, on the public interest and third parties, of upholding an unlawful statement will in some instances outweigh the individual's reasonable expectations and reliance. Reform of administrative law principles will not therefore be sufficient in and of itself.

The solution is, second, to provide compensation in those instances where unlawful representations are not upheld by the principle of substantive legitimate expectations, and where the individual's reliance was reasonable.[106] For example, a landowner who incurs expenses in reliance upon incorrect planning advice should be compensated for those expenses if, on a balancing of the harm

[103] See Ch. 5.4.A.V. [104] See Ch. 4.7.C. [105] Ibid.

[106] See A. W. Bradley, 'Administrative Justice and the Binding Effect of Official Acts' (1981) CLP 1, 18–20; JUSTICE—All Souls Review Committee, *Administrative Justice: Some Necessary Reforms* (Oxford, 1988), 173–5; Lord Woolf, *Protection of the Public—A New Challenge* (London, 1990), 56; Craig 649–50.

caused to him and affected neighbours, it is decided that the planned development should not take place. It may be that English courts will be reluctant to liberalize the *Hedley Byrne* principle to the extent which would be necessary to implement this proposal. If this was found to be true, there is a strong case for the adoption of a system of statutory compensation which does not require the individual to prove negligence or an assumption of responsibility by the relevant officer.[107]

It is important to examine two objections which might be raised against these proposals for reform. One objection which might be made is that it would be preferable to give compensation rather then *ever* allowing an unlawful representation to bind through the principle of substantive legitimate expectations.[108] This objection does not withstand scrutiny. Compensation is a valuable complement to the principle of legitimate expectations, but it is, for the following reasons, not a suitable alternative.

First, compensation is not a sufficient remedy in and of itself.[109] The rationale for the protection of legitimate expectations derives from autonomy, planning, and trust in government.[110] People's plans and their trust in government may be undermined when authorities go back on representations, although no loss calculable in money is suffered. An example may illustrate this point.[111] Imagine that X is informed incorrectly about the criteria which apply to adoption of family members from abroad, that he fulfils these criteria, and that he informs his orphaned nephew that permission to adopt is likely to be granted. Should we deny X the very *possibility* of legal protection simply because he did not rely financially on the unlawful representation, say, by travelling to bring the happy message in person?[112]

Second, to provide compensation is simply a waste of scarce resources if it can be shown, in a particular instance, that the public interest would not be harmed by upholding the expectation in substance.[113] An example may, again, illustrate the point.[114] Imagine that a company Y is incorrectly informed about licensing policy in relation to aviation, and that it invests £10 million in new aircraft and employees in reliance on this information. Why pay Y this large amount of compensation if on the facts it can be shown that the public interest, and other licensees, would not be harmed significantly if Y was allowed to carry out the planned operation? Letting Y hold the administration

[107] Ibid.

[108] See Wade 375–8; Brown, above n. 99, 335–6.

[109] See R. Pagone, 'Estoppel in Public Law: Theory, Fact and Fiction' (1984) UNSWLJ 267, 278.

[110] See Ch. 1.

[111] This example has analogies with *R v Home Secretary, ex p Kahn* [1984] 1 WLR 1337.

[112] The point may be expressed differently: disappointment of expectations is, in the absence of financial reliance, extremely difficult to quantify. How would we compensate X for the disappointment of his plans to adopt and his lost chance of forming emotionally rewarding bonds with an adopted child?

[113] See Craig 649–50.

[114] This example has analogies with *Laker Airways Ltd v Department of Trade* [1977] QB 643.

to its representation would be less wasteful than paying it to lay off its aircraft and employees.

Third, it has been argued that compensation is preferable to substantive protection of legitimate expectations because it does not restrict (or 'fetter') the administration's discretionary powers. The authority which has induced an expectation is free to depart from it if that is felt necessary to make a lawful decision in the public interest.[115] This argument ignores the economic reality of modern administration.[116] Public authorities have strictly limited financial resources, and they must act so as to minimize liability.[117] The threat of liability therefore acts as a *de facto* restriction on discretionary powers which may be as strong, or even stronger, than the principle of substantive legitimate expectations.

Another objection, which might be made against the proposals put forward above, is that the imposition of liability for administrative misrepresentations—based either on a more liberal application of *Hedley Byrne* principles or on statutory provisions—would adversely affect the exercise of statutory advisory functions: officials would be less willing to give advice and to publish policies if they could be liable in damages for doing so.[118] It was argued in Chapter 1 that the fear of such a 'chilling effect' is largely unfounded, and that a loss in the quantity of information may be offset by a gain in quality.[119] It may be added at this point that there is no evidence that the imposition of a relatively strict liability for misrepresentations in French law has had a significant and adverse effect on the exercise of the administration's advisory functions.

[115] See Wade 376.

[116] See E. Campbell, 'Agreements About the Exercise of Statutory Powers' (1971) ALJ 338, 340; P. D. Finn and K. J. Smith, 'The Citizen, The Government and Reasonable Expectations' (1992) ALJ 139, 147.

[117] This applies also to authorities which take out legal liability insurance, as insurance premiums reflect liabilities over time.

[118] See *Welton v North Cornwall DC* [1997] 1 WLR 570, 580–1; *Harris v Evans* [1998] 1 WLR 1285, 1298, 1301; *W v Essex CC* [1998] 3 WLR 534, 547.

[119] See Ch. 1.2.C.I.

Conclusion

How and in what circumstances should English law protect expectations created by administrative decisions and representations? I have sought to answer this broad question by addressing three more specific questions.

The first question was 'why should administrative law protect expectations at all?' The proposed answer was that expectations should be protected to respect the principle of fairness. Fairness requires protection of expectations for two reasons. On the one hand, the disappointment of an expectation may cause considerable harm to an individual who has relied upon its fulfilment (the reliance theory). On the other hand, expectations are a central aspect of legal certainty and therefore of individual autonomy (the Rule of Law theory). Protection of legitimate expectations also promotes trust in public authorities and thereby their perceived legitimacy and efficacy. However, fairness and trust must be balanced against the principle of lawful government in the public interest. To determine the right balance between these principles, it is necessary to distinguish between four scenarios: revocation of final decisions, departure from individualized assurances, departure from policy in particular instances, and general changes of policy (Situations 1–4). The rationale for protection of expectations differs in these four situations, and different degrees of legal protection are therefore required.

'How are expectations protected by administrative law today?' That was the second question addressed in this book. The answer was based on an analytical and comparative study of English, French, and EC law. It was seen that the three legal systems protect expectations by different combinations of procedural, substantive, and compensatory rules. Three main findings emerged from the comparative study.

First, there is a different emphasis on procedural, substantive, and compensatory protection of expectations in English, French, and EC law. Traditionally, English law only provided procedural protection of expectations, and the development of substantive protection has been slow and difficult. By way of contrast, the Community courts have had little difficulty accepting that expectations deserve substantive protection. In French law, there is no explicit concept of reasonable or legitimate expectations at all. The CE has generally preferred to compensate loss, caused by reliance on administrative decisions and representations, rather than to impose procedural and substantive limitations on the administrations' discretionary powers.

Second, the marked conceptual differences between English, French, and EC administrative laws do not always lead to different outcomes in decided cases.[1] The difference between EC law and English law (which have principles of legitimate expectations) and French law (which has no such principle) is smaller than might be expected. The three legal systems differ most markedly in relation to *procedural* protection of expectations. Revocation of favourable and final decisions (Situation 1) is normally subject to hearing and reasoning requirements in all three of the legal systems,[2] but procedural protection of expectations created by informal representations is only available in English law (Situations 2–4). The difference between English, French, and EC law is smaller as far as *substantive* protection of expectations is concerned. Although French law does not recognize the concept of substantive legitimate expectations as such, expectations are protected indirectly by the principle of irrevocability of decisions which create rights (Situation 1)[3] and the principle of equal treatment (Situation 3).[4] These principles are supplemented by important statutory provisions in the areas of tax and land planning (Situation 2).[5] In the context of *compensatory* protection, the differences between English, French, and EC law are, once again, significant but smaller than the markedly different concepts and principles would suggest. The French and the EC administration's liability for unlawful decision-making and misrepresentations is not restricted by the concept of duty of care, but the French and the EC courts limit liability to some extent by a pragmatic 'variation' of the concept of illegality and a strict application of the requirements of direct causation, certain damage, and contributory fault.[6]

Third, EC law provides overall more protection of expectations than English and French law. English law and EC law have converged in recent years as it is now recognized in English law that expectations may be enforced substantively.[7] However, two important differences remain. On the one hand, the English courts are still reluctant to intervene when expectations are disappointed by general changes of policy. The Community courts are more willing to impose temporal limitations on policy changes to uphold the expectations of affected individuals (Situation 4). On the other hand, the extremely narrow English damages liability for unlawful decision-making and misrepresentations leaves victims of administrative error without effective compensatory protection. The EC law principles of liability in fault are somewhat more generous.[8] The extensive procedural protection of expectations provided by English law does not offset the relative weakness of substantive and compensatory protections.

The third and final question addressed in this book was whether 'the current approach in English law to protection of expectations is satisfactory'.[9] In other

[1] This confirms the findings of many comparative studies of private law. See K. Zweigert and H. Kötz, *An Introduction to Comparative Law*, 3rd edn. (Oxford, 1998), 39–40.

[2] See Ch. 2.3.B.

[3] The principle of *intangibilité de décision créatrices de droits*. See Ch. 3.2.B.

[4] The principle of *égalité de traitement*. See Ch. 4.4.

[5] See Ch. 4.3.C.

[6] See Chs. 5.4.B and 6.4–6.5.

[7] See Ch. 4.2.A.

[8] See Chs. 5.4.C and 6.4–6.5.

[9] See the final sections of Chs. 2–6.

words, does English law meet the requirement of fairness and trust in administration? It was argued that this is not the case. The existing procedural, substantive, and compensatory principles do not protect expectations adequately and there is, therefore, a strong case for legal reform. The comparative study of French and EC law was used as a source of inspiration for such reform, and three types of recommendations were made.

First, the administration should be placed under a duty to consult prior to general changes of policy which will affect individuals who have a reasonable expectation that the existing policy will be continued until further notice (Situation 4).[10]

Second, it should be recognized that favourable and lawful administrative decisions are irrevocable, and that favourable unlawful decisions are irrevocable if the affected person's reasonable expectations outweigh the public interest in seeing the decision revoked (Situation 1).[11] The rhetoric of *Wednesbury* unreasonableness should be abandoned in substantive legitimate expectations cases to the advantage of a 'significant imbalance' test, and it should be recognized that unlawful representations may create legitimate expectations protected by law (Situation 2–4).[12]

Third, the administration should adopt a practice of granting *ex gratia* compensation for grave and special harm caused by lawful administrative decisions (Situation 1). The English courts should adopt a more generous approach to damages liability for unlawful decision-making (Situation 1) and administrative misrepresentations (Situation 2–4). In the context of unlawful decision-making, legal reform should draw on the 'sufficiently serious breach' test adopted in EC law.[13]

What is, then, the answer to the question 'how and in what circumstances should English law protect expectations created by administrative decisions and representations'? It is this. Expectations cannot be adequately protected by a single legal principle; a combination of procedural, substantive, and compensatory rules is required. The particular combination favoured by this author is set out in Table 1.

[10] See Ch. 2.5. [11] See Ch. 3.5. [12] See Ch. 4.7. [13] See Chs. 5.5 and 6.6.

Table 1. *Legitimate expectations in administrative decisions making: the principles which should be applied*

The Source of the Expectation	*Legality*	*The Specific Nature of the Expectation*	*Procedural Principle*	*Substantive Principle*	*Compensatory Principle*
Formal Decision (Situation 1)	Lawful	Favourable, unconditional, and communicated decision	Protections apply on grounds of rights or interests. The affected person should not have to show a legitimate expectation.	Decision is irrevocable (unless statutory basis for revocation). The concept of expectations has no role.	Revocation without a statutory basis: Fault based liability. Revocation with a statutory basis: Statutory or *ex gratia* no-fault compensation for special harm.
Formal Decision (Situation 1)	Lawful	Decision which is not favourable, unconditional, and communicated	Protections may apply on grounds of rights or interests. Otherwise, if a legitimate expectation is shown.	Decision is *prima facie* revocable subject to substantive legitimate expectations. Balancing of expectations and public policy arguments.	Revocation in violation of reasonable expectations, and not justified by public policy considerations: Fault based damages liability. Revocation in violation of reasonable expectations, but justified by public policy considerations: no-fault compensation for special harm.
Formal Decision (Situation 1)	Unlawful	Favourable, unconditional, and communicated decision	Protections may apply on grounds of rights or interests. Otherwise, if a legitimate expectation is shown.	Decision is *prima facie* revocable subject to substantive legitimate expectations. Balancing of expectations, public policy arguments and legality.	Revocation without statutory basis: Fault based damages liability subject to critical causation requirement. Revocation with statutory basis: Statutory or *ex gratia* no-fault compensation for special harm.
Formal Decision (Situation 1)	Unlawful	Decision which is not favourable, unconditional, and communicated	Protections may apply on grounds of rights or interests. Otherwise, if a legitimate expectation is shown.	Decision is *prima facie* revocable subject to substantive legitimate expectations. Balancing of expectations, public policy arguments and legality.	Revocation in violation of reasonable expectations, and not justified by legality and public policy considerations: Fault based damages liability. Revocation in violation of reasonable expectations, but justified by legality and public policy considerations: no-fault compensation for special harm.

Informal Representation (Situation 2)	Lawful	Individualized representation	Protections apply if a legitimate expectation is shown. No requirement of reliance.	Subjective Principle: Representation may be binding on grounds of substantive legitimate expectations. Balancing of expectations and public policy arguments. Detrimental reliance is normally required.	Violation of reasonable expectations not justified by public policy considerations: Fault based damages liability. Violation of reasonable expectations justified by public policy considerations: no-fault compensation for special harm.
Informal Representation (Situation 2)	Unlawful	Individualized representation	Protections apply if a legitimate expectation is shown. No requirement of reliance.	Representation may be binding on grounds of substantive legitimate expectations. Balancing of expectations, public policy arguments and legality. Detrimental reliance is always required.	Revocation in violation of reasonable expectations, and not justified by legality and public policy considerations: Fault based damages liability. Revocation in violation of reasonable expectations, but justified by legality and public policy considerations: no-fault compensation for special harm.
Informal Representation (Situation 3)	Lawful	Generalized Representation: Departure in individual case	Protections apply if a legitimate expectation is shown. No requirement of reliance.	Representation is binding on grounds of substantive legitimate expectations and formal equality. Balancing of expectations, equality and public policy arguments for departure. Detrimental reliance is not required.	Violation of reasonable expectations not justified by public policy considerations: Fault based damages liability. Violation of reasonable expectations justified by public policy considerations: no-fault compensation for special harm.

(continued)

Table 1. *Continued*

The Source of the Expectation	*Legality*	*The Specific Nature of the Expectation*	*Procedural Principle*	*Substantive Principle*	*Compensatory Principle*
Informal Representation (Situation 3)	Unlawful	Generalized representation: Departure in individual case	Protections apply if a legitimate expectation is shown. No requirement of reliance.	Representation may be binding on grounds of substantive legitimate expectations and formal equality. Balancing of expectations, equality, public policy arguments and legality. Detrimental reliance is always required.	Revocation in violation of reasonable expectations, and not justified by legality and public policy considerations: Fault based damages liability. Revocation in violation of reasonable expectations, but justified by legality and public policy considerations: no-fault compensation for special harm.
Informal Representation (Situation 4)	Lawful	Generalized representation: Change of policy	Protections apply if a legitimate expectation is shown. No requirement of reliance.	Representation is binding on grounds of substantive legitimate expectations. Balancing of expectations and public policy arguments for departure. Detrimental reliance is normally required.	Violation of reasonable expectations not justified by public policy considerations: Fault based damages liability. Violation of reasonable expectations justified by public policy considerations: no-fault compensation for special harm.
Informal Representation (Situation 4)	Unlawful	Generalized representation: Change of policy	Protections apply if a legitimate expectation is shown. No requirement of reliance.	Representation may be binding on grounds of substantive legitimate expectations. Balancing of expectations and public policy arguments and legality. Detrimental reliance is always required.	Revocation in violation of reasonable expectations, and not justified by legality and public policy considerations: Fault based damages liability. Revocation in violation of reasonable expectations, but justified by legality and public policy considerations: no-fault compensation for special harm.

Bibliography

ABRAHAM, H., *The Judicial Process*, 6th edn. (New York, 1993).
AKEHURST, M., 'Revocation of Administrative Decisions' (1982) PL 613.
ALDOUS, G., and ALDER, J., *Applications for Judicial Review: Law and Practice of the Crown Office*, 2nd edn. (London, 1993).
ALEXY, R., 'Habermas's Paradigm of Law' (1994) Ratio Juris 231.
ALLAN, T. R. S., 'Pragmatism and Theory in Public Law' (1988) LQR 422.
—— *Law, Liberty, and Justice: The Legal Foundations of British Constitutionalism* (Oxford, 1993).
—— Case Notes (1997) CLJ 246.
—— 'Procedural Fairness and the Duty of Respect' (1998) OJLS 497.
—— 'Fairness, Equality, Rationality: Constitutional Theory and Judicial Review', in C. Forsyth and I. Hare (eds.), *The Golden Metwand and the Crooked Cord: Essays in Honour of Sir William Wade* (Oxford, 1998), 15.
ALLEN, D. K., '*Audi Alterem Partem* in France' (1980) PL 288.
ALLISON, J. W. F., 'The Procedural Reason for Judicial Restraint' (1994) PL 452.
—— 'Fuller's Analysis of Polycentric Disputes and the Limits of Adjudication' (1994) CLJ 367.
—— *A Continental Distinction in the Common Law: A Historical and Comparative Perspective on English Public Law* (Oxford, 1996).
—— 'Transplantation and Cross-fertilisation', in J. Beatson and T. Tridimas (eds.), *New Directions in European Public Law* (Oxford, 1998).
AMOS, M., 'The Parliamentary Commissioner for Administration, Redress and Damages for Wrongful Administrative Action' (2000) PL 21.
AMSELEK, P., 'La Responsabilité sans faute des personnes publiques d'après la jurisprudence administrative', in *Mélanges Eisenmann* (Paris, 1975).
—— 'Le rôle de la pratique dans la formation du droit: aperçus à propos de l'exemple du droit public français', RDP 1983, 1471.
AMSON, R., and LINDON, D., 'Un Ombudsman en France', JCP 1970, 2322.
ANDENAS, M., and FAIRGRIEVE, D., 'Sufficiently Serious? Judicial Restraint in Tortious Liability of Public Authorities and the European Influence', in M. Andenas (ed.), *English Public Law and the Common Law of Europe* (London, 1998), 285.
ANDRÉ, J.-M. 'La responsabilité de la puissance publique du fait des diverses formes d'engagements non contractuels de l'administration', AJDA 1976, 20.
ANSELL, F., 'Unauthorised Conduct of Government Agents: A Restrictive Rule of Equitable Estoppel Against the Government' (1986) Univ Chicago LR 1026.
APPRILL, C., 'La notion de "droit acquis" dans le droit de la fonction publique internationale', RGDIP 1983, 315.
ARCHBOLD, J. F., RICHARDSON, P. J., THOMAS, D. A., BOWES, M., and MOYS, E. M., *Criminal Pleading, Evidence and Practice* (London, 1998).
ARNULL, A., 'Liability for Legislative Acts under Article 215(2) EC', in T. Heukels and A. McDonnell (eds.), *The Action for Damages in Community Law* (The Hague, 1997).
ARROWSMITH, S., *Civil Liability and Public Authorities* (South Humberside, 1992).

ARTHURS, H. W., 'Rethinking Administrative Law: A Slightly Dicey Business' (1979) Osgoode LJ 1.

—— *'Without the Law', Administrative Justice and Legal Pluralism in Nineteenth Century England* (Toronto, 1985).

ASIMOV, M., 'Delegated Legislation: United States and United Kingdom' (1983) OJLS 253.

AUBY, J.-B., 'Responsabilité en matière d'urbanisme', in F. Gazier and R. Drago (eds.), *Encyclopédie Dalloz: Répertoire de la responsabilité de la puissance publique* (Paris, 1996).

AUBY, J.-M., *L'inexistence des actes administratifs: étude de contentieux administratifs* (Paris, 1951).

—— 'L'incompétence ratione temporis. Recherches sur l'application des actes administratifs dans le temps', RDP 1953, 5.

—— 'Les Moyens inopérants dans la jurisprudence administrative', AJDA 1966, 5.

—— 'L'abrogation des actes administratifs', AJDA 1967, 131.

AUVRET, P., 'La notion de droit acquis en droit administratif français', RDP 1985, 53.

AZIBERT, M., and DE BOISDEFFRE, M., 'Chronique générale de jurisprudence administrative française', AJDA 1987, 86.

BAILEY, S. H., and BOWMAN, M. J., 'The Policy/Operational Dichotomy—A Cuckoo in the Nest' (1986) CLJ 430.

BAILEY-HARRIS, R., and HARRIS, M., 'The Immunity of Local Authorities in Child Protection Functions—Is the Door Now Ajar?' (1998) CFLQ 227.

BALDWIN, R., 'Ministerial Responsibility and Government by Agency' (1988) MLR 622.

—— 'Governing with Rules', in G. Richardson and H. Genn (eds.), *Administrative Law and Government Action* (Oxford, 1994).

—— *Rules and Government* (Oxford, 1995).

—— and HAWKINS, K., 'Discretionary Justice: Davis Reconsidered' (1984) PL 570

—— and HORNE, D., 'Expectations in a Joyless Landscape' (1986) MLR 685.

—— and HOUGHTON, J., 'Circular Arguments: The Status and Legitimacy of Administrative Rules' (1986) PL 239.

—— and MCCRUDDEN, C., *Regulation and Public Law* (London, 1987).

BAMFORTH, N., 'Fairness and Legitimate Expectation in Judicial Review' (1997) CLJ 1.

BANAKAS, E. K., 'Public Authority Liability for Pure Economic Loss: A Comparative Study of English, French and German Law', in *Afieroma Eton Andrea A. Gaze* (Athens, 1994).

BARAV, A., 'Damages in Domestic Courts', in T. Heukels and A. McDonnell (eds.), *The Action for Damages in Community Law* (The Hague, 1997).

BARKER, A., 'The Impact of Judicial Review: Perspectives from Whitehall and the Courts' (1996) PL 612.

BARKER, K., 'Unreliable Assumptions in the Modern Law of Negligence' (1993) LQR 461.

BARTHELEMY, J., *Juris Classeur Administratif*, Fasc 590 (Paris, 1987).

BASSETT, M., 'Le principe dit de "l'acte contraire" en droit administratif français', Doctoral thesis (Paris, 1967), 217–45.

BATAILLER, F., 'Les *Beati Possidentes* du droit administratif', RDP 1965, 1072.

BECK, U., *Risk Society: Towards a New Modernity* (London, 1992).

BELL, J. S., 'The Law of England and Wales', in J. S. Bell and A. W. Bradley (eds.), *Governmental Liability: A Comparative Study*, UKCLS vol 13 (London, 1991), 17.

—— 'Reflections on the Procedure of the Conseil d'État', in G. Hand and J. McBride (eds.), *Droit sans frontières: Essays in Honour of L. Neville Brown* (Birmingham, 1991), 211.

—— *French Constitutional Law* (Oxford, 1992).

—— 'English Law and French Law—Not So Different?' (1995) CLP 63.

—— 'Administrative Liability in French Law' (1996) EPL 337.

—— 'Mechanisms for Cross-fertilisation of Administrative Law in Europe', in J. Beatson and T. Tridimas (eds.), *New Directions in European Public Law* (Oxford, 1998), 147.

BELLOUBET-FRIER, N., 'Le principe d'égalité', AJDA 1998 Ed. spéciale 152.

BELOFF, M., 'Natural Justice and Fairness—the Audi Alterem Partem Rule', in M. Supperstone and J. Goudie (eds.), *Judicial Review*, 2nd edn. (London, 1997).

—— and MOUNTFIELD, H., 'Unconventional behaviour? Judicial Uses of the Convention in England and Wales' (1996) EHRLR 5.

BENNION, F. A. R., *Statutory Interpretation*, 3rd edn. (London, 1997).

BERGE, J. B. J. M. TEN, and WIDDERSHOVEN, R., 'The Principle of Legitimate Expectations in Dutch Constitutional and Administrative Law', in *Dutch National Reports to the XV International Congress of Comparative Law,* University of Bristol July 1998.

BERGER, R., 'Estoppel Against the Government' (1954) Univ Chicago LR 680.

BEVERIDGE F., and NOTT, S., 'A Hard Look at Soft Law', in P. Craig and C. Harlow (eds.), *Lawmaking in the European Union* (The Hague, 1998), 285.

BINGHAM, L. J., 'Should Public Law Remedies be Discretionary?' (1991) PL 64.

BLACK, J., 'Reviewing Regulatory Rules', in J. Black, P. Muchlinski and P. Walker (eds.), *Commercial Regulation and Judicial Review* (Oxford, 1998).

BLOM-COOPER, L., 'Lawyers and Public Administrators, Separate and Unequal' (1984) PL 215.

BLUMANN, C., *La renonciation en droit administratif français* (Paris, 1974).

BOCKHARDT, K., 'Vertrauensschutz im europäischen Gemeinschaftsrecht' (1988) EuGRZ 309.

BON, P., 'La responsabilité de l'État dans l'exercise dans sa fonction de contrôle de la légalité des actes locaux', RFDA 1999, 1032.

BORRIE, G., 'The Regulation of Public and Private Power' (1989) PL 552.

BOULOUIS, J., 'Sur une catégorie nouvelle d'actes juridiques: les "directives"', in *Receuil d'études en hommage à Charles Eisenmann* (Paris, 1975), 192.

—— 'Quelques observations à propos de la sécurité juridique', in F. Capotorti, C. Ehlermann, J. Frowein, F. Jacobs, R. Joliet, T. Koopmans, and R. Kovar (eds.), *Liber Amicorum Pierre Pescatore* (Baden-Baden, 1987).

BOUYSSOU, F., 'Nature juridique et force véritable du certificat d'urbanisme: la fin des illusions', JCP Ed. Notariale, 1977 I 33.

BOYLE, A. E., 'Sovereignty, Accountability, and the Reform of Administrative Law', in G. Richardson and H. Genn (eds.), *Administrative Law and Government Action* (Oxford, 1994).

BOYRON, S., 'Proportionality in English Administrative Law: A Faulty Translation?' (1992) OJLS 237.

BRADLEY, A. W., 'Estoppel—Statutory Discretion—Ultra Vires' (1961) CLJ 139.

BRADLEY, A. W., 'Estoppel—Administrative Discretion—Informal Delegation' (1971) CLJ 3.

—— 'Administrative Justice and the Binding Effect of Official Acts' (1981) CLP 1.

—— 'Revocation of a Discretionary Grant, Departmental Rules and Natural Justice' (1987) PL 141.

BRAUNSTEIN, M., 'In Defense of Traditional Immunity—Toward an Economic Rationale for not Estopping the Government' (1982) Rutgers LJ 1.

BRAZIER, M. R., *et al.*, *Clerk and Lindsell on Torts*, 17th edn. (London, 1995).

BRIDGES, L., Mezaros, G., and Sunkin, M., *Judicial Review in Perspective*, 2nd edn. (London, 1995).

BRISSAUD, J., *A History of French Public Law* (New York, 1969).

BRODIE, D., 'Public Authorities and the Duty of Care' (1996) JR 127.

—— 'Public Authorities—Negligence Actions—Control Devices' (1998) Legal Studies 1.

BRONKHORST, H. J., 'The Valid Legislative Act as a Cause of Liability of the Communities', in T. Heukels and A. McDonnell (eds.), *The Action for Damages in Community Law* (The Hague, 1997).

BROWN, L. N., 'Tribunal Adjudication in Britain: Model Rules of Procedure' (1993) ERPL special edn. 287.

—— and BELL, J. S., *French Administrative Law*, 5th edn. (Oxford, 1998).

BROWN, P. M., 'Estoppel by Representation in Administrative Law', Ph.D. thesis (University of Cambridge, 1989).

—— 'The Ombudsmen, Remedies for Misinformation', in G. Richardson and H. Genn (eds.), *Administrative Law and Government Action* (Oxford, 1994).

BROWNE-WILKINSON, Lord, 'The Impact of European Law on English Human Rights and Public Law', in B. S. Markesinis (ed.), *The Gradual Convergence, Foreign Ideas, Foreign and English Law on the Eve of the 21st Century* (Oxford, 1994).

CADENAT, P. , 'Chronique de jurisprudence des cours admistratives d'appel', AJDA 1997, 275.

CALDWELL, J. 'Legitimate Expectation and the Rules of Natural Justice' (1983) Canterbury LR 45.

CALVET, H., 'Droit administratif de la responsabilité et droit communautaire', AJDA 1996 Ed. spéciale, 92.

CAMPBELL, E., 'Agreements About the Exercise of Statutory Powers' (1971) ALJ 338.

CANE, P., 'Public Law and Private Law: A Study of the Analysis and Use of a Legal Concept', in J. Eekelaar and J. Bell (eds.), *Oxford Essays in Jurisprudence* (Oxford, 1987), 57.

—— *An Introduction to Administrative Law*, 3rd edn. (Oxford, 1996).

—— 'Suing Public Authorities in Tort' (1996) LQR 13.

—— 'The Constitutional and Legal Framework of Policy-Making', in C. Forsyth and I. Hare (eds.), *The Golden Metwand and the Crooked Cord: Essays in Honour of Sir William Wade* (Oxford, 1998).

CAPPELLETTI, M.. *The Judicial Process in Comparative Perspective* (Oxford, 1989).

CARBAJO, J., *L'application dans le temps des décisions administratives exécutoires* (Paris, 1980).

CARBONNIER, J., *Flexible Droit*, 7th edn. (Paris, 1992).

CARTIER, G., 'La théorie des attentes légitimes en droit administratif' (1992) Revue de Droit Université Sherbrooke 75.

CARTWRIGHT, J., 'Remoteness of Damage in Contract and Tort: A Reconsideration' (1996) CLJ 488.
CHAPUS, R., *Responsabilité publique et responsabilité privée* (Paris, 1957).
—— 'De l'office du juge: contentieux administratif et nouvelle procédure civile', 1977–8 EDCE, 11.
—— *Droit administratif général*, vol. i, 12th edn. (Paris, 1998).
—— *Droit administratif général*, vol. ii, 11th edn. (Paris, 1998).
—— *Droit du contentieux administratif*, 6th edn. (Paris, 1996).
CHAYES, A., 'The Role of the Judge in Public Law Litigation' (1976) Harvard LR 1281.
CLARK, D. H., 'Natural Justice: Substance and Shadow' (1975) PL 27.
CLAYTON, R., and TOMLINSON, H., *Judicial Review Procedure* (Chichester, 1997).
CLIQUENNOIS, M., 'Que reste-t-il des directives? A propos du vingtième anniversaire de l'arrêt "Crédit foncier de France"', AJDA 1992, 3.
COHEN, D., and SMITH, J. C., 'Entitlement and the Body Politic: Rethinking Negligence in Public Law' (1986) Canadian Bar Review 1.
CONVERY, J., 'Public or Private? Duty of Care in a Statutory Framework: *Stovin v Wise* in the House of Lords' (1997) MLR 559.
—— 'State liability in the United Kingdom after Brasserie du Pêcheur' (1997) CMLRev 603.
COUNCIL OF EUROPE, *La responsabilité de l'État et des collectivités publiques régionales et locales pour les dommages causés par leurs agents et leurs services administratifs*, Actes du neuvième colloque de droit européen, Université Complutense, Madrid 2–4 October 1979 (Strasbourg, 1980).
COUZINET, J. F., 'La notion de faute lourde administrative', RDP 1977, 283.
COTTERELL, R., *Law's Community: Legal Theory in Sociological Perspective* (Oxford, 1995).
CRAIG, P. P., 'Negligent Misstatements, Negligent Acts and Economic Loss' (1976) LQR 213.
—— 'Representations by Public Bodies' (1977) LQR 398.
—— 'Negligence in the Exercise of a Statutory Power' (1978) LQR 428.
—— 'Compensation in Public Law' (1980) LQR 413.
—— *Public Law and Democracy in the United Kingdom and the United States of America* (Oxford, 1990).
—— 'Legitimate Expectations: A Conceptual Analysis' (1992) LQR 79.
—— 'The Common Law, Reasons and Administrative Justice' (1994) CLJ 282.
—— 'Substantive Legitimate Expectations in Domestic and European Law' (1996) CLJ 289.
—— 'Once More unto the Breach: The Community, the State and Damages Liability' (1997) LQR 67.
—— 'Public Law and Private Power', in M. Taggart (ed.), *The Province of Administrative Law* (Oxford, 1997), 196.
—— 'Formal and Substantive Conceptions of the Rule of Law: An Analytical Framework' (1997) PL 467.
—— '*Ultra Vires* and the Foundations of Judicial Review' (1998) CLJ 63.
—— 'The Domestic Liability of Public Authorities in Damages: Lessons from the European Community?', in J. Beatson and T. Tridimas (eds.), *New Directions in European Public Law* (Oxford, 1998), 75.

CRAIG, P. P., 'Substantive Legitimate Expectations and the Principles of Judicial Review', in M. Andenas (ed.), *English Public Law and the Common Law of Europe* (London, 1998), 23.
—— *Administrative Law*, 4th edn. (London, 1999).
—— 'Competing Models of Judicial Review' (1999) PL 428.
—— 'Unreasonableness and Proportionality in UK Law', in E. Ellis (ed.), *The Principle of Proportionality in the Laws of the EU* (Oxford, 1999), 85.
—— and DE BÚRCA, G., *EU Law: Text and Materials*, 2nd edn. (Oxford, 1998).
—— and FAIRGRIEVE, D., 'Barrett, Negligence and Discretionary Powers' (1999) PL 626.
CRANSTON, R., 'Reviewing Judicial Review', in G. Richardson and H. Genn (eds.), *Administrative Law and Government Action* (Oxford, 1994), 45.
CRAWFORD, C., 'Estoppel in Public Law—the Final Nail in the Coffin?' (1982) MLR 87
—— 'A Public Law Issue?' (1990) MLR 814.
—— and REID, T., 'Planning Officers' Advice and Undertakings: Estoppel and Personal Bar in Public Law' (1982) 3 Scottish Planning Law and Practice Occasional Papers.
CURTIN, D., 'Constitutionalism in the European Community. The Right to Fair Procedures in Administrative Law', in J. O'Reilly (ed.), *Human Rights and Constitutional Law: Essays in Honour of Brian Walsh* (Dublin, 1992), 293.
DE BÚRCA, G., 'The Principle of Proportionality and its Application in Community Law' (1993) YEL 105.
—— 'Proportionality and Wednesbury Unreasonableness' (1997) EPL 561.
DE CRUZ, P., *Comparative Law in a Changing World* (London, 1995).
DEGUERGUE, M., *Jurisprudence et doctrine dans l'élaboration du droit de la responsabilité administrative* (Paris, 1994).
DEHOUSSE, R., 'Comparing National and EC Law: The Problem of the Level of Analysis' (1994) AJCL 761.
DE LAUBADÈRE, A., VENEZIA, J. C., and GAUDEMET, Y., *Traité de droit administratif*, vol. i, 14th edn. (Paris, 1996).
DELVOLVÉ, P., *Le principe de l'égalité devant les charges publiques* (Paris, 1969).
—— 'Le principe de non-rétroactivité dans la jurisprudence économique du Conseil d'État', in *Mélanges Marcel Waline*, vol. ii, (Paris, 1974), 355.
—— 'La notion de directive', AJDA 1974, 461.
—— 'Acte administratif', in F. Gazier and R. Drago (eds.), *Encyclopédie Dalloz: Répertoire de contentieux administratif* (Paris, 1996).
DE SMITH, S. A., LORD WOOLF, JOWELL, J. L., and LE SUEUR, A. P., *Judicial Review of Administrative Action*, 5th edn. (London, 1995), with *1st Supplement* (London, 1998).
DICEY, A. V., *Introduction to the Study of the Law of the Constitution*, 10th edn. (London, 1959).
DI MALTA, M., 'Les renseignements administratifs', D 1964 chron 33, 225
DOTAN, Y., 'Why Administrators should be Bound by their Policies' (1997) OJLS 23.
DOUET, F., *Contribution à l'étude de la sécurité juridique en droit fiscal interne français* (Paris, 1997).
DREWRY, G., 'Public Lawyers and Public Administrators: Prospects for an Alliance?' (1986) Public Administration 173.
—— 'The Ombudsman, Parochial Stopgap or Global Panacea?', in P. Leyland and T. Woods (eds.), *Administrative Law Facing the Future: Old Constraints and New Horizons* (London, 1997), 83.

DUE, O., 'Le respect des droits de la défense dans le droit administratif communautaire', CDE 1987, 383.

DUVAL, C., 'Les justifications de la raison d'être et du maintient de la jurisdiction administrative en France au 19e siècle' (1998) Jahrbuch für europäische Verwaltungsgeschichte 55.

DWORKIN, R. M. *Political Judges and the Rule of Law* (London, 1980).

—— *A Matter of Principle* (Oxford, 1985).

—— *Law's Empire* (London, 1986).

EHRMANN, H. W., *Comparative Legal Cultures* (Englewood Cliffs, 1976).

EHLERMANN, C.-D., and OLDEKOP, D., 'Due Process in Administrative Procedure', in *Reports to 8th F.I.D.E. Congress*, vol. iii (1978), 11.1–11.20.

ELIAS, P., 'Legitimate Expectations and Judicial Review', in J. L. Jowell and D. Oliver (eds.), *New Directions in Judicial Review* (London, 1988).

ELLIS, E., 'The Concept of Proportionality in European Sex Discrimination Law', in E. Ellis (ed.), *The Principle of Proportionality in the Laws of the EU* (Oxford, 1999).

ELVIN, D., 'Misfeasance in Public Office' (1998) JR 26.

EMILIOU, N., *The Principle of Proportionality in European Law* (The Hague, 1996).

ENDICOTT, T. A. O., 'The Impossibility of the Rule of Law' (1999) OJLS 1.

ENGLARD, I., *The Philosophy of Tort Law* (Aldershot, 1993).

ERRERA, R., 'The Scope and Meaning of No-Fault Liability in French Administrative Law' (1986) CLP 157.

EUDE-GUIAS, C., *Juris Classeur Administratif*, Fasc. 107–20 (Paris, 1998).

EVANS, A., *EC Law of State Aid* (Oxford, 1997).

EVANS, J. M., 'Delegation and Estoppel in Administrative Law' (1971) MLR 335.

EVANS, R. C., 'Damages for Unlawful Administrative Action: The Remedy for Misfeasance in Public Office' (1982) ICLQ 640.

EWALD, W., 'The Logic of Legal Transplants' (1995) AJCL 489.

FARRER, 'A Prerogative Fallacy—That the Crown is not Bound by Estoppel' (1933) LQR 511.

FATÔME, E., and LEFONDRÉ, M., *Le Certificat d'urbanisme* (Paris, 1983).

FAZAL, M. A., 'Reliability of Official Acts and Advice' (1972) PL 43.

—— 'Estoppel in English Administrative Law' (1994) Journal of the Indian Law Institute 455

FELDMAN, D., 'Judicial Review: a Way of Controlling Government?' (1988) Public Administration 2.

—— 'Proportionality and the Human Rights Act', in E. Ellis (ed.), *The Principle of Proportionality in the Laws of the EU* (Oxford, 1999), 117.

FENNELLY, N., 'Legal Interpenetration—Towards Freedom of Movement of Principles', in M. Andenas (ed.), *English Public Law and the Common Law of Europe* (London, 1998), 7.

FICKLER-DESPRES, O., 'Les promesses de l'administration', JCP 1998 I no 104.

FINES, F., *Étude de la responsabilité extracontractuelle de la Communauté Économique Européenne* (Paris, 1997).

FINN, P. D., and SMITH, K. J., 'The Citizen, The Government and Reasonable Expectations' (1992) ALJ 139.

FINNIS, J., 'Law as Co-ordination' (1989) Ratio Juris 97.

FLOGAITIS, S., *Administrative law et droit administratif* (Paris, 1986).

FORDHAM, M., 'Anxious Scrutiny' (1996) JR 81.
—— *Judicial Review Handbook*, 2nd edn. (London, 1997).
—— 'Reasons: The Third Dimension' (1998) JR 158.
FORSTHOFF, E., 'Rechtsstaat oder Richterstaat?', in *Rechtsstaat im Wandel: Verfassungsrechtlische Abhandlunger 1954–1973* (Munich, 1976).
FORSYTH, C. F., 'The Provenance and Protection of Legitimate Expectations' (1988) CLJ 238.
—— 'Of Fig Leaves and Fairy Tales: the Ultra Vires Doctrine, the Sovereignty of Parliament and Judicial Review' (1996) CLJ 122.
—— 'Wednesbury Protection of Substantive Legitimate Expectations' (1997) PL 375.
FOSTER, S., 'Legitimate Expectations and Prisoners' Rights' (1997) MLR 727.
FOULKES, D., *Administrative Law*, 8th edn. (London, 1995).
FRANCE, S., 'Legitimate Expectations in New Zealand' (1990) NZULR 123.
FRIDMANN, G. H. L., 'Malice in the Law of Torts' (1958) MLR 484.
FROMONT, M., Note CE 24/4–64, *Société des huileries de Chauny*, D 1964, 579.
—— 'Le principe de sécurité juridique', AJDA 1996 Ed. spéciale, 178.
FULLER, L. L., *The Morality of Law*, Rev. edn. (New Haven, 1969).
—— 'The Forms and Limits of Adjudication' (1978) Harvard LR 353.
GALLIGAN, D. J., 'The Nature and Function of Policies Within Discretionary Power' (1976) PL 332.
—— 'Judicial Review and the Textbook Writers' (1982) OJLS 257.
—— *Discretionary Powers: A Legal Study of Official Discretion* (Oxford, 1986) (reprinted with corrections 1990).
—— *Due Process and Fair Procedures: A Study of Administrative Procedures* (Oxford, 1996).
GANZ, G., 'The Limits of Judicial Control over the Exercise of Discretion' (1964) PL 367
—— 'Estoppel and *Res Iudicata* in Administrative Law' (1965) PL 237.
—— 'Legitimate Expectation', in C. Harlow (ed.), *Public Law and Politics* (London, 1986), 145.
—— *Quasi Legislation: Recent Developments in Secondary Legislation* (London, 1987).
GAUDEMET, Y., 'Remarques à propos des circulaires administratives', in *Mélanges Stassinopoulos* (Paris, 1974).
GAZIER, F., and DRAGO, R. (eds.), *Encyclopédie Dalloz: Répertoire de la responsibilaté de la puissance publique* (Paris, 1996).
GENEVOIS, B., 'Principes géneraux du droit', in F. Gazier, R. Drago and A. Dupie (eds.), *Encyclopédie Dalloz: Répertoire de contentieux administratif* (Paris, 1996).
GERAPETRITIS, G., *Proportionality in Administrative Law: Judicial Review in France, Greece, England and in the European Community* (Athens, 1997).
GESSNER, V., Hoeland, A., and Varga, C. (eds.), *European Legal Cultures* (Aldershot, 1996)
GEUTTIER, C., *La responsabilité administrative* (Paris, 1996).
GIDDENS, A., *The Third Way,* (Cambridge, 1998).
—— 'Reith Lectures 1999', available at http: //www.bbc.co.uk/reith99.
GIDDINGS, P., 'The Parliamentary Ombudsman: A Successful Alternative?', in D. Oliver and G. Drewry (eds.), *The Law and Parliament* (London, 1999), 125.
GIRARDOT, T.-X., and RAYNAUD, F., 'Chronique génerale de jurisprudence administrative française', AJDA 1997, 936, AJDA 1998 pp. 97, 553.

GILTARD, D., *Juris Classeur Procedures Fiscale*, Fasc. 170–4 (Paris, 1994).
GLIDEWELL, I., 'Immigration Law and Practice in the United Kingdom', in *Bridging the Channel: The Clifford Chance Lectures*, vol. i (Oxford, 1996), 193.
GOODE, R., 'International Restatements of Contract and English Contract Law' (1997) Uniform LR 231.
GOODHART, C. E., 'Economics and the Law: Too Much One-Way Traffic?' (1997) MLR 1.
GOODIN, R. E., 'Welfare, Rights and Discretion' (1986) OJLS 231.
GOODNOW, F. J., *Comparative Administrative Law* (New York, 1893).
GORDON, R. J. F., *Judicial Review: Law and Procedure*, 2nd edn. (London, 1996).
—— and WARD, T., 'The Billowing Fog' (1996) NLJ 1663.
GÖTZ, V., 'Protection of Legitimate Expectations', in *German Reports on Public Law, Presented to the XV International Congress of Comparative Law* (University of Bristol, July 1998).
GOULD, B. C., 'Damages as a Remedy in Administrative Law' (1972) NZULR 105.
GREEN, L., *The Authority of the State* (Oxford, 1990).
GREEN, N., 'Proportionality and the Supremacy of Parliament in the UK', in E. Ellis (ed.), *The Principle of Proportionality in the laws of the EU* (Oxford, 1999).
GRIFFITH, J. A. G., 'Judicial Decision Making in Public Law' (1985) PL 564.
—— *The Politics of the Judiciary*, 5th edn. (London, 1997).
GROSSFELD, B., *The Strength and Weakness Of Comparative Law* (Oxford, 1990).
HABERMAS, J., *The Theory of Communicative Action* (Boston, 1984).
—— *Between Facts and Norms* (Cambridge, 1996).
HADFIELD, B., 'Judge-proofing Reviewable Decisions—Should Judges be Entrusted with Review?', in B. Hadfield (ed.), *Judicial Review: A Thematic Approach* (Dublin, 1995), 257.
HADJIEMMANUIL, C., 'Civil Liability of Regulatory Authorities after the *Three Rivers* Case' (1997) PL 32.
HALLIDAY, S., 'The Influence of Judicial Review on Bureaucratic Decision-Making' (2000) PL 110.
HAMMOND, A. H., 'Judicial Review: The Continuing Interplay between Law and Policy' (1998) PL 34.
HAMSON, C. J., *Executive Discretion and Judicial Control: An Aspect of the French Conseil d'État*, The Hamlyn Lectures (London, 1954).
HANDLER, J. F., *The Conditions of Discretion: Autonomy, Community, Bureaucracy* (New York, 1986).
—— 'Discretion: Power, Quiescence, and Trust', in K. Hawkins (ed.), *The Uses of Discretion* (Oxford, 1992), 331.
HARDEN, I., and LEWIS, N., *The Noble Lie: The British Constitution and the Rule of Law* (London, 1986).
HARLOW, C., 'Fault Liability in French and English Law' (1976) MLR 516.
—— 'Administrative Reaction to Judicial Review' (1976) PL 116.
—— 'Remedies in French Law' (1977) PL 227.
—— 'Administrative Liability: A Comparative Study of French and English Law', PhD thesis (London School of Economics, 1979).
—— '"Public" and "Private Law": Definition Without Distinction' (1980) MLR 241.
—— *Compensation and Government Torts* (London, 1982).

HARLOW, C., *Understanding Tort Law*, 2nd edn. (London, 1995).
—— 'Why Public Law is Private Law: An Invitation to Lord Woolf', in A. A. S. Zuckerman and R. Cranston (eds.), *Reform of Civil Procedure: Essays on 'Access to Justice'* (Oxford, 1995), 201.
—— 'A Special Relationship?', in I. Loveland (ed.), *A Special Relationship? American Influences on Public Law in the UK* (Oxford, 1995).
—— 'State Liability: Problem Without Solution' (1995–6) NJCL 67.
—— 'Francovich and the Problem of the Disobedient State' (1996) ELJ 199.
—— 'Back to Basics: Reinventing Administrative Law' (1997) PL 245.
—— 'Droit Privé—*English Style*' (1997) OJLS 517.
—— 'European Administrative Law and the Global Challenge', in P. Craig and G. De Búrca (eds.), *The Evolution of EU Law* (Oxford, 1999).
—— and RAWLINGS, R., *Pressure Through Law* (London, 1992).
—— *Law and Administration*, 2nd edn. (London, 1997).
HARTLEY, T., *The Foundations of European Community Law*, 4th edn. (Oxford, 1998).
HAWKINS, K., 'The Use of Legal Discretion: Perspectives From Law and Social Science', in K. Hawkins (ed.), *The Uses of Discretion* (Oxford, 1992), 11.
HEERS, M., 'La sécurité juridique en droit administratif français: Vers un consécration du principe de confiance légitime?', RFDA 1995, 963.
HELIN, J.-C., and HOSTIOU, R., *Droit des enquêtes publiques* (Paris, 1993).
HEPPLE, B., 'The Search for Coherence' (1997) CLP 67.
HÉRON, J., *Principes du droit transitoire* (Paris, 1996).
HEUSTON, R. F. V., and BUCKLEY, R. A., *Salmond and Heuston on the Law of Torts*, 21st edn. (London, 1996).
HEY, J., *Uncertainty in Microeconomics* (Oxford, 1979).
HILL, J., 'Comparative Law, Law Reform and Legal Theory' (1989) OJLS 101.
HIMSWORTH, C., 'Legitimately Expecting Proportionality?' (1996) PL 46.
HINDS, W., 'Third Party Objections to Planning Applications: An Expectation of Fairness?' (1988) JPL 742.
—— 'Estopping the Taxman' (1991) BTR 191.
HOFFMANN, LORD, 'A Sense of Proportion', John Maurice Kelly Memorial Lecture, Published by the faculty of Law, University College Dublin 1997.
—— 'Human Rights and the House of Lords' (1999) MLR 159.
HONORÉ, A. M., 'Causation and Remoteness of Damage', *International Encyclopaedia of Comparative Law*, vol. xi, ch. 7 (New York, 1971).
HOPPER, M., 'Financial Services Regulation and Judicial Review', in J. Black, P. Muchlinski and P. Walker (eds.), *Commercial Regulation and Judicial Review* (Oxford, 1998).
HOSKINS, E., 'Snakebite and Estoppel' (1987) VAT Intelligence 407.
HOSTIOU, R., *Procédures et formes de l'acte administratif uniltéral en droit français* (Paris, 1974).
HOWARTH, D., 'My Brother's Keeper? Liability for Acts of Third Parties' (1994) Legal Studies 88.
HUBEAU, F., 'Le principe de la protection de la confiance légitime dans la jurisprudence de la Cour de Justice des Communautés Européennes', CDE 1983, 143.
HUNT, M., *Using Human Rights Law in English Courts* (Oxford, 1997)

HUTCHINSON, A., 'The Rise and Ruse of Administrative Law and Scholarship' (1985) MLR 293.

IRVINE OF LAIRG, LORD, 'Judges and Decision-Makers: The Theory and Practice of *Wednesbury* Review' (1996) PL 59.

—— 'The Development of Human Rights in Britain under an Incorporated Convention on Human Rights' (1998) PL 221.

ISRAEL, J.-J., *La régularisation en droit administratif français* (Paris, 1981).

JACKSON, P., 'Legitimate Expectations and Good Administration' (1983) LQR 499.

JACOBINI, H. B., *An Introduction to Comparative Administrative Law* (New York, 1991).

JACOBS, F. G. 'The Principle of Legality—Towards a European Standard?', in G. Hand and J. McBride (eds.), *Droit sans frontières: Essays in Honour of L. Neville Brown* (Birmingham, 1991), 277.

—— 'Public Law—The Impact of Europe' (1999) PL 232.

—— 'Recent Developments in the Principle of Proportionality in EC Law', in E. Ellis (ed.), *The Principle of Proportionality in the Laws of the EU* (Oxford, 1999).

JAMES, S., 'The Political and Administrative Consequences of Judicial Review' (1996) Public Administration 613.

JANSEN, N., 'The Idea of a Lost Chance' (1999) OJLS 271.

JÈZE, G., 'Du retrait des actes juridiques', RDP 1913, 225.

—— 'Essai d'une théorie générale des fonctionnaires de fait', RDP 1914, 48.

JOLOWICZ, J. A., and ROGERS, W. H. V., *Winfield and Rogers on Tort*, 15th edn. (London, 1998).

JOUVE, V., 'Recherches sur la notion d'apperance en droit administratif français', RDP 1968, 283.

JOWELL, J. L., 'The Rule of Law Today', in J. L. Jowell and L. Oliver (eds.), *The Changing Constitution*, 3rd edn. (London, 1994), 57.

—— 'Is Proportionality an Alien Concept?' (1996) EPL 401, 410.

—— 'Politics, Principle, and Judicial Review' (1997) CLP 189.

—— and LESTER, A., 'Beyond Wednesbury, Substantive Principles and Administrative Law' (1987) PL 368.

—— —— 'Proportionality: Neither Novel nor Dangerous', in J. L. Jowell and D. Oliver (eds.), *New Directions in Judicial Review* (London, 1988).

JUSTICE—All Souls Review Committee, *Administrative Justice: Some Necessary Reforms* (Oxford, 1988).

KAHN-FREUND, Sir O., 'On the Uses and Misuses of Comparative Law' (1974) MLR 1.

KAMBA, W. J., 'Comparative Law: A Theoretical Framework' (1974) ICLQ 485.

KERR, M., 'Administrative Law and the Administrator' (1983) Management in Government 168.

KERRY, M., 'Administrative Law and Judicial Review' (1986) Public Administration 163.

KLABBERS, J., 'Informal Instruments before the European Court of Justice' (1994) CML-Rev 997.

KLUG, F., and STARMER, F., 'Incorporation through the Back Door?' (1997) PL 223.

KOOPMANS, T., 'European Public Law: Reality and Prospects' (1991) PL 53.

—— 'Judicial Activism and Procedural Law' (1993) European Review of Private Law 67.

KORAH, V., 'The Rights of Defence in Administrative Proceedings Under Community Law' (1980) CLP 73.

KRITZER, H. M., 'Courts, Justice and Politics in England', in H. Jacob (ed.), *Courts, Law, and Politics in Comparative Perspective* (New Haven, 1996), 81.

LABETOULLE, D., 'Principe de légalité et principe de sécurité', in *Mélanges Guy Braibant* (Paris, 1996), 403.

LACEY, N., 'The Jurisprudence of Discretion: Escaping the Legal Paradigm', in K. Hawkins (ed.), *The Uses of Discretion* (Oxford, 1992).

LANG, J. Temple, 'Legal Certainty and Legitimate Expectations as General Principles of Law', Paper presented at the Conference on General Principles of Community Law (Malmö 27–28 Aug. 1999).

LANGROD, G. (ed.), *La consultation dans l'administration contemporaine* (Paris, 1972).

LANZA, A., 'Le certificat d'urbanisme', AJDA 1984, 294.

LASOK, D., *The European Court of Justice: Practice and Procedure*, 2nd edn. (London, 1994).

LATOURNERIE, M.-A., 'The Law of France', in J. S. Bell and A. W. Bradley (eds.), *Governmental Liability: A Comparative Study*, UKCLS vol. 13 (London, 1991), 198.

LAUWAARS, R. W., *Lawfulness and Legal Force of Community Decisions* (Leiden, 1973).

LAWS, Sir J., 'Judicial Remedies and the Constitution' (1994) MLR 213.

—— 'Law and Democracy' (1995) PL 72.

—— 'The Constitution: Morals and Rights' (1996) PL 622.

—— 'Wednesbury', in C. Forsyth and I. Hare (eds.), *The Golden Metwand and the Crooked Cord: Essays in Honour of Sir William Wade* (Oxford, 1998), 185.

LAWSON, F. H., and MARKESINIS, B. S., *Tortious Liability for Unintentional Harm in the Common Law and the Civil Law*, vols. i–ii (Cambridge, 1982).

LE CHATELIER, G., 'Les Incidences du droit communautaire sur le droit du contentieux administratif', AJDA 1996 Ed. spéciale, 97.

LEDOUX, L. 'Essai d'une théorie sur la fonction de fait', Revue générale d'administration 1912 II 397, III 22.

LEFONDRE, M., 'Le retrait des aides financières publiques aux enterprises privées' (1993) Révue Administratif 131.

LEGRAND, P., 'European Legal Systems are not Converging' (1996) ICLQ 52.

—— The Impossibility of 'Legal Transplants' (1997) MJ 111.

LEMASURIER, J., 'Vers une démocratie administrative: du refus d'informer au droit d'être informé', RDP 1980, 1239.

LE MIRE, P., 'La stabilité des situations juridiques', AJDA 1980, 203.

LENAERTS, K., and VANHAMME, J., 'Procedural Right of Private Parties in the Community Administrative Process' (1997) CMLRev 531.

LESTER, A., 'Government Compliance with International Human Rights Law: A New Year's Legitimate Expectation' (1996) PL 187.

LE SUEUR, A. P., 'Justifying Judicial Caution: Jurisdiction, Justiciability and Policy', in B. Hadfield (ed.), *Judicial Review: A Thematic Approach* (Dublin, 1995), 228

—— 'Legal Duties to Give Reasons' (1999) CLP 150, 161–6.

LETEMENDIA, M., *Retrait et abrogation des actes administratifs individuels en droit communautaire et droit anglais* (Brussels, 1987).

LÉVY, D., *La responsabilité de la puissance publique et de ses agents en Angleterre* (Paris, 1957).

LEWIS, C., 'Fairness, Legitimate Expectations and Estoppel' (1986) MLR 251.

—— 'Damages and the Right to an Effective Remedy for Breach of European Community

Law', in C. Forsyth and I. Hare (eds.), *The Golden Metwand and the Crooked Cord: Essays in Honour of Sir William Wade* (Oxford, 1998), 319.

LINDBLOM, C., 'The Science of Muddling Through' (1959) Public Administration Review 79.

LOCHAK, 'Réflexion sur les fonctions sociales de la responsabilité administrative', in J. Chevallier (ed.), *Le droit administratif en mutation* (Paris, 1993).

LOMBARD, M., 'Recherches sur le rôle de la bonne et mauvaise foi en droit administratif français', Doctoral thesis (Univerity of Strasbourg III, 1978).

LONG, M., WEIL, P., BRAIBANT, G., DELVOLVÉ, P., and GENEVOIS, B., *Les grands arrêts de la jurisprudence administrative*, 10th edn. (Paris, 1993).

LOUGHLIN, M. 'Procedural Fairness: A Study of the Crisis in Administrative Law' (1978) Univ. Toronto LJ 215.

—— 'Innovation Financing in Local Government: The Limits of Legal Instrumentalism—Part 2' (1991) PL 568.

—— *Public Law and Political Theory* (Oxford, 1992).

—— *Legality and Locality: the Role of Law in Central-Local Government Relations* (Oxford, 1996).

LOVELAND, I., *Housing Homeless Persons* (Oxford, 1995).

LUCAS, J. R., *The Principles of Politics* (Oxford, 1966).

LUHMANN, N., *A Sociological Theory of Law* (London, 1985).

MCBRIDE, J., 'Damages as a Remedy for Unlawful Administrative Action' (1979) CLJ 323.

MACCORMICK, N., 'Voluntary Obligations and Normative Powers' (1972) Proceedings of the Aristotelian Society, Supplement 46, 59.

MACKIE, K., 'Expectations and Natural Justice' (1985) ALJ 33.

MCLEOD, I., 'Local Authorities, Estoppel and the Ombudsman' (1989) LGR 505.

MACPHERSON, P. A., 'The Legitimate Expectation Doctrine and Its Application to Administrative Policy' (1995–6) Canadian Journal of Administrative Law and Practice 141.

MARCH, J. G., SIMON, H. A., and GUETZKOW, H., *Organisations*, 2nd edn. (London, 1993).

MARIANI-BENIGNI, I., 'L'"exception de risque accepté" dans le contentieux administratif de la responsabilité', RDP 1997, 841.

MARKESINIS, B. S., *Foreign Law and Comparative Methodology* (Oxford, 1997).

—— and DEAKIN, S. F., *Tort Law*, 4th edn. (Oxford, 1999).

—— AUBY, J.-B., COESTER-WALTJEN, D. C., and DEAKIN, S. F., *Tortious Liability of Statutory Bodies: A Comparative and Economic Analysis of Five English Cases* (Oxford, 1999).

MARKUS, K., and WESTGATE, M., '*Unilever* and *Hargreaves*: A Cross-Analysis' (1997) JR 220.

—— 'The Duty to Follow Guidance' (1997) Judicial Review 154.

MARSH, D., and RHODES, R. A. W., *Policy Networks in British Government* (Oxford, 1992).

MAS-COLELL, A., WHINSTON, M. D., and GREEN, J. R., *Microeconomic Theory* (Oxford, 1995).

MASHAW, J. L., *Due Process in the Administrative State* (New Haven, 1985).

MASON, A., 'Negligence and the Liability of Public Authorities' (1998) Edinburgh LR 3.

MASSOT, J., and MARIMBERT, J., *Le Conseil d'État* (Paris, 1988).

MAURER, H., *Droit administratif allemand*, tr. M. Fromont (Paris, 1995).
MAURICI, J., 'The Meaning of Policy: A Question for the Court?' (1998) JR 85.
MEGARRY, R. E., 'Administrative Quasi-legislation' (1944) LQR 125.
—— Note on *Re 56 Denton Road, Twickenham, Middlesex* [1952] 2 ALL ER 799 (1953) LQR 13.
MEREDITH, P., 'Legitimate Expectation and School Closures' (1988) PL 4.
MERRYMAN, J. H., 'The French Deviation' (1997) AJCL 109.
MESTRE, J., *Introduction historique au droit administratif français* (Paris, 1985).
MILL, J. S., *On Liberty*, 1859 (reprinted by The Everyman Library, London 1993).
MITCHELL, J. D. B., *Contracts of Public Authorities* (London, 1954).
—— 'The Causes and Effects of the Absence of a System of Public Law in the United Kingdom' (1965) PL 95.
MONTI, G., '*Osman* v. *UK*—Transforming English Negligence Law into French Administrative Law?' (1999) ICLQ 757.
MOREAU, J., *L'influence de la situation et du comportement de la victime sur la responsabilité administrative* (Paris, 1957).
—— 'L'influence du développement de la construction européenne sur le droit français de la responsabilité de la puissance publique', in *Mélanges J. Boulouis* (Paris, 1991).
—— 'Les conséquences des illégalités procédurales en droit administratif français' (1993) ERPL special edn. 85.
MORRELL, J., and FOSTER, R., *Local Authority Liability* (Bristol, 1998).
MOSLER, H. (ed.), *Liability of the State for Illegal Conduct of its Organs*, Heidelberg Colloquium, Max Planck Institut 1964, (Cologne, 1967).
MOUSTAKAS, M. M., 'La confiance de l'administré et son influence sur le régime juridique des actes administratifs unilateraux', Doctoral thesis (Paris II, 1993).
MOWBRAY, A. R., 'Administrative Guidance and Judicial Review' (1985) PL 558.
—— 'Legitimate Expectations and Departmental Representations' (1990) LQR 568.
—— 'A Right to Official Advice: The Parliamentary Commissioner's Perspective' (1990) PL 68.
MULLENDER, R., 'Negligent Misstatement, Threats, and the Scope of the *Hedley Byrne* Principle' (1999) MLR 425.
MUZELLEC, R., 'Le principe d'intangbilité des actes administratifs individuels en droit administratif français', Doctoral thesis (Rennes, 1971).
NAÔMÉ, C., 'La notion de sécurité juridique dans la jurisprudence de la Cour de Justice et du Tribunal de Première Instance des Communautés Européennes', RDPE 1993, 223.
NAUWELAERS, M., and FABIUS, L., 'Chronique générale de jurisprudence administrative française', AJDA 1976, 557.
NEHL, H. P., *Principles of Administrative Procedure in EC Law* (Oxford, 1999).
NEIL, P. , 'The Duty to Give Reasons', in C. Forsyth and I. Hare (eds.), *The Golden Metwand and the Crooked Cord: Essays in Honour of Sir William Wade* (Oxford, 1968).
'Never Trust a Bureaucrat, Estoppel Against the Government', unsigned casenote (1969) Southern California LR 391.
NEWMAN, F. C., 'Should Official Advice Be Reliable? Proposals as to Estoppel and Related Doctrines in Administrative Law' (1953) Columbia LR 374.
NÖCKER, T., and FRENCH, G., 'Estoppel: What's the Government's Word Worth? An Analysis of German Law, Common Law Jurisdictions, and of the Practice of International Arbitral Tribunals' (1990) The International Lawyer 409.

NOLTE, G., 'General Principles of German and European Administrative Law—A Comparison in a Historical Perspective' (1994) MLR 191.

NOTT, S. M., and MORGAN, P. H., 'The Significance of Department of the Environment Circulars in the Planning Process' (1984) Journal of Planning and Environmental Law 624.

ODENT, R., 'Les droits de la défense', EDCE 1953, 55.

—— 'De la décision Trompier-Gravier à la décision Garysas', EDCE 1962, 43.

OLIVER, D., 'Is the *Ultra Vires* Rule the Basis of Judicial Review?' (1987) PL 543.

—— 'Underlying Values of Public and Private Law', in M. Taggart (ed.), *The Province of Administrative Law* (Oxford, 1997), 217.

O'TOOLE, B., 'Treating Networks Seriously' (1997) Public Administration 45.

PACTEAU, B., *Excès de pouvoir et motifs de l'acte administratif* (Paris, 1977).

—— 'La sécurité juridique, un principe qui nous manque?', AJDA 1995 Ed. spéciale, 131.

PAGONE, R., 'Estoppel in Public Law: Theory, Fact and Fiction' (1984) UNSWLJ 267.

PAILLET, M., *La responsabilité administrative* (Paris, 1996).

PANNICK, D., 'The Law Lords and the Needs of Contemporary Society' (1982) Political Quarterly 318.

PAPADOPOULOU, R.-C., *Principes généraux du droit et droit Communautaire* (Brussels, 1996).

PAVLOPOULOS, C., *La directive en droit administratif* (Paris, 1978).

PAYRE, J. P., 'Faute et fait de la victime dans le contentieux de la responsabilité administrative extra-contractuelle', AJDA 1980, 398.

PEIRIS, G. L., 'Wednesbury Unreasonableness: The Expanding Canvas' (1987) CLJ 53.

PÉLISSIER, G., *Le principe d'égalité en droit public* (Paris, 1996).

PESCATORE, P., 'Les principes généraux du droit en tant que source du droit communautaire', in *Reports to 12th F. I. D. E. Congress* 1986, 17.

PETIT, J., 'Contribtion à l'étude des conflits de lois dans le temps en droit public interne', Doctoral thesis (Paris II, 1993).

PEYRICAL, J.-M., 'Le juge administratif et la sauvegarde des actes de l'administration', AJDA 1996, 22.

PICARD, E., *La notion de police administrative* (Paris, 1984).

PICKARD, R. D., 'The Doctrine of Estoppel Within Development Control', Ph.D., thesis (Newcastle upon Tyne Polytechnic, 1990).

PLANCHON, M.-H., 'Le principe de la confiance légitime devant la Cour de Justice des Communatés Européennes', Revue de la Recherche Juridique—Droit Prospectif 1994, 447.

POOLE, M., 'Legitimate Expectations and Substantive Fairness: Beyond the Limits of Procedural Propriety' (1995) NZLR 426.

POSNER, R. A., *Economic Analysis of Law*, 4th edn. (Boston, 1992).

POSTEMA, G. J., 'Coordination and Convention at the Foundations of Law' (1982) Journal of Legal Studies 165.

PROSSER, T., 'Poverty, Ideology and Legality' (1977) BJLS 39.

—— 'Regulation, Markets and Legitimacy', in J. L. Jowell and L. Oliver (eds.), *The Changing Constitution*, 3rd edn. (London, 1994).

PROVINE, D. M. 'Courts in the Political Process in France', in H. Jacob (ed.), *Courts, Law, and Politics in Comparative Perspective* (New Haven, 1996), 177.

PUISSOCHET, J.-P., '"Vous avez dit confiance légitime?"', in *Mélanges Guy Braibant* (Paris, 1996), 581.

PURDUE, M., 'The Scope for Fact-Finding in Judicial Review', in G. Hand and J. McBride (eds.), *Droit sans frontières: Essays in Honour of L. Neville Brown* (Birmingham, 1991), 193.

RADFORD, M., 'Mitigating the Democratic Deficit? Judicial Review and Ministerial Accountability', in P. Leyland and T. Woods (eds.), *Administrative Law Facing the Future: Old Constants and New Horizons* (London, 1997).

RAGNEMALM, H., 'Confiance légitime et délai raisonnable', in G. C. Rodríguez Iglesias, O. Due, R. Schintgen and C. Elsen (eds.), *Mélanges en hommage à Fernand Schockweiler* (Baden-Baden, 1999), 511.

RASMUSSEN, H., *On Law and Policy in the European Court of Justice* (The Hague, 1986).

RAWLINGS, R., 'Courts and Interests', in I. Loveland (ed.), *A Special Relationship? American Influences on Public Law in the UK* (Oxford, 1995).

RAWLS, J., *A Theory of Justice* (Cambridge, Massachusetts, 1971).

RAYNAUD, F., and FOMBEUR, P., 'Chronique générale de jurisprudence administrative', AJDA 1998, 403.

RAZ, J., 'Voluntary Obligations and Normative Powers' (1972) Proceedings of the Aristotelian Society, Supplement 46, 79.

—— 'The Rule of Law and its Virtue' (1977) LQR 195.

—— *The Authority of Law* (Oxford, 1979).

—— *The Morality of Freedom* (Oxford, 1986).

—— The Politics of the Rule of Law (1990) Ratio Juris 331.

—— *Ethics in the Public Domain* (Oxford, 1994).

RAYNAUD, J., *La Cour des Comptes* (Paris, 1980).

RICHARDSON, G., 'The Duty to Give Reasons: Potential and Practice' (1986) PL 437.

—— 'The Legal Regulation of Process', in G. Richardson and H. Genn (eds.), *Administrative Law and Government Action* (Oxford, 1994).

—— and SUNKIN, M., 'Judicial Review: Questions of Impact' (1996) PL 79.

RICHER, L., *La faute du service public dans la jurisprudence du Conseil d'État* (Paris, 1978).

RIGGS, R. E., 'Legitimate Expectations and Procedural Fairness in English Law' (1988) AJCL 395.

ROSENBERG, D., 'The Causal Connection in Mass Expose Cases: A Public Law Vision of the Tort System' (1984) Harvard LR 851.

ROSS, M., 'Behind Proportionality: The Cultural and Constitutional Context', in M. Adenas (ed.), *English Public Law and the Common Law of Europe* (London, 1998).

ROY, C., *La théorie de l'expectative légitime en droit administratif* (Cowansville, 1993).

RUBINSTEIN, A., *Jurisdiction and Illegality* (Oxford, 1965).

SALLET, F., *La perte de chance dans la jurisprudence administrative relative à la responsabilité de la puissance publique* (Paris, 1994).

SAMUEL, G., 'Comparative Law and Jurisprudence' (1998) ICLQ 817.

SANDERS, A., and YOUNG, R., *Criminal Justice*, 2nd edn. (London, 1998).

SANDLER, D., 'The Revenue Giveth—the Revenue Taketh Away' (1994) CLJ 273.

SCHERMERS, H. G., HEUKELS, T., and MEAD, P. (eds.), *Non-Contractual Liability of the European Communities* (The Hague, 1988).

—— and WAELBROECK, D., *Judicial Protection in the EC*, 5th edn. (Deventer, 1992).

SCHOCKWEILER, F., WIVÉNES C., and GODART, J.-M., 'Le régime de la responsabilité extra-contractuelle du fait d'actes juridiques dans la Communauté européenne', RTDE 1990, 27.

SCHWARZE, J., *European Administrative Law* (London, 1992).

—— *Administrative Law under European Influence* (Baden-Baden, 1996).

SCHWEHR, B., 'A Study in Fairness in the Field of Community Care' (1997) Journal of Social Welfare and Family Law 159, 247.

—— and BROWN, P., 'Legitimate Expectations—Snuffed Out?' (1991) PL 163.

SCOTT, C., 'The Jurifidication of Regulatory Relation in the UK Utilities Sector', in J. Black, P. Muchlinski and P. Walker (eds.), *Commercial Regulation and Judicial Review* (Oxford, 1998).

SHARPSTON, E., 'Legitimate Expectations and Economic Reality' (1990) ELR 103.

SINGH, R., 'Making Legitimate Use of Legitimate Expectations' (1994) NLJ 1215.

—— and STEYN, K., 'Legitimate Expectations in 1996: Where Now' (1996) JR 17.

—— —— 'Legitimate Expectation Update 1997' (1997) JR 33.

SLAPPER, G., 'Modernising Justice' (1999) SLR 31.

SLYNN, G., '"But in England There is No . . ."', in *Festschrift für Wolfgang Zeidler*, vol. i (Berlin, 1987), 397.

SMITH, K. J., 'The Developing Doctrine of Legitimate or Reasonable Expectations in the Public and Private Law of England and Australia', Ph.D. thesis (University of Cambridge, 1994).

SPENCE, M. J., *Protecting Reliance: The Emergent Doctrine of Equitable Estoppel* (Oxford, 1999).

STANTON, K., *Breach of Statutory Duty in Tort* (London, 1986).

—— 'Incremental Approaches to the Duty of Care', in N. J. Mullan (ed.), *Torts in the Nineties* (North Ryde, Australia, 1997), 34.

STAPLETON, J., 'Duty of Care and Economic Loss, A Wider Agenda' (1991) LQR 249.

—— 'The Condition of the Law of Tort', in P. Birks (ed.),*The Frontiers of Liability* (Oxford, 1994).

—— 'Duty of Care, Peripheral Parties and Alternative Opportunities for Deterrence' (1995) LQR 301.

STEVENS, D., 'The "Comfort Letter": Old Problems, New Developments' (1994) ECLR 81.

STEYN, K., 'Consistency—A Principle of Public Law?' (1997) JR 22.

STEYN, LORD, 'The Weakest and Least Dangerous Department of Government' (1997) PL 84.

STREET, H., *Governmental Liability: A Comparative Study* (Cambridge, 1953).

STREIT, M. E., 'Economic Order, Private Law and Public Policy' (1992) Journal of Institutional and Theoretical Economics 675.

STUART, LORD MACKENZIE, 'Legitimate Expectations and Estoppel in Community Law and English Administrative Law' (1983) LIEI 53.

—— 'Recent Developments in English Administrative Law—The Impact of Europe?', in F. Capotorti *et al.* (eds.), *Liber Amicorum Pierre Pescatore* (Baden-Baden, 1987).

SUMMERS, R. S., 'A Formal Theory of the Rule of Law' (1993) Ratio Juris 127.

TAGOURDEAU, J.-P., 'Le caractère certain et direct du préjudice en matière de responsabilité extra-contractuelle de la puissance administrative', AJDA 1974, 508.

TALLINEAU, L., 'Les actes particuliers non créateurs de droit', Doctoral thesis (Poitiers, 1972).

—— 'Les tolérances administratives', AJDA 1978, 3.

TAVERNIER, P, 'Le juge Communautaire et l'application dans le temp des règlements CEE', AFDI 1976, 169.

TEBOUL, G., *Usages et coutume dans la jurisprudence administrative* (Paris, 1989).

TEUBNER, G., 'Legal Irritants: Good Faith in British Law or How Unifying Law Ends Up in New Divergences' (1998) MLR 11.

TOTH, A. G., *The Oxford Encyclopaedia of European Community Law*, vol. i (Oxford 1990).

—— 'The Concepts of Damage and Causality as Elements of Non-Contractual Liability', in T. Heukels and A. McDonnell (eds.), *The Action for Damages in Community Law* (The Hague, 1997).

TOUBE, D., 'Requiring Reasons at Common Law' (1997) JR 68.

TOUCHARD, J. F., 'A propos de la responsabilté pour faute de l'administration fiscale', RDP 1992, 785.

TREITEL, G., 'Crown Proceedings: Some Recent Developments' (1957) PL 321.

TRIDIMAS, T., *The General Principles of EC Law* (Oxford, 1999).

TROPER, M., 'Le concept d'État de droit', in M. Troper (ed.), *L'État de droit* (Caen, 1993).

UNGER, R. M., *Law in Modern Society* (New York, 1976).

USHER, J., 'The Influence of National Concepts on Decisions of the European Court' (1976) ELR 359.

—— 'Tide or Flood?—The influence of Concept of European Community Law in English Law', in G. Hand and J. McBride (eds.), *Droit sans frontières: Essays in Honour of L. Neville Brown* (Birmingham, 1991), 277.

—— *General Principles of EC Law* (Harlow, 1998).

VAJDA, C., 'Some Aspects of Judicial Review within the Common Agricultural Policy' (1979) ELR 244, 341.

VAN GERVEN, W., 'Mutual Permeation of Public and Private Law at the National and Supranational Level' (1998) MJ 7.

VAN HOECKE, M., and WARRINGTON, M., 'Legal Cultures and Legal Paradigms: a New Model for Comparative Law' (1998) ICLQ 495.

VEDEL, G., and DELVOLVÉ, P., *Droit administratif*, 12th edn. (Paris, 1992).

VELJANOVSKI, C. G., 'The New Law-and-Economics: A Research Review', in A. I. Ogus and C. G. Veljanovski, *Readings in the Economics of Law and Regulation* (Oxford, 1984), 12.

VIALLE, P., 'Lien de causalité et dommage direct dans la responsabilité administrative', RDP 1974, 1243.

VINCENT, J.-Y., 'Le retrait des actes administratifs unilatéraux', RTDE 1974, 31.

VINCENT, P. , 'Chronique de jurisprudence', AJDA 1999.

VINEY, G., 'Modération et limitation des résponsabilité et des indemnisations', in J. Spier (ed.), *The Limit of Liability: Keeping the Floodgates Shut* (The Hague, 1996), 127.

VLACHOS, G., *Les principes généraux du droit administratif* (Paris, 1993).

WADE, H. W. R., 'The Concept of Legal Certainty. A Preliminary Skirmish' (1940–1) MLR 183.

—— 'Law, Opinion and Administration' (1962) LQR 188.

—— 'Public Law, Private Law and Judicial Review' (1983) LQR 166.
—— and FORSYTH, C. F., *Administrative Law*, 7th edn. (Oxford, 1994).
WALDRON, J., 'The Rule of Law in Contemporary Liberal Theory' (1989) Ratio Juris 79.
—— 'Vagueness in Law and Language: Some Philosophical Issues' (1994) California LR 509.
WALINE, M., '*Audi Alterem Partem*', in *Livre Jubilaire du Conseil d'État du Grand-Duché de Luxembourg* (Luxembourg, 1957), 495.
—— Note CE 24/4–64, *Société des huileries de Chauny*, RDP 1964, 799.
WALKER, P., 'What's Wrong With Irrationality?' (1995) PL 556.
WARD, I., 'The Anomalous, the Wrong, and the Unhappy: UK Administrative Law in a European Perspective' (1994) NILQ 46.
WATSON, A., *Legal Transplants: An Approach to Comparative Law* (Edinburgh, 1974)
—— 'Legal Transplants and Law Reform' (1976) LQR 79.
—— 'Comparative Law and Legal Change' (1978) CLJ 313.
—— 'From Legal Transplants to Legal Formants' (1995) AJCL 469.
—— 'Aspects of Reception of Law' (1996) AJCL 335.
WEATHERILL, S., and BEAUMONT, P., *EU Law* (London, 1999).
WEBER, M., *Economie et société*, vol. i (Paris, 1971).
—— *L'éthique protestant et l'esprit du capitalism* (Paris, 1981).
WEBER, Y., 'Promesses, renseignements, retards', in F. Gazier, R. Drago and C. Kaufmann (eds.), *Encyclopédie Dalloz—Répetoire de la responsabilité de la puissance publique* (Paris, 1992).
WEILER, J. H. H., 'Eurocracy and Distrust' (1986) Washington LR 1103.
WEIR, T., 'Governmental Liability' (1989) PL 40.
WELLENS, G., and BORCHARDT, G., 'Soft Law in European Community Law' (1989) ELR 267.
WIGNALL, G., 'Legitimate Expectation and the Abuse of Power' (1994) NLJ 1038.
WILKEN, S., and VILLIERS, T., *Waiver, Variation and Estoppel* (Chichester, 1998).
WILKINSON, H. W., 'The Place of Estoppel in Planning Law' (1990) NLJ 168.
WILLIAMS, D. G. T., 'Discretion and Estoppel' (1981) CLJ 198.
WOEHRLING, J. M., 'Le principe de confiance légitime dans la jurisprudence des tribunaux', in *General Reports to the XV International Congress of Comparative Law* (University of Bristol, 1998).
WONG, G., 'Towards the Nutcracker Principle: Reconsidering the Objections to Proportionality' (2000) PL 92.
WOODHOUSE, D., *In Pursuit of Good Administration: Ministers, Civil Servants and Judges* (Oxford, 1997).
WOOLF, J., Case Notes (1989) Tax J no 33, 4.
—— Case Notes (1994) Tax J no 254, 6.
WOOLF, LORD, 'Public Law—Private Law: Why the Divide?' (1986) PL 220.
—— '*Protection of the Public—A New Challenge*', 41st Hamlyn Lecture (London, 1990).
—— 'Judicial Review: A Possible Programme for Reform' (1992) PL 221.
—— '*Droit Public*—English style' (1995) PL 57.
—— 'Judicial Review—The Tensions Between the Executive and the Judiciary' (1998) LQR 579.

WRIGHT, D., 'Rethinking the Doctrine of Legitimate Expectations in Canadian Administrative Law (1997) Osgoode Hall LJ 139.

WRIGHT, J., 'Local Authorities, the Duty of Care and the European Convention on Human Rights' (1998) OJLS 1.

WYATT, D., and DASHWOOD, A., *European Community Law*, 3rd edn. (London, 1992).

—— 'European Community Law and Public Law in the UK', in B. S. Markesinis (ed.), *The Gradual Convergence, Foreign Ideas, Foreign and English Law on the Eve of the 21st Century* (Oxford, 1994).

ZEGHBIB, H., 'Principe du contradictoire et procédure administrative non contentieuse', RDP 1998, 467.

ZELLICK, G., 'Government Beyond Law' (1985) PL 283.

ZWEIGERT, K., and KÖTZ, H., *An Introduction to Comparative Law*, 3rd edn. (Oxford, 1998).

YANNAKOPOULOS, C., *La notion de droits acquis en droit administratif français* (Paris, 1997).

Reports, Studies, and Official Publications

CHANCELLOR'S DEPARTMENT, *Your Right to Know. Freedom of Information*, White Book Cm 3818, 1997.

HANSARD COMMISSION, *Making the Law: The Report of the Hansard Society Commission on the Legislative Process*, Chairman Lord Rippon of Hexham (London, 1992).

LAW COMMISSION, *Aggravated, Exemplary and Restitutionary Damages*, Report no. 132, HMSO 1993.

—— *Administrative Law: Judicial Review and Statutory Powers*, Report no. 226, HMSO 1994.

LORD NOLAN, *First Report of the Committee on Standards in Public Life*, Cm 2850, 1995.

LORD WOOLF, *Access to Justice: Final Report to the Lord Chancellor on the Civil Justice System in England and Wales* (London, 1996).

SELECT COMMITTEE ON THE PARLIAMENTARY COMMISSIONER FOR ADMINISTRATION, *Maladministration and Redress*, First Report, 1994–1995, HC 112, January 1995.

TREASURY SOLICITOR'S DEPARTMENT, *Judge Over Your Shoulder*, May 1995.

—— *Ombudsman in Your Files*, February 1995.

Index